Up Your OWN Organization!

Up Your OWN Organization!

A Handbook on How To Start and Finance a New Business

by

Donald M. Dible

Introduction by
Robert Townsend
Former Chairman of the Board, Avis Rent a Car Corporation

Foreword by
William P. Lear
Chairman of the Board, Lear Motors Corporation

Preface by
John L. Komives
Director, Center for Venture Management

 The Entrepreneur Press

This publication is designed to provide accurate and authoritative information in regard to the subject matter covered. It is sold with the understanding that the publisher is not engaged in rendering legal, accounting or other professional service. If legal advice or other expert assistance is required, the services of a competent professional person should be sought.

——*From a Declaration of Principles jointly adopted by a Committee of the American Bar Association and a Committee of Publishers.*

Printed in the United States of America

Copyright © 1971, 1974 by Donald M. Dible

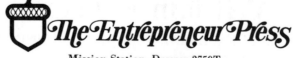

Mission Station, Drawer 2759T
Santa Clara, California 95051

Current printing (last digit):
14 13 12 11 10 9 8 7

Library of Congress Catalog Card Number: 76-177261

To Alice

Introduction

C. Northcote Parkinson is the discoverer of Parkinson's Law—"Work expands so as to fill the time available for its completion." He has also written about the automatic growth that takes place in organizations. For instance, he related the number of ships in the British Navy to the number of people working in their equivalent of the Navy Department. He discovered that when the number of ships began to decline, the number of people continued to grow. Ten years after that discovery, the number of ships is still declining and the number of people is still growing. When the British Empire began to dissolve, he discovered that the number of people employed to administer the affairs of the Empire continued to grow; to this day the number is still rising even though the Empire has disappeared. His most recent discovery is that, if everything continues on course, by the year 2195 everyone in Britain will be working for the government. One of our large banks got interested in this, did some research, and came to the conclusion that if the trends of the last 10 years continue, everyone in America will be working for the government by the year 2049. That's only 78 years from now. Meanwhile the concentration of economic power continues.

Anthony Jay, in his new book *Corporation Man*, published by Random House, concludes, "It seems almost inevitable that well before the end of this century most of the wealth of the Western world will be controlled by 3 to 6 hundred giant international corporations. The only argument now is about the exact number."

As an escapee from both the American Express Co. and the International Telephone & Telegraph Co., as a long-time non-admirer of big government, and as an ardent lover of human beings as individuals, I must confess that I'd almost rather see the kids reduce the country to rubble than see it pass into the clammy hands of a few hundred politicians and top corporation executives.

The only thing standing in the way may be the man with enough guts to chuck security and start his own business. *Up Your OWN Organization* is for that man. To me, he and his ilk are the last remnants of humanity—the only real human beings left. Don Dible's book is *not* for *homo corporationis docilis boob tuberus*, nor for the sick, thwarted, empire-building, power-mad manager who thrives on his growing collection of warm bodies. Not for them. It's for the individual who's been wondering for a long time whether life has to be the way it is in that big organization he or she works for—10% chicken salad and 90% chicken you-know-what. "Wouldn't it be fun," asks this individual, "to see if we could start a new company, dedicated to chicken salad—chicken salad for the customer, for all the shareholders, and for the employees, most of whom will be shareholders too?"

Let's hope if it's a man, and if he asks his wife, that she'll have the same pioneer instincts mine did when I came home one night and asked her to vote on the choice of my staying in a secure senior officer's berth with American Express or quitting to become president of Avis at a sharp reduction in salary and investing our life savings in that company with its dismal track record of 13 consecutive loss years. She thought for awhile and then said, "Look, you're 41 years old. Next time you get a chance to try out your own ideas, you may not have any guts left. Take the job with Avis. If it doesn't work, we'll take the five kids to the Yucatan Peninsula and teach them all to speak Spanish and live on fish, bananas, and coconuts." What a wife! What a woman! What a human being! Bless her heart. And bless the hearts of all you people out there with any guts left.

Robert Townsend

Foreword

Mr. Dible's book is very readable, interesting, and well organized, interspersed with many humorous and very appropriate stories and anecdotes. It covers *every* aspect of business enterprise and all its many functions in layman's language.

I personally don't know of any work as complete without laboring through many volumes on the subject matter. Mr. Dible has obviously done a tremendous amount of research and has added his own considerable personal knowledge to the contents of his book. I feel that it will be of great value to every small-businessman or potential entrepreneur and recommend that it be read from cover to cover.

William P. Lear
Chairman of the Board
Lear Motors Corporation

Preface

This year we begin the American Revolution Bicentennial Celebration. The American Revolution was based upon the philosophy that humans can be trusted to look after themselves and to do it in the spirit of fair play. We no longer needed or wanted a government ideology that provided for a God anointed King or a birthright House of Lords. And, if an upright man wanted to engage in business to make or trade items of use to someone else, he could certainly do it as his birthright. The flowering of the free enterprise system and rewarding those who enterprised and only tolerating those who merely inherited money or contacts, was a hallmark of the American Experience.

This book details how that System can be worked in today's society. We live in a highly complex and integrated social setting. Everywhere we turn, we find new rules and sub-systems, and we also find that the entire U.S. or the whole world is within the market planning of even smaller firms. This book was written for today's entrepreneur in today's sophisticated world. It is written for the entrepreneurs of 1976 and later, who are reaffirming that American Revolution.

The world of new enterprise is filled with all sorts of people from all sorts of life styles, ideas, human values, etc. There is a myth that most people who start a business are people who, if they knew what they were getting into, wouldn't do it. I suspect that the same could be said for parents. However, to start your own business has the same intrigue for the human psyche as enjoying sex, listening to good music or eating a well prepared and presented meal, or enjoying all the other intrinsic pleasures of human existence. Thus we find that big business executives, farmers, students, doctors, lawyers, accountants and consultants all start their own businesses; as do hamburger and soft water and gasoline franchisees; as do housewives who open antique stores or boutiques; and nowadays, other types of businesses, as do minorities—who not only want to escape from stifling employment, but want seriously to get a piece of the action for themselves.

Starting your own business is as much a part of the American social and political scene as the White House, apple pie or driving a car. For years, many established businesses have preached the 'Free Enterprise System'; and they meant it in the marketplace, especially for consumer goods. However, as this book amply points out, the Free Enterprise System really means starting your own business, and testing your ideas and products and services out there in that marketplace where customers will either put up their money or they won't. Free enterprise also means putting your own resources and your own body and time into an enterprise and testing yourself out there in that marketplace.

If you fail, that is part of the process; and if you make it, you are rewarded—in today's high taxes and all too numerous government regulations. Ironically, these regulations—which are designed to control big business—actually do harm to the *new* small business by posing sometimes insurmountable obstacles for the fledgling enterprise and occasionally regulating it right OUT of business.

Reading this book won't guarantee you success, but it'll make you a lot smarter and potentially a lot more successful. Don has thought through all the details about a new venture, and he has passed them along to you. In fact, he has tested many of these ideas himself in his own new company—The Entrepreneur Press. The company has survived into its third year and promises to become even more successful in the future.

In noting that this is a book for all men and all seasons, it is interesting to see that the original edition has been adopted in new courses and classes on starting your own business. The finest Ivy League schools, as well as other universities where there are imaginative faculties, are starting this course all over the countryside. Some 600 courses were taught in this general area of new and small business in the 1973-1974 school year. This book is one of the major reference texts in these courses. Venture capitalists, Small Business Administration officials, economic development officials, lawyers, account- ants, consultants, and entrepreneurs all have this book in their professional library— another sign of the catholicity of readers of *Up Your OWN Organization!*

The Center for Venture Management has counted Don Dible and his work among the best tools of venture formation ever since it was written. It has proven to be a very useful and helpful source and resource for all types of persons and reasons. We sincerely hope and express the good wishes that this new edition will live on and continue to be useful to all.

John L. Komives

xi

Contents

PROLOGUE

SECTION ONE — THE MAN, THE IDEA, THE COMPANY IMAGE

CHAPTER 1. CONTEMPORARY ENTREPRENEURSHIP—PROFILES AND CASE HISTORIES   1

     DETECTIVE STORY   2
     PERT-O-GRAPH *IS* PERTINENT!   8
     CARPET CRITTERS 'N THINGS   14
     ELEPHANTS, LASERS, AND MOON ROCKS: TALK ABOUT A
       MIXED BAG!   18
     RECOMMENDED READING   24

CHAPTER 2. WHAT MOTIVATES THE ENTREPRENEUR?   25

     FACTORS EXTERNAL TO THE CORPORATION   29
       The Desire to be His Own Boss   29
       The Desire for Fame   30
       The Desire for a Personal Fortune   30
       The Pure Joy of Winning   31
     FACTORS INTERNAL TO THE CORPORATION   32
       Inadequate Corporate Communications   32
       Inequity Between Major Contributions and Financial Rewards   33
       Promotion and Salary Policies   33
       Employee Security?   34
       Corporate Politics and Nepotism   35
       Red Tape   35
       Orphan Products   36
       Questionably Relevant Educational Requirements   37
     RECOMMENDED READING   39

CHAPTER 3. PERSONAL RESOURCES CHECKLIST   41

     COMPETENCE   41

MOTIVATION AND THE THREE D's: DESIRE, DETERMINATION, AND DEDICATION   42
FIRST-HAND KNOWLEDGE OF THE PRODUCT OR SERVICE TO BE OFFERED   43
ABILITY TO MANAGE PEOPLE AND RESOURCES   44
BROAD, WELL-ROUNDED EXPERIENCE   45
STAMINA AND PHYSICAL WELL-BEING   46
FINANCIAL RESOURCES   47
RECOMMENDED READING   49

CHAPTER 4.   INCREASED RESPONSIBILITY—THE PRICE OF SUCCESS   51

MISTRESSES AND mistresses   52
SESAME STREET MAY BE FINE, BUT . . .   54
THE MYTH OF WORKING FOR YOURSELF   54
RECOMMENDED READING   56

CHAPTER 5.   RECRUITING PARTNERS   57

FORMER BUSINESS ASSOCIATES   57
FRIENDS   58
BUSINESS CONSULTANTS   58
COMPETITOR'S STAFF   58
REFERRALS   59
CLASSIFIED ADVERTISING   59
AN OWL, A GOOSE, AND THE LITTLE RED HEN   60
RECOMMENDED READING   62

CHAPTER 6.   A TRAINING PROGRAM FOR SUCCESS   63

PHYSICAL CONDITIONING   63
ACQUIRING THE PROPER MENTAL ATTITUDE   64
MAKE YOUR WIFE THE HEAD CHEERLEADER IN YOUR ROOTING SECTION   64
INVESTIGATE SEMINARS   64
The U. S. Department of Commerce   65
The Small Business Administration   65
Trade Associations   65
The American Management Association   66
Colleges and Universities   66
Seminars for Pure Profit   66
Donald M. Dible Seminars   68

xiv

REDISCOVER BOOKS   70
   Community Libraries   71
   College and University Libraries   71
   Professional and Trade Association Libraries   72
   Bookstores   72
   Book Clubs   73
PERIODICALS, TOO   73
   Trade Journals   74
   Bank Publications   74
   Financial Papers   75
   Business Magazines   75
   Newsletters   75
   Community Newspapers   76
UNCLE SAM WANTS (To Help) YOU!   76
   The U. S. Department of Commerce   76
   The Small Business Administration   77
PUBLIC SPEAKING   78
   Toastmasters Clubs   78
   Community Colleges and University Extension Courses   79
   Commercial Institutions   79
RECOMMENDED READING   80

CHAPTER 7.   MANY PEOPLE ARE GLAD TO HELP YOU—JUST ASK THEM!   81

ENTREPRENEURS WHO HAVE ALREADY GOTTEN STARTED   82
TRADESMEN IN YOUR INDUSTRY   83
   Suppliers   83
   Customers   83
   Manufacturers' Representatives   83
   Distributors   84
BANKERS   84
STOCKBROKERS   85
COLLEGE FACULTY MEMBERS   85
RECOMMENDED READING   87

**CHAPTER 8.   THE CONCEPTION AND PROTECTION OF A PRODUCT
        IDEA**   89

MOMMY, WHERE DO PRODUCT IDEAS COME FROM?   89
   Former Employers   90
   New Partners   91

New Product Periodicals   91
Doctoral Dissertations   92
Idea Books   93
Trade Shows   94
State Invention Expositions   95
Patent Brokers   96
National Information Referral and Exchange Centers   97
PROTECTION   99
Patents   100
Unpatentable Ideas   102
WARNING TO INVENTORS   102
RECOMMENDED READING   105

CHAPTER 9.   PROJECTING A GOOD IMAGE   107

THE IMPORTANCE OF IMAGE TO THE ENTREPRENEUR   108
SELECTION OF A COMPANY NAME   109
POINTERS ON BUSINESS STATIONERY   109
COMMENTARY BY ROBERT TOWNSEND   110
RECOMMENDED READING   113

SECTION TWO — THE BUSINESS PLAN

CHAPTER 10.   THE IMPORTANCE OF A BUSINESS PLAN   117

THE BUSINESS PLAN IS A SALES DOCUMENT   118
Credibility   118
Authority   118
Ingenuity   119
THE BUSINESS PLAN AND FOUNDER RESPONSIBILITY   119
SOURCES OF ASSISTANCE IN PREPARING YOUR BUSINESS
PLAN   120
Public Offering Prospectuses   120
The Business Plan of Another Company   121
Business Consultants   121
Lawyers and Certified Public Accountants   121
Public Relations Firms   121
Books on Writing Effective Sales Letters   121
Trial Runs   122
PACKAGING THE BUSINESS PLAN   122
Investors Prefer Virgins   122
Busy Investors May Unintentionally Waste Your Time   123

FORGET EVERYTHING I'VE SAID!!   123
   Back-of-the-Envelope Advocates   124
   The Unbelievers   124
   "We Want to Help, Too!"   124
SUPER-SERENDIPITY   125
RECOMMENDED READING   126

CHAPTER 11.   THE MINI-PROPOSAL   **129**

INVESTOR PREFERENCES   130
   Initial Capitalization Required   130
   Maturity of the Enterprise   130
   Preferred Industrial Sectors   132
EMPHASIZE THE HIGHLIGHTS   132
   Niche in the Market   132
   Superior Qualifications of the Founders   133
   Market Characteristics   133
KEEP IT SHORT AND SWEET   133
RECOMMENDED READING   135

CHAPTER 12.   THE FORMAL BUSINESS PLAN   **137**

INTRODUCTION   138
TABLE OF CONTENTS   138
THE MANAGEMENT TEAM   138
   Capsule Resumes of the Founders   138
   References   139
   Organization Chart   139
   Who Does What, With Which, and to Whom   139
   Synergy of the Founding Team   140
   Management Assistance Required   140
   Watch the Birdie   140
THE BOARD OF DIRECTORS   140
   How Many?   142
   Composition—Who?   142
   Recruiting   144
   Compensation   144
SUPPORTING PROFESSIONAL SERVICE AGENCIES   144
   How to Select a Law Firm   145
   How to Select an Accounting Firm   146
   How to Select a Commercial Bank   148
   How to Select an Insurance Agency   150

THE MARKET TO BE SERVED   151
    Document Your Assertions   152
    List Major Potential Customers   152
    Analyze Major Competitors   153
    Estimate Market Share   153
    Polish Your Crystal Ball   153
    Discuss Product-Timing   153
THE PRODUCTS AND/OR SERVICES   154
    Competitive Features   154
    Pictures   158
    Manufacturing Process   158
    Cost Breakdowns   158
    State-of-the-Art   158
MARKETING STRATEGY   159
    Promotional Methods   159
    Advertising Efforts   159
    Distribution   160
    Terms of Sale   162
    Delivery/Performance Timing   163
    A New Twist   163
RESEARCH AND DEVELOPMENT PROGRAM   164
    Product Improvement   164
    Process Improvement   164
    Development of New Products   165
    Who Pays?   165
PLANT LOCATION AND RELATED CONSIDERATIONS   166
    Founders' Backyard   166
    Customer Proximity   166
    Supplier Proximity   167
    Manpower Availability   167
    Transportation Service   167
    Educational Facilities   168
    Investor Preferences   168
    Tax Climate   168
CONCEPT IN A CAPSULE   168
RECOMMENDED READING   170

CHAPTER 13.   APPENDIX TO THE FORMAL BUSINESS PLAN   175

    SALES FORECAST   175
    PRO FORMA FINANCIAL STATEMENTS   176

Cash Flow Statement   177
Profit and Loss Statement   178
Balance Sheet   178
PROJECTED STAFF AND PLANT REQUIREMENTS   179
Head Count   179
Floor Space   179
Leasehold Improvements   179
Major Capital Equipment   179
LEGAL STRUCTURE OF THE COMPANY   179
Sole Proprietorship   180
Partnership   180
Corporation   181
FOUNDERS' RESUMES   181
"TO WHOM IT MAY CONCERN:"   182
KEY ARTICLES BY MEMBERS OF THE FOUNDING STAFF   182
FOUNDERS' PERSONAL FINANCIAL STATEMENTS   182
FOUNDERS' COMPENSATION   182
Tax Aspects   183
Salaries   183
Equity Formula   184
SUPPORTING DOCUMENTATION   185
Market Surveys and Reports   185
Newspaper and Magazine Articles   186
Credit Reports and/or Annual Reports on Competitors   186
RECOMMENDED READING   187

SECTION THREE — ALI BABA AND THE FORTY MONEY SOURCES

CHAPTER 14.   INTRODUCTION TO MONEY SOURCES   191

MONEY CONCEPTS   192
Salt, Beads and Grain   192
Supply and Demand   192
Debt Versus Equity Financing   193
Comparison Shopping   194
ARE VENTURE CAPITALISTS *REALLY* THIEVES?   195
WHAT TO LOOK FOR IN A VENTURE CAPITAL PARTNER   195
Money   195
More Money   196
Availability of Managerial Assistance   196
Compatibility of Objectives   197

Investors Who Can Keep Their Cool   198
Confidence in Team and Concept   198
Reasonable Expectations Regarding Capital Appreciation   199
Some Knowledge of the Market to be Served   199
TERMS OF THE DEAL   199
Risk-Reward Ratios   200
Return on Investment   201
Earned Equity   202
"Getting Out"   203
RECOMMENDED READING   204

CHAPTER 15.   FORTY MONEY SOURCES

   205

CLOSED-END INVESTMENT COMPANIES   206
COLLEGES, UNIVERSITIES AND OTHER ENDOWED
     INSTITUTIONS   208
COMMERCIAL BANKS   209
COMMERCIAL FINANCE COMPANIES   211
CONSUMER FINANCE COMPANIES   212
CORPORATE VENTURE CAPITAL DEPARTMENTS OR
     SUBSIDIARIES   213
CREDIT UNIONS   215
CUSTOMERS   215
ECONOMIC DEVELOPMENT ADMINISTRATION   217
EMPLOYEES   220
EQUIPMENT MANUFACTURERS   222
FACTORING COMPANIES   223
FAMILY INVESTMENT COMPANIES   225
FINANCIAL CONSULTANTS, FINDERS, AND OTHER
     INTERMEDIARIES   226
FOUNDERS   228
INDUSTRIAL BANKS   230
INSURANCE COMPANIES   231
INVESTMENT ADVISERS   232
INVESTMENT BANKERS   234
INVESTMENT CLUBS   237
LEASING COMPANIES   238
MUTUAL FUNDS   240
MUTUAL SAVINGS BANKS   241
PARENT COMPANIES   241
PENSION FUNDS   242

PRIVATE INDIVIDUAL INVESTORS   243
PRIVATE INVESTMENT PARTNERSHIPS   245
PRIVATELY OWNED VENTURE CAPITAL CORPORATIONS   246
RELATIVES AND FRIENDS   247
SALES FINANCE COMPANIES   249
SAVINGS AND LOAN ASSOCIATIONS   250
SECURITIES DEALERS   251
SELF UNDERWRITING   253
SMALL BUSINESS ADMINISTRATION   255
SMALL BUSINESS INVESTMENT COMPANIES   257
STATE AND LOCAL INDUSTRIAL DEVELOPMENT
    COMMISSIONS   258
TAX-EXEMPT FOUNDATIONS AND CHARITABLE TRUSTS   259
TRADE SUPPLIERS   260
TRUST COMPANIES AND BANK TRUST DEPARTMENTS   262
VETERANS ADMINISTRATION   262

NOTES   265

APPENDIX

APPENDIX 1.   ANNOTATED LIST OF DIRECTORIES & GUIDES TO
               VENTURE CAPITAL SOURCES   269

APPENDIX 2.   SEMINARS AND WORKSHOPS ATTENDED BY THE
               AUTHOR WHICH INFLUENCED THE CONTENT OF
               THIS MANUSCRIPT   293

APPENDIX 3.   DIRECTORY OF THE MEMBERSHIP OF THE
               NATIONAL ASSOCIATION OF SMALL BUSINESS
               INVESTMENT COMPANIES   295

APPENDIX 4.   SIX BUSINESS START-UP CHECKLISTS   331

APPENDIX 5.   SMALL BUSINESS ADMINISTRATION AND U. S.
               DEPARTMENT OF COMMERCE FIELD OFFICE
               LOCATIONS   354

APPENDIX 6.   BUSINESS AND FINANCIAL PERIODICALS   359

APPLAUSE   361

INDEX   363

Prologue — First Edition

This book is written for today's pioneers: the men and women who have the desire *and* the ability to transform their dream of owning a business into the reality of a vital new enterprise. To these modern frontiersmen belong the financial gains and the personal satisfaction that are the just and proper rewards for creative effort.

In the process of establishing a company of my own, I have spent many hours doing research in various libraries. In this research, I found in the library stacks many tall shelves of books that analyzed the techniques and styles for managing all sizes of *established* business entities. But there was a curious shortage of literature on the fundamentals of *organizing and assembling* the resources necessary to *launch* a new enterprise.

I have also spent many dollars in travel expenses and admission fees to attend seminars on how to start a business and/or how to raise venture capital. While in attendance at these seminars, I noted the similarity of the questions asked by session attendees, whether the conference was held in Boston or Los Angeles, New York or San Francisco. They all wanted to know, in some form or another, "How?"

A dearth of information exists, then, to answer questions that are asked by everyone who thinks seriously about opening a business of his own. Three basic steps are involved in the creation of a new enterprise: (1) recognition and objective evaluation of one's personal needs *and* abilities, including the identification of one's marketable product and/or service; (2) preparation of a plan for the attainment of one's goal; and (3) acquisition of the financial resources necessary to make the plans a reality.

Although my own working experience is largely in the area of electronics products—and many of the examples given here unavoidably reflect this fact—I have made a sustained effort to produce a book that would have the widest possible utility to any entrepreneur—employed, unemployed (and there are all too many capable men and women in this category today) and self-employed—whether in the product or service field or in manufacturing, wholesaling, or retailing. It was gratifying indeed to have William Lear observe in the Foreword that this book "will be of great value to every small businessman or potential entrepreneur." If this proves to be the case, I will have accomplished what I set out to do.

Donald M. Dible
November, 1971

Prologue — Second Edition

The publication of this book truly has been an entrepreneurial venture; for in addition to writing *Up Your OWN Organization!*, I also organized The Entrepreneur Press to publish it. This is not to say that a major publisher couldn't be found to undertake the project. It's just that the search for a publisher can take six months to a year. Then, most publishing companies spend as much as a full year — or more — to shepherd a business book from manuscript form to bound copies. Then, it may be another year before the author begins to receive any royalty income. That's a possible two and a half to three year wait for payoff! Furthermore, if the publisher fails to mount a major marketing effort, the author's returns can be small indeed. It is a fact that many business books produced by major publishers sell fewer than 5,000 copies. That is why we chose to publish *Up Your OWN Organization!* ourselves. It seemed the entrepreneurial thing to do.

Sales of the first edition now exceed 30,000 copies and represent more than $500,000 in retail sales. With this second edition, in an effort to further broaden our sales base, we are producing a quality paperback version. Whether you buy your copy in hard or soft cover, we sincerely hope that you will find *Up Your OWN Organization!* a valuable and helpful addition to your business library.

As you start your business and make it grow, we would greatly appreciate hearing from you. In particular, if you would let us know your feelings about *Up Your OWN Organization!* and send us any suggestions for improvement you may think of, we would be very grateful.

Since this book was first published, we have received many wonderful letters. Readers have told us about their success in raising money and starting their own businesses making use of the principles described here. One man raised more than a million dollars for his business following our guidelines. Many others have raised thousands of dollars for their ventures.

In an effort to expand our services to the small business community, we have recently initiated a series of seminars in cooperation with universities, trade and professional associations and civic groups. For more details on these programs, please see page 68.

Finally, we now have an audio-tape cassette series on "How to Start and Finance a New Business" consisting of sixteen half-hour talks by attorneys, accountants, commercial bankers, commercial factors, investment bankers, venture capitalists, equipment leasing specialists, marketing consultants and business advisors. If you would like to receive information on these or *any* of our present or future product offerings, please write to us at The Entrepreneur Press, Mission Station, Drawer 2759T, Santa Clara, California 95051.

Donald M. Dible
September, 1974

Section One

THE MAN

THE IDEA

THE COMPANY IMAGE

Chapter 1

Contemporary Entrepreneurship- Profiles and Case Histories

In his timely book *The Age of Discontinuity*, internationally acclaimed business consultant Peter F. Drucker observes:

> Now we are entering again an era in which emphasis will be on entrepreneurship. However, it will not be the entrepreneurship of a century ago, that is, the ability of a single man to organize a business he himself could run, control, embrace. It will rather be the ability to create and direct an organization for the new. We need men who can build a new structure of entrepreneurship on the managerial foundations laid these last fifty years. History, it has often been observed, moves in a spiral; one returns to the preceding position, or to the preceding problem, but on a higher level, and by a corkscrew-like path. In this fashion we are going to return to entrepreneurship on a path that led out from a lower level, that of a single entrepreneur, to the manager, and now back, though upward, to entrepreneurship again.[1]

The following profiles and case histories represent a few of the structural beams, short ones and long ones, in this new edifice of entrepreneurship.

1

DETECTIVE
STORY

2134 Old Middlefield Way, Mountain View, California 94043 ▪ (415) 968-8775

"If you aren't a hard-ass—a real bastard—when it comes to collecting your accounts receivable, you'll be out of business in no time." You'll have to agree, that's pretty sage advice. The remarkable thing is that it comes from 29 year old Richard Bauer, Jr., vice president of DTI Security. Two years ago, Dick teamed up with David Schuldt, now the 30 year old president of DTI, to start a company in the burgeoning residential security industry. Since that time, both young men have undergone a forced transformation from salaried, big company employees to seasoned executives in their own successful enterprise.

The idea for the venture sprang from a working relationship Dave and Dick developed when they were both employed by Ampex Corporation. When that giant company fell upon hard times, they started thinking seriously as to whether they should seek other employment or set out to start a business of their own. Since both of them had relatives who were in business for themselves, the notion of collaborating to start a new company didn't seem like an unreasonable alternative.

Interestingly, their decision to go into their own business followed the publication of the first edition of the book you are now reading by only a few months. On the recommendation of some friends, they bought a copy, even though the original price was $24.95 plus tax. Dave, Dick, and their wives each took turns reading the book. Since they regarded the decision to go into business as a serious one, they wanted to give themselves every possible chance for success. In particular, the wives found the discussions regarding personal sacrifice and the "business as mistress" point of view especially sobering. Clearly, they were not contemplating a get rich scheme. (Dave Schuldt now describes the DTI attitude toward business as simply "Spartan.")

The next several months were spent trying to identify a suitable product with which to launch the company. Since their work at Ampex involved selling tape recording equipment to a variety of government agencies in the security and surveillance area, it isn't surprising that the security market received their close attention.

They studied a number of market surveys covering the residential and industrial security business and learned that very substantial market growth was projected. Further study of trade journals and industry association information confirmed these projections.

Having done their marketing homework, DTI's founders then had to decide whether to go after the residential or industrial markets. They learned that it would be least costly to direct their initial efforts in the area of residential security since product development and acceptance costs—as well as selling costs—would be much lower than in the industrial market.

DTI's initial base of operations—"World Headquarters," they called it—was located in Dave Schuldt's two-car garage. The floor was scrubbed, the windows were covered with curtains, a desk and telephone were installed, and a workbench was built.

Working evenings and weekends over a nine month period, Dave and Dick produced their first product, an intrusion and fire detection network called the DSS-10 Security System. It was designed for installation by any of the 6,000 home security system dealers across the country.

Once its solid state system has been activated, the DSS-10 sounds a loud alarm if any window or door in a home is opened or broken. The alarm also sounds if a special sensor detects smoke or fire. In order to compete in a market served by almost two hundred other manufacturers, the product was designed with low cost, reliability, and ease of installation in mind. From a consumer appeal standpoint, however, a primary competitive advantage is the physical design of the DSS-10. In an industry where most products are covered by unattractive gray metal boxes, the DSS-10 is housed in a handsomely styled wall unit no more obtrusive than a thermostat.

Having completed the design and testing of the first product, a pilot run of twenty units was assembled to demonstrate reproducibility. All went well; a major milestone had been reached.

Now the time had come to formulate and implement a business plan. Making use of Section Two of this book, a formal plan was prepared. It was determined that $75,000 would be needed to reach the next milestone.

Once again, our information services came along at just the right time. A "Donald M. Dible Seminar" on "How to Start and Finance a New Business" (See page 68) was presented in a nearby city, attended by more than 225 entrepreneurs. Included in the audience were Dave and Dick.

Armed with their business plan and the information received at the seminar, Dave and Dick succeeded in selling a thirty per cent interest in DTI Security for $75,000 within a very short period of time. Roughly half of this money was invested by friends, relatives and acquaintances while the balance was obtained from referrals. Shortly afterward, "World Headquarters" was moved to its present location, a modest 1,000 square foot rented facility.

Since starting DTI, Dave and Dick have learned the vital lesson that cash is the lifeblood of any business. "The sale isn't made until you get paid," says Dave. Success requires not only that you produce a large sales volume, but you've also got to be tight fisted when it comes to your expenses. DTI has used a great many techniques to control its costs. To start with, Dave and Dick both took a 33 per cent cut in pay when they started their own company; after all, equity capital is too scarce a commodity to be used for anything as unproductive as officers' salaries!

Whenever a major purchase is to be made, competitive bids are always obtained. Recently, when an injection mold was required to make a critical part, the Yellow Pages of Telephone Books for all communities within a 100 mile radius were consulted to locate prospective bidders. The lowest bidder's price was less than sixty per cent of the next highest bid. The savings were well over $1,500.

Another way in which DTI saves money is by subcontracting with housewives for assembly work to be done in their own homes. The women, acting as private contractors, pick up parts from the company on Mondays and deliver the finished goods on Fridays. The assembled hardware is inspected, tested, and subjected to a 48 hour "burn-in" period at DTI before being placed into inventory or shipped directly to a customer.

The use of such a labor force enables DTI to avoid many of the problems and expenses associated with a large labor force: vacation pay, sick pay, paid holidays, dental and medical insurance, employer-matched Social Security payments, income tax collection, workmen's compensation, and unemployment compensation to say nothing of the cost of larger facilities, workbenches, chairs, and other amenities. There is much to be said in favor of a subcontract work force for a small company that wants to handle rapid growth, or variations, in sales volume with minimum increases in overhead.

When I asked Dave and Dick what they felt was the most important personal element leading to their success, they both agreed that the moral support and active involvement of their wives in the business was essential. Since starting the company, Dave and Dick's working time has averaged sixteen hours a day, five days a week plus nine hours on Saturday. Sunday's are reserved for their families. With a work schedule like that, you can appreciate the strain on their wives. One of the keys to promoting harmony on the home front has been actively to involve the wives in the business. Dave's wife spends twenty hours a week as the company bookkeeper while Dick's wife spends a comparable amount of time handling the correspondence of the marketing department and acting as watch-dog over the accounts receivable. Not only does the involvement of the wives make for a more harmonious home life, it is also another very effective way of minimizing the company's expenses. (Remember, not only do the wives share the burden of their husbands' heavy work schedules, they also share the joys and triumphs of seeing the big sales closed and watching the business grow. It is truly a family team effort.)

A little over one year has elapsed since DTI moved its "World Headquarters" out of Dave's garage. In its first fiscal year, the company has come within fifteen per cent of meeting its original sales and profit forecasts. On the sales front, DTI is moving ahead into several major markets.

While exhibiting at an important industry trade show in Chicago, Dave and Dick met the manufacturer of a non-competing line of security hardware. This led to their subsequent introduction to a key export broker. DTI now indicates that export sales will account for thirty per cent of their total sales volume next year.

Another area that has opened up for DTI is private label manufacturing. Many major merchandise outlets such as catalog and department stores have outside companies specially make products bearing their own labels. For instance, some gas station chains sell tires carrying the name of the chain, when, in fact, the tires were manufactured by a major tire producer that also markets tires under its own brand name.

At the present time, DTI is negotiating with one of the largest retail operations in the country for a substantial purchase order for security systems to be produced on a private label basis. This retail operation has its own nationwide service organization capable of installing the systems right in the customer's home in much the same way as a washing machine or custom draperies might be installed. Another advantage that marketing through this outlet offers is the ability of the retail chain to offer its customers easy financing—a sure-fire way to increase consumer sales.

Penetration of these markets was by no means automatic. Dick described the preparations for exhibiting at their first major trade show, the International Security Conference, last February. For four days and nights, Dick and Dave labored over the construction of their display. When it was arranged to their satisfaction, they loaded it into Dick's little Pinto station wagon along with their samples, brochures, personal luggage and themselves. The load was so heavy that the frame of the station wagon nearly rested on the rear axle. It was Saturday afternoon, the day before the exhibits were to be erected. They set off on their 350 mile trek to Los Angeles, site of the trade show.

When they arrived at the hotel where the show was being held, they offered up a small "Prayer of Thanks" that the springs on the car had not broken. Then, they offered up the $550 rental fee on their eight by ten foot booth PLUS an additional $180 for rented chairs, side tables and drapes for the three day show. Hurriedly, amid the bedlam of hundreds of other exhibitors readying their booths, they set up their display.

Weary but proud, Dave and Dick admired their completed exhibit. Next on the agenda: the formal Exhibitors' Reception. Here is where much of the real trade show "action" occurs. Contacts are made, referrals are noted, and sell, sell, sell is the order of business. It was three in the morning on Monday—official opening day, when Dave and Dick finally got to bed. In the next three days, they each got a *total* of less than ten hours sleep. That's the way it is at trade shows.

Slightly over one year old, DTI has been through a lot. The sales backlog is close to $100,000 and should double in the next month when some "ready to hatch" orders materialize. Membership in two important trade associations is being arranged. Most important, a second round of financing is being negotiated. A major investor is considering the purchase of a one-third interest in the company for around $250,000. This should place DTI in a much more viable position in the marketplace, enabling it to respond quickly to customer demands and serve the needs of even their largest dealers.

Legislation presently under consideration promises substantial industry growth in the next few years. Already, many communities require that fire detection equipment be installed in apartment buildings and multiple story dwellings. Much of the rest of the nation is expected to follow suit in the near future. Also, insurance companies are beginning to offer significant premium reductions to policy holders who have security and/or fire detection systems installed. As far as David Schuldt and Richard Bauer, Jr. are concerned, there's nowhere to go but up!

HALCOMB ASSOCIATES

PERT-O-GRAPH
IS PERTINENT!

149 San Lazaro Avenue, Sunnyvale, California 94086 Telephone (408) 245-3131

Cold steel rings as it drives nails into structural studs, and saw blades whine as they slice through fir 2 by 4's—workmen are constructing a classroom of the future under the roof of Halcomb Associates, an industrial consulting firm on the San Francisco peninsula. Amidst the cacophony of progress, the man who got the outfit moving reluctantly parted with a three-hour chunk of irretrievable, evanescent time to reminisce for this story. "Let's see," he muses, "How *did* it all start?"

Actually, it was Mr. Bowers who did it. . .planted the seed, that is, of Jim Halcomb's entrepreneurship. Bowers was the high-school teacher who gave Jim his first glimpse of the inner workings of business. Hardly a "General Business" class meeting would go by without the students hearing the exhortation, "Differentiate the product! Differentiate the product! Differentiate the product!" Jim got the message. Jim contends that today there are hundreds of look-alike small businesses in the highly specialized industrial consulting field of Program Evaluation and Review Technique/Critical Path Method (PERT/CPM), a unique approach to project planning that was first employed in a major program in 1958 by Admiral William F. (Red) Raborn when he scheduled the hugely successful Navy Polaris Missile Project. The unusual and atypical success of this government-sponsored effort resulted in enormous world-wide interest in the new planning process, and in the space of just a few years, more than 3,000 trade-journal articles appeared on the subject of PERT/CPM.

In commenting on the need for "differentiating the product," Jim points out that as many as 99 out of every 100 companies in the industrial consulting field project the same image; he attributes his own remarkable success to his never-ending efforts to be unique and different. This effort is reflected in the extensive selection of products and services offered by Halcomb Associates, including:

> The Pert-O-Graph Kit (a do-it-yourself management tool for project planning). Built around the Pert-O-Graph II Computer, this kit is so highly thought of as a time and money saver by the president of a major Florida electronics firm that he supplies one to every engineer and scientist on his staff.[2]
>
> The Pert-O-Graph Computer Watch (a Longines-Wittnauer precision timepiece equipped with the Pert-O-Graph Computer) for convenient rapid-fire project forecasting.
>
> Management Consulting to assist in PERT/CPM planning of any project, from a sales campaign to a major real-estate development (clients include hundreds of corporations in North America, Europe, and Asia).
>
> Project Management Seminars offered periodically in major cities in the United States and Canada, featuring instruction in the use of advanced project-planning techniques.

Most recently, Jim has added in-house education to his service offerings—thus the noisy construction of a uniquely equipped classroom designed to make Halcomb-style education a "total experience." In fact, when ready for use, the facility will be reminiscent of a set from the movie *2001: A Space Odyssey*, replete with the most modern of visual and audio aids. There will even be a servomechanism-actuated moving whiteboard (not *blackboard,* mind you!) that will slide into the wall when the rear-image projection screen is in use. Additionally, two room-filling, horseshoe-shaped desks have been built to accommodate a class of roughly 20 students. Of course, air-conditioning rounds out the amenities.

This facility was initiated because Halcomb won a $58,932 contract for the purpose of retraining a select group of jobless aerospace engineers who have highly specialized but out-of-demand skills. The curriculum is intended to qualify them for management posts in Operation Breakthrough, a federal program set up under the auspices of the U. S. Department of Housing and Urban Development. Operation Breakthrough is a national program, designed to provide, in this decade alone, 26 million new homes for low- and moderate-income families; the project will make use of the most progressive production techniques devised thus far.

Jim is particularly well qualified to conduct such a training program. He is a former aerospace engineer himself; accordingly, he should relate extremely well to his students. In addition, his 10-year-old firm has handled more than 200 projects in the housing and construction field. In fact, as a building trades consultant, Jim has participated in such diverse projects as planning the development and building of Foster City (a major real-estate complex on the shores of San Francisco Bay) and the construction of Harrah's Casino at South Lake Tahoe, Nevada.

However, unlike the students he will soon be teaching, Jim left the aerospace community because he had a carefully conceived plan (long since drastically revised!). Recognizing the enormous difficulty that most engineering managers have in getting a shot at a corporate management position, Jim decided that he would resign, go into the "management consulting" business for two years, and then return to the aerospace industry as a "qualified" top-echelon manager. (Obviously, that's not the way things have worked out, but I don't think Jim has any regrets!)

For three years prior to starting his company, Jim had been a project manager in the PERT/CPM field at Varian Associates, a leading high-technology electronics firm. While at Varian, Jim developed the Pert-O-Graph Computer, a circular slide rule for scientifically estimating program schedules. However, unlike its big, expensive, and complicated electronic counterparts, the Pert-O-Graph Computer is so simple to operate that most laymen wouldn't call it a computer at all! Therefore, because of the enormous and still-growing resentment against computers and the increasing public desire to "fight it," evidenced by a national flood of cartoons and jokes that point an accusing finger at The Dumb Computer, Jim's brainchild has earned him a lot of friends who rejected the electronic colossus and its priests, the programmers.

Articles describing Halcomb's new device appeared in numerous trade magazines. Varian literally gave away thousands of cardboard models of the Pert-O-Graph at trade shows as a goodwill gesture. Finally, someone on the staff of *Business Week,* a highly respected businessmen's magazine with a worldwide circulation, heard about the Pert-O-Graph. Recognizing widespread interest in PERT, the magazine sent a staff reporter over to Varian to get a news story. The response to the subsequent article was staggering. Requests for additional information came in by the tens of thousands, and even IBM wanted to know how to get a sample!

Mail volume was so tremendous that Varian transferred Halcomb to its public relations department to assist with responding to the inquiries. As a result, he decided that there were an awful lot of people—inside and outside of the electronics industry—who wanted to hear more about PERT; and he suggested a market expansion program to the Varian management. Properly, the company pointed out that its not unlimited resources should be confined to the electronics field. The customers for Jim's proposed products simply did not represent a large enough market to interest a multi-million dollar corporation.

Not long afterward, Jim expressed the desire to go into business for himself; he offered to buy the trademark for his creation. The enlightened Varian management (entrepreneurs themselves) authorized the necessary transfer of title free of charge and, although dubious about his prospects for success, gave Jim their blessing. In fact, to this day, Varian remains one of Jim's industrial clients.

With a chuckle, Jim recalls that his "first office, equipped with a loudly clanking radiator, would have served nicely as an anteroom for a broom closet." Its size, however, was simply symptomatic of the magnitude of his "venture" capital, a mere $500 that he obtained by taking out a loan against his life insurance policy. (Today, he is a strong advocate of a regular program of personal savings. He contends that "good luck is where preparedness meets opportunity," and "financial preparedness can only be achieved by consciously planning for it.")

In reviewing the progress of his company over the last decade, Jim sums up his feelings regarding the essence of what makes for success: Persistence and audacity, coupled with a very healthy measure of publicity. After listening to him for several hours, I am satisfied that Jim is persistence personified. He voices resounding agreement with the philosopher who said "Men don't fail; they just stop trying" and asserts that "If you try *enough* different things, sooner or later something has *got* to break. Pick a direction and stick with it." In pursuing such a program, *time* becomes one of your most precious resources, and Jim maintains that you must "learn to be a steward of your own time. You must learn how to say 'No' firmly but politely to the unending stream of requests for 'just a few minutes of your time'."

To insure that he is never wanting for something new to try, Jim has maintained an idea file since his teenage years. Whenever he encounters *anything* of interest in his reading or conversations that he thinks *may* be of value at some future date, the concept is catalogued for easy accessibility and stored in his idea file. In discussing the value of such a file, Jim can provide a veritable verbal parade of examples of unusual successful ideas that have resulted from the amalgamation of two or more quite different disciplines. For example, consider the bringing together of ink and the roughly surfaced steel ball to make up the ballpoint pen; the packaging together of a timepiece and a receiver to make a clock-radio; and, going further back in time, the then-absurd idea of designing a radio for use in an automobile—one of countless ideas originally laughed at and now accepted as routine and commonplace. Persistence in his quest for creativity and persistence in his efforts to develop and exploit the products and services he offers are of primary significance in Jim's remarkable achievements in his highly competitive field.

Jim recalls with pleasure a time when he learned of a construction firm that had just been awarded a $2 million contract. The company general manager had never heard of PERT and was not particularly receptive to Jim's overtures. However, in the face of Jim's unrelenting onslaught, the contractor finally consented to give him a try. Following the ahead-of-schedule and under-budget completion of the program, Jim's very pleased client indicated, "I sure am glad you kept dinging me." Jim observes that in many instances people appreciate a persistent seller. Frequently, they want what you have to sell—in fact, they may desperately need what you have to sell—but they don't know how to make the time available to listen to what you have to say and to acquire an understanding of your product.

Because Halcomb recognizes that he has a large number of satisfied customers, many of whom had to be persuaded to buy his service in the first place, he is a strong believer in the importance of audacity in bringing your products and services to the attention of potential clients. With a twinkle in his eye, he says, "I could write a book on how to get past the girl in the lobby. One trick is to ride the elevator to the fourth floor and take the staircase to the third if that's where your quarry hides." On a more serious note, however, Halcomb acknowledges that there is a very fine balance between being persistent and being discourteous—a balance to which he is keenly attuned.

In discussing the fact that he is primarily engaged in the marketing of a professional service, Jim points out that you can't *sell* a professional service. You reach your market through *exposure*. This is where publicity gets into the act. Jim has written numerous articles on the subject of PERT/CPM for leading trade magazines and journals. Whenever anything new or unusual happens around the Halcomb headquarters, a news release is prepared and distributed to the communications media. Although such news items do not always come to the attention of individuals in top management slots, substantial numbers of middle-level managers regularly and methodically review professional and trade journals.

To illustrate the value of reaching large numbers of middle managers, consider this event in Halcomb's history. Several years ago, Jim received a call from the Comptroller of the Columbia Broadcasting System Television Division. At the time, CBS had been renting movies from Metro-Goldwyn-Mayer, Paramount, and other major movie producers for use on CBS TV. Since the CBS management was unhappy in their role as a movie broker, they decided to build a studio of their own. At the time this decision was formalized, it was recognized that an all-out effort would have to be made in order to ready the proposed facility. Very little time remained in which to film programs for the upcoming fall season. Several of the CBS top staffers had a passing acquaintance with the PERT concept and recognized its potential value in the resolution of this timing problem. However, they needed an expert; and they needed one fast! There was no time for canvassing the industry to find their man. When the problem was brought up at a CBS staff meeting, one of the middle-management attendees, having read many of Jim's articles, indicated that, insofar as he knew, Halcomb was one of the best consultants in the industry. Subsequently, Jim got the contract; and the new Hollywood film-making facility, known as "Studio Center," was built and staffed (Jim even helped in programming a schedule for satisfying the staffing requirements) in record time. Thus, one can fully appreciate the importance of publicity in the marketing of a professional service. Other professionals such as lawyers and accountants, who recognize the importance and value of publicity in building a clientele, regularly accept speaking invitations whenever they are afforded the opportunity.

When asked how his family has weathered the events of the last 10 years, Jim beams, grinning from ear to ear. Peering into the wings of his mind, he invites his wife, Eleanor, on stage. Eleanor has borne primary responsibility for the rearing of five bright, rambunctious young men (now aged six through sixteen). Furthermore, she has been the company controller since its inception.

One of the Halcomb family pastimes is weekend boating on the delta of the Sacramento River, sometimes called the Everglades of the West. The family got started on the boating kick by renting teacup-sized sailboats at $1 per hour when the boys and the budget were thimble-sized. Today they own a 37-foot cabin cruiser. Another regular family event is the annual trout fishing trip Jim shares with his sturdy sons, angling on chill Sierra streams on the opening day of trout season—a pleasure he has enjoyed every season for the last 12 years.

Although Jim concedes that he does not have as much time for his family as he would like to have, it is obvious that his waking hours are filled with truly satisfying work *and* play. We may assume that in his nightly slumbers, he is persistently PERTing the next day's exciting events!

John Philip Company   1070 Florence Way • Campbell, Calif. 95008 • Phone (408) 378-7522

CARPET CRITTERS
'N THINGS

In one corner of the spacious, richly carpeted office stands a lone putter. On the floor beside it lie three white, dimpled spheres and a practice putting cup. A compartmentalized cabinet graces the far wall, housing file drawers, telephone, tape recorder, and a modest reference library that is dominated by several large volumes—tax guides. An inviting black leather and chrome chair and a clutter-free oval work table that rests on a single pedestal complete the equipment with which John Philip Maltby, president and founder of the John Philip Company, administers his rapidly growing novelty and giftwares empire. It hasn't always been this way for Maltby, but I don't want to get ahead of my story. . . .

It all started nine years ago when J. P., as Maltby prefers to be called, was a hard-working manufacturers' representative in the giftwares field. A family friend read something called the "Parents' Creed" in her church newsletter and gave the Maltbys a copy. J. P. and his wife Shirley liked it so well that they had an artist make a rendering of it on parchment. They then made it the featured work of art on their family-room wall. For the next year, this poetry-on-parchment received rave reviews from every single visitor to the Maltby home. Everyone, and especially Shirley, indicated that a wall hanging designed around the "Parents' Creed" would be an overnight best seller.

When the arm-twisting he was getting finally neared the pain level, J. P. said "Uncle" and reluctantly agreed to give the idea a try—"Parents' Creed" was to make its market debut.

In order that you may appreciate this narrative more fully, J. P. has consented to the inclusion of the text of the "Parents' Creed" in this work:

CHILDREN LEARN WHAT THEY LIVE

If a child lives with criticism, He learns to condemn.
If a child lives with hostility, He learns to fight.
If a child lives with ridicule, He learns to be shy.
If a child lives with shame, He learns to feel guilty.
If a child lives with tolerance, He learns to be patient.
If a child lives with encouragement, He learns confidence.
If a child lives with praise, He learns to appreciate.
If a child lives with fairness, He learns justice.
If a child lives with security, He learns to have faith.
If a child lives with approval, He learns to like himself.
If a child lives with acceptance and friendship,
He learns to find love in the world.

Dorothy Law Nolte[3]

One final detail required serious attention before J. P. could proceed with his plans. An intensive search was mounted to locate Dorothy Law Nolte, authoress of the "Creed," for the purpose of formalizing a royalty agreement. J. P.'s attorney was successful in making these arrangements, affording J. P. the protection of the copyright laws before he committed his resources to the promotion of the "Creed."

While maintaining his job as an independent manufacturers' representative, J. P. invested his savings in raw materials and arranged to have several subcontractors (called "farmers" since he was "farming" the work out) prepare an initial production run of a few hundred pieces with which to test the market.

Early acceptance was far beyond his expectations, and within three years J. P. was not only working a routine 80-plus hours a week (by this time he had given up his "rep" job); but his farmers couldn't harvest the crop fast enough. Almost as reluctantly as he had made the decision to launch his venture, J. P. decided that he was forced to open his own shop and handle the entire operation himself—new-product selection, marketing, *and* manufacturing.

To do this, however, required far more capital than J. P. could readily acquire through normal banking circles because any significant expansion in a small company is commonly regarded as a speculative and risky proposition. Enter the United States Small Business Administration, (sometime) champion of the entrepreneur and bolsterer of beleaguered baby business battlements.

J. P. filed a five-year business plan with the local SBA Field Office and requested a $10,000 loan. In it, he provided detailed information on the three cardinal points that should be covered in *any* loan request from *any* source:

1) How much do you need
2) What do you want it for, i.e., to what use will you put it?

And, most important,

3) *How do you propose to pay it back?*

Shortly afterward, in an afternoon when business matters were particularly hectic, J. P. was at his home workshop struggling to get a large order ready for shipment. When the doorbell rang, it was an unshaven, T-shirt-clad Maltby who greeted the representative of the Small Business Administration. (J. P. maintains that there was some mixup about their appointment.) He invited his visitor up to the spare-bedroom headquarters for a two-hour conference and a first-hand look at pure pandemonium. J. P. to this day can't believe it, but he *did* get a five-year, 5-percent SBA direct loan for $10,000. He was told that his history of sustained profits placed his loan in a very low-risk category. All he had to do to qualify was put up his house, his car, his file cabinets, and even his portable typewriter for collateral. Without this loan, the John Philip Company undoubtedly would not be as successful as it is today.

Later bank credit ran thin due to continued rapid growth and a resulting shortage of working captial. J. P. then found it necessary to employ the services of a commercial factor in borrowing against his accounts receivable to secure additional capital. Again, he acknowledges, without this critical financing, his company could not have managed to sustain its satisfying growth rate.

In reviewing the last eight years, J. P. recalls another high point. After the birth of cinema actress Sophia Loren's son, she was deluged with gifts from well-wishers. In an interview with a reporter for one of our leading women's magazines, Miss Loren commented that she and her husband, Carlo Ponti, were delighted with many of the gifts their son received, but the remembrance that they treasured most was sent by a friend in New York City—a copy of the "Parents' Creed."

Maltby attributes the success of his "Parents' Creed" to the fact that it is a "philosophy for raising children that has universal appeal." He is now exporting special foreign editions of it to Australia, Puerto Rico, and many European countries; supply channels for additional overseas markets are in the planning stages.

Today he employs a staff of close to 40 people for the production of such items as "Carpet Critters" (do-it-yourself kits for making cute hippopotamuses and elephants out of scrap carpeting and yarn), the "Teen Creed" (a decorator wall hanging bearing a message intended to bridge the generation gap), and a small galaxy of colorful pillows, bean bags, dolls, pajama storage cases, and artistic cloth calendars.

Daily company operations are supervised by a general manager who has been added to the staff. J. P. relies primarily on weekly meetings with his supervisors and general manager for routine reporting requirements. Thus, he is free to devote his enormous creative talent and shrewd knowledge of his market to planning and guiding a steady program of expansion. (There is even time for golf these days!)

Although he relies heavily on his staff, J. P. says that the most important and valuable resource he has is his wife and right-hand lady, Shirley. Even now, she spends two days a week at the factory updating the books and handling the payroll accounts. (As a sign of their corporate progress, though, she is now ably assisted by a new mini-computer.) Shirley's background as a graduate of the New York School of Interior Design makes her an invaluable assistant in the conception and evaluation of new products. More important, though, is the firm commitment and steadfast devotion with which she has supported and encouraged her husband through the adventure of building their own enterprise.

LASER TECHNOLOGY, INC.

10624 VENTURA BOULEVARD · TELEPHONE (213) 763-7091 · NORTH HOLLYWOOD, CALIFORNIA 91604

ELEPHANTS, LASERS, AND MOON ROCKS: TALK ABOUT A MIXED BAG!

The Asiatic elephant has a gestation period that lasts from 21 to 22 months—the longest in a living species of animal. However, the performance of the pachyderm and, for that matter, the rest of the animal kingdom pales in comparison with the gestation period for some of Man's ideas. Consider the case of Laser Technology, Incorporated of North Hollywood, California, which took more than 35 years to reach maturity as the brainchild of founder H. B. McLaughlin; and, even at that, the labor was forced!

After 35 years of faithful service with a major aircraft manufacturer, McLaughlin found himself the loser in a post-merger management shuffle. At the age of 63, he landed smack in the middle of a recession labor market; and, since almost all companies in his industry operate under a forced-retirement-at-age-65 policy, he found it virtually impossible to locate employment related to his extensive professional background. In his own words, "Thomas Alva Edison couldn't get a job in California today if he applied over the age of 50."

Eight months elapsed before this former aerospace executive finally accepted a position as a laboratory technician. In the interim, he had sustained a vigorous campaign, characterized by remarkable persistence and ingenuity, in search of work. Because of his long and varied experience, he felt qualified for positions from purchasing agent to president. In total, he responded to hundreds of classified advertisements.

In his responses, he put his highly developed organizational talents to use and prepared a master form letter. With his wife's secretarial support, he responded to various openings with combinations of nearly 75 different number-coded paragraphs, each a description of one facet of his prior experience and each suitably tailored to the requirements of a particular job. Composition instructions to his spouse might read: "Honey, send this one a 12, 19, 37, 63 letter." In response, he received 14 different offers of employment. However, in his application letters, he intentionally omitted any reference to his age; and, when he appeared for his interviews, he was typically greeted with the embarrassed hospitality a leper might expect as the uninvited guest at a nudists' picnic.

After his ordeal with unemployment, McLaughlin realized that he had developed some very clear ideas regarding his future plans. For more than 35 years, his daydreams had been occupied with thoughts of going into business for himself. In fact, he had contemplated the prospect of turning his hobby of gemstone growing, cutting, and polishing (known as lapidary work) into a source of income to supplement his expected retirement pension.

Now his major objective was to lay the groundwork for his own company during the evenings and weekends while he sustained himself with a regular five-day-a-week job. He says "I wanted to guarantee myself a place to work for as long as I was physically and mentally able to do so."

Fortunately, while McLaughlin was filling his garage with equipment and developing his hobby of growing and processing single crystal gemstones, the space age was making new demands on industry for exotic materials and processes. The groundwork for

McLaughlin's new business was closely tied to the emergence of the semiconductor industry (transistors and integrated circuits) and the superconductor industry (study of newly discovered magnetic phenomena and research in computer memories), along with advances in the field of insulator manufacturing. However, the single most significant development was the emergence of the laser market, with its demands for ultra-high-purity crystals and optically ground surfaces. Here was a field in which all of the equipment that McLaughlin had spent more than 14 years perfecting and accumulating could be utilized. Assessing his position, he determined that he had some basis for a company (equipment), the means for economic survival (a steady job), a market to serve (the laser industry), and guts. He next set out to implement what he refers to as his eight-point program:

1. Selection of Associates

In choosing his associates, McLaughlin tried to select those individuals who had backgrounds that were suitable to the new business but that were unlike his own background. He has a very great appreciation for the valuable insights a heterogeneous team may provide a business that serves markets as diverse as jewelry and high technology.

2. Raising Venture Capital

McLaughlin and his new associates held a meeting and invited all of the individuals who had expressed interest in the new business and who were in a position to contribute either money, equipment, time, or knowledge in exchange for stock. Enthusiasm controlled the meeting; at one point a man stood up and announced "I'll take $1,600 worth," without even indicating how many shares of stock he expected to receive in return for this investment. By the end of the meeting, which lasted an hour and a half, the decision to proceed with incorporation of the business was finalized in spite of the fact that the initial capitalization was only $20,200.

On several occasions shortly after this momentous meeting, McLaughlin was told by astute businessmen "You won't last out your first year;" "Within six months you'll have to locate additional financing;" and, when McLaughlin's planned sales organization was described, "It's *impossible* to sell a thousand-dollar item by mail!" With justifiable pride, McLaughlin points out that he has indeed lasted more than a year. In fact, the company recently celebrated its seventh anniversary. Growth has been sustained through earnings without any additional financing, and several hundreds of thousands of dollars worth of products have been sold exclusively through the use of direct mail, display advertising, and publicity releases in trade journals, all of which goes to prove that the experts can be wrong. One of the most difficult factors to evaluate in weighing the potential for success of a new enterprise is the determination of the founders.

Not very long after the initial meeting, permission was obtained from the Commissioner of Corporations of the State of California to issue stock in the new enterprise and collect the money pledged. When he called on one man for his money, he was told "Mac, I know I pledged $1,000, and I don't know why I did it. I guess the enthusiasm ran so high at the meeting that I got carried away. I'm 48 years old and I've never had $1,000 at one time in my whole life." Fortunately, this was the only instance of inability to honor a pledge, and the financing was satisfactorily completed.

3. . Setting Up Shop

Next, a building was leased and the business was effectively launched. Everyone but the stenographer (McLaughlin's wife) had another full-time job outside. All of the original employees agreed to accept a $2-per-hour salary, to be paid annually in stock.

4. Building a Prototype

Part of the assets McLaughlin contributed to the new enterprise in exchange for founders' equity were models of several different pieces of equipment. However, the first product that produced an order was a prototype of a new piece of equipment called a Wire Saw. In McLaughlin's words, "This unit was a winner!" Interestingly enough, McLaughlin was still employed at this point by the University of Southern California, and this same institution was Laser Technology's first customer.

As McLaughlin emphasizes, not only is a prototype necessary for the procurement of new orders, but it can also be of inestimable value in garnering free publicity for the enterprise and generating interest in the product. The Wire Saw, the product that launched Laser Technology, functions in much the same way as a common hack-saw. However, instead of using an ordinary metal blade, the cutting blade of the Wire Saw is a specially formulated metal alloy imbedded with industrial diamond dust; this combination proved to be a technical breakthrough for slicing crystals and very high-density metals. Borrowing from the words of Neil Armstrong, our first astronaut to set foot on the moon, the accomplishment proved to be not only one small step for mankind but also one giant leap for Laser Technology for, subsequent to the return of this lunar vehicle, the Laser Technology Wire Saw proved to be one of the most satisfactory means available for cutting the moon rocks that the astronauts brought back with them.

5. Solicit Publicity

Typically, a small new company is long on enthusiasm and short on cash. Laser Technology periodically supplies news releases to more than 300 trade publications that serve industries representing potential clients for their products. The key to obtaining free publicity in a publication is to persuade the editor that your message is of sufficient general interest to their readership to warrant the use of the space allocated for news. In McLaughlin's opinion, a properly handled news release may garner more free publicity than a far more expensive, paid advertisement.

6. Respond to Inquiries

As a result of the news releases issued to trade publications, Laser Technology received a substantial number of mail inquiries from potential customers. By promptly responding to each inquiry with brochures and additional information describing the entire line of product offerings of Laser Technology, a substantial amount of new business resulted; and the customer list for the new company was significantly enlarged.

7. Secure Sales

Profitable sales represent the life blood of any business, large or small. In the first year of operation, sales for Laser Technology amounted to only $3,000, certainly not much by aerospace standards. However, due to the fact that the business had no employees on the payroll who were working for more than stock in the company, the drain on assets normally represented by a corporate payroll was nil. Since the first year, annual sales have doubled each year, representing a growth rate with which any company should be pleased.

One of the primary factors to which McLaughlin attributes the success of his company is its unconditional money-back guarantee on all of its products. Such a customer service program is virtually unheard of in industry circles dominated by large corporations.

The Laser Technology sales organization is run by McLaughlin's 69-year-old wife (he is now 70 years of age). She also serves as Secretary-Treasurer for the corporation. As McLaughlin puts it, "My wife didn't know that you couldn't sell a $1,000 item by direct mail; and, therefore, she has been quite successful in doing it for six years." He asserts that he is confident of her ability to sell the latest product, the Environmental Diamond Wheel Chemical Polishing Machine, which carries a price tag in the $7,000 range.

8. Don't Neglect Research and Development

In McLaughlin's words, "All my life I wanted to have a company where sales would bring in sufficient money to enable us to do intensive research and development work. The success of work you do today is what keeps you in business two, three, four, or even 10 years from now." Presently, Laser Technology has no less than 15 different products in various stages of development. One of their newer products is a unique, composite synthetic gemstone made of Metastrontion Titanate and cut into a diamond shape. This unique stone is characterized by multiple interior reflections exceeding those of real diamonds. However, because the basic material is slightly less hard than a real diamond, McLaughlin crowns each synthetic gem with a very thin slice of sapphire. Since diamond is the only material that will scratch sapphire, the brilliance of the underlying synthetic stone is preserved.

Another significant factor in a well-coordinated research and development program is the investigation of new applications for existing products. For example, recently the diamond-impregnated Wire Saw was found uniquely well suited to the fabrication of honeycomb cavities for use in air-frame structures; and the aircraft industry was provided with an entirely new manufacturing technique. As a result of this new application, the Wire Saw was entered in the recent Industrial Research "100" competition. Every year, thousands of inventions and ideas are evaluated by a select industry committee for the purpose of choosing the 100 best entries for an award. The McLaughlins were notified that their entry in the competition had been selected as one of the top 100 submitted. Included in the letter of notification was an invitation to attend the awards banquet in New York to accept the honor. Feeling that a trip to New York merely to accept an award represented an unjustifiable expenditure of time and money, the McLaughlins requested that Industrial Research mail the award. With unconcealed pride, McLaughlin produces a copy of the letter he received in reply and, pointing to the last paragraph, reads, "An Industrial Research '100' Award is to applied research what a Nobel prize is to basic research. You should be proud of the research and development achievement of your company." Never having won a Nobel prize or anything close to it, the McLaughlins decided that they would *make* the time necessary to attend the banquet.

Among the fellow recipients of this honor were such goliaths as General Electric, Westinghouse, RCA, Union Carbide, Bell Laboratories, General Telephone, Hewlett-Packard, Honeywell, IBM, and Bendix. At the banquet, the featured speaker indicated that the average cost of development of the items that had won awards that year was $240,000. Since such a figure represented 10 times the total assets of Laser Technology, McLaughlin offers his listener assurances that development cost for the Wire Saw was substantially less than $240,000.

Today, seven years after start-up, Laser Technology employs a staff of 20, most of whom have regular eight-hour-a-day jobs in the aerospace industry. To accommodate such a staff, Laser Technology runs two shifts, and McLaughlin works from 7:00 a.m. to 10:00 p.m. five days a week and puts in substantial additional time every weekend. As I sat in McLaughlin's office surveying the shelf-lined walls and the storage racks suspended from the ceiling and listening to the clicking of a homemade automatic wire-processing machine in the background, McLaughlin beamed and said, "I am now 70 years old and I have a place to work. In fact, I'm working 70 hours a week and enjoying every minute of it. I'm so happy in my work that I wouldn't trade my opportunity here for a berth in heaven." Amen!

Recommended Reading

Allen, Frederick Lewis. *The Great Pierpont Morgan.* Perennial Library. New York: Harper & Row, Publishers, 1965.

Burlingame, Roger. *Henry Ford.* Quadrangle Paperbacks. Chicago: Quadrangle Books, 1970.

Chamberlain, John. *The Enterprising Americans.* Perennial Library. New York: Harper & Row, Publishers, 1967.

Cossman, E. Joseph. *How I Made $1,000,000 in Mail Order.* Englewood Cliffs, N.J.: Prentice-Hall, Inc., 1963.

Fortune Magazine Staff, ed. *Adventures in Small Business.* New York: McGraw-Hill Book Company, 1957.

Frasca, John. *Con Man or Saint?* Anderson, S.C.: Droke House, Publishers, Inc., 1969.

Josephson, Matthew. *Edison.* New York: McGraw-Hill Book Company, 1959.

Lay, Beirne, Jr. *Someone Has to Make It Happen; the Inside Story of Tex Thornton, the Man Who Built Litton Industries.* Englewood Cliffs, N.J.: Prentice-Hall, Inc., 1969.

Miller, William, ed. *Men in Business.* Torchbook Edition. New York: Harper & Row, 1962.

Paulucci, Jeno F., with Rich, Les. *How It Was to Make $100,000,000 in a Hurry; the Tale of Jeno and the Bean Sprout.* New York: Grosset and Dunlap, 1969.

Rae, John B., ed. *Henry Ford.* A Spectrum Book. Englewood Cliffs, N.J.: Prentice-Hall, Inc., 1969.

Rodgers, William. *Think; A Biography of the Watsons and IBM.* A Signet Book. New York: Stein and Day Publishers, 1969.

Sarnoff, Paul. *Russell Sage.* New York: Ivan Obolensky, Inc., 1965.

Schafer, R. C. *How Millionaires Made Their Fortunes and How You Can Make Yours.* Pyramid Books. New York: Pyramid Publications, 1970.

Sevard, Keith. *The Legend of Henry Ford.* New York: Athenaeum, 1968.

Sloan, Alfred P., Jr. *My Years With General Motors.* New York: Macfadden-Bartell Corporation, 1965.

Uhlan, Edward. *The Rogue of Publishers' Row,* 20th ed. A Banner Book. Jericho, N.Y.: Exposition Press, Inc., 1970.

Wright, Esmond, ed. *Benjamin Franklin, A Profile.* New York: Hill and Wang, 1970.

Chapter 2

What Motivates
the Entrepreneur?

Many academic treatises and theses have been written for the purpose of identifying and analyzing the factors that motivate the entrepreneur. In this chapter, we will address the subject in a style with which you personally may identify or which may closely relate to the situation of someone you know well.

A Sunny Day

Dear Boss,

I, Jack B. Nimble, hereby give notice of my formal resignation, effective two weeks from today.

I've been a designer with the Gargantuan Growth Group, Incorporated (G Cubed) ever since I finished college. My work here has been very educational, although I do confess to occasional bewilderment regarding big business management decisions. This example should illustrate what I mean: Once at a bitch session the Director of Manufacturing responded to a question of mine by telling a story about the "Mushroom" Theory of Management. He said that you should always keep your employees in the dark, feed them lots of horseshit, and, when they grow up, cut them off at the ankles and can them. Everybody thought it was a funny story; but by the time the meeting was over I still didn't have an answer to my question.

However, I'm not writing this letter to complain. I'd like to take this opportunity to thank you and the company for all you have done for me.

That $100 bonus I got last Christmas in exchange for patent rights on my 14th invention was a welcome addition to my son's college fund. And I get a real kick out of seeing the Production Department turning out thousands of my little gadgets every day, even if my name isn't on the label. I only regret that I had to spend two years and write three fat proposals before persuading you and the division manager that it was a good product idea in the first place.

In case you think that my decision to leave has anything to do with the layoff of Larry Longtimer last week, I want to put your mind at ease. I had been wondering why Larry was still on the payroll. His enthusiasm and drive really went to hell after he was promoted to Vice President of Historical Planning. I just didn't feel he was doing the company any good in that new position. Confidentially, though, something has been puzzling me. Why did the top brass transfer him out of the Stockholders' Delight Division he started 12 years ago, especially right after they racked up their 10th straight record year? The new manager, Mr. Presidentson, isn't doing nearly as well.

At Larry's farewell luncheon last Friday, I was really moved by the company's generosity in giving him a solid gold 25-year service pin with a real diamond in it. It's too bad Larry couldn't hold out until he was eligible for retirement next year, though. I guess it couldn't be helped, what with the big losses this year in the Stockholders' Delight Division. Anyway, that check for two weeks' severance pay should tide him over until he qualifies for unemployment compensation. I understand you can get as high as $75 per week nowadays.

I'd also like to say that my resignation is in no way related to my having to terminate those "summer-hire" students last year just two weeks after they started working. (Remember how long it took me to persuade you to let me hire them in the first place?) I guess the company's sudden realization that it was in a cash bind and required immediate layoffs couldn't be helped. I sure had a tough time explaining to those students, though. They went away grumbling some terrible things about their first introduction to big business.

Boss, I remember your explaining that the last 6 percent raise you gave me was the largest in the whole department, that I'm the youngest guy in the company's history to have the responsibilities I hold, and that my salary is the highest in the company for my job classification. I also recall that to be eligible for my next promotion to Novice Manager, I have to put in at least two more years with the company.

Boss, you've gotta understand! Each month, I get a copy of the *Alumni Review* from my *alma mater*. My wife reads me the class news at bedtime every evening after that damn thing comes in the mail. You wouldn't believe the jerks I used to have for classmates and lab partners who have started businesses of their own and are making out pretty well. One has launched a successful magazine with an international circulation, another has his own real estate development corporation. Still another has a computer peripheral company with 500 people on the payroll and grossed $10 million last year while our "most likely to fail" is a *bona fide* magnate in the alfalfa exporting business. Phil Anthrope, my former class president, just made a $100,000 Alumni Fund donation to establish a perpetual scholarship bearing his name. With competition like this, you can understand why I was too ashamed of my career progress to go to last year's reunion. I *know* I'm at least as good as most of these guys, and I've got to prove it to my wife, my friends, and most of all, *myself*. G Cubed timetables just don't hack it!

By now, I'll bet you're wondering what my plans are. I want you to know that I am not going to work for a competitor. You remember that new electromechanator Willie Whizbanger recently finished an 18-month development program on? You know, the one you circulated a memo about, saying the company was going to abandon it because there was no market for it? (You even let Willie buy the sole patent rights for $1.) Guess what? The Vice President of Corporate Development at Upward Spiral Industries read Willie's recent professional society article about it and called our Marketing Department to see if he could buy some electromechanators from G Cubed. When he learned we weren't going to make any here, the Upward Spiral man asked if they might buy the patent rights. That's when Marketing referred the call to Willie.

Later that evening Willie telephoned me at home to say that if I wanted to start a company with him to make electromechanators, Upward Spiral had indicated they would be our first customer. Willie said that the man at Upward Spiral even told him that he could help us get some venture capital if we would prepare a business proposal. He mentioned the possibility of our being a subsidiary or some such thing, but Willie and I are going to get more details after we finish working on our business plan. Incidentally, we will probably be calling our new company Nimble Whizbanger Laboratories. I'm going to be the President and Willie is going to be the Vice President of Engineering.

The main reason Willie and I feel so confident about our prospects for success is the way Fred Faithless and his group made out when they spun off to start Levitation Laboratories two years ago. They were just acquired last month by Colossal Conglomerate in a stock swap deal, and we understand that Fred has now retired to a cattle ranch in the Canadian Rockies at the tender age of 37.

Of the seven or eight companies started by former G Cubed staff members, the only one we know of that has failed was started by Stanley Spleen and Gilbert Gall. As near as we can reckon, their difficulties were basically due to walnut paneling, palace revolts, and the 35-hour work week.

Willie and I have built a new prototype of our electromechanator at my uncle's auto repair shop using parts we bought at the Spleen and Gall bankruptcy sale. Also, we went to one of these new seminars on how to get started. Willie and I have talked to our wives about this, and last night we came to our final decision. Boss, it has been a pleasure working for you, and if you decide you might like to join us in about six months, we'd be glad to talk it over.

Sincerely,

Jack B. Nimble

A Clear Day

Dear Readers,

If I have been successful, Jack's letter should sum up most of the factors which prompt a man to consider starting a business of his own. There are two categories in which these factors can be classified:

1. Those elements outside the corporation walls that irresistibly lure the entrepreneur to test his mettle in his own enterprise. They include:

a)   The desire to be his own boss
b)   The desire for fame
c)   The desire for personal fortune
d)   The pure joy of winning

2. Those elements in the corporate experience which provoke the entrepreneur to run screaming for the exit. They include:

a)   Inadequate corporate communications
b)   Inequity between major contributions and financial rewards
c)   Promotion and salary policies
d)   Employment security?
e)   Corporate politics and nepotism
f)   Red tape
g)   Orphan products
h)   Questionably relevant educational requirements

Let's examine each of these in detail.

FACTORS EXTERNAL TO THE CORPORATION

The Desire to be His Own Boss

When corporate decisions and fortunes appear to be most capricious, a man may feel an ungovernable desire to do his own thing. He wants to feel that, if he fails, it was his doing and his doing *alone*. The essence of entrepreneurship is the charting of one's own course on the high seas of tomorrow's business world.

Obviously the degree of autonomy an entrepreneur can enjoy depends largely on his stockholders or partners (if he has any), his customers, his financial condition, and even his products. With careful planning, the entrepreneur can weigh autonomy against his other entrepreneurial objectives and arrive at an acceptable compromise *before* he commits his financial, physical, and emotional resources to the enterprise.

A very important aspect of being your own boss is the freedom to choose those projects to which you will devote your efforts. Should you wish to spend part of your time literally building sand castles at the beach, this option may be yours to pursue, *if* you work things right. The satisfaction in *doing* instead of *proposing* or *justifying* can be quite liberating. Successful entrepreneurs derive some of their greatest satisfaction from watering, *without* first having to perform a rain dance for the corporate demigods, their ideas and concepts until they flower and bear fruit.

The Desire for Fame

I have no statistics on the number of companies that bear in some form the names of their founders, but a look through any business directory suggests that companies that do include founders' names substantially outnumber those that do not. And consider that a large percentage of those that do not are the result of the desire for trademark protection not possible or practical with the use of the founder(s)' name(s). For example, the familiar name of the Kodak film company was specifically selected, in the words of its founder, George Eastman, "because I knew a trade name must be short, vigorous, incapable of being misspelled to an extent that will destroy its identity, and, in order to satisfy trademark laws, it must mean absolutely nothing."[4]

I seriously doubt that the desire to see one's name on a billboard is the sole reason for the inception of any corporation, but the opportunity for obtaining some degree of fame certainly enhances the attractiveness of the my-own-business undertaking. The identification of the founder with his creation is a major incentive in goading him to superhuman efforts. He often feels that both his reputation and that of his whole family depend on the success of his efforts. Significant achievement in the business and social community, with its attendant prestige and honor for the entrepreneur *and* his family, serves as justification for undertaking the risks involved.

The Desire for a Personal Fortune

There are other financial factors at work in the motivation of an entrepreneur apart from score-keeping of rewards for work performed. For example:

In school, a perfect mark is 100 points out of 100 possible points. Measuring the worth of an idea without access to such a simplistic yardstick is a fundamental enigma. Obviously, 100 percent of all the money there is in the world (or in the company treasury, for that matter) is an impractical prize for perfect business performance. Some slightly smaller apportionment will have to make do. The amount of money available with which, then, to "keep score" is usually in grossly inadequate supply, particularly if corporate structure has the key to the counting house. As the expression goes, "you'll never get rich working for somebody else."

Accordingly, after working several years in industry, the potential entrepreneur begins simultaneously to discover that his salary growth *and* his promotion rate are running along with very short steps. And he begins to recognize that people who launch their *own* successful businesses often make a *lot* of money in the process. The realization comes to him about the time when: the no-money-down, GI-Bill-financed tract house with its tar and gravel roof is beginning to need repairs; the property taxes have doubled in the last five years; the kids are reaching school age or are far enough along so that college tuition has ceased to be a nebulous future concern; the balancing of the family budget requires more and more time and proves less and less encouraging a task than it was when the expense/income ratio was a lot more reasonable.

And suddenly other symptoms of latent entrepreneurship begin to manifest themselves. Instead of devoting all of the evening reading to trade and industry publications, the stricken entrepreneur-to-be makes time for a review of *The Wall Street Journal* and *Business Week.* Here to dazzle him are success stories of new glamour companies with 50-to-1 price/earnings ratios (Chapter XI dying-company obituaries seem to appear on a space-available basis as column fillers, if they appear at all). As the captivated company founder of the future continues to grapple with his personal finances, he begins to visualize how much more he could be enjoying life if he had no money worries. He begins to evaluate his own potential in comparison with the examples he has been reading about. And he decides that he's got as much success serum in his veins as the guys in those articles he's been reading. Why shouldn't he, like "those guys," enjoy a new house, a yacht, that great new sports car, a Paris-designer wardrobe for his wife, Ivy League colleges for his kids? He could even set up a charitable foundation, like the Fords and the Rockefellers. All he's got to do is put together a company and hire a good tax man to keep Uncle Sam from taking all of the profits. Right? Well, not quite, but such decisions are rarely reached on a rational basis, anyway.

The Pure Joy of Winning

It's pretty tough for a corporation to supply continuing opportunities that can satisfy the consuming, emotional need to *win* that possesses the soul of the embryonic entrepreneur. Dr. Stanley F. Kaisel, founder and former President of what is now the MEC Division of Teledyne, addressed a group of young MIT alumni by stating, with the authority of the business veteran, "Victories come from doing things *better* than other people. Victories are what provide the fun in having a company of your own."[5]

And indeed the *élan* of intense competition and the heady feeling of victory *is* a very significant motivational factor in the creation of new companies. As a member of a large corporation, the soul of the entrepreneur often feels like a handicapped race horse, bearing a greater burden than his less able counterparts. In the case of race horses, handicapping ostensibly provides for an "equitable" contest; it gives the older, albeit more feeble, a crack at the finish line. How frustrating to watch the trophies and glory accrue only to senior or better-entrenched colleagues! Conversely, excessive competitive zeal has no place in either a large *or* small company. A delicate balance between internal cooperation and external competition is an essential element of long-term survival in any corporate entity. Recently a 14-month-old company *and* $350,000 of an investor's money were almost totally dissipated by the disaster of internal competition. Today, only one of the six founders (not the president) remains to administer intensive care to the corporate dream turned nightmare.

Fortunately, I have observed far more business success stories than I have instances of failure. These successes have resulted in no small degree from the ability of the members of each founding group constructively to channel their competitive energies. The point I wish to make is that there was enough *room* in their new corporate structure for each to expend his energies to the limit without colliding with ceilings *or* colleagues. A story which magnificently illustrates this theme is that of Thomas Alva Edison. Because he was his own boss, he was free to devote his enormous inventive talent to damn near any project he wanted to work on. As a result, he became one of the most prolific technological creators of all time. We are indebted to him for his work on such diverse products as the radio, the phonograph recording, the motion picture camera, the telephone, and the electric light. Edison also left us his statement on the subject of winning: "I don't care so much about making my fortune as I do for getting ahead of the other fellows."[6]

FACTORS INTERNAL TO THE CORPORATION

Inadequate Corporate Communications

Entrepreneurs are often impatient with and confused by the typical communications problems of the large corporation. The only viable solution to this problem (as far as guys like Jack B. Nimble are concerned) is for Jack to call the shots himself. But his lack of patience with The System makes it highly improbable that he will stick around long enough to gain the vantage point in the corporate hierarchy where the visibility is 100 percent. What Jack must do, then, is build his own corporate structure beneath him (where, ironically, if the enterprise is successful, the ponderous insensitivity of the large corporation will reassert itself to annoy the frustrated entrepreneurs in Jack's employ). The Gordian knot of corporate communications has been the subject of many books and many studies. There is only one conclusion, however, upon which everyone agrees—the sword is most efficiently wielded from the *top* of the knot.

Inequity Between Major Contributions and Financial Rewards

When Jack's new product is commercially successful, all the diamonds in Africa wouldn't represent sufficient compensation for his efforts. Totally his is the product—memories of budget over-runs in research and development; projects written off as failures; tens of thousands of dollars invested in capital equipment; the assisting small army of purchasing men, production workers, machinists, technical writers, draftsmen, stockroom clerks, sheet-metal workers; the librarian; and the secretary who every Friday faithfully watered his philodendron fade from consciousness. They were, he rationalizes, only doing their jobs. So was that marketing guy who had to pander his wife to close the big sale. But the invention, the idea that became a successful *thing*—that, thinks Jack, is a horse of a different color, and he should be the one to receive first and foremost consideration in the distribution of the rewards.

In the typical corporate structure, the Jacks of this world may expect little more than a relatively comfortable salary plus a token bonus in recognition of their occasional and unpredictable inventive output. The company attitude seems to be: "We're paying you to invent, so why should we give you additional incentives simply because you manage to do what we hired you to do in the first place?"

On the other hand, companies are rarely equipped adequately to reward the innovative and pioneering achievements of genuinely creative minds. Company standards are established on the expectation of mediocrity in innovation. Often, incentives are structured to provide bonuses based solely on the number of patents applied for, regardless of commercial or scientific merit.

However, in the hands of a resourceful entrepreneur, a worthwhile innovation may provide a sound basis for a new enterprise. The resulting financial rewards may be a more realistic quantification of the merit of a genuine contribution to the industry and may provide the entrepreneur with a substantially greater return for his efforts than he could ever have expected from a corporation.

As I see it, if a creative guy (be he inventor, scientist, marketing innovator, or manufacturing genius) is willing really to take a chance on the commercial merits of his output, if he is willing and able to *risk*, then founding a company of his own can provide him with a well-deserved return. On the other hand, if he is comfortable only with the resources of a large corporation backing his longshot ideas, then, like the race track tipster's, his "equitable" return is the price of a tout sheet.

Promotion and Salary Policies

My friends, you got trouble. Right here in Corporation City. Trouble starts with a "T" and that rhymes with "P" and that stands for Prejudice—*age* prejudice. Yeah!

Are expressions like "time in grade," "Yes, but he's too young," or "he ain't old enough to be makin' that kind of money" creeping into your vocabulary? Are you set on keepin' these smart-assed whippersnappers down in their proper place? My friend, you got trouble, trouble, Trouble! That Music Man's gonna lead 'em right down Route 128 to the first vacant shop they can find. I've seen plenty of young engineers who "weren't ready" for increased corporate responsibility resign and subsequently succeed in mastering far more demanding problems in starting their own company. These young cockerels simply said "To hell with the incubator! Let me at the hen yard!"

When it comes to the compensation of exceptional young men, corporate practice is baffling. Why is it that companies are so reluctant to flex their salary guidelines for promising, productive men? Ultimately, such men quit in frustration to take a higher-paying position elsewhere or to start their own business. Then—and this is the grabber—the first company often will pay the man's replacement a *higher* salary to fill the opening and pay the head-hunter a 10-percent-of-annual-salary bounty to boot! (Remember, the bump a guy gets when he hits his head on a salary ceiling injures more than just his cranium.)

Employee Security?

There is no such thing. Security comes from keeping your skills sharp enough (up-to-date enough) and versatile enough to weather the fickle winds of corporate fate. Personal resourcefulness is far more valuable an asset than any narrow skill (What do you do when they stop making anything resembling the only computer you know how to operate?). Furthermore, it is hard to conceive of any endeavor that can tax your personal resourcefulness more than running a company of your own and that has the potential for rewarding you more handsomely with the kind of reward that means the money-in-the-bank security *most* people have in mind when they talk about security.

This security thing is a slippery concept. To paraphrase the late Mike Todd: "I've never been insecure, only broke. Being insecure is a frame of mind, while being broke is only a temporary situation." For the spirited entrepreneur, reversals and setbacks are merely pebbles and short detours on the road to success. Security results from the self-knowledge that *you* and not some impersonal corporate entity are responsible for your own destiny. Security results from positive personal action to insure that you acquire and maintain skills and attitudes for which there is a continuing demand. *Real* personal security is measured by the confidence with which you undertake difficult new challenges and the ease with which you adjust to adversity. Hand-wringing worry-warts will *never* be secure, with or without a company job.

In summary, as long as you have a skill or talent for which there is a professional demand, you may look forward to "security." To expect to be retained in *any* position after you cease to be able to contribute effectively toward the goals of that organization is to pay a terrible penalty in terms of self-respect and the real security that comes from knowing that your contributions are important.

Corporate Politics and Nepotism

Most companies, and particularly the small ones that guys like J. B. Nimble start, are patterned in the image of their creators. From what I have seen, the Laws of Relativity (Nepotism) and corporate politics are at least as virulent in the small, closely held corporations as they are in their bigger brothers. The expression "Blood is thicker than water" must surely have emerged from the small-company milieu. As long as companies are run by people, politics will have to be reckoned with as a factor of corporate reality. Therefore, you may as well be the nepotor instead of the nepotee.

Red Tape

No matter how you hack at it, red tape is a pain in the ass! It is a disease endemic to large corporations, being symptomatic of procrastination and indecision. The originator of red tape, called "the corporate coward," is characterized by a fear of making decisions. His *modus operandi* is his insistence on including any and all steps effective in producing delay. The problem is thereby dissipated until it is too vague to require a decision and, thus, the risk involved in general decision-making is brought to its nadir. The progress-minded employee finds it necessary to negotiate the complex administrative labyrinth that *his idea*—the bureaucracy's *problem*—has become, which frustrates his efforts to advance his programs and destroys or seriously impairs his initiative. And, as may be expected, his productivity is similarly affected.

Red tape also includes the corporate coward's ability to insulate himself from responsibility. The insulating material is in the form of voluminous data from various studies and reports; any decision that he reaches limps forth from under the crush of background material and is ready at any moment, should its efficacy be questioned, to scuttle again beneath the bulging dossier as the corporate coward mumbles "Well, I did everything *I* could to insure that the decision was correct." (In effect, he is only saying, "Don't I deserve an 'A' for effort?")

I am reminded of a situation I experienced while in the military service, when I ran a one-man office in a records-retirement warehouse. The lighting in the building was terrible, and I felt that my efficiency could be considerably enhanced (*and* my eyesight preserved) if I had the benefit of fluorescent lighting. I discussed the problem with my boss, a Chief Warrant Officer of many years' experience. Although he indicated that my suggestion was worthwhile, he pointed out that it would be necessary to document the merits of my request in order to secure approval to have the work done. I therefore spent the next hour carefully preparing a concise, half-page report to justify the installation of the lighting and submitted it.

Approximately one week later, I received notification that my request had been turned down for insufficient supporting information. At this point, I revised and resubmitted the request, giving an elaborate discussion of the savings in time and money and the increased efficiency which would result from the added lighting. Naturally, many of the figures were slanted to obtain the necessary approval. Later, I was told that the second request I had submitted was one of the best the authorizing officer had ever seen. He further indicated that if every request that came to his attention was as carefully documented as the one representing my second attempt, every one of them would qualify for his approval. Needless to say, I did not dare question him as to what impact this rationale might have on his budget or the manpower available to him.

In the preparation of this kind of justification, I was, in effect, placed in the position of making the decision *for* the responsible individual; and, thus, the desired goal was achieved. I got what I wanted, and he didn't have to make the decision.

I was quite appalled, however, when subsequently it took two men one and one-half days to install the two fluorescent lights in my small office. It turned out that they had very little to do; their backlog was very low, and they were simply stretching out their work to fill in the hours on their time cards.

Orphan Products

Let's take a closer look at Willie Whizbanger, the engineer to whom we referred above. Willie was an enthusiastic guy, very bright and very creative and very involved with his projects. Whenever he was assigned a particularly challenging task, he would jump up and down (discreetly, mind you) and rub his hands with glee! His eyes would twinkle and his customary mask of deep preoccupation with theoretical considerations would give way to an ear-lobe-to-ear-lobe grin. He would even be polite to the company salesmen when they annoyed him with questions about when he might finish his project and how much the end product might cost to make.

Often the night watchman would wonder about this man who stayed up until it was nearly dawn fiddling with the knobs on his expensive instruments and marking strange symbols in his notebook. Now and then, the watchman would write little notes to the day-shift Security Officer, seeking assurances that all was well.

Willie, working until dawn, was very happy. He was doing just what he spent six years in college studying to do.

Finally the prototype was complete. Every design objective had been achieved and the final reports had been painstakingly written. All that remained was to tool up in Production and turn out thousands more just like the first. Willie offered cigars around. "Willie," his boss said, placing his arm around the young man's shoulders, "you've done a fine job; I'm really proud of you. Now let's go into my office for a few minutes. I want to bring you up to date on a few changes we've just made in the Marketing Department."

Minutes later, Willie and his boss were luxuriating in the fine aroma of Jamaican tobacco and the comfort of heavy leather chairs. "Willie, I know how much this latest project has meant to you. I personally feel it represents the most creative work you've done for me to date.

"However, I've spent the last two days in discussions with our new Vice President of Marketing and the Controller, reviewing the new product promotion budgets. Now I know the previous Marketing Honcho was looking forward to a big campaign to introduce your new product; but, as you know, he recently resigned—another company offered him a salary we couldn't meet. Anyway, the new marketeer just isn't convinced the market is ready for your product. His budget is tight, so he's asked us in Engineering to put the idea on the shelf for a year or two. I hope you'll understand, Willie. If you want to, take the rest of the day off, and we'll talk about a new project tomorrow morning."

In a blue funk and with a lump in this throat, Willie dumped the remaining cigars into his briefcase and prepared to go home. Just then, his phone rang. The gal on the switchboard said, "Mr. Vector of Upward Spiral Industries is calling."

It is unreasonable to expect one or two entrepreneurs to personify *all* of the reasons people have for starting a business of their own. Therefore, the next section will cover additional motivations not mentioned in Jack's letter.

Questionably Relevant Educational Requirements

Within the corporate compound, a manager candidate lacking a college degree (a "mustang," in Navy parlance) has the deck stacked against him. In many cases, degree snobbery is so great that less-capable college-educated men will refuse to work for very capable mustangs. The college-graduates spent four years preparing for their career; evidently they don't want to let anyone else into the circle of the elite unless he too antes up the four-year membership fee. Like the old days of fraternity hazing, the attitude seems to be "I had to put up with it; why should the new candidates get off any lighter?" Given such a set of circumstances, the degree-deficient man either takes the time to complete his college education, resigns himself to mediocre career progress, or starts a business of his own.

Everyone knows of individuals who have studied several years in night school for an advanced college degree. Have you ever noticed the large salary increase they often receive after they finish the last three lousy units needed to complete the degree requirements? Ask yourself: Are they being paid for capability or for a slip of parchment?

Unfortunately, a college education serves too often as a ball and chain, preparing a man for a lifetime career as a corporation employee. Listen to him speak: "Hell, I spent four years of my life getting this degree in Synergistic-Heuristic Invalid Technology, and I'll be damned if I'm going to give that up to go into any *new* field, *regardless* of how promising it may appear to be. So what if I haven't had a raise in two years? I've got security."

Contrast this with the talented high-school graduate who goes into fast-food franchising, real-estate development, or garment retailing. If he is modestly successful, his income will be comparable to that of the college-educated corporation employee. If his success is more than modest, his lifetime earnings will exceed the corporation employee's by several times over.

Without a doubt, the reader can conjure up a list of entrepreneurial motivations twice as long as mine. To treat this topic exhaustively, however, would be the subject of an entire book. The references at the end of this chapter should be of help to those wishing to study this fascinating phenomenon further.

Recommended Reading

Brooks, John. *Business Adventures.* Bantam Books. New York: Weybright and Talley, Inc., 1970.

Collins, Orvis F. and Moore, David G. *The Organization Makers; a Behavioral Study of Independent Entrepreneurs.* New York: Appleton-Century-Crofts, 1970.

Guzzardi, Walter, Jr. *The Young Executives.* A Mentor Executive Library Book. New York: The New American Library, Inc., 1966.

Jay, Anthony. *Management and Machiavelli, an Inquiry into the Politics of Corporate Life.* Bantam Books. New York: Holt, Rinehart and Winston, 1969.

Komives, John L. *Some Characteristics of Selected Entrepreneurs.* Ph.D. Thesis, Michigan State University. Ann Arbor, Michigan: University Microfilms, 1965.

McClelland, David C. *The Achieving Society.* Princeton, New Jersey: D. Van Nostrand Company, 1961.

McGregor, Douglas. *The Human Side of Enterprise.* New York: McGraw-Hill and Co., 1960.

Parkinson, C. Northcote. *Parkinson's Law.* Ballentine Books. Boston: Houghton Mifflin Company, 1964.

Peter, Laurence J. and Hull, Raymond *The Peter Principle.* Bantam Books. New York: William Morrow and Co., 1970.

Rand, Ayn. *Capitalism: The Unknown Ideal.* A Signet Book. New York: The New American Library, 1967.

Townsend, Robert. *Up the Organization: How to Stop the Corporation from Stifling People and Strangling Profits.* New York: Alfred A. Knopf, 1970.

Wechsberg, Joseph. *The Merchant Bankers.* Pocket Books. New York: Little, Brown and Company, 1968.

Chapter 3

Personal Resources Checklist

"The single most important factor in the success or failure of a new enterprise is the *people*."[7] Do *you* have the personal resources necessary successfully to withstand the rigors of starting a business of your own? Measure yourself and see.

Many of the topics to be covered below will appear to be just plain common sense. Yet, on the average, more than 1,000 firms are discontinued *every day* of the year.[8] The single greatest underlying cause of business failure, or *bankruptcy*, is incompetence, which accounts for approximately 45 percent of the total failures. Before you take the chance of becoming one of the 1,000, consider *your* personal capabilities.

COMPETENCE

There is no one who can be completely objective in evaluating his own competence. Competence constitutes a measure of one's ability to gather

41

information, evaluate it, and arrive at operational decisions with a high percentage of right answers quickly, in order to render these decisions maximally effective. Generally, the information that must be evaluated is less than complete. Accordingly, imagination, an ability to "read between the lines," the maturity of judgment necessary to recognize when a decision *must* be made (with or *without* all the facts), and the guts to say "We'll do it this way," are the marks of the competent manager.

Fear of making a wrong judgment causes the administrative paralysis that is a sure sign of incompetence. Consider this story of a baseball player: It was the bottom of the ninth inning. The score was six to five. Runners were on second and third. Any base hit would bring in two runs and win the ball game. There were already two outs. The count on the batter was three and two. The crowd in the packed stands watched with pounding pulses and bated breath as the pitcher delivered a hard, fast ball right down the middle. "Strike three," the umpire roared. The game was over.

"Why didn't you swing at that last pitch?" the red-faced coach demanded of his retired batter.

"Well, sir," responded the batter, "I was afraid I'd miss it."

MOTIVATION AND THE THREE D'S: DESIRE, DETERMINATION, AND DEDICATION

Starting a new firm is not a recommended pastime for the dilettante. Desire, determination, and dedication, the three ingredients in my personal definition of motivation, are essential qualities that enable the entrepreneur to continue to function effectively in the face of crushing disappointments and reversals. Motivation is the catalyst that facilitates the application of one's talents to the resolution of seemingly insoluble problems.

There is a vast literature that has popularized the subject of motivation. We have all heard of people such as Norman Vincent Peale, Bishop Fulton J. Sheen, Napoleon Hill, and Maxwell Maltz. In the writings of all of these men, one theme prevails: You get more satisfaction out of life by deciding what it is you want from life and then pursuing that goal with single-minded devotion. One businessman of my acquaintance is so motivated that he has prepared a formal, written life plan. This plan includes all of the major goals this man has scheduled for himself and a listing of the carefully thought-out steps necessary to enable him to obtain his life's objectives. Anyone contemplating a business of his own must decide what it is he hopes to achieve by his actions. (A review of the earlier section that discussed "What Motivates the Entrepreneur" should be of some help in making your personal evaluation.)

To illustrate the power of motivation, consider the tale of the young swain out one evening in the family car with the girl of his dreams. As the lovers admired the twinkling lights of the city below from their mountain-top parking spot, the girl looked deeply into her escort's eyes and said, "I'd feel much more in the mood for love if you'd put the top down." He did.

The next day, when the young man was talking with a buddy, he mentioned that it took him nearly 20 minutes to get that damned top down. "How come?" his friend asked. "On my convertible, I can put the top down in about *three* minutes." "Well, you see," our friend replied, "my car isn't a convertible!" *That's* what I mean by the power of motivation!

FIRST-HAND KNOWLEDGE OF THE PRODUCT OR SERVICE TO BE OFFERED

The concept of apprenticeship is older than recorded history. Although a man may learn the ropes the hard way by starting in a new field without any relevant experience, the knowledge gained at the knee of a master is worth a full-tuition scholarship in the School of Hard Knocks.

I recall the time between my freshman and sophomore years in college. Summer jobs were scarce; and, after several days of fruitless searching, I finally managed to secure a promising position as an ice cream vendor. The work entailed hawking my wares from a small refrigerated truck in the finest tradition of the Good Humor Man. Based on my second week's sales, I judged my competence level to be pretty high. In spite of the fact that my training consisted of verification of my driver's license and the posting of a $50 bond, I was selling a lot more than many of the guys who had been "in the business" for a much longer period of time than I had.

Also, my motivation was of the most basic kind—I needed the money to pay rent on my $46.50-per-month basement apartment. And I wanted to have the highest weekly sales volume in the organization by the end of the season. But, despite working seven days a week, 12 hours a day (counting the routine three-hour round trip from Boston to my Cape Cod resort market), I found that my sales were peaking out at a level which brought me a net before taxes of about 75 cents an hour.

Then Fortune smiled upon me. Papa Fortune. Papa Fortune was five-feet-six and 250 pounds. (He liked ice cream.) Winters, he sold heating oil from his own truck (*not* his *ice cream* truck), and summers he was the Assistant Manager at the ice-cream vending plant. Papa decided that any kid who worked as hard as I did should be able to sell a hell of a lot more goods than I was managing to sell.

One night as I was plugging my refrigeration unit into the outdoor receptacle after another grueling day's work, Papa called me aside for a consultation. "Wad chew take in terday, kid?" When I told him, he said, "Tomorrow, I'm goin out wit cha. I'll show ya da ropes."

When we arrived at the "front" the next day, I watched and listened and was stupefied by what I observed. "Lady, yew don't want yer kids to rot dere teeth on those color'd water sticks (5 cents) when dey could be injoyin de healt-given goodness of a frozin oringe jooce bar wit Vitamin C (10 cents), do ya?"

"Sonny (quarter in hand), you'd rather have a choclit sundy (25 cents) dan an ice creem bar (10 cents), wooden ya? Dey lass fibe times longer, an' yewl still have yers wen de udder kids finish deir ice creem bars."

"Mister, yew doan wan ate ice creem bars (80 cents total) for yer kid's birfday pardy. Make it a reel treet and git um a haff gallin ($1.75) of de bess ice cream money kin buy!"

To little girl loitering around the truck: "Hi, Sis, watt wood yew like?" Answer: "I don't have any money, Mister." Rejoinder: "Well, run ask yer Mommy fer sum. We'll catch yew at the nex block." (In most instances, this non-buyer would become a huffing-puffing, beaming little tyke dropping a dime in Papa's pudgy paw on the next street stop. Not only that, but on future days she would be prepared for my visit with a dime tied inside a corner of the handkerchief pinned to her dress.

Our sales for the day were about double my previous average; and the next day (the one that really counted as far as I was concerned), my sales were 50 percent higher than they had been before my "apprenticeship." I seriously doubt whether I could have come close to realizing those sales results by the end of the summer had it not been for Papa's training. He had enabled me to obtain a substantial gain in *first-hand knowledge* of my job.

ABILITY TO MANAGE PEOPLE AND RESOURCES

We have all heard of or seen cases of craftsmen, salesmen, designers, or other non-managers who were promoted to a position of managerial responsibility and failed miserably. Clearly, the optimum time for an entrepreneur to test his capabilities as a manager is *before* he goes into a business of his own.

Management weaknesses in a large firm are generally remedied by what is known as the "horizontal promotion," where, in Peter-Principle[9] terms, a man who has reached his Level of Incompetence is simply placed aside the pathway of progress and into a new but nonfunctional position. Usually this ploy involves no cut in salary and ostensibly no change in prestige; rather, it is like removing a barnacle from the hull of a ship and stowing it in the cargo area so that it can enjoy the voyage without continuing to slow the vessel. In a firm of your own, however, stowaways are unwelcome regardless of the circumstances, and they must be promptly excised to protect the corporate ship from foundering without hope of salvage.

In the framework of a new enterprise, the availability of people and resources is usually extremely limited. The ability of the president initially to achieve dramatic results in output per manhour and per invested dollar will profoundly affect the ensuing rate of company growth.

When the amount of information available on a fledgling company is scarce (and this is typically the case), the evaluations made by customers, suppliers, bankers, investors, and even prospective employees tend greatly to magnify any slight indications of trouble. The willingness of customers to buy a company's products, the order size to which they are willing to commit themselves and the frequency of their reorders, the amount of credit a supplier is willing to extend, the willingness of bankers to lend money and the level of risk indicated in the interest rate charged, and investor confidence reflected in stock valuation all reveal a careful review by the parties concerned of the early performance of the new company. Deficiency in the specialty of managing people and resources currently ranks as the third largest cause of business failure. Thus, an objective evaluation of these management skills is of crucial importance.

BROAD, WELL-ROUNDED EXPERIENCE

As mentioned earlier, the founder of a new company rarely has the good fortune to start out with a large, seasoned staff. Not only, then, must he possess substantial expertise in at least one business area (preferably that which represents the main thrust of his operation) but he should also be familiar enough with the other areas to insure survival and growth of the firm until additional staff can be added to bolster any weaknesses.

The new business will probably demand that the founder possess *some* experience or knowledge in sales, purchasing, manufacturing, engineering, and certainly finance. The *degree* of expertise required will obviously depend on whether the business deals in a product or in a service. Furthermore, the nature of the products or services will also determine the skills required. The manufacturer who supplies products, such as motors, to other firms has markedly different problems than the manufacturer of, say, household furniture, who offers his goods for sale to the public. The hairstyling salon operator with a staff of six beauticians also has problems quite unlike those of the president of a drayage concern with a fleet of trucks.

If possible, the prospective entrepreneur should structure his work experience prior to starting his own business so that he has an opportunity for exposure to those key areas that will dramatically influence the success of the enterprise he launches. The minimum requirement is the development of an ability to communicate effectively and intelligently with people who are experts in their specialties.

Should the president-to-be decide, after careful analysis, that he needs a partner or two to complement his skills, he has probably done himself and his business a great favor. There is only one thing worse than a new company president with serious deficiencies in his key areas of operation, and that is the individual who fails to recognize these deficiencies so that he can compensate for them. Cultivation of the ability to identify personal deficiencies and, further, to be able to recognize and evaluate other individuals who have the desired expertise is the mark of a man who has a high probability of building his company from a garage-shop operation into a major competitor in its industry.

For contrast, consider the unfortunate case of the corporation that had an excellent product concept, a fantastic marketing capability, a manufacturing organization that was the envy of all the competition, and a record of timely deliveries that made it the darling of the market place. The product pricing afforded the company a very nice profit, but still it failed. How could such a thing happen you ask. Quite simply: If the accounts receivable don't turn quickly enough to provide the necessary cash flow for meeting the payroll and giving the government its pound of flesh, the sheriff will soon visit with a padlock for the door. It's happened to thousands and thousands of businesses in the past, and it will continue to happen. Failure in this one critical area can cost the company its life and the founders their jobs, their dreams, and quite possibly their personal financial solvency. The time-worn but time-honored cliche about a chain being only as strong as its weakest link has justifiably earned its place in business parlance.

One more observation before moving on: In the operation of a small, new company, there is precious little time. If you are contemplating starting a business and if you recognize a deficiency in a given area and if you decide that you can brush up by referring to a textbook or some other source once the clock starts running, forget it. The race will be over before you remove that pebble from your track shoes.

STAMINA AND PHYSICAL WELL-BEING

If you ever have an opportunity to meet with a group of entrepreneurs shortly after they have started their business or if you see a photograph of such a group, take note of their eyes. If they are true entrepreneurs, their eyes will be bloodshot; and large, black rings will have taken up residence just underneath.

Starting a business and handling the hundreds of details necessary to get it firmly established is probably one of the most grueling tasks a man can undertake. A work week of 80 to 100 hours on the job is quite common for the dedicated entrepreneur. One president told me that his weekly work record, attained during the first weeks after the start-up of his second company, was 135 hours. This man, needless to say, had a cot in his office.

The justification for working such long hours stems from the requirement that every dollar invested in the business has to do the work of at least three. This is partly the result of the excessive optimism so common in forecasting the cash requirements of the new firm. Typically, money is the most limited resource of all in any new enterprise.

Until products are delivered or services are performed to generate accounts receivable, the young company must sustain itself with its meager cash reserves. The fixed expenses, which include taxes, rent, utilities, and the payroll for the hourly workers (if things are going well, the founders *may* also get paid), provide a steady drain on the financial reserves of the enterprise. What the firm's treasury lacks must be compensated for by the stamina of the founders.

Stamina requires two things: excellent physical health and an inflexible determination to drive your body to whatever lengths are necessary to meet the demands of the moment. It is not my intention to peddle physical culture or promulgate pious platitudes regarding the virtue of having a healthy body. This is a no-nonsense subject that warrants the serious consideration of anyone contemplating a business of his own.

One of the occupational diseases of entrepreneurship is the duodenal ulcer. Having one can be a nasty, miserable experience. The entrepreneur cannot afford the inefficiencies that favoring such a problem requires; nor can a fledgling business endure, without serious penalty, the burden of a bedridden president. To overlook the importance of proper diet (a supper of candy bars from the vending machine is not exactly the ideal meal), adequate regular sleep (insomnia is a common problem of young presidents), and regular exercise is foolhardy. You can demand far more of a robust, healthy person than of one who is run down and out of shape. Giving your body the proper attention it deserves is one of the wisest investments an entrepreneur can make.

An added benefit of good physical health is the forceful, dynamic image you project of your company when speaking with customers, suppliers, or investors. No matter how good your product is, it's tough to dazzle a buyer when fatigue has you bushed, beat, and befuddled. I have heard more than one venture capitalist tell of a company president he knew who had to spend time in the hospital every time things got rough at the factory. This is not an undertaking for weak sisters or tender tummies.

FINANCIAL RESOURCES

Even a shoestring operation requires a shoestring for a start, and we all know that shoestrings today cost a lot more than they used to. For most entrepreneurs, the process of starting a business will probably entail making the largest cash investment he has made thus far in his life.

A start-up situation in which a significant amount of funding is not provided by the founders themselves, from their personal resources, is quite rare. Thus, a person contemplating a business of his own should consider the economic demands such a decision will make upon him and his family. If he has been particularly successful in a corporation career, with the attendant handsome salary and expense-account travel, he is going to have quite an adjustment to make in the early years of operating his new business. This change in life style may prove to be quite traumatic for the entrepreneur and even more so for his family. (But canned beans aren't nearly so bad as they're made out to be. Try the B&M brand Brick Oven variety.)

When and if the new enterprise needs financial assistance from outside sources, a record of personal fiscal responsibility will be most helpful. Almost invariably, any investor contemplating a major equity position in a new company will very thoroughly investigate the financial circumstances of the officers of the company. At the outset, modest salaries and even more modest expense accounts should be programmed as a matter of company policy.

In those instances where a very small-scale beginning is planned and the initial capitalization is modest, only minor adjustments in life style will be necessary.

However, the rate of return one can reasonably expect from such limited financial commitment will also be modest.

First-hand experience with members of the financial community is of considerable value and importance to any businessman. At the very least, the entrepreneur should cultivate an association with the commercial banker where he maintains his checking account. If the bank has been properly chosen, its bankers should be able to provide considerable assistance later on in locating additional financing, if needed. A substantial part of this book is devoted to an in-depth analysis of the many sources of financing available to the young businessman, including his commercial banker.

Recommended Reading

Allen, Louis L. *Starting and Succeeding In Your Own Small Business.* New York: Grosset & Dunlap, 1968.

Bank of America National Trust and Savings Association. "Opening Your Own Business." *Small Business Reporter,* Vol. 7, No. 7, 1966.

Bank of America National Trust and Savings Association. "Small Business Success." *Small Business Reporter,* Vol. 7, No. 5, 1966.

Bureau of Business and Economic Research. *A Study of the Problems of Small Electronics Manufacturing Companies in Southern California.* San Diego: School of Business Administration, San Diego State College, 1962.

Greenwalt, Crawford H. *The Uncommon Man.* New York: McGraw-Hill Book Co.,Inc., 1959.

Jewkes, John; Sawers, David; Stillerman, Richard. *The Sources of Invention.* New York: W. W. Norton & Company, Inc., 1969.

King, Joseph E. "Psychological Testing for Small Business." *Management Aids for Small Business, Annual No. 3.* Washington, D.C.: Small Business Administration, Government Printing Office, 1957, pp. 38-45.

Levinson, Robert E. "Checking Your Management Methods." *Management Aids for Small Manufacturers, Annual No. 11.* Washington, D.C.: Small Business Administration, Government Printing Office, 1965, pp. 8-14.

Maltz, Maxwell. *Psycho-Cybernetics.* Pocket Book Edition. Englewood Cliffs, New Jersey: Prentice-Hall, 1969.

Martin, Clement G. *Managing Your Health: Profits Without Losses.* Homewood, Illinois: Dow Jones-Irwin, Inc., 1971.

Maslow, Abraham H. *Eupsychian Management: A Journal.* Homewood, Illinois: Richard D. Irwin, Inc. and The Dorsey Press, 1965.

Maslow, Abraham H. *Toward a Psychology of Being.* An Insight Book. Princeton, New Jersey: D. Van Nostrand Co., Inc., 1968.

Metcalf, Wendell O. *Starting and Managing a Small Business of Your Own.* Starting & Managing Series, No. l. Washington, D.C.: Small Business Administration, Government Printing Office, 1962.

Pickle, Hal. B. *Personality and Success; an Evaluation of Personal Characteristics of Successful Small Business Managers.* Small Business Research Series, No. 4. Washington, D.C.: Small Business Administration, Government Printing Office, 1964.

Schwartz, David J. *The Magic of Thinking Big.* Cornerstone Library Publications. Englewood Cliffs, New Jersey: Prentice-Hall, 1965.

Small Business Administration. *A Study of the Small Business in the Electronics Industry.* Washington, D.C.: Small Business Administration, Government Printing Office, 1962.

Steinmetz, Kline, & Stegall. *Managing the Small Business.* Homewood, Illinois: Richard D. Irwin, Inc., 1968.

Chapter 4

Increased Responsibility-
The Price of Success

With the founding of a new company, the entrepreneur will discover a small army of interest groups and individuals making heavy demands on his time and resources. The price of neglect of any of these groups can be a catastrophe. One of the easiest to overlook when formulating your business plan is the interest group represented by your wife and children. Yet your family represents a host of things which give meaning and substance to your personal life.

To the entrepreneur, the founding of a successful company represents the fulfillment of a life-long dream. Frequently, the entrepreneur has failed to recognize that many of the glowing stories he has heard regarding the concept of "working for yourself" are fictional. Let's explore for a moment these complex relationships between the family, the new firm, and the founder.

51

One company president of my acquaintance has devised a near-perfect situation. His company is in the manufacturing business, and in recent years has grown steadily; today he has a staff of about 50 employees. His products are proprietary in nature, thus giving him a unique competitive advantage—his products lend themselves well to distribution in regional markets. One factor this company president is considering is the possibility of opening subsidiary plants (carbon copies of the parent plant) in these regional areas.

It is the president's feeling, however, that at this time he is not personally disposed to making the personal sacrifices in time and effort to make this expansion. He believes that it will take several years for him to develop a cadre of capable lieutenants whom he can send into the field to open the subsidiaries and that his responsibilities to his family are of sufficient importance that he is unwilling to apportion more of his own energies to his company.

One unique factor in this man's situation is that the company of which he is president is one he totally owns. He has no other stockholders. Other stockholders would probably recognize significant potential for capital appreciation if the company were to expand significantly right now, taking advantage of their technological lead in the proprietary products the company manufactures. Stockholders might feel that, if this particular man cannot handle the responsibilities of an expansion, he should consider stepping aside into an ancillary position, thus permitting the stockholders to bring in a stronger administrator able to pilot a rapidly growing company. But by structuring his company as he has, this president is able to satisfy all of his personal needs. He is deriving from his company all that he wishes. It has reached a size that is satisfying to him and he does not wish to compromise his marital responsibilities at the altar of greater corporate success.

MISTRESSES AND mistresses

Whenever the subject of entrepreneurship comes up, someone is bound to make the observation that a company of your own can be a demanding mistress. Carrying the analogy further, there is rarely room in a marriage for both a wife and a mistress (particularly a full-time mistress). There are no statistics regarding how much higher than the national average is the divorce rate among new company founders. However, the difference is significant; and it has two causes. Early in the formation of a company, if the husband works 100 hours a week, he will have very little opportunity to nurture and nourish his marital relationship. It takes a very strong, devoted woman indeed to withstand the rigors of being married to a near stranger.

To manage successfully the demands of marriage and possibly a growing family while simultaneously meeting the insistent demands of a young company requires a very deep personal understanding of the relative importance of these two elements of life. The syndrome of the discontented, disillusioned woman married to a man totally consumed by and involved with his own business is unfortunately an all-too-common one. It is a wise founder who makes ample provision for his wife in his plans for business success.

One alternative is to permit your wife to become a member of your staff, possibly your personal secretary. But this is difficult to manage successfully, particularly if your company grows to large size very quickly; and few couples are equal to the challenge. The jealousy of other employees and the vulnerability to charges of nepotism pose too great a potential corporate morale problem. Furthermore, once you hire your mate to work in the office, the task of firing her (should the need arise) can prove to be a damned unpleasant bit of housekeeping.

The entrepreneur may decide that a more acceptable solution is to encourage his wife to pursue career opportunities of her own. Or she may interest herself in activities outside of the business world from which she may derive satisfaction and a sense of involvement and achievement.

A further, or supplementary, solution to the problem may take the form of mini-vacations or mini-honeymoons. Several entrepreneurs of my acquaintance successfully manage this feat by setting aside at least once or twice a month a full day that is the exclusive property of the spouse. Once established, this commitment should be honored faithfully; worrying about company problems during this break is not allowed. No note paper or tape recorders are permitted for catching the elusive solutions to work problems; escape the telephone, if you can. You're not *supposed* to be thinking about work on these days off.

Close on the heels of the neglected-wife syndrome comes the problem of handling newly acquired riches. A thrice-married friend of mine advised me that the number of beautiful gold-diggers in the world is legion. (Having followed the "Milestones" column in *Time* magazine for years, I have been intrigued by the regularity with which wealthy men shed and acquire mates.) This matter is obviously a highly personal one, but it should certainly be considered before embarking on a career of entrepreneurship.

Contemplating this problem from the corporate point of view provides still another perspective. Divorce almost invariably is a traumatic experience for all parties involved. Consider the new company president who gives every last iota of his resources to the new operation to make it a success. Should he subsequently find his marriage breaking up, his effectiveness in handling corporate problems will suffer. His ability to give his company his all will be severely compromised, and his subsequent handling of corporate problems will reflect the difficult personal adjustments he has made. The workload he managed to handle on a 16-hour-a-day regimen cannot possibly receive satisfactory treatment from a half-hearted, listless, and dispirited president. Late shipments, forgotten commitments, and neglected staff can only bring about unavoidable and possibly irreparable corporate financial problems. To protect the company, the marriage, and the well-being of the president as well, he *must* give due regard to the delicate balance to be struck in handling the sometimes unreasonable demands of the two rivals in his life.

SESAME STREET MAY BE FINE, BUT KIDS NEED A *DADDY*, TOO

After the wives comes another special group that frequently suffers from the ambitions of new company presidents—children. Many sociological studies have been conducted on children who are reared in a fatherless household. Unfortunately, too little study has been done to document the problems of youngsters caught in a situation where father is always at work.

It has been suggested that the entrepreneur's wife actively cultivate the friendship of the wives of other company founders. Consideration might also be given to the possibility of moving the family to an area where there is a high percentage of families whose husbands have their own businesses. In this way, the wives can commiserate and the children will have playmates who share their parental situation. When all of Tommy's friends have daddies who are home by six o'clock, Tommy may feel a sense of deprivation due to his father's work habits. If, however, most of Tommy's friends have fathers who are similarly engaged, the circumstances are regarded as normal and the childhood trauma is somewhat diminished.

The solutions entrepreneurs devise to cope with their family obligations are as varied as the men themselves. Some men insist on spending at least two days a week with their families, engaged in communal recreation. Some of these men adamantly refuse to discuss one thing with their families regarding the pressures of their business. Other men spend less time with their families and frequently talk about nothing during those infrequent reunions but their business problems.

Doing justice both to a marriage and a company is one of the most commonly overlooked difficulties of starting a business. Yet many men who contemplate a business of their own would state without hesitation that the success of their marriage was very important to them. Reviewing the divorce statistics, one can only conclude that either these men understand themselves poorly or the price of honesty is something they would rather put on their credit card.

THE MYTH OF WORKING FOR YOURSELF

Another commonly overlooked pitfall in establishing a business of your own is the mistaken idea that as a company president you will enjoy a heretofore unimagined degree of independence. Consider the following list for a few minutes and then analyze once again your expectations for independence.

Interest Groups Which Compromise the Independence of the Entrepreneur

Stockholders
Members of the Board of Directors

> Partners
> Customers
> Suppliers
> Manufacturer's Representatives
> Service Agencies
> Consumer Protection Groups
> Governmental Agencies, including city, county, state, and federal jurisdictions
> Trade Associations
> Creditors

In his book *The Small Businessman and His Problems*, lawyer-author L. Charles Burlage illustrates the entrepreneur's dilemma with the following letter, reproduced here with the author's kind permission.

Dear Creditor:

> In reply to your request to send a check, I wish to inform you that the present condition of my bank account makes it almost impossible. My shattered financial condition is due to Federal laws, state laws, county laws, brother-in-laws, sister-in-laws, and outlaws.

> Through these laws I am compelled to pay a business tax, amusement tax, head tax, school tax, gas tax, water tax, sales tax, liquor tax, income tax, food tax, furniture tax, excise tax, and now the Princess Anne County tax. I am required to get a business license, car license.

> I am also required to contribute to every society and organization which the genius of man is capable of bringing to life.

> For my own safety, I am required to carry health insurance, life insurance, fire insurance, earthquake insurance, tornado insurance, unemployment compensation insurance and old age insurance.

> My business is so governed that it is no easy matter to find out who owns it. I am expected, inspected, suspected, disrespected, rejected, defected, examined, re-examined, informed, required, summoned, fined, commanded, and compelled, until I provide an inexhaustible supply of money for every known need, desire or hope of the human race.

> Simply because I refuse to donate to something or other, I am boycotted, talked about, lied about, held up, held down, and robbed, until I am almost ruined.

> I can tell you honestly that except for a miracle that happened, I could not enclose this check. The wolf that comes to my door nowadays just had pups in my kitchen; I sold them, and here is the money.[10]

Recommended Reading

Burlage, L. Charles. *The Small Businessman and His Problems.* New York: Vantage Press, 1958.

Carnegie, Dale. *How to Stop Worrying and Start Living.* New York: Pocket Books, 1953.

Fish, George, ed. "Entrepreneurial Psychology of Facing Conflict in Organization." *The Frontiers of Management Psychology.* New York: Harper and Row, 1964.

Getty, J. Paul. *How to Be Rich.* A Playboy Pocket Book. Chicago: Playboy Press, 1965.

Kirstein, George G. *The Rich: Are They Different?* A Tower Book. Boston: Houghton Mifflin Co., 1970.

Mandino, Og. *The Greatest Salesman in the World.* New York: Frederick Fell, Inc., 1968.

Peale, Norman Vincent. *A Guide to Confident Living.* A Fawcett Crest Book. Greenwich, Conn.: Fawcett Publications, Inc., (Prentice-Hall, 1948).

Piper, Watty. *The Little Engine that Could.* New York: Platt & Munk, Publishers, 1961.

Scanzoni, John H. *Opportunity and the Family.* New York: The Free Press (Macmillan), 1970.

Smith, Norman R. *The Entrepreneur and His Firm: The Relationship between Type of Man and Type of Company.* East Lansing, Michigan: Michigan State University Press, 1967.

Chapter 5

Recruiting Partners

I don't know of any sector of the business community in which it is possible to develop a large sales volume without having to rely on the services of others. This reliance involves relinquishing to your assistants or associates the necessary controls to enable them effectively to discharge their responsibilities. One former company founder (now a venture capitalist) says that, in distilling his years of experience, the best advice he had to offer is: "Pick your partners as carefully as you would pick a wife. Furthermore, insofar as possible, choose people who complement your business and personal strengths." Now this book does not presume to tell you how to pick a spouse. But it will give you some ideas on partner selection that you will find of value.

FORMER BUSINESS ASSOCIATES

The most common candidates for partnership are former business associates. Dr. John L. Komives, Director of the Center for Venture Management (a Milwaukee-based, not-for-profit research and educational organization),[11] speculates that at least 80 percent of all new multiple-founder businesses involve circumstances where two or more members of the founding team were employed by the *same* firm prior to starting their own company. If you have previously been associated with your proposed partner, you will have had an opportunity to test your ability to work with him and to arrive at as objective an evaluation of his capabilities as is possible before he goes on your payroll.

FRIENDS

Depending on the kind of talent required to produce a well-rounded, broadly experienced management team, it is possible that a new company president may find one or more of his friends suitable for the role of co-founder. Objectivity in the evaluation of a friend's capabilities is, however, frequently difficult. Furthermore, subsequent performance appraisals of those staff members numbered among the president's friends becomes difficult and sometimes unpleasant. This kind of relationship warrants very careful scrutiny *before* it is entered into.

You must also consider the possibility that your circle of business acquaintances and friends may not be large enough to include the full staff you require to man your company adequately. Recruiting your partners from a group limited to friends and acquaintances is a little bit like marrying your high-school sweetheart. When you get to college you may discover a lot of coeds the likes of which you never dreamed of.

BUSINESS CONSULTANTS

A number of entrepreneurially inclined professionals set themselves up as consultants in their specialty fields. Frequently, this role of consultant is an interim one, halfway between working for a corporation and finding a position as a corporate founder. Often these men can be employed by a new business on a limited contract basis, receiving payment in cash, stock warrants, or other negotiated form of compensation. Should this "trial marriage" prove satisfactory, the consultant can be smoothly integrated into the staff. In the event the trial marriage does not prove satisfactory, the relationship can be terminated neatly without recrimination and without the trauma commonly associated with partnership upheavals in a small firm.

COMPETITOR'S STAFF

Qualified experts for the new enterprise may often be men from the staff of a competing firm. The recruiting of these men is commonly referred to as "raiding," and this practice entails some risk of legal action. However, in most instances, any judicial shenanigans are limited in their effect and can usually be disregarded. (Fortunately, serfdom went out of vogue some time ago.) Nowadays the courts don't take very kindly to limiting the freedom of an individual to pursue any legitimate career and employer of his choosing.

REFERRALS

By letting your friends and business associates know of your requirements in rounding out your staff, you should be able to obtain a prescreened list of qualified contenders. This list can be an extremely helpful source of information in your quest for a competent team.

CLASSIFIED ADVERTISING

Every day the major metropolitan and financial newspapers serve as clearing houses for people with a broad range of skills, qualifications, and interests. I prefer to group the classified headings into two categories: (1) Those listing people who are looking for positions or situations and (2) Those listing situations that are looking for people.

An intriguing array of apparently gifted people regularly appears under the headings: Positions Wanted, Situations Wanted, or Business Opportunities. Entries range all the way from a disenchanted super-corporation vice president looking for a position as a general manager through the inventor with a new product he would like to help you manufacture and exploit to the Harvard MBA with $50,000 or $100,000 cash who would like to become a partner in some new enterprise. In the other category, Positions Available or Business Opportunities, you will find ads placed by companies that are offering a handsome salary-stock option package to the right man who is willing to take the position of vice president of manufacturing and ads placed by companies that are seeking a marketing manager with a track record and money to invest in the chance of a lifetime.

For a particularly helpful booklet on this subject, write to

The New York Times
Classified Advertising Department
Times Square
New York, New York 10036

and request a complimentary copy of "How to Write a Better *Business Opportunities* Advertisement."

AN OWL, A GOOSE, AND THE LITTLE RED HEN

In closing this section on how to recruit partners, I am reminded of a story from my childhood. As I recall, it went something like this:

Once upon a time in Pawtucket, Rhode Island there lived a Little Red Hen. This chick decided that she would like to go into business and make a lot of bread. She surveyed the market and decided that public demand for the whole-wheat variety was inadequately served by the present suppliers. So she called a meeting of several of her friends to try to interest them in helping with her project. She started off the meeting by saying, "Friends, I have quite a proposition for all of you today. How would you like to go into business with me and really make a lot of bread?"

"I think that's a swingin' idea," said a little banty from his perch on one of the rafters.

The cock-of-the-walk puffed up his chest and said to the group, "My missus is always complaining about a shortage of dough in our house. I think the Little Red Hen really has something here. Count me in." And so it went; every one of the Little Red Hen's friends volunteered to participate in this bread-making venture.

The next meeting of our little group was held two weeks later, and the first thing on the agenda was the selection of the company name. After much debate, everyone decided that the "Doughty Dough Makers" was a real pip. So with that important item of business concluded, it was time to assign responsibilities to various members of the new firm in order to get the enterprise under way.

However, from this point on, very strange things began to happen—the new founders became restless and fidgety. Every time the Little Red Hen asked one of her partners to undertake a certain task toward implementing their plans, problems arose.

The bantam rooster indicated that his regular job as a night club bouncer made him too tired to work on anything else. He needed the daylight hours to rest up for the next night's work. Furthermore, he said that his life style was such that he simply couldn't afford the financial risk of quitting his steady job and waiting until the Doughty Dough Makers could pay him a regular salary. However, once the company got rolling, he'd be glad to work as the night watchman. Salarywise, he said he'd be content with a stock option *plus* the same money he was getting now at the night club. "After all," he said, "you're entitled to some kind of a raise when you change employers, aren't you?"

The cock-of-the-walk complained that his duties as president of the Strut and Show-Off Marching Band Society were getting very hectic because of a convention the Society was planning. He wouldn't really be able to help out until this event was over, about eight weeks from now.

The brooding hen said that she had decided she couldn't spare the time away from her babies; but later on, when the company needed someone to assist with counting the profits, her chicks would be old enough to stay by themselves and she would try to find time to come out and lend a helping wing.

By this time, the Little Red Hen was in a foul mood; and she bit the cock-of-the-walk right on the tail. His screech sharply brought the attention of the bickering attendees back to their leader, who requested that only those founders able to start working for the new company immediately remain at the meeting. The rest of the founders (the really chicken-hearted) were asked to leave and told that they would later be notified about the future role they might play in the company.

Well, as you might have guessed, everyone left the meeting coop except the Little Red Hen. However, don't despair, dear reader. Our heroine (Women's Lib Groups: Attention!) teamed up with a Wise Owl on the east coast and an Old Lady Goose on the west coast, and now they're all making a bundle selling potato chips.

Recommended Reading

Bank of America National Trust and Savings Association. "Personnel for the Small Business." *Small Business Reporter,* Vol. 9, No. 8, 1970.

Bruce, Martin M. "Providing Management Replacements in Small Business." *Small Marketers Aids, Annual No. 1.* Washington, D.C.: Small Business Administration, Government Printing Office, 1959, pp. 64-70.

Cowan, Donald R. G. *The Small Manufacturer and His Specialized Staff.* Washington, D.C.: Small Business Administration, Government Printing Office, 1954.

Elliott, John M. "Employee Selection and Placement Methods for Small Plants." *Management Aids for Small Business, Annual No. 1.* Washington, D.C.: Small Business Administration, Government Printing Office, Rev. 1958, pp. 144-151.

Fast, Julius. *Body Language.* New York: Pocket Books, 1971.

Freeman, G. L. and Taylor, E. K. *How to Pick Leaders.* New York: Funk and Wagnalls, 1950.

Leon, Ernest L. *Personnel Management Guides for Small Business.* Small Business Management Series, No. 26. Washington, D.C.: Small Business Administration, Government Printing Office, 1961.

Masterson, Thomas R. " 'Tailor-Make' Your Executive Staff." *Management Aids for Small Manufacturers, Annual No. 8.* Washington, D.C.: Small Business Administration, Government Printing Office, 1962, pp. 27-34.

Perry, John. "Hiring a Key Executive for Your Small Plant." *Management Aids for Small Manufacturers, Annual No. 7.* Washington, D.C.: Small Business Administration, Government Printing Office, 1961, pp. 9-16.

Chapter 6

A Training Program for Success

The decision to start a company of your own will have as profound an effect on your life as your marriage or the arrival of your first child. It is not a matter that should be taken lightly. Just as an athlete preparing for a major contest must condition his body for the stress ahead, just as a scholar contemplating year-end examinations must force-feed his mind with facts and information, just as a medical doctor must undergo a period of internship before entering into formal practice, the prospective entrepreneur must plan and pursue a program of self-improvement so that he will be in optimum condition for the demanding, challenging experiences he will encounter in the formation of his own business. In planning your own program for success, take time to consider each of the following points:

PHYSICAL CONDITIONING

The importance and value of stamina and good physical condition to the founder of the new firm was discussed earlier. The regular programs that are offered by YMCAs and various health clubs, spas, and gymnasiums are ideal for this purpose.

Now I'm not suggesting that you approach this regimen with the expectation of becoming the next Mr. America. Endurance and stamina are the objectives, and the conditioning might even improve your sex life!

ACQUIRING THE PROPER MENTAL ATTITUDE

The concept of motivation is a very important element in business success. Reference was made earlier to the vast body of literature on the subject of personal motivation; the would-be entrepreneur should read one or two of these books so that he may vicariously experience the success of others. If you don't come away from this reading with the conviction that you've got at least twice as much going for you as some of those other formerly poor bastards who made it to the top of the heap, then ask yourself what kind of dynamite it *takes* to get you excited.

If your "Hot Button" isn't in the full-on position, there's an excellent possibility that the stuff of which company presidents are made does not lie dormant in your breast. You let it die there when Daddy gave you a spanking for taking the alarm clock apart with your little screwdriver, and you might as well sign off. But, if you're among the *living*, read on.

MAKE YOUR WIFE THE HEAD CHEERLEADER IN YOUR ROOTING SECTION

Earlier, we discussed the importance and value of marital stability in enabling the entrepreneur to devote his attention to the problems of his business. Remember the popular observation that "Behind every great man, there stands a woman." With this thought in mind, if you've got fence mending to do, do it *before* you start your business.

INVESTIGATE SEMINARS

One of the most convenient and readily assimilated forms of education is the seminar. Typically, such courses are of short duration (one or two days is the rule); and, since most seminar speakers have a reputation to maintain (and a handsome income to preserve), their talks are not only informative but they are also usually entertaining. Unlike many of their academic counterparts who deliver a lecture designed to fill the allotted fifty-five minutes, a seminar speaker is confronted with the problem of distilling and refining his vast knowledge in an effort to convey the very essence of it in an hour.

A large number of different groups and organizations sponsor seminars:

The U. S. Department of Commerce

Most branches offer short courses, lecture programs, and movie presentations of primary concern to the businessman interested in domestic and international trade. A surprisingly large number of small businessmen are active in the import-export field, handling products of their own manufacture or acting as brokers or agents for other manufacturers. The limited amount of capital necessary to get into selected areas of this fascinating industry makes it ideal for the small entrepreneur. Advance notice of U. S. Department of Commerce seminars may be obtained by contacting your nearest Field Office and requesting that your name be added to their regular mailing list. Admission fees, if any, are nominal.

The Small Business Administration

Regular programs including short courses, conferences, problem-solving clinics, and workshops tailored to the needs of the small businessman are offered by all major field offices of the SBA. Offerings cover, for example, personnel problems, taxation, sales, marketing, manufacturing, and inventory control. In some cases, special topics of concern to businessmen in a particular geographic or industrial sector are scheduled in areas where interest level warrants their discussion. Session speakers include lawyers, accountants, bankers, university professors, and management consultants. As in the case of Department of Commerce offerings, admission fees, if any, are nominal.

Trade Associations

Every trade association I know of has a big wing-ding of a convention at least once a year. At these gatherings, conferences, seminars, panel-discussions, guest lecturers, movie and slide programs, and other such presentations are profusely provided. Convention programs generally are planned to include sessions dealing with engineering, marketing, manufacturing, and financial problems as they relate to the needs of the industry sponsoring the convention. Many conventions, particularly those sponsored by associations serving high-technology industries, offer seminars dealing specifically with the problems of starting a new business.

It is customary that convention registration fees provide not only for admission to the main exhibits but also for admission to any or all seminars. Since trade associations are almost always non-profit organizations, convention admission fees are typically quite modest.

For a comprehensive directory of trade associations, your library should have a copy of the *Gale Research Company Encyclopedia of American Associations,* a guide to the trade, business, professional, labor, scientific, educational, fraternal, and social organizations of the United States.

The American Management Association

This association is a non-profit, educational membership organization devoted to developing and sharing better methods of management throughout the management community. Every year, the AMA presents more than 2,000 seminars, conferences, briefing sessions, and courses treating almost every conceivable topic of management concern. A representative list of the Association divisions includes:

Manufacturing
Marketing
Packaging
Personnel
Purchasing
Research and Development
Finance
General Management
General Services
Insurance
International Management
Management Systems and Licenses

Programs are offered in most principal cities in the United States and Canada. For the latest information on scheduled presentations and membership benefits and fees, write to the AMA Membership Department, The American Management Association Building, 135 West 50th Street, New York, New York, 10020.

Colleges and Universities

Many colleges and universities offer business programs for alumni; others extend their hospitality to the community at large. Most of these institutions send out advance announcements of course and seminar offerings to individuals who have asked to be placed on their mailing lists. A letter or phone call to the appropriate school office should insure your receiving future mailings.

The admission fee for these seminars covers a very broad range, depending on the school. Usually, privately supported institutions charge more than schools supported by the taxpayers. Based on my recent experience, fees for a two-day seminar may run from a low of $45 to a high of $300. Some private universities conduct regular seminar series as a supplementary source of revenue.

Seminars for Pure Profit

There is an industry made up of private companies that offer seminars purely for profit. Some of the most professional and worthwhile presentations in the seminar field are conducted by these groups. Often, the program offerings of these "seminar companies" include speakers who have garnered world renown in the business and financial community. A few of the many firms active in this field include:

AMR International, Inc.
280 Park Avenue
New York, New York 10017
(212) 697-3700

CPC Seminars
10 South LaSalle Street
Chicago, Illinois 60603
(312) 641-0922

The Corporate Growth Institute
P. O. Box 363
Princeton, New Jersey 08540
(609) 921-7117

Corporate Seminars, Inc.
575 Madison Avenue
New York, New York 10022

Cossman International Programs
13451 Ventura Boulevard
Sherman Oaks, California 91403
(213) 789-1400

The Institute for Advanced Technology
(A Division of Control Data Corp.)
5272 River Road
Washington, D. C. 20016
(301) 652-2268, Ext. 245-248

The Management Training Center, Inc.
87 Terrace Hall Avenue
Burlington, Massachusetts 01803
(617) 273-0997

In weighing the decision to attend a particular seminar, the problem of determining cost-versus-value will eventually steal into your mind. Cost is not limited to registration fees, transportation, and food and lodging, for another very real cost is the *time* you spend in attending the seminar. In other words, if your bag is real-estate development or personnel problems in manufacturing, what the hell are you doing at a seminar on nuclear physics?

To derive the greatest value from a seminar, you should determine the suitability of your education, experience, and interest relative to the subject matter to be presented. (Of the dozens of seminars I have attended, I have never been to one from which I didn't get at least five valuable new ideas that I was subsequently able to employ for my personal advantage.) It is your responsibility to obtain value from a seminar. The speakers will do their part to convey knowledge and experience; absorbing and applying this knowledge and experience is up to you.

Three other factors to be considered in evaluating the merits of seminar attendance are these:

1. Seminars should afford you an excellent opportunity to meet large numbers of people with interests similar to or complementary to yours. You should make a concerted effort to interact with other attendees during the intermission and break periods for the purpose of cultivating new and potentially rewarding acquaintances.

2. In many cases, the sponsor of the seminar will provide all registrants with a listing of other attendees, frequently including their company affiliation, address, and telephone number. This courtesy list significantly enhances your opportunity for developing valuable contacts.

3. Seminars should also serve to stimulate new ideas. Information delivered by the speakers should produce a synergistic, catalytic interaction with the knowledge and experience you already possess—in other words, you should end up with a $1 + 1 = 3$ result.

Donald M. Dible Seminars

I just finished telling you how valuable seminars can be to anyone who wants to succeed in his own business. Therefore, you shouldn't be too surprised to learn that in addition to writing books and operating three businesses, I have started giving seminars to better enable me to spread the gospel of entrepreneurship.

These seminars can be conducted in your community on either a private or sponsored basis. On a private basis, The Entrepreneur Press may present seminars in metropolitan areas where high interest and attendance are probable without the endorsement of a sponsor. In other situations, the endorsement of a sponsoring organization may be necessary to insure a worthwhile turnout in order to meet normal expenses. (Without exception, organization sponsorship significantly improves the chances of high seminar attendance and minimizes financial risk for all concerned.)

Here is how my seminar presentations got started. Since *Up Your OWN Organization!* was first published, many convention, government, trade, professional and college audiences have invited me to speak on a wide variety of small business subjects. In the process, a series of sixteen one-hour talks on small business have been developed. These talks are divided up into two one-day programs:

HOW TO START AND FINANCE A NEW BUSINESS

ADVENTURES IN ENTREPRENEURSHIP
  Starting the Business
  Raising the Capital
  Supplier Relationships
  Marketing the Product
  Personal and Financial Rewards
HOW TO PREPARE A BUSINESS PLAN
  The Mini-Proposal
  Optimum Format
  The Formal Business Plan
  Free Sources of Help and Guidance
  How to Get the Most Out of Your Business
    Plan
HOW TO CONDUCT A LOW-COST MARKET
SURVEY
  The Role of Trade Associations
  How to Get Free Help From Magazine
    Editors
  Making Use of Government Surveys
  Finding Low-Cost Marketing Reports
  Review of Market Research Companies
TWENTY-ONE CHANNELS OF
DISTRIBUTION — NEW MARKETS FOR
YOUR PRODUCTS
  Definitions and Examples
  Directories of Buyers and Sales Outlets
  Trade Association Assistance
  How Double & Triple Your Sales
  Case Histories

CHARACTERISTICS OF THE SUCCESSFUL
ENTREPRENEUR
  Size of Total U.S. Business Community
  Number of Companies Having
    Regularly-Traded Stock
  Personality Traits of Entrepreneurs
  Ideal Educational Background
  Nature of Successful Small Businesses
PROPRIETORSHIPS, PARTNERSHIPS &
CORPORATIONS AS BUSINESS FORMS
  Personal Financial Liability Considerations
  Tax Considerations
  Personal Income Alternatives
  Opportunities to Build a Personal Estate
  Opportunity to Become a Stock Market
    Millionaire
OBJECTIVES OF THE VENTURE
CAPITALIST
  The Golden Rule of Venture Capital
  Determining Mutual Objectives
  Necessary Return on Investment
  Methods of Liquidating Investment
  Determining Value of Founder's Equity
HOW AND WHERE TO RAISE BUSINESS
CAPITAL
  Definitions of Loan *Versus* Equity Financing
  What Lenders Want to Know
  Raising Equity Money for Partnerships &
    Corporations
  Public *Versus* Private Financings
  Directories of Money Sources

CONVERTING YOUR IDEAS INTO DOLLARS

HOW TO GET WHAT YOU WANT THROUGH
SALESMANSHIP
  Analyzing the Cost of Failure *Versus* the
    Rewards of Success
  How to Build Your Self Image
  Homework—Sales Insurance
  Persuasion Through Other People
  The Hidden Power of: I Love You
THE MECHANICS OF SETTING UP YOUR
OWN BUSINESS
  Business License
  Sales Tax Obligations
  Internal Revenue Service
  Selection and Registration of Company Name
  Letterheads and Stationery
BOOTSTRAP FINANCING
  Analyzing Your Money Requirements
  Unusual Ways to Economize
  How to Establish Supplier Credit
  Getting Your Customers to Help
  The Magic of Credit Cards
HOW TO FIND NEW PRODUCTS
  Finding Out About Important Trade Shows
    and Expositions

Where to Find Little-Known Directories of
  New Products
How to Locate Products From Foreign
  Countries
How to Get Information About Invention
  Shows
Government Patents Available for License
PATENTS, TRADEMARKS AND
COPYRIGHTS
  Definitions and Differences
  Time Period of Protection Available
  The Application Process—How to "Do It
    Yourself"
  How to Keep Records That Prove Your
    Claims
  Invention Rackets
VALUABLE, FREE GOVERNMENT
SERVICES FOR SMALL BUSINESS
  Small Business Administration Loans and
    Services
  Small Business Administration Publications
  Department of Commerce Services
  Department of Commerce Publications
  Congressional Handbook for Small
    Business—Key to a Treasure Chest

HOW TO GET FREE PUBLICITY
  How to Write a News Release
  Where to Get Promotional Photographs
  Reproduced at Low Cost
  Where to Send Your News Releases for Best
  Results
  How to Get on Television
  How to Get Newspaper Articles and
  Interviews
  How to Get Free Write-Ups in Trade
  Magazines

HOW TO MARKET PRODUCTS AND IDEAS
  Who Will Buy Ideas
  How to Package Products & Ideas for
  Maximum Sales
  Ways to Minimize Financial Risk in
  Advertising
  How to Get Others to Market Your Products
  Unravelling the Mysteries of Discounts,
  Commissions, and Gross Margin

People who attend these programs come from all walks of life. We get college students, presidents of million dollar companies, inventors with new gadgets, housewives looking for spare time income, and old folks looking for a way to find fulfillment in their autumn years. We get high powered sales executives, accountants, lawyers, teachers, investors, and engineers. We also get people who have spent their careers working for big corporations and who have been thinking, "There's got to be a better way to live my life." We get lots and lots of people in this last category. They leave our seminars KNOWING there's a better way.

Any organization—trade, professional, government or college—wishing to sponsor one or both of these seminars for its members may secure more information by writing to The Entrepreneur Press, Mission Station, Drawer 2759T, Santa Clara, California 95051.

REDISCOVER BOOKS

The entrepreneur is typically a maverick, more interested in *doing* things than in thinking about them, studying them, or planning them. No bookworm is he! Probably the poor guy found schoolwork something to be endured rather than enjoyed. Thus, the process of learning the business of business from books is not something he anticipates with delight. The midnight oil he burns is far more likely to illuminate his sweating brow than a treatise on how someone else solved his problems. He likes to be in the thick of things, where the action is. "Hell," he says, "why be content with Front Row Center when you can be the Star of the Show?"

Overlooked is the fact that the Star studies; even the understudy studies. So forget the klieg lights and get your hindquarters down to the library, the repository of *Mistakes to Avoid*, *Dragons I Have Slain*, and *Accounting for the Simpleton* (for when it comes to accounting, most entrepreneurs are just that). Let your education commence!

The wealth of information contained in books and the opportunities that this packaged knowledge represents remind me of a story that Zig Ziglar,[12] one of America's super-salesmen, delights in telling. Back in the days of the general store with its cracker barrels and kegs of black-strap molasses, there was a storekeeper who had a vexing problem. A mischievous little boy took to loitering in his shop; whenever no one was looking, the lad would lift the lid on the keg of molasses, dip his fingers into the sweet sticky mess, and get himself a hand-to-mouthful. One day the suspicious proprietor caught the lad in the act, and said "Sonny, if I ever catch you doing that again, I'm going to dunk you, clothes and all, into that very keg."

It wasn't long afterward that temptation overcame the boy and he was back to the store and into the molasses. The storekeeper had a hunch as to what was going on and snuck up on the little thief.

"I've caught you again, you rapscallion," the proprietor said, picking him up by the seat of the pants and the scruff of the neck. He gave the little shaver a mighty shake and then said to him, "Do you have any last words to say before I drop you into this-here keg? Remember, the Lord has mercy on those sinners who repent."

Wide-eyed, the lad looked at the nearly full keg, then gazed into the proprietor's eyes and said, "Yes, Sir, I do. Lord, please grant me a tongue large enough to equal this opportunity."

I hope that the entrepreneur will feel a little of this anticipatory delight when he discovers the opportunities in the world of books. I know of damn few *successful* entrepreneurs, college-educated or not, who have failed to avail themselves of the wisdom of their predecessors, the men who have taken the time and trouble to record what they have learned for the benefit of their "heirs" who have been stricken with the do-your-own-thing malady. Let's have a look at a few of the more common types of libraries and bookstores available to you.

Community Libraries

Do you live in a community so intellectually impoverished that it doesn't have a library? If that's the case and if your criterion of success is more than mere economic survival, then the burg you live in is probably a terrible location in which to open your business. However, if yours is a more typical situation, there will at least be a county and/or city library to which you will have access. The extent of the library collection that is of specific interest to the small businessman largely depends on the support of the citizenry. The composition of the collection is one of the most important responsibilities of the library staff. Rather than make their acquisition decisions in a vacuum, libraries greatly appreciate hearing specific requests and recommendations from their patrons. Provided that there is sufficient demand for the type of information included in the books you request and that the library budget permits, the staff will be glad to order them for you.

College and University Libraries

Although these libraries are primarily intended for the use of the faculty and student body, most institutions make provision for the use of their facilities by the community at large. Depending on whether or not the institution is privately or publicly supported, the cost of library privileges will vary widely. (In spite of the fact that the practice is frowned upon, a few of the more pragmatic and resourceful entrepreneurs I have known have been successful in persuading some of their student friends to take out university library books for their use.) If you are fortunate enough to have access to a business school library, you should find their collection to be an enormously valuable resource.

Professional and Trade Association Libraries

Many trade associations and professional organizations maintain book collections which are specifically related to subjects of primary interest to the association members.

Provided there exists such a library to serve your industry and access to it is practical from a geographical standpoint, you should not fail to investigate the services the facility has to offer.

One facility which should be of particular interest to the entrepreneur is the American Management Association Library and Management Information Service, available at no additional charge to members of the AMA. A free brochure describing these services may be obtained by writing to the Management Information Service, American Management Association, The American Management Association Building, 135 West 50th Street, New York, New York 10020, or telephone (212) 586-8100, Extensions 172, 163, or 164.

Bookstores

First cousin to the library is the bookstore, and you will find that there is a surprising number of bookstores that limit their stock to a particular subject area. Some shops specialize in religious books, some in legal or medical reference works, others in best-sellers, and still others in pornography. Fortunately for the businessman, a few of them concentrate their efforts in the field of business books. In spite of this penchant for specialization, however, most bookstores are in business to provide their owners with a livelihood. Thus, they are usually quite accommodating in ordering books in print from any legitimate trade publisher whose offerings you request.

In the event you encounter difficulty in obtaining a particular book, there is a process you can employ to bring results. First, consult a copy of *Books in Print*,[13] a two-volume reference published by the R. R. Bowker Co. and available in most libraries. Obtain the author's name, title, and publisher of the book you wish. Then contact a major metropolitan bookseller, such as Brentano's, Inc., 20 University Place, New York, New York 10003, to place your order. The cost to you will probably include the regular list price plus postage, sales taxes where applicable, and nominal handling charges.

Book Clubs

Many book clubs (and some trade and professional associations) provide their members with a wide selection of offerings, usually at a cost discounted below normal publisher's list price. Once you get on the mailing list of some of these firms, you'll be hearing from them regularly for a long, long time.

One business-book seller that has been recommended to me by a satisfied customer is The Executive Program, Riverside, New Jersey 08075. A trade association which offers business books at special membership prices is the American Management Association, American Management Association Building, 135 West 50th Street, New York, New York 10020. Write a letter of inquiry to either or both of these firms for a brochure describing the services they offer.

Still another source of information on book dealers who are offering volumes at prices lower than retail may be found in the "Book Exchange" section of *The New York Times Book Review,* a feature section of the Sunday edition of this newspaper.

PERIODICALS, TOO

Unending sources of information of interest to the small businessman are the periodicals. At the present time, there are more than 50,000 different periodicals offered for sale in this country. These publications afford the entrepreneur an excellent opportunity for acquiring the latest information available in any subject area that may be of interest to him.

Several directories that list business periodicals exist; with luck, you should find at least one of them in your library. Two of the more commonly available directories are:

Business Publication Rates and Data, published monthly by Standard Rate and Data Service, Inc., contains a descriptive listing of business magazines and is indexed by name of magazine and by business fields covered.

Standard Periodical Directory, published by the Oxbridge Publishing Company, Inc., gives comprehensive coverage to periodicals in the United States and Canada. It contains over 53,000 entries, including magazines, journals, newsletters, house organs, government publications, advisory services, directories, transactions and proceedings of professional societies, yearbooks, and major-city daily newspapers.

Another publication *any* information seeker should treasure is the *Readers' Guide to Periodical Literature,* published semi-monthly (monthly in July and August) by the H. W. Wilson Company. This guide provides a complete, up-to-date index of all articles, listed by subject, in leading periodicals including *The New York Times Magazine, Time, Newsweek, Fortune, Business Week, Forbes, Harvard Business Review,* and *Nation's*

Business. (See Appendix 6 for an extensive listing of business and financial periodicals.)

To obtain specialized information on business periodicals serving any particular industry, additional assistance may be obtained by corresponding with one of the following organizations:

Ayer Press
West Washington Square
Philadelphia, Pennsylvania 19106

Associated Business Press, Inc.
205 East 42nd Street
New York, New York 10017

R. R. Bowker Company
1180 Avenue of the Americas
New York, New York 10036

Many organizations offer subscriptions to leading magazines at discounted prices. One such firm is Publishers Clearing House, 382 Channel Drive, Port Washington, New York 11050. A free brochure is available on request.

Trade Journals

Trade journals are some of the most authoritative sources available of timely, specialized industrial information. Announcements of the latest commercial products, analyses of major innovations in marketing, and discussions on manufacturing, research, and development activities are regular editorial subjects. Invaluable market survey and market forecast information is frequently printed in these publications before it is promulgated by any other news medium. Meeting and convention calendars are also commonly included as a convenience to the readers.

A study of trade journal advertising affords the marketeer and designer one of the most valuable sources of information about competitors in his industry. These advertisements typically extol the virtues of brand-new products and provide the entrepreneur with useful information on the sort of competition he can expect to encounter.

Bank Publications

Several major banks offer free of charge or at nominal cost publications of interest to the businessman. A particularly fine service is offered through the Bank of America publication *Small Business Reporter*. Information on subscription rates and reprints can be had by writing to *Small Business Reporter,* Department 3120, Bank of America N. T. & S. A., San Francisco, California 94120. A description of the publication, from the *Small Business Reporter* publication index, "What is the *Small Business Reporter?*" follows.

> The *Small Business Reporter* studies specific small businesses as well as various areas of business operation. Through research, including extensive field interviewing over a period of months, it makes these reports practical and objective. A communicative style makes them easy to read and understand.

Financial Papers

Such periodicals as the *Wall Street Journal, Barrons,* and the financial sections of the major metropolitan dailies provide small businessmen with an excellent source of up-to-date information on events of interest in the financial community. In addition to providing up-to-date information on stock prices and market trading volume, business papers also serve as a source of information with regard to broad, national economic trends; and they occasionally provide analyses of specific industries.

Business Magazines

Magazines such as *Business Week, Forbes,* and *Nation's Business* provide the entrepreneur with considerable information on the condition of the business community which is useful in determining in a broad sense the availability of capital in capital markets; also published occasionally are in-depth stories on selected sectors of industry.

Newsletters

There are more than 1500 different newsletters currently published in the United States. Almost any subject you can conceive has a voice through the medium of a newsletter. There are newsletters dealing with automotive parts retailing and newsletters dealing with zoo management.

The survival of any newsletter depends on the ability of its editors to address their special subject with authority, consistency, and a timeliness usually not found in any other information source outside of a full-time staff consultant.

Newsletters, typically, are *not* low in cost. They rarely include paid advertising; thus, the full cost of research, preparation, and distribution must be borne by the readers. Usually, the no-advertising policy assures a minimum of bias and a maximum of objectivity in the material covered. In addition, when the cost of hiring consultants or maintaining the staff necessary to acquire the specialized information made available in newsletters is weighed against the subscription rate, most people would agree that the newsletter editor is the lowest paid "employee" on the staff. For a direct pipeline into virtually any commercial field, newsletters are hard to beat for being "firstest with the mostest" at the lowest practical cost. The *National Directory of Newsletters and Reporting Services,* published by the Gale Research Company of Detroit, lists every major publication and can be found in most major library reference collections.

Community Newspapers

The editors of most community newspapers pride themselves on being the first to offer their readers news of recent developments on the local business scene. Therefore, community newspapers eagerly solicit newsworthy items regarding product development, contract awards, and personnel changes from businesses in and around their major area of circulation.

Businesses also recognize the public relations value of keeping the local newspaper informed of significant developments. Furthermore, by keeping their local editors up to date and providing news releases to community newspapers, these businesses avail themselves of free advertising and succeed in enhancing their corporate image.

When a local paper has an aggressive staff, even information unfavorable to a local business may be ferreted out and served up to the voracious appetite of its readership. Regardless of the circumstances, community newspapers represent an informative and inexpensive source of business intelligence within a limited geographical area.

UNCLE SAM WANTS (TO HELP) YOU

Many government agencies produce enormous quantities of timely, worthwhile information of interest to the entrepreneur. One remarkable aspect of this service is that the government publications are available free of charge or for a very nominal fee. The U.S. Department of Commerce and the Small Business Administration are the front-runners in the race to supply the entrepreneur with all the tools-in-print that he can effectively use in launching and operating his own business. Consider the publications these two agencies offer:

The U. S. Department of Commerce

In 1970, the Department of Commerce established the National Technical Information Service (NTIS) to coordinate and consolidate the Department's business and technical information activities and to serve as the primary focal point within the federal government for the collection, announcement, and dissemination of technical reports and data. The NTIS makes available reports summarizing the research work supported by federal funds in more than 150 agencies within the federal government. Material covered in these reports ranges through all levels of scientific, social, and economic research.

In addition to making announcements and distributing information, NTIS performs a specialized reference service. A staff is maintained to assist the public in locating specific literature and information on specialized centers of expertise.

Currently, information available through NTIS includes Census Bureau statistics on population, housing, and industry; also included are marketing reports for specific industries for the purpose of promoting domestic and international commerce.

More than 20 different products and services are made available through NTIS on a charge basis. The fee covers the costs of the reproduction and handling required to make the different products available. The key announcement services of NTIS are listed below:

U. S. Government Research & Development Report: A semi-monthly abstract journal announcing all NTIS documents as they become available for release to the public.

U. S. Government Research & Development Reports Index: Companion publication to the *Bulletin,* indexing each issue by subject, corporate and personal author, and contract and report numbers.

Clearinghouse Announcements in Science & Technology: A current-awareness service announcing NTIS reports in 35 different fields of technology. Published semi-monthly.

Fast Announcement Service: Features reports selected for their potential high interest to business, industry, and science. Published in 57 categories and covers about 10 percent of the NTIS document input.

The Small Business Administration

Every year the Small Business Administration literally gives away millions of leaflets and pamphlets relating to various topics of interest to the small businessman. The SBA form "Free Management Assistance Publications" (SBA Form 115a) includes a listing of more than 150 different publications available free from the SBA. These publications include such series as Management Aids, Technical Aids, Small Marketers Aids, and Small Business Bibliographies.

The SBA form "For Sale Booklets" is SBA Form 115b. This form includes the Small Business Management Series, the Starting and Managing Series, Small Business Research Series, Management Aids Annuals, and several non-series publications.

Taken as a whole, the publications offered by the SBA will present encyclopedic coverage of every major program a small businessman can expect to encounter. The cost of the "For Sale Booklets" is often no more than 50 cents; no booklet costs more than $2.

In addition to the enormous reservoir of information represented by the SBA publications, the SBA makes a further offering of the booklet "A Survey of Federal

Government Publications of Interest to Small Business." This bibliography includes the various publications of 28 different government agencies and deals principally with nontechnical literature. Entries have been selected, annotated, and arranged both by subject and by issuing agency.

PUBLIC SPEAKING

The entrepreneur who has the ability to express his thoughts effectively before an audience possesses an extremely valuable asset. This ability is part of the "charisma" that so many venture capitalists and other members of the financial community look for in the people in whom they consider investing money.

People who say they are not capable of addressing a large group generally lack confidence in their ability to do so. Formalized programs of instruction afford the bashful orator the opportunity to overcome this fear. Public speaking is an ability that readily lends itself to cultivation through practice and experience. Participation in a formally structured program of public speaking repeatedly forces a student to test his wings. Pretty soon he is saying "Look, Ma, I can fly!" and another one of life's problems has been turned into a talent of substantial worth. There are many ways in which the entrepreneur can cultivate speaking skills:

Toastmasters Clubs

According to a Toastmasters International brochure, "Even experienced speakers have butterflies in their stomachs—this is natural—but the Toastmasters program will help you make them fly in formation." To be maximally effective in discharging his newly assumed responsibilities, the entrepreneur should develop the ability to present his ideas and thoughts persuasively and confidently. One of the finest and least expensive programs for attaining this goal is that provided by Toastmasters International, which is an organization devoted to helping its members master the art of effective oral communication and dynamic leadership.

Meetings are usually held once a week; they afford the members opportunities for delivering prepared speeches and extemporaneous monologues and for cultivating the hard-to-master ability to *listen* to what other people say while making critical evaluations of their ideas. A typical Toastmasters meeting is charged with an air of camaraderie as the members share their experiences and enjoy the pleasure and satisfaction of helping one another.

As you progress through the Toastmasters program, you will overcome the nervousness common to most inexperienced speakers and progress via a series of projects toward the development of techniques, speech preparation, voice modulation, the use of word pictures, and enhancement of your vocabulary.

The enthusiasm with which graduates of the Toastmasters program describe their experiences has made a believer of me. I am presently enrolled in the Toastmasters program myself, and I highly recommend it to you. For a descriptive brochure and further information on how to become a Toastmaster, you may write to Toastmasters International World Headquarters, 2200 North Grand Avenue, Santa Ana, California 92711.

Community Colleges and University Extension Courses

Many educational institutions offer courses of instruction in public speaking at very low cost. On the college campus, one can expect experienced, professional assistance in the development of one's oratory talents.

Commercial Institutions

Schools devoted to the teaching of public speaking, sales techniques, and "personality improvement" can be found in every major city. Probably the best known of these is the Dale Carnegie Institute, which offers the famous Dale Carnegie courses in cities around the world.

I have spoken to many people who have availed themselves of some form of organized public speaking instruction through Toastmasters International, university evening programs, and commercial schools such as the Dale Carnegie Institute. Invariably the comments I have received have been extremely favorable. The people involved indicate consistently that their public speaking ability and their self confidence have been significantly enhanced as a result of participation in the programs' regimens.

Recommended Reading

Bunn, Verne A. *Buying and Selling a Small Business*. Washington, D.C.: Small Business Administration, Government Printing Office, 1969.

Burger, Ninki Hart. *The Executive's Wife*. Collier Books Edition. New York: The Macmillan Company, 1970.

Cossman, E. Joseph. *How to Get $50,000 Worth of Services Free, Each Year, from the U.S. Government*, rev. ed. New York: Frederick Fell, Inc., 1969.

Cooper, Kenneth H. *Aerobics*. New York: M. Evans and Company, Inc., 1968.

Drucker, Peter F. *Managing for Results: Economic Tasks and Risk-taking Decisions*. New York: Harper & Row, Publishers, Inc., 1964.

Elton, Reuel W. "How Trade Associations Help Small Business." *Management Aids for Small Business, Annual No. 2*. Washington, D.C.: Small Business Administration, Government Printing Office, Rev. 1958.

Janezick, Elizabeth G., comp. *A Survey of Federal Government Publications of Interest to Small Business*, 3rd ed. Washington, D.C.: Small Business Administration, Government Printing Office, 1969.

Kepner, Charles H. and Tregoe, Benjamin G. *The Rational Manager; a Systematic Approach to Problem Solving and Decision Making*. New York: McGraw-Hill Book Company, 1965.

Lederman, Martin. *The Slim Gourmet*. New York: Simon and Schuster, Inc., 1955.

Martin, Clement G., M. D. *Managing Your Health: Profits without Losses*. Homewood, Illinois: Dow Jones-Irwin, Inc., 1970.

McGregor, Douglas. *The Human Side of Enterprise*. New York: McGraw-Hill, 1960.

Peale, Norman Vincent. *The Power of Positive Thinking*. A Fawcett Crest Book. New York: Fawcett World Library, 1956.

Phair, W. A. "How Business Publications Help Small Business." *Management Aids for Small Manufacturers, Annual No. 6*. Washington, D. C.: Small Business Administration, Government Printing Office, 1960, pp. 67-73.

Shefter, Harry. *How to Prepare Talks and Oral Reports*. New York: Washington Square Press, Inc., 1963.

Sweetland, Ben. *I Can! The Key to Life's Golden Secrets*. New York: Cadillac Publishing Company, Inc., 1953.

Chapter 7

Many People are Glad to Help You - Just Ask Them

When I started writing this book, I could hardly wait to get to this section because I wanted to share with you my discovery of how unselfish other people were in their willingness to help. I used to feel, as most of us do, that my pride would not let me ask for help. Asking for other people's assistance struck me as being much like seeking charity. But as I see it now, other people are usually delighted to help, that is, if they are convinced that you will make effective use of their advice. You must project to others your capability and willingness to implement their suggestions. You must convey the spirit of your worthiness to receive the benefits of their knowledge and experience. This is the *real* measure of pride: *the self-knowledge that you are worthy of other people's help.*

Have you ever heard of anyone getting a hernia while pulling himself up by his own bootstraps? I haven't. First, you must make a sincere effort at getting started in your chosen business. Then, when you need help, when you really start looking for help, when you are in a position to turn help to good use, you *will* find it. And bear in mind: it is highly unlikely that anyone is going to seek you out to spoon feed it to you—you've got to go prospecting for it on your own.

One crackerjack entrepreneur I know states that there are two qualities never found lacking in the president of a successful new business: *persistence* and *audacity*. When it comes to getting the help you need—help to turn your business idea into a commercial enterprise—these characteristics are musts. You should find them extremely valuable when seeking advice and guidance from the suggested sources listed below.

ENTREPRENEURS WHO HAVE ALREADY GOTTEN STARTED

Men already active in businesses of their own represent one of the best possible sources of general, first-hand information on what it is like to have your own show. As a rule, they are most willing to discuss the mixed blessings their work affords them.

A typical conversation might go something like this: "Mr. Businessman, what was it like when you got your initial big contract? How did you finagle it?"

"Well, young man, I had all my relatives come down early in the morning the day my best customer came to town for his first plant tour. All the women put on white smocks and sat on folding chairs in front of door panel/saw-horse work benches. They quadrupled the size of our assembly line. Next, I borrowed some test equipment for the day from a friend of mine who owns a TV repair shop. We also brought in half a dozen job-shop draftsmen just for the occasion. Needless to say, our customer was satisfied with our capability because we got the contract and our bank loaned us the money we needed to do the job."

"What happened after you finished that order?"

"Well, we didn't get another big one for six months, so we had to let half our people go. My nerves got so bad I could hardly sleep and I started working on an ulcer. Once we got our second big job, though, things settled down. We've had a very encouraging sales growth ever since, and I've been very careful not to hire more people than our order backlog would justify."

This example is merely representative of the typical nitty-gritty insight such interviews can offer. Another way you can benefit is through referrals. Usually, successful businessmen have a wide circle of colleagues and can suggest several who might take an interest in helping you along. Other business contacts may be cultivated at community service clubs, such as the Junior Chamber of Commerce, Rotary International, and Kiwanis International. The members of such clubs are dedicated to helping others and to serving society constructively. Frequently, a club officer can direct you to a businessman willing to take a personal interest in you. Fraternal organizations such as the Elks, Moose, Odd Fellows, Masonic Groups, Knights of Columbus, and B'nai B'rith have served as meeting grounds for developing business contacts over many years. College fraternity and alumni associations, professional and trade associations, political organizations such as the Young Republicans and Young Democrats, and church groups also fill the bill. In fact, whenever and wherever people meet, an opportunity usually exists for the development of business relationships.

TRADESMEN IN YOUR INDUSTRY

Tradesmen are also fine sources of information and assistance. Tradesmen include the suppliers, customers, manufacturers' representatives, and distributors in your chosen industrial field.

Suppliers

In prospecting for information, you will undoubtedly discover that suppliers are very much interested in helping a potential customer develop and grow. And their assistance won't be limited only to market savvy, either. It may also include piece-part and subassembly quotations for use in your business proposal, free parts and material samples, and contract and customer leads.

Customers

While you're at it, don't overlook potential customers as another source of help. You must understand that the customer desires greater competition among his suppliers. It is his hope that competition will spur them on to better quality, lower prices, and more timely deliveries. When it comes to new product specifications and market forecasting, customers can provide really valuable advice. New order down-payments or deposits and progress payments constitute another area where customers can be of help. Thousands and tens of thousands of companies owe their starts to a good-sized contract from an understanding customer who was willing to gamble on the new guy.

Manufacturers' Representatives

Another group in the cheering section is made up of manufacturers' representatives, usually an entrepreneurially inclined bunch themselves. These guys often operate as sole proprietorships or partnerships and earn their bagels and butter hustling products for small- and medium-sized companies. Usually their principals (companies whose products they sell) can't afford a large network of direct sales offices, so a marriage of convenience is contracted. You pay the "Rep" a commission on each order he gets; and, with proper factory support, he'll work his fanny off for you.

At the outset, though, even before your company gets started, the Rep can be a big help. Most Reps are constantly on the lookout for principals offering new lines to complement (not compete with) the products they already handle. The opportunity to "sign up" a promising new firm with a hot product line is a powerful attraction.

Since Reps work with small- to medium-sized companies constantly, they can often provide a whale of a lot of information on market size, product pricing, and desirable product characteristics. Their income is almost entirely dependent on their business contacts and perpetually renewed supply of "leads." In my own experience, I have found Reps to be a congenial, hardworking, and helpful group with a first-hand knowledge of the markets they serve.

Distributors

Distributors comprise still another unique group that may be of help to you. Usually operating as wholesale outlets specializing in a particular industry, distributors tend to have much larger organizations than manufacturers' representatives have. Distributors typically maintain inventories of finished merchandise; the Reps, on the other hand, act primarily as marriage brokers in placing customer contracts directly with manufacturing suppliers. Inventory maintenance incurs substantial costs in the operation of a Distributorship. Understandably, then, distributors must operate on a much larger commission or discount than does a Rep.

Distributors can be of help to the new businessman in providing product, pricing, and marketing suggestions. From the small businessman's point of view, the distributor is a hybrid—part salesman and part customer.

In essence, the difference between Reps and distributors is in the type of product handled. Most Reps specialize in the custom or job-shop field, where substantial supplier-customer liaison is necessary. Usually the product sold is tailor-made to the customer's specifications. Most distributors handle standardized products which (hopefully) are not overly vulnerable to obsolescence while in the warehouse.

BANKERS

An often maligned and much misunderstood group of new-business helpers is the banking community. Banks don't spend millions of dollars every year advertising their services solely to get their message across to the Ford Motor Company and Bethlehem Steel. They really do have an interest in working with the little guy. Several of the larger institutions have developed extensive literature in brochure and pamphlet form for this express purpose.

When it comes to juicy industry "insider" stories, bankers' ethics forbid their divulging any information about their clients. However, they can serve as a valuable reference point in evaluating the business climate in almost any area of commercial specialization, be it beauty salons or ecological systems manufacturing. Bankers deserve a section of their own later on, so for now let's move on to the next source of help.

STOCKBROKERS

Stockbrokers spend five days a week functioning as croupiers in the nation's largest game of chance—the investing public's confidence level in the future of American Business. Many of them have wealthy clients or business contacts who can either help in locating private investors for a new company or can commit funds themselves. Your broker can be an excellent contact in furthering your plans.

All of the major brokerage firms maintain research departments to provide the latest information on pivotal companies, "market indicators," and key industries. Although you may find their augury a little heavily spiced with *if's*, *and's*, and *but's*, their expertise in this wizardry is probably a hell of a lot better than yours or mine.

COLLEGE FACULTY MEMBERS

The next group of baby-business boosters may be found in our universities. College professors and teachers, particularly those in business schools, colleges of pure and applied science, and engineering schools, are often veritable clearing houses of information for new companies. Many professors have extensive consulting practices in addition to their teaching duties. They are thus afforded a firsthand look at new applications of technology to commercial markets. Most professors sincerely enjoy their vocation of communicating knowledge to people, including entrepreneurs. Some teachers have gone to great lengths to assist and encourage their graduate students and research associates in starting small companies. In fact, for years a number of large university laboratories have served as spawning grounds for high technology companies.

In most cases, it is safe to say that your request for a conference with a former professor to discuss your new enterprise plans will be greeted with warm enthusiasm. Over a luncheon at the faculty club, you will be pleased and delighted to discover how poorly you had estimated your old prof's interests outside of the classroom. You will probably find yourself committed for days simply to the task of following up on leads and suggestions he may offer. Furthermore, it's likely he won't even permit you to pay for the meal—"Club rules, you understand," he says with a grin as he signs the chit.

Would you have believed there was such a mighty reservoir of willing, qualified assistance ready to respond to your needs for help? Let me tell you, it was a welcome surprise to me. These broadly defined groups operate largely with the expectation that some day you may be able to return or pass on the favor. This may take the form of your future patronage or of a spirit of "Go thou and do likewise."

On the assumption that the small businessman does not often suffer the burden of a surfeit of cash, the preceding list purposely omitted such service groups as attorneys, certified public accountants, and business consultants. *I do not intend to suggest that professional services are unnecessary.* To do so would be foolhardy of me and a disservice to you. I simply have chosen to discuss them as a separate group.

Let's take a moment now to catalog, for ready reference, the many helpers that tomorrow's businessman can turn to:

1.   Other entrepreneurs, who can be reached through

   a.   Community service clubs such as

   i.   The Junior Chamber of Commerce
   ii.   Rotary International
   iii. Lions International
   iv.   Kiwanis International

   b.   Fraternal organizations such as

   i.   Elks
   ii.   Moose
   iii. Odd Fellows
   iv.   Masonic Clubs
   v.   Knights of Columbus
   vi.   B'nai B'rith

   c.   College related organizations including

   i.   Fraternities
   ii.   Alumni Associations

   d.   Professional and Trade Associations

   e.   Political organizations typified by the

   i.   Young Democrats
   ii.   Young Republicans

   f.   Church groups

2.   Tradesmen, broken down into groups of

   a.   Suppliers
   b.   Customers
   c.   Manufacturers' Representatives
   d.   Distributors

3.   Bankers

4.   Stockbrokers

5.   College Faculty Members.

Recommended Reading

American Management Association. *Directory of Consultant Members*. New York: American Management Association, 1966 ed.

Association of Consulting Management Engineers, Inc. *Directory of Membership and Services, 1970-71*. New York: Association of Consulting Engineers, Inc., 1970/71.

Bennett, E. I. H. "Using Your Banker's Advisory Services." *Management Aids for Small Manufacturers, Annual No. 4*. Washington, D.C.: Small Business Administration, Government Printing Office, 1958, pp. 65-71.

Bettger, Frank. *How One Idea Multiplied My Income and Happiness*. Wynnewood, Pa.: By the Author, 1129 Montgomery Avenue, 1953.

Carnegie, Dale. *How to Win Friends and Influence People*. Cardinal Edition. New York: Pocket Books, 1940.

Cruger, Frank M. "How Industrial Distributors Help Small Manufacturers." *Management Aids for Small Manufacturers, Annual No. 4*. Washington, D. C.: Small Business Administration, Government Printing Office, 1958, pp. 72-78.

Dunn, Clark A.; Poehle, Herbert F.; and Murray, Donald S. *Research Relations between Engineering Educational Institutions and Industrial Organizations*. Small Business Management Series, No. 23. Washington, D. C.: Small Business Administration, Government Printing Office, 1959.

Hicks, Tyler. *How to Start Your Own Business on a Shoestring and Make up to $100,000 a Year*. Award Books. New York: Parker Publishing Company, Inc., 1970.

Hill, Napoleon, and Keown, E. Harold. *Succeed and Grow Rich through Persuasion*. A Fawcett Crest Book. Greenwich, Conn.: Fawcett Publications, Inc., 1970.

The J.K. Lasser Institute. *How to Start and Build a Successful Business*. Larchmont, New York: American Research Council, 1961.

National Trade and Professional Associations of the U.S. *Annual*. Washington, D.C.: Columbia Books.

Staudt, Thomas A. "How Manufacturers' Agents Help Small Business." *Management Aids for Small Business, Annual No. 2*. Washington, D.C.: Small Business Administration, Government Printing Office, Rev. 1958, pp. 127-133.

White, L. T. "How Big Companies Help Small Marketers." *Small Marketers Aids, Annual No. 3*. Washington, D. C.: Small Business Administration, Government Printing Office, 1961, pp. 56-64.

Chapter 8

The Conception and Protection of a Product Idea: "After All, You've Got to Have *Something* to Sell!"

Having made the decision to go into business for yourself in spite of the hardships and pitfalls discussed in preceding chapters, you must next give consideration to your business vehicle: a product or service to be offered for sale. This chapter will treat the subject of product selection and its protection.

MOMMY, WHERE DO PRODUCT IDEAS COME FROM?

Contrary to the teachings of our wealthy friends from Chapter 5, the Wise Owl, the Old Lady Goose, and the Little Red Hen, I must point out that the Stork does *not* bring product ideas. These ideas originate in many different ways and places, including:

Former Employers

Very often, product ideas are "adopted," bought, or licensed from former employers. Now it may interest many of you to learn, in passing, that the body of law which treats the relationship between an employer and his employees comes under the legal heading of "Master and Servant." (Remember our *Olde English* heritage!) This section of the law covers those things which an employer *may* require of his employees (such as patent agreements and employment contracts) and those things which guarantee the rights of an employee to earn his daily bread in any *reasonable* area of his choice. Under the safeguards in our Constitution, an employer may not make indentured servants of his employees.

An employer may not, for instance, extract a promise from a plumber on his staff that would preclude that plumber's working for another employer if he chose to do so. Such a covenant would be unenforceable. However, if the plumber-employee were taught by his former employer, in confidence, a "secret" way of clearing stopped-up drains and agreed not to use this technique when working for any other employer, he could be legally obliged to honor his commitment provided it did not stop him from earning a livelihood as a plumber.

To illustrate this point further, an employee may resign from his job and legally set up a business of his own to manufacture products identical to, and in competition with, those made by his former employer provided that (1) the products are not protected by patents, (2) the elements of the manufacture and operation of the product are evident from an examination of the finished product (dismantled if necessary) by anyone reasonably skilled in that product discipline, and (3) the employee had not previously consented, as a consideration of his employment, not to compete with his former employer for a specified period of time after termination of employment.

On the other hand, an employee who takes "trade secrets" from his former employer when his former employer has followed the necessary procedure for communicating these secrets in confidence is vulnerable to legal action. A few examples of trade secrets are (1) the formula for, or ingredients in, Coca-Cola soft-drink syrup, (2) the technique used to cut sheets of plastic film into thin strips for use in tape recorders or as gummed tape, and (3) a process for annealing the steel alloys used in ball bearings to attain the desired hardness.

Note: The foregoing is not intended to serve as a substitute for competent legal counsel. In any case where vulnerability to legal action from a former employer may exist, the services of a skilled attorney should be retained. *As a bare minimum*, where a signed employment or patent agreement was a condition of hire demanded by a former employer, counsel for the entrepreneur should be given the opportunity to examine the document.

One further note on this subject: Individual states regulate their own corporate laws, and practices regarding trade secrets and their protection *do* vary from state to state. Again, competent legal counsel is a must!

On a friendlier note, many companies are willing to sell patent rights on certain products to former employees or, in some cases, even to make them available to *any* interested buyer. Alternatively, various licensing agreements may be drawn up providing for the use (exclusive or nonexclusive) of the patent on a royalty basis. An example of the transfer of trademark rights by an employer to an employee is the Pert-O-Graph, discussed in Chapter 1.

In recent years, a number of employers have decided to "join them (the entrepreneurs) rather than fight them," and they now encourage spin-offs in the form of subsidiaries. In this way, the entrepreneur receives the help of a large company in getting established; and the parent company retains a stock position in the new firm. Thus, the parent company realizes a gain where otherwise there would have been a net loss of employee talent and product revenue.

In those instances where the form of company organization is a sole proprietorship or partnership, an entrepreneurially inclined employee may succeed in persuading the company owner(s) to make him a partner rather than resign to start his own company. In the position of partner, the entrepreneur should then have greatly increased latitude in promoting the products in which he is especially interested.

New Partners

There is an increasing tendency today for *teams* of entrepreneurs to found new companies. Thus, the product idea may have originated with only one of the partners; but it provides the revenue-producing article for exploitation by all of them. In this context, I will long remember a graduation-time bulletin-board notice I saw at MIT when I was an undergraduate there. It went something like this:

> Two Harvard MBA candidates wish to discuss partnership possibilities with MIT degree candidate or laboratory assistant with a commercial product concept. Purpose: join forces and start a new company.

Similar advertisements may be found regularly in the classified section of *The Wall Street Journal.*

New-Product Periodicals

Many periodicals offer specialized information of considerable value in the quest for product ideas. Several are listed below.

1. The Small Business Administration offers a monthly booklet, *Products List Circular,* describing recent patents the owners of which wish to commercialize. Listing in the Circular is available to patent owners at no

charge. Single copies are 20 cents; annual subscriptions are $1.50 from the Superintendent of Documents, Washington, D.C. 20402.

2. The U. S. Patent Office publishes the *Official Gazette* every Tuesday; this paper gives a brief summary, one claim, and one picture, if there are any illustrations, of every patent issued that week. Since this publication is large and may contain many entries of no practical interest to you, a visit to one of the numerous libraries around the country which subscribe to the *Gazette* may serve to satisfy your curiosity. Copies of desired patents may be obtained from the Patent Office for 50 cents each.

3. The famous New York advertising agency Batten, Barton, Durstine and Osborn, Inc. publishes the *New Products Digest*, a monthly compilation of new products and services being introduced in the United States. Since all material in the publication comes from other than public sources, it serves as a nice supplement to the government publications listed above. Annual subscriptions are $50; however, complimentary copies may be obtained by writing (on your letterhead) to the agency at 383 Madison Avenue, New York, N. Y. 10017.

4. The Institute for New Products, also in New York, publishes a semi-monthly *New Products Newsletter* listing product offerings in the United States and several foreign countries. A particularly valuable feature of this newsletter is the section "Licensing Opportunities," which lists patents offered for license or sale and companies and individuals seeking products. Annual subscriptions are $50; however, complimentary copies may be obtained by writing (on your letterhead) to the Institute at 135 East 44th Street, New York, N. Y. 10017.

Regular review of any or all of these publications should unleash a flood of commercially viable new product ideas in the mind of the entrepreneur, any one of which could be adapted to his business plans or vice versa.

Doctoral Dissertations

Every year thousands and thousands of bright young men and women compose dissertations as part of the requirement for the doctoral degree. These dissertations represent original work in almost any subject area you can imagine, from accounting to zoology.

Since several hundred thousand doctoral dissertations have been written in the last 30 years, there is an excellent probability that a student has labored for years doing research on a subject of interest to your business and has summarized his findings in a doctoral dissertation that may be available to you for the mere cost of reproducing it.

Many corporations today recognize the value of doctoral dissertations as a resource material in locating new products and ideas. The cost of doctoral dissertations is modest; as a business resource, such papers are often, unfortunately, neglected. Here are two particularly useful ways of determining the availability of doctoral dissertations covering subjects relevant to your business.

Various University Libraries

Copies of doctoral dissertations are often available through the library services of universities that offer doctoral programs. Either by corresponding with or by visiting a university that has a particularly strong department in the subject area of interest to you, you may buy copies of the doctoral dissertations you want.

University Microfilms

This organization, a Xerox company, offers microfilm or Xerox copies of more than 150,000 dissertations in all fields, representing the work of graduate students from more than 260 North American and European universities.

Because of the enormous amount of information represented in this library, a specialized information retrieval system called Datrix (Direct Access to Reference Information: a Xerox service) has been implemented. The Datrix computer's memory is enriched with a constant input of key words selected from the titles, authors, subject headings, and other relevant portions of the paper. A University Microfilms client simply provides the company with a list of key words that are matched against a list of the entries in the Datrix computer. The computer subsequently prints out a listing of all dissertations containing the key words supplied, and this list is forwarded to the client for his evaluation. Titles of desired manuscripts may be selected from this list and copies of the dissertations may be ordered from the company. Bound Xerox copies of complete dissertations are a minimum of $10 a copy. For further information on this unique resource service, write to University Microfilms, 300 North Zeeb Road, Ann Arbor, Michigan 48106.

Idea Books

Another wellspring of embryo businesses is idea source books. You may not necessarily use one of the ideas in these books "as is," but you may add your individual novel twist to it to provide the basis for your new enterprise. Several such books are listed below:

1. *New Products and New Sales Ideas* is a regularly revised compilation of entries taken from *The Journal of Commerce*. This pamphlet, published

by one of the leading newspapers of business and international commerce, includes listings of hundreds of new domestic products as well as products originating in Australia, Denmark, England, Japan, West Germany, and many other countries. Copies of this publication may be obtained by sending 50 cents to Twin Coast Newspapers, Inc., 99 Wall Street, New York, N. Y. 10005.

2. *Design News Annual* is a problem-solution idea file for design engineers. It includes a Product Directory and a Supplier Locator. Revised annually and issued in June, it is available from the Cahners Books Division of the Cahners Publishing Co., Inc., at 221 Columbus Avenue, Boston, Massachusetts 02116, for $25.

3. *999 Little-Known Businesses,* by William Carruthers, is a fascinating collection of business ideas, primarily suitable for cottage industries (product manufacturing in the home) and moonlighting activities. Copies may be obtained by sending $9.99 to the Plymouth Publishing Company, 310 Beverley Road, Brooklyn, N. Y. 11218.

4. *The Millionaire Book of Businesses, Plans, and Know-How,* by David Magee, is similar in format and content to book #3 and also lists 999 novel ideas for businesses. The descriptions are not quite as extensive as in the case of book #3; however, the contents of the two books *are different*! A copy of this book may be obtained by sending $10 to National Counselor Reports, Kerrville, Texas 78028.

5. *300 Ways to Moonlight,* by Jerry LeBlanc, is another compendium of product and service ideas, a number of which could evolve into full-time businesses. The last chapter of this book gives a cursory treatment of the subject of starting your own business. Copies of this Paperback Library book may be obtained at your neighborhood bookstore for 75 cents.

6. *How to Earn (a lot of) Money in College, the Student Guide to Employment,* published by the Harvard Student Agencies, Inc. This unusual paperback book includes many ideas which, with a little imagination, could be adapted into full-fledged businesses. As an example, one item discusses the origin of computer dating, the brainchild of two Harvard Juniors and a Cornell dropout which has now evolved into a multi-million-dollar industry. Copies should be available at your local bookstore at $1.95 or may be obtained by writing to the Agencies at 993 Massachusetts Avenue, Cambridge, Massachusetts 02138. Include 25 cents for postage and handling.

Trade Shows

Every year many millions of dollars are spent by major industry association members to exhibit their products at national and international trade shows. These shows afford the alert visitor unique opportunities to identify and recognize new product ideas and marketing trends. Provided the entrepreneur does not have to spend an inordinate amount of money in traveling to get to the location of the trade show, he should find that the expense of attending is quite nominal.

If a new trade show is sponsored by an industrial sector with which the entrepreneur is not intimately familiar, he should avail himself of the many opportunities that will be available for discovering new products and concepts which may be applicable to fields not obvious to the trade show sponsors and exhibitors.

Your local library should have a copy of *Exhibits Schedule*, an annual directory of trade and industrial shows produced by *Sales Meetings* magazine in cooperation with Exhibit Designers and Producers Association. In the event your local library does not have a copy, further information may be obtained by writing to Exhibits Schedule, 1212 Chestnut Street, Philadelphia, Pennslyvania 19107. Subscription rates are $35 per year for this complete, worldwide guide to exhibits, trade shows, state fairs, trade fairs, industrial shows, and public exhibitions.

Your library may also have copies of *World Meetings: United States and Canada* and/or *World Meetings: Outside United States and Canada*. Each of these directories provides information on more than 1,000 meetings of scientific, technical, and medical interest held at various locations in the world. Each of these directories may be obtained from the CCM Information Group, a subsidiary of Crowell-Collier and MacMillan, 909 Third Avenue, New York, New York 10022, at $35 each. Further information including a descriptive brochure may be obtained by writing to this organization.

State Invention Expositions

A unique opportunity awaits the product-seeking entrepreneur at annual state invention expositions. According to a brochure titled *State Invention Expositions* and offered by the U. S. Department of Commerce, Office of Invention & Innovation, an invention

> exposition involves a two or three day meeting which brings together inventors, patent owners, manufacturers, distributors, investors and others for the purpose of negotiating the sale or license of patents and arranging for the production and distribution of new inventions and new products. It may also provide educational functions which enable the inventor to visualize and cope with the many problems he will face in promoting his inventions!

> The state invention exposition is frequently staged under other names such as Inventors Congress, Inventors Fair and Inventors Show. Irrespective of the name attached to the activity, the basic objective is the same—to bring forth new inventions, products and processes which will create new jobs through new or expanded production and distribution.[14]

The Office of Invention & Innovation publishes a regularly revised *Calendar of State Invention Programs*. To obtain the latest issue of this calendar and to determine when such an exposition is planned within your state, send your inquiry to the above Office in Washington, D. C. 20234. You may also obtain a copy of *State Invention Expositions* by writing to the same office. This brochure is also available at your local U. S. Department of Commerce field office.

Patent Brokers

A patent broker makes the patents or ideas of inventors available for examination by individuals who are seeking new products for commercial exploitation. The patent broker operates in much the same way as a real estate broker; he brings together the patent owner (usually the inventor) and the prospective buyers or licensees of the patent rights.

Patent brokerage firms may operate in any number of the following ways:

Seller's Agent

An inventor or patent-holding client may engage the services of a patent broker in order to locate a buyer for the patent or salable idea.

Buyer's Agent

An individual or corporation wishing to purchase or license rights to a patent or idea may engage the services of a patent broker to locate the desired patent idea or process.

Independent Dealer

In some instances, a patent broker or a patent brokerage firm may elect to purchase patent rights outright from the inventor or patent holder, with the intention of subsequently selling or licensing the patent rights to a buyer. The patent broker then takes legal possession of the patent (in the case of the seller's agent or the buyer's agent, the broker merely acts as an intermediary to introduce the buyer to the seller or vice versa).

Patent brokers may be of considerable help to an inventor in marketing his patent. A good patent broker will be able to assist the inventor in preparing a marketing plan that will enable him to obtain the highest possible price for his patent.

Patent brokers may receive remuneration for their services in any combination of the following ways:

Simple Fees

The patent broker may exact a fee, either a fixed amount or a percentage of the cash transaction involved, from the buyer, the seller, or both. The patent broker is often paid in much the same way that a stock broker is paid—he receives a commission on both the purchase and the sale of any given item.

Royalties

In some instances, a patent broker will receive his remuneration in the form of a royalty levied against the licensed or sold patent or process.

Retainers

The services of a patent brokerage firm are sometimes permanently retained by industrial clients. In these instances, the industrial concern may simply indicate to the patent broker their particular area of interest. Thus, the patent broker will be on the alert for any products or processes which might be useful to his client. Conversely, a client company may periodically provide the patent broker with a listing of the latest products and processes that the corporation is interested in licensing or selling.

The patent broker receives a retainer for performing his marketing services regardless of whether or not he is successful in his efforts. Obviously, the long-term failure of a patent broker effectively to perform a service for his client may result in discontinuance of the relationship.

National Information Referral and Exchange Centers

Two little-known, national services of particular interest to the information and idea seeker are those offered by the National Referral Center and the Science Information Exchange.

National Referral Center

The Center, part of the Science and Technology Division of the Library of Congress, is a clearinghouse for information in any field related to science and technology; and in these days of heart transplants and space exploration, that covers *plenty* of subject matter. A brochure offered by the Center indicates that it

> provides a single place to which anyone may turn for advice on where and how to obtain information on specific topics in science and technology.
> The Center does not provide technical details in answer to inquiries, nor does it furnish bibliographic assistance. Functioning as an intermediary, it directs those who have a

question concerning a particular subject to organizations or individuals with specialized knowledge of that subject.

In discussing the interpretation of the term "information resources," the Center explains that its extremely broad definition

> extends to any organization, institution, group, or individual with specialized knowledge in a given field and a willingness to share this knowledge with others. Through a continuing survey, the Center is building up a central inventory of detailed data on such resources in terms of their areas of interest and the services they provide. Included in this inventory are professional societies, university research bureaus and institutes, Federal and state agencies and units within them, industrial laboratories, museum specimen collections, testing stations, and individual experts, as well as more traditional sources of information, such as technical libraries, information and document centers, and abstracting and indexing services. The Center's criterion for registering a resource is not size but the ability and willingness to supply information to others within reasonable limitations.

Requests for information from the Center should be limited to one topic in order to facilitate prompt, efficient handling. Inquiries should also include reference to information resources already explored in order to avoid needless duplication of effort. It is also helpful if the inquirer states his special qualifications, such as researcher, member of a professional society, etc., to assist the Center staff in assessing the potential utility of recommended information sources to the end-user.

I have personally made use of the Center's services on two occasions and was pleasantly surprised and quite pleased with the prompt, efficient, and helpful assistance rendered by their fine staff. Best of all, the service is provided free of charge to all of us poor taxpayers. To avail yourself of this service or to secure a copy of the Center's descriptive brochure, write to the Library of Congress, Science and Technology Division, National Referral Center, 10 First Street S. E., Washington, D. C. 20540.

Science Information Exchange

The Exchange is a service agency of the Smithsonian Institution and serves the scientific community as a national registry of research in progress. Presently, SIE lists 100,000 one-page records of research each year, representing research projects that are planned or in progress. According to an Exchange brochure,

> These are unpublished descriptions of work funded by all sources of support, public and private. They are updated annually. Each describes who supports the project, who does it, where, and when, and each has a technical summary of the planned work.
> In the two decades of continuous operation of the Exchange, research investigators and administrators have found this type of information, retrieved in response to their specific questions, to be of value both scientifically and economically. Knowing of even a single similar research project has occasionally led to a direct cost saving.

The services of the Exchange are designed for the purpose of helping the user:

To keep up with new research.

To avoid duplication in planning new work or in the preparation of proposals for grants or contracts.

To find out what a given investigator is now working on.

To find out the research activity in a department, research unit or research organization.

To detect trends and shifts in research interests.

To update invitation lists for symposia and conferences or identify prospective discussion leaders.

To help plan itineraries for onsite visits by foreign scientists.

To compare and coordinate projects and programs among agencies with overlapping interests and missions.

To observe the distribution of projects geographically by sponsors, by performers, by subject fields or any combination thereof.

To help define and describe new programs of complex multi-disciplinary content by tabulation of research already in progress.

To identify research activities of fellows and grantees.

To help find possible sources of grant support.

The services of the Exchange are offered at nominal charge. For additional information on the Exchange, a descriptive brochure may be obtained by writing to the Science Information Exchange, Smithsonian Institution, 300 Madison National Bank Building, 1730 M Street, N. W., Washington, D. C. 20036.

PROTECTION

The mortality rate for new businesses is consistently and alarmingly high. One primary cause of business failure is the inability of a new company to cope effectively with vigorous, well-entrenched competition. Here is where the concept of *protection* comes into play.

In formulating his business plans, the entrepreneur should give very careful consideration to questions such as: "What unique characteristics do my products have that, when compared with the offerings of my competitors, will prompt customers to give my product preferential consideration?" and "What can I do to *protect* this advantage?"

The most commonly recognized form of product protection is a patent. In other instances, protection can be obtained through possession of trade secrets such as special manufacturing processes, "secret formulas," or the use of exotic materials. Still another form of protection can be realized through the use of proper timing: being the first entrant with an innovative concept into a new (but *ready*) market. This latter case requires swift establishment of the new product as "*the* one to buy" in the target virgin market before the competition has an opportunity to develop and obtain distribution for a rival product.

Patents

When reviewing any business proposition, a professional, experienced investor will always want to know what means the entrepreneur intends to use to protect his product and, at the same time, safeguard the investor's money. The new businessman certainly owes it to himself and his backers to do all he can to secure the competitive advantage a patent affords.

Although it is far beyond the scope of this book to offer an in-depth study of patent law and procedures, a brief discussion of the subject is certainly in order. The following material was obtained from the Patent Office publication *Q & A About Patents*. For further information on patents, consult the references indicated at the end of this chapter.

> A patent is a grant issued by the United States Government giving an inventor the right to exclude all others from making, using, or selling his invention within the United States, its territories and possessions.
>
> The term of a patent is seventeen years from the date on which it was issued; except for patents on ornamental designs, which are granted for terms of 3½, 7, or 14 years.[15]

And, finally,

> A patent may be granted to the inventor or discoverer of any new and useful process, machine, manufacture, or composition of matter, or any new and useful improvement thereof, or on any distinct and new variety of plant, which is asexually reproduced, or on any new, original, and ornamental design for an article of manufacture.[16]

Ordinarily, the services of a competent patent attorney should be obtained to assure maximum protection for any valuable idea, patentable or not. However, lawyers usually prefer to work on a cash basis instead of taking a "piece of the action" or working on a contingency arrangement. Therefore, the entrepreneur with a patentable idea and severely limited resources who wishes to establish a record of the time or origination and nature of his idea may do so by making use of the Patent Office's "Disclosure Document Program." The following excerpt is taken from a Patent Office brochure:

> A paper disclosing an invention and signed by the inventor or inventors may be forwarded to the Patent Office by the inventor (or by any one of the inventors when there are joint inventors), by the owner of the invention, or by the attorney or agent of

the inventor(s) or owner. It will be retained for two years and then be destroyed unless it is referred to in a related patent application filed within two years.

The Disclosure Document is not a patent application, and the date of its receipt in the Patent Office will not become the effective filing date of any patent application subsequently filed. However, like patent applications, these documents will be kept in confidence by the Patent Office.

This program does not diminish the value of the conventional witnessed and notarized records as evidence of conception of an invention, but it should provide a more creditable form of evidence than that provided by the popular practice of mailing a disclosure to oneself or another person by registered mail.[17]

In closing this section on patents, I should quote Thomas A. Edison, who opined, "A patent is a license for a lawsuit." Quoting the Patent Office publication *General Information Concerning Patents*:

The Patent Office has no jurisdiction over questions of infringement and the enforcement of patents, nor over matters relating to the promotion or utilization of patents or inventions.[18]

For the typically under-financed entrepreneur, these words simply mean that if you get a humdinger of an idea for a product and protect it with a patent, you must consider the possible expenses of protracted litigation to defend your patent property. Now it may turn out that some industrial colossus decides that your patented product would make a very nice addition to its line. A not uncommon practice is for such companies to employ highly skilled patent attorneys on a full-time basis for the purpose of suggesting ways of "designing around" a particular patent. I have heard several attorneys assert that unless the subject of a patent represents a truly new and basic innovation, it is virtually impossible to prevent infringement either directly or as a result of this "designing around" process.

Any attorney can acquaint the legal neophyte with facts on the expense of protracted litigation and the frequency with which some large corporations resort to this ploy as a means of circumventing the rights of a patent holder. It is not an uncommon thing for a small patent holder simply to abandon the defense of his rights due to an inability to afford the necessary legal fees.

In this country, we have an elaborate legal system for the enforcement of our laws and the apprehension and prosecution of offenders. In the case of patent infringements, however, the expenses of protecting and enforcing patent rights must be borne by the patent holder. The primary deterrent to patent infringement is the award of triple damages for provable losses *provided* the patent holder can afford the time and expense of the necessary litigation. One of the most practical solutions I have repeatedly heard suggested is the licensing or outright sale of the patent to a large corporation which can afford to exploit, promote, and *protect* this valuable property.

Another risk the holder of a patent may encounter has to do with the possibility that, after spending substantial sums of money and considerable time fighting alleged infringement of his patent, a court may decide that his patent is invalid. Any monies he has spent on litigation and even on the acquisition of the patent are subsequently lost.

This aspect of patent law can be likened to other areas of law as well. Simply because a law is on the books does not mean that it is necessarily constitutional. Its verity may possibly hinge on the results of an actual test in the courts.

Unpatentable Ideas

Unfortunately, many ideas and concepts of potential commercial value are not readily protectable (if they are protectable at all) by a patent umbrella. They may, however, be turned to profitable use at some future date. In the meantime, steps must be taken to protect them from careless disclosure until the opportunity arrives for exploitation by the originator or his designee.

The publication *Small Business Profits from Unpatentable Ideas*, referenced at the end of this chapter, treats this problem in detail. In that publication, the author explains that:

(1) An idea made public, either by word of mouth or in writing, immediately becomes common property, and unless the plan is revealed under contract or by confidential disclosure, anyone can make use of that property without infringing any rights;

(2) the voluntary submission of an idea does not set up a contractual relationship between the originator and the other party;

(3) because of the lack of contract, no action of any kind can be brought by the originator for breach of trust or contract;

(4) ideas can be protected, provided the originator follows certain procedures governed by the law of contracts.[19]

In the same publication, the following form is suggested for the submission and review of an idea while affording the originator the protection of the law of contracts:

John Doe Co.
123 Fourth Street
Anytown, U. S. A.

Gentlemen:

I have developed a new idea for the packaging of your product which I believe would greatly increase your sales and profits. The new method of packaging would not raise production costs.

If you are interested in details of the idea, I shall be glad to forward you complete information if you will kindly sign the enclosed agreement form. Promptly upon receipt of the signed form, I shall forward to you all information I have regarding the idea.

Sincerely,

Robert Roe

AGREEMENT TO REVIEW IDEA

We, the undersigned, agree to receive in confidence full details about an idea for product packaging to be submitted for our consideration by Robert Roe.

It is further understood that we assume no responsibility whatever with respect to features which can be demonstrated to be already known to us. We also agree not to divulge any details of the idea submitted without permission of Robert Roe or to make use of any feature or information of which the said Robert Roe is the originator, without payment of compensation to be fixed by negotiation with the said Robert Roe or his lawful representative.

It is specifically understood that, in receiving the idea of Robert Roe, the idea is being received and will be reviewed in confidence and that, within a period of 30 days, we will report to said Robert Roe the results of our findings and will advise whether or not we are interested in negotiating for the purchase of the right to use said idea.

Company _____

Street and Number _____

City _____ Zone _____ State _____

Official to receive disclosures (please type)

_____ Title _____

Date _____ Signature _____

Accepted: _____

Robert Roe, Inventor

WARNING TO INVENTORS

Inventors typically make poor businessmen and even worse managers. The eccentricities and volatile temperament that usually characterize the creative genius are almost invariably irreconcilable with the unflappable personality and judgmental constancy required of a good manager. Thus, the inventor who would realize financial reward from his mind's offspring would be well advised to give serious thought to the following alternatives to founding a company with the intention of single-handedly presiding over the enterprise:

Outright Sale

The inventor may sell his patent for a fixed amount, thereby formally assigning his right, title, and interest in the patent to the buyer. The inventor may assign either the patent itself or the patent application, in the event the patent is still pending. Upon proper notification, the U. S. Patent Office will then take the necessary steps to record the assignment on the patent document.

License for a Flat Fee or Royalty

The inventor who does not wish to sell his patent interest outright may license its use to another individual or firm in consideration of a flat fee or royalty. In the case of a flat fee arrangement, the patent "renter" agrees to pay a negotiated sum in exchange for the right to use the patent for a fixed period of time on an exclusive or nonexclusive basis. In the case of a royalty arrangement, the patent "renter" agrees to pay the inventor a piece rate for the number of items manufactured or the number of items sold. Alternatively, the "renter" may pay the inventor a percentage of the manufacturer's wholesale price or a percentage of the retail price. In other instances, an agreement may include flat fees *plus* royalties. In the case of patent licensing, the Patent Office makes no provision for registering the licensee on the patent document.

These two alternatives may prove to be infinitely more rewarding financially, to the inventor than the launching of a business which he is psychologically, educationally, and emotionally ill equipped to handle. If the inventor *must* start a business, then he would be wise to consider hiring a qualified general manager to "run the store" while he isolates himself in the laboratory where he can most effectively apply his creative talents for the benefit of the enterprise. (Remember that qualified general managers are far more plentiful than truly creative inventors.)

Recommended Reading

Allison, David, ed. *The R & D Game: Technical Men, Technical Managers, and Research Productivity*. Cambridge, Massachusetts and London, England: The M. I. T. Press, 1969.

Amerongen, C. van, trans. *The Way Things Work; an Illustrated Encyclopedia of Technology*. New York: Simon and Schuster, 1967.

Auslander, M. Arthur. *Protecting and Profiting from Your Business Ideas*. Pilot Books. New York: Pilot Industries, Inc., 1969.

Campbell, Hannah. *Why Did They Name It . . . ?* Ace Books. New York: Fleet Publishing Corporation, 1964.

Dock, M. Russell, and Sanderson, William R. *A Fortune in Your Head*. New York: Clark Boardman Company, Ltd., 1963.

Fenner, Terrence W. *Inventor's Handbook*. New Orleans, Louisiana: Associated Ideas International.

Fisher, Austin W., Jr. "Wishing Won't Get Profitable New Products." *Management Aids for Small Manufacturers, Annual No. 6*. Washington, D. C.: Small Business Administration, Government Printing Office, 1960, pp. 16-22.

Horowitz, Ira, and Alcott, James A. *Small Business and Government Research and Development*. Small Business Management Series, No. 28. Washington, D. C.: Small Business Administration, Government Printing Office, 1962.

Inventor's Services Company. *Inventor's Guide 1971*. Burlingame, California: Inventor's Services Company, 1971.

Jones, Stacy V. *You Ought to Patent That*. New York: The Dial Press, Inc., 1962.

Josephs, Ray. *How to Make Money from Your Ideas*. Garden City, New York: Doubleday & Company, Inc., 1954.

Kessler, K.O., and Carlisle, Norman. *The Successful Inventor's Guide: How to Develop, Protect and Sell Your Invention Profitably*. Englewood Cliffs, New Jersey: Prentice-Hall, Inc., 1965.

Malley, John W. "Buying and Selling a Patent." *Management Aids for Small Manufacturers, Annual No. 11*. Washington, D. C.: Small Business Administration, Government Printing Office, 1965, pp. 42-48.

Mann, C. Howard. "Small Business Profits from Unpatentable Ideas." *Management Aids for Small Business, Annual No. 3*. Washington, D.C.: Small Business Administration, Government Printing Office, 1957, pp. 45-51.

Null, Gary, and Simonson, Richard. *How to Turn Ideas into Dollars*. Pilot Books. New York: Pilot Industries, Inc., 1969.

Rines, Robert H. *Create or Perish; the Case for Inventions and Patents.* Washington, D. C.: Acropolis Books, 1969.

Sanderson, William R. *Patent Your Invention and Make It Pay.* New York: Grosset & Dunlap (by arrangement with American Research Council, Larchmont, New York), 1966.

Schwartztrauber, Evelyn M. "Know Your Patenting Procedures." *Management Aids for Small Business, Annual No. 2.* Washington, D. C.: Small Business Administration, Government Printing Office, Rev. 1958, pp. 1-8.

Smith, Alan A. *Technology and Your New Products.* Small Business Management Series, No. 19 (2d Edition). Washington, D. C.: Small Business Administration, Government Printing Office, 1967.

TTA Information Services Company. *Guide to Locating New Products.* San Mateo, California: TTA Information Services Company, an Affiliate of Technology Transfer Associates, Inc., 1971.

Uman, David B. *New Product Programs, Their Planning and Control.* New York: American Management Association, 1969.

U. S. Department of Commerce/Patent Office. *Directory of Registered Patent Attorneys & Agents; Arranged by State and Counties, 1969.* Washington, D. C.: U. S. Department of Commerce/Patent Office, 1969.

U. S. Department of Commerce. *Patents: Spur to American Progress.* Washington, D. C.: U. S. Department of Commerce, Government Printing Office, 1969 revision.

Chapter 9

Projecting a Good Image

Every year, untold millions of dollars are spent by the nation's leading firms for the purpose of enhancing and perpetuating their corporate images. Generally speaking, the factors which motivate these companies to consider such enormous expenditures stem from the simple desire that they be thought well of. The idea is to persuade the customers, suppliers, creditors, employees, and stockholders that the XYZ Corporation is progressive, technologically and professionally capable, provides products and services of the highest quality, and has a fundamental concern for the well-being of the community it serves. Hopefully, the result of such a campaign will be increased sales, creditor confidence, improved profits, *and* job security for the corporate officers and directors.

A favorable corporate image typically has a profound effect on stockholder confidence and, hence, on the trading-price of a company's securities. In economic terms, the difference between the aggregate market

107

value of the outstanding stock in a company and its net worth is defined as "good will." This balance-sheet term uniquely identifies stockholder confidence and is an excellent measure of the effectiveness of a company's public-relations efforts. A high price-to-earnings ratio or a high stock-valuation-to-net-worth ratio simply means that the company is successful in projecting a good *image*.

THE IMPORTANCE OF IMAGE TO THE ENTREPRENEUR

In the case of an entrepreneur eager to establish a business of his own, the concept of projected image is of enormous importance. Usually, none of the company founders will have had first-hand experience as the president or founder of another company. In other words, they don't have "track records." In lieu of this, they must possess and/or perfect the ability to communicate their enthusiasm and professional capabilities to investors, suppliers, and customers alike. In short, they must project a *good image*.

Image is the "wrapper" in which you present your product or service. The quality of this product or service is far from being the only element important to the customer; the customer wants and *expects image* with his purchase. If a customer is considering the merits of competing offers, it is impossible to eliminate the subjective factors which obscure objective comparison. Velvet and satin lined boxes for precious jewelry, artistically designed crystal flacons for exotic perfumes, "imported" gifts (probably made in a garage in Germany instead of a garage in Hoboken), "secret" ingredients in franchised fried chicken, tuxedoed headwaiters, and a host of other examples attest to the importance of image in the marketplace. *This is a fact:* You can sell damn near anything if you surround it with the right image!

What I am driving at is this: If the entrepreneur has something *worthwhile* to offer, he must build an image around it merely to compete *unhandicapped* against the crappy service and crummy merchandise the other image builders are successfully merchandising. What's more distressing, the buyers *know* they're paying for image. False front stores are older than our Old West; and any society that will countenance annual automobile model changes for as long as ours has isn't about to scuttle image overnight. Honest, Willie and Jack, that's the way it is. Those are the house rules. If you don't like them, you'll have to look for another table or maybe even another casino.

Consider Alexander Graham Bell. The poor guy had one hell of a time persuading people that his telephone gadget had any merit. Had he been a better image builder, he would have found it much easier to garner the support he needed to get his idea off the ground.

I don't care how good your product is; I don't care how wonderful your service can be. If you can't sell it, it isn't worth a tinker's damn—to you *or* to the public. Who knows how many worthwhile products and services society has been deprived of due to the promotional ineptitude of their champions? If it takes image to get the dunderhead buyer to try a good thing, then give it to him. With both barrels. Don't futsy around simply because promotion is a bad word. Sell! Then you'll have the opportunity to show what you can *really* do. *But* you gotta get the order *first*!

Summary:

1. Ya gotta be a Barnum to get 'em into the tent.

2. Then give 'em their money's worth, or you'll screw things up for everybody else in the biz.

SELECTION OF A COMPANY NAME

Having decided on the initial product or service he wishes to market and having readied himself to solicit customers or investors, the entrepreneur is very quickly going to experience the need for a company name.

In those instances where a new company will be serving the fields of science and technology, the founders will often select a company name with endings which include scientific or technological "buzz words." The staff of companies serving the consumer market may select names such as "Quality Gismos" or "Superior Widgets Company." Still other companies in the service fields may stress speed of performance or low-cost service. Typical names for such enterprises might be "Speedy Spade-Work Gardening" or "Economy Photographic Service."

Another factor to be considered in the selection of a company name is the possibility that the one chosen may resemble, or be identical to, the name of a previously established business. The company attorney can arrange to have a search made to insure against the possibility that the proposed name is currently being used by another firm.

Having selected a name which is both satisfactory to the founders and legally acceptable in that it neither duplicates the name of an existing company nor misleads the public (for instance, one cannot establish a business suggesting that he is a doctor or a lawyer without having the appropriate credentials), the next step involved is the registration of this name with some public agency. Again, the company attorney can provide the appropriate assistance in handling this matter. Since licensing regulations vary between different municipalities, counties, and states, the assistance of a lawyer in handling this formality is usually advisable. Alternatively, information on business licensing can be obtained by getting in touch with your local municipal or county clerk's office.

POINTERS ON BUSINESS STATIONERY

With the formality of name selection and registration completed, the entrepreneur is ready for the next step in public relations. Business stationery is a *must* in image building. A well-executed logotype ("logo") and its embellishment upon your business cards, letterheads, and envelopes does much to enhance the initial impression a new company and its founders make on a prospective customer or investor.

Often, the founders will know an artist who would be willing to design a company trademark or logo for a nominal charge. If one of the founders is artistically gifted, he may even design it himself. Otherwise, many commercial art firms (and a few souls in the printing trade still qualify to do more than merely reproduce *other* people's art work) will be able and happy to undertake the task.

A number of local printers in this field advertise their services in the classified section of major metropolitan newspapers and in the ubiquitous Yellow Pages of the telephone book. Still others offer highly specialized printing service (business cards only or envelopes only) by mail. A few sources of supply and ideas are listed below. Samples and catalogs may be obtained by addressing your inquiries to:

Idea Art
30 East 10th Street
New York, New York 10003
(212) LF 3-6622

Hammermill Paper Company
1475 East Lake Road
Erie, Pennsylvania 16500
(814) 456-8811

Goes Lithography Company
42 West 61st Street
Chicago, Illinois 60621
(312) 684-6700

Whiting Plover Paper Company
Stevens Point, Wisconsin 54482
(715) 344-3100

COMMENTARY BY ROBERT TOWNSEND

I disagree with this chapter. It seems to me that image is one of the most dangerous concepts in modern organizations. One of the great advantages that a small, new company has over a big, mature one is that the small, new company knows the difference between form and substance, between appearance and reality. Image is not a goal. It's a by-product. A good image has to be earned by performance.

Now, having said all this, I could be pushed into letting a small, new company spend a little more for embossed letterheads, for example; but I can't be pushed much further than that. In any event, there ought to be some kind of a tickler file in the chief executive's desk that comes up every 30 days and says "Image is a by-product. Let's not chase image any more. Let's go earn one by our performance and by chasing the real goal of customer satisfaction, employee satisfaction, and shareholder satisfaction."

As a service to those entrepreneurs who have never worked in a gigantic business, or as a reminder to those who have and might otherwise be tempted to forget their experience, I'd like to give you a reading list of books which show in one light or another the enormous triviality, waste, and phoniness of the big organization.

Arnold, Thurman. The Folklore of Capitalism. *New Haven, Connecticut: Yale University Press, 1937.*

Ayers, Edward. What's Good for GM. *Nashville, Tennessee: Aurora Publishing, 1970.*

Bannock, Graham. The Juggernauts: The Age of the Big Corporations. *Indianapolis: Bobbs-Merrill Co., 1971.*

Dahl, Robert A. After the Revolution: Authority in a Good Society. *New Haven, Connecticut: Yale University Press, 1970.*

Galbraith, John K. The New Industrial State. *New York: Signet, 1967.*
  (With the proviso that he is all wet on the inevitability of large organizations.)

Goodman, Paul. New Reformation: Notes of a Neolithic Conservative. *New York: Random House, 1970.*

Goodman, Paul. People or Personnel *and* Like a Conquered Province. *New York: Vantage Press, 1965 and 1967.*
  (Two titles in one paperback.)

Harrington, Alan. Life in the Crystal Palace. *New York: Alfred A. Knopf, 1959.*

Jay, Anthony. Corporation Man. *New York: Random House, 1971.*

Lundberg, Ferdinand. The Rich and the Super-Rich. *New York: Bantam Books, 1968.*

Mills, C. Wright. The Power Elite. *Oxford, England: Oxford University Press, 1959.*

Mintz, M., and Cohen, J. S. America, Inc.: Who Owns and Operates the United States. *New York: Dial Press, 1971.*

Nossiter, Bernard. The Mythmakers: An Essay on Power and Wealth. *Boston: Houghton Mifflin Company, 1964.*

Parkinson, C. Northcote. Parkinson's Law and other Studies in Administration. *Ballentine Books. Boston: Houghton Mifflin Company, 1964.*

Peter, Laurence J., and Hull, Raymond. The Peter Principle. *Bantam Books, New York: William Morrow and Co., 1970.*

Quinn, Theodore K. Giant Business: Threat to Democracy. *New York: Exposition Press, 1954.*

Raskin, M. Being and Doing. *New York: Random House, 1971.*

Slater, Philip. The Pursuit of Loneliness: American Culture at the Breaking Point. *Boston: Beacon Press, 1970.*

(Author unknown; it drifted up in a bottle). Up the Organization: How to Stop the Corporation from Stifling People and Strangling Profits. *New York: Alfred A. Knopf, 1970.*

Whyte, William H., Jr. The Organization Man. *New York: Simon and Schuster, 1956.*

That's a pretty good reading list, which will tend to remind you of what goes on in large organizations and, hopefully, will lead you to fight nonsense, waste, phoniness and triviality.

Recommended Reading

Bank of America National Trust & Savings Association. "Advertising." *Small Business Reporter,* Vol. 9, No. 1., 1969.

Miller, Raymond W., and Miller, Robert W. "Public Relations for Small Business Owners." *Small Marketers Aids, Annual No. 3.* Washington, D. C.: Small Business Administration, Government Printing Office, 1961, pp. 48-55.

Norins, Hanley. *The Compleat Copywriter; a Comprehensive Guide to All Phases of Advertising Communication.* New York: McGraw-Hill Book Company, 1966.

Section Two

THE BUSINESS PLAN

Chapter 10

The Importance of a Business Plan

If an entrepreneur couples the marvelous mechanism of persistence with his talent and his determination to start a business of his own, he has a high probability both of establishing the business and of succeeding in it. However, by first formulating a thoughtful, carefully prepared plan of his objective, the entrepreneur can economize in the use of his financial resources and personal efforts. A well-prepared business plan is like a scholarship in the School or Hard Knocks; it reduces what might otherwise be a prohibitive tuition to a manageable one.

117

THE BUSINESS PLAN IS A SALES DOCUMENT

Fundamentally, a business plan (also referred to as a proposal, a prospectus, or a brochure) is the primary vehicle for giving credibility to an idea. In order effectively to organize the resources required for the establishment of a new business, it is usually necessary to persuade a great many people that the business concept is viable. Oftentimes the willingness of suppliers to extend credit, the willingness of customers to place orders, and, usually most important for the beginning businessman, the willingness of investors to invest in a new enterprise will depend on the care with which the business plan has been prepared.

Most often a business plan outlines a process for "combining your money with my brains so we can both get rich." A properly prepared plan, then, will clearly outline the process for the efficient exploitation of the business concept and explain the attendant multiplication of those monies invested. The plan is a scenario briefly describing the principal characters and milieu (marketplace) in which they will function.

A business plan prepared for the scrutiny of a professional, seasoned venture capitalist should be able to provide all the answers *any* investor, from your rich aunt to a Wall Street underwriter, might ask. The business plan as a sales document must be prepared for the most sophisticated investor and must incorporate many subtle characteristics, including the important factors of credibility, authority, and ingenuity.

Credibility

The plan must convey a sense of optimism regarding the success of the intended venture tempered by the realities of the marketplace. Obviously it would be foolhardy to propose a venture in which the principal participants did not anticipate a substantial measure of success, but the concepts embodied in the plan should be sufficiently documented in order to inspire not only optimism but also confidence.

The use of professionally prepared market surveys and reports that discuss present demand and provide detailed projections of future requirements for the proposed product or service are of great value in communicating a sense of credibility to the reader. Relating your planned enterprise to such factors as population growth (for predicting an agricultural market), far-reaching legislation on environmental pollution (for predicting a water- or air-filtering process market), or a new but accepted technological breakthrough such as television (for estimating the demand for TV antennas) enormously enhances the believability of a proposed business idea.

Authority

The plan must convey the image of the founders as possessing an unusually sophisticated knowledge of the market they intend to serve and the maturity of judgment necessary to respond to the challenges of a dynamic marketplace.

Ordinarily, such a characteristic is established by having a "track-record" in a related field of business or an unusually distinguished educational background. For instance, if the success of the new enterprise will be heavily determined by the excellence of its engineering talent, one or more of the founders must have a record of numerous successful and profitable innovations in products or processes. Presumably this background would have been obtained while in the employ of some other company, while at a university laboratory, or under some other set of circumstances that would afford the individual the opportunity simultaneously to gain experience and demonstrate his creativity.

Obviously, excellence in the areas of marketing, sales, finance, and manufacturing is also expected of the founders in a measure proportional to the demands of the business areas they contemplate exploring. A background in cosmetics marketing would be ideal for a businessman planning to supply the beauty industry, but it might very probably be wasted on a company planning to make custom parts for the automotive industry.

Ingenuity

Invariably, the entrepreneur who solicits constructive criticism will encounter the question "What have you got that nobody else has got that will make you, your company, and its products and/or services outstanding in the marketplace?" Your idea must have *pizzazz*, that exciting ingredient that inspires the imagination and fires the enthusiasm of all who behold it.

A low-cost computer that works five times as fast as the best one currently being sold on the market, an economical new process for softening household water, and a cheap four-channel audio system or home video tape player are all characterized by the pizzazz that is bound to win the heart and the purse of some investor. The application of a proven idea, technique, or product to a new, previously unrecognized but waiting market might also qualify for a financial encomium.

Most investors, to summarize, are looking for a ground-floor, 10-cents-a-share shot at the next Xerox or Polaroid. It is up to you to demonstrate that your idea has at least a little of the potential of ideas such as these.

THE BUSINESS PLAN AND THE RESPONSIBILITY OF THE FOUNDER

In organizing the resources necessary for the formation of a new enterprise, the founders take upon themselves a very great responsibility to every individual and every business that their plan may affect. A conscientious, responsible effort, including careful research and investigation, in the preparation of the plan will do much to insure against financial injury to employees, suppliers, customers, investors, and even the founders themselves.

A properly researched business plan will represent a "dry run" of the early years following the formation of the business and should expose the founders to every major problem they can reasonably expect to encounter. Obviously, not all problems can be foreseen. But, by anticipating and preparing for *some* problems, more of the energies and resources of the founders will be available for solving the hidden difficulties. The entrepreneur who takes the time and trouble conscientiously to prepare his business plan can know that he has done his best to honor his responsibilities to the business community. He will also, because he has familiarized himself with every aspect of what he proposes to do, acquire the self-confidence that is so essential in persuading others that his proposed endeavor will be successful.

None of the sources of assistance listed in the next section are suggested as substitutes for your own hard work. Your business plan should, again, represent your finest efforts and capabilities. You are the one who is going to manage the new enterprise. In doing so, you will have available to you the assistance and counsel of many individuals. However, the responsibility for the results of your actions rests solely upon your shoulders. The business plan, like your business, must represent an extension of your ideas, moulded and modified by the most competent assistance you can acquire.

You properly expect to enjoy a substantial percentage of the rewards of success in your venture; therefore, you must also be prepared to bear the brunt of the blame and hardship in the event of failure. As Harry S. Truman, once the president of a *very* large organization, was fond of saying, "The buck stops here."

SOURCES OF ASSISTANCE IN PREPARING YOUR BUSINESS PLAN

There are a number of ways in which an entrepreneur can acquire a first-hand knowledge of the characteristics of a well-prepared business plan. The following list includes many of them, but your own imagination will provide you with many others.

Public-Offering Prospectuses

Any time a public offering of stock is made, the document which describes the offering (called a prospectus) must be registered and approved either by the Corporation Commissioner, or a similar agency within the state in which the offering is tendered, or the Securities and Exchange Commission. Since the offering of stock for sale to the public is a rather common occurrence, most stockbrokers have a ready supply of prospectuses describing current offerings. Your broker will be happy to give you one or two samples, which will give you a number of ideas regarding the kind of information you should expect to provide in your business plan.

The Business Plan of Another Company

Your attorney may have had recent experience with other clients successful in starting their own businesses. If so, there is a high probability that he will have copies of the business plans of these companies in his files. In those instances where no possibility of a conflict of interest exists and where the subject company gives its permission, your attorney may afford you an opportunity to examine copies of these plans. It is unlikely, however, that you will be permitted to remove them from his office.

Business Consultants

A number of individuals billing themselves as business consultants may be of assistance to you in the formulation and preparation of your business plan. Provided you rely on their services only as advisors and insure that the finished business plan is truly a representation of your *own* concepts, such assistance can prove to be quite worthwhile.

Lawyers and Certified Public Accountants

A competent attorney can provide a critical, objective evaluation of your business plan. Furthermore, if there are elements of the plan which may make you vulnerable to a lawsuit, your attorney's counsel is valuable insurance.

Another professional who can assist you in obtaining an objective evaluation of your business plan is the CPA. Of course, his comments will be particularly appropriate in evaluating the merit of your financial projections.

Public Relations Firms

Some public relations firms occasionally undertake the task of preparing business plans. Provided the entrepreneur recognizes that such a firm may be tempted to oversell the business' potential and inject excessive optimism into the business plan, their services can be of value.

Books on Writing Effective Sales Letters

Your business plan is a sort of sales letter because the *best* ideas do not always represent the basis for a new business; instead, new businesses grow upon ideas that can be effectively *promoted*, first in the investor's office, later in the marketplace.

Assuming that your business idea has *some* merit, the very least you can do for it is to learn how properly to promote it. A number of books exist on the subject of writing effective sales letters. Your local library undoubtedly has several. If you have not already been exposed to such books, you will find them quite educational and informative.

Trial Runs

Although you feel that your initial written plan is ready for exposure, you may find after your first few contacts that it needs some revision. Incorporation of new ideas that have resulted from suggestions and criticism offered during what otherwise might be termed "false starts" can prove to be beneficial in producing a polished, professional plan.

PACKAGING THE BUSINESS PLAN

The business plan is of critical importance in establishing your corporate image. Depending on the nature of the intended recipient, the business plan may range all the way from a neatly typed presentation bound in a manila report folio all the way up to a four-color, heavy-stock pamphlet printed on the finest coated paper. In the cosmetics of the business plan as well as in the content, the judgment of the entrepreneur will be evident. Too lavish a format will frighten off a penny-pinching millionaire who made his money the hard way or an ulcer-prone banker just as quickly as will a sloppily typed, mimeographed document.

Investors Prefer Virgins

The entrepreneur who is seeking capital with which to start his business will very quickly discover that every investor wants to be the first person on this planet to cast his greedy, beady little eyes upon your proposal—to feel that he is having the first crack at "cutting a fat hawg." A number of seasoned venture capitalists will invariably inquire after the names of other investors who have been afforded an opportunity to review your business plan. Some may even ask you to fill out a form listing the members of the investment community to whom you have already presented the plan. In the event these other investors have declined to participate in funding the plan, the interviewing investor may also be expected to ask *why* they declined. The business plan that has been reviewed and rejected by a number of venture capitalists is referred to as a "shopped" or "shop-worn" proposal. The fund-raising entrepreneur, then, must develop the capability for shopping his proposal *discreetly*.

Busy Investors May Unintentionally Waste Your Time

Busy investors will spend anywhere from two weeks to two months making a preliminary review of your business plan. Obviously, approaching investors on a one-at-a-time basis can prove extremely costly in terms of time; in addition, a small minority of the investing community may not even accord you the courtesy of responding to an inquiry. Therefore, you must learn how to distribute many copies of your plan both simultaneously and discreetly, without over-exposing and hence "shopping" it.

In order to keep track of the proposals that you have distributed, it is advisable to number each copy. However, an investor will not be flattered if he receives a copy numbered 97. This investor may not give your proposal more than a cursory review on the assumption that, if it has merit, some other investor may have already initiated action to finance the company or on the alternative assumption that, if 96 other knowledgeable investors have already rejected the proposal, it certainly does not warrant the expenditure of his valuable time.

If you do submit a relatively large number of proposals to groups of sophisticated investors in geographically and financially diverse areas, you will undoubtedly wish to keep track of each individual copy. In this event, you may wish to try the suggestions of a panelist on one of the many seminars I have attended:

1. use different colored inks to identify different series;
2. set numbers off by outlining, circling, enclosing in parentheses, following by hyphens, etc.;
3. spell out the numbers;
4. use Roman numerals;
5. treat letters as numerals;

and hope that two of the investors to whom you have given your proposals don't get together for a business discussion.

Note: Before presenting *any* copies of your business plan to potential investors, *see your attorney*. If you distribute it indiscriminately, you may be guilty (knowingly or otherwise) of making a *public offering* without proper registration, a crime under civil law punishable by fines *and* imprisonment!

FORGET EVERYTHING I'VE SAID!!

Regardless of the subject, exceptions to the rule almost invariably exist.

Back-of-the-Envelope Advocates

The president of a particularly successful electronics firm I know of has his own approach to fund raising and investor solicitation—the "back-of-an-envelope" philosophy. This individual perfected an excellent prototype of a new device; and, with nothing more than his track record as a scientist and manager, unbounded enthusiasm, and a damn good product, he was able to raise more than $100,000 with which to launch his enterprise. In his fund-raising campaign, he conveyed the attitude, "If you don't like my approach, I'll find someone who does. I don't have time to fool around with elaborate proposals; I want to get in on the action *now*!"

The problems he has encountered since commencing operation have been handled as they arose by the growing cadre of capable lieutenants he has been able to attract. He concedes that he had a number of problems early in the game due to inadequate financial planning, but his business volume is now such that he can afford the full-time services of a professional financial planner.

The Unbelievers

The investment community has more than its fair share of cynics. In my own fund-raising efforts, I had the dubious honor of having a seasoned venture capitalist compliment me on the excellence of my business plan and then inquire regarding the name of the public relations firm that I had hired to prepare it for me. To this day I don't believe I was successful in persuading this particular gentleman that the proposal represented my own work exclusively, although it was extremely well received in the rest of the financial community. If you have never had a business of your own and your business plan looks too good, you might run the risk of this kind of rejection.

"We Want to Help, Too!"

A number of investors (entrepreneurs themselves) are unwilling to become involved in any new business that does not at the outset exhibit a definite need for their special talents, whether in the area of finance, engineering, manufacturing, sales/marketing, or management. The entrepreneur, in dealing with such a situation, should seek to locate investors with whom a long-term, harmonious relationship may be anticipated. If your investor insists on telling you how to run the store before the doors are even open, he may be in there actually running it himself not too long afterward.

On the other hand, there is a good chance that you have a lot to learn in running your first business; and it doesn't hurt to have someone handy who knows some of the answers and is willing to give you help over the rough spots.

SUPER-SERENDIPITY

As has been stated earlier, careful planning can prove to be of enormous value in the founders' effort to guarantee the success of the new venture. Furthermore, by securing the services of a good insurance underwriter, the founders may take steps to minimize the effects of unanticipated and possibly catastrophic occurrences. However, a very significant element that cannot be integrated into the founders' plans is the ability to *recognize* and *exploit* unexpected opportunities when they present themselves. This element I call *super-serendipity*.

Take the case of the man who wins the Irish sweepstakes. Given this substantial windfall, a winner unaccustomed to and unprepared for a life of wealth may squander all of his winnings within a short time. Nevertheless, his good fortune in winning the sweepstakes *is* serendipity. But, if he were to take his prize and suitably invest it in a growth opportunity, the same windfall might become super-serendipitous.

As another example of super-serendipity, consider this story taken from my own recent past. An inventor acquaintance solicited my services to assist him in marketing one of his latest creations. Subsequently, while attending a seminar, I heard a venture capitalist indicate that one of his portfolio companies was engaged in the manufacture of products related to the invention I had recently been asked to market. This is an example of serendipity. Had I then simply forgotten about this potential opportunity, I would never have realized the return the situation potentially offered. However, by asking the speaker what the name of the portfolio company was and by subsequently tracking down the founders of this company, I was able successfully to market the invention and thus realize a commission. It is virtually impossible to plan for super-serendipity in the preparation of a business proposal or in formulating the growth projections for a proposed venture. However, it would serve the founders well to emphasize their ability to exploit new opportunities, for it is the recognition of unanticipated opportunity that has resulted in the substantial success of many businesses.

In summary, a group of founders capable of demonstrating that they have the sophistication and maturity necessary to recognize and exploit unanticipated opportunities enjoy a unique advantage when trying to inspire investor confidence in a highly competitive capital market. After all the "hard data" has been favorably evaluated, it is the hint of the existence of this founder quality that gives rise to the "gut-feel" upon which many investors ultimately base an affirmative investment decision.

Recommended Reading

Bank of America National Trust & Savings Association. "Small Business—a Look Ahead." *Small Business Reporter*, Vol. 8, No. 1, 1967.

Bank of America National Trust & Savings Association. "Steps to Starting a Business." *Small Business Reporter*, Vol. 8, No. 8, 1969.

Bursk, Edward C., ed. "Pointers on Meeting Competition." *Management Aids for Small Manufacturers, Annual No. 10.* Washington, D.C.: Small Business Administration, Government Printing Office, 1964, pp. 17-23.

Committee on Definitions, American Marketing Association, Ralph S. Alexander, Chairman. "Key Marketing Words—What They Mean." *Management Aids for Small Manufacturers, Annual No. 10.* Washington, D.C.: Small Business Administration, Government Printing Office, 1964, pp. 24-31.

Daenzer, Bernard J. *Fact-Finding Techniques in Risk Analysis.* New York: American Management Association, 1970.

Friant, Ray J., Jr. *Preparing Effective Presentations; How to Make Presentations Pay Off!* Pilot Books. New York: Pilot Industries, 1971.

Goodpasture, Bruce. "Creative Thinking: A Commonsense Approach." *Small Marketers Aids, Annual No. 8.* Washington, D.C.: Small Business Administration, Government Printing Office, 1966, pp. 1-8.

Mayer, Kurt B., and Goldstein, Sidney. *The First Two Years: Problems of Small Firm Growth and Survival.* Small Business Research Series No. 2. Washington, D.C.: Small Business Administration, Government Printing Office, 1961.

Nierenberg, Gerard I. *The Art of Negotiating; Psychological Strategies for Gaining Advantageous Bargains.* New York: Hawthorne Books, Inc., 1968.

Price, Selwin E. "Financial Facts that Lenders Require." *Management Aids for Small Manufacturers, Annual No. 12.* Washington, D.C.: Small Business Administration, Government Printing Office, 1966, pp. 56-62.

Roberts, Frank L. "Reducing the Risks in Product Development." *Management Aids for Small Manufacturers, Annual No. 5.* Washington, D.C.: Small Business Administration, Government Printing Office, 1959, pp. 15-22.

Roth, Charles B. *Secrets of Closing Sales,* 4th ed. Englewood Cliffs, New Jersey: Prentice-Hall, Inc., 1970.

Schwartz, Eugene. *Breakthrough Advertising: How to Write Ads that Shatter Tradition and Sales Records.* Englewood Cliffs, New Jersey: Prentice-Hall, Inc., 1966.

Steere, Ralph E. "Easy-To-Make Flip Charts Provide Selling Tools." *Management Aids for Small Manufacturers, Annual No. 13.* Washington, D.C.: Small Business Administration, Government Printing Office, 1967, pp. 9-16.

Williams, Robert E. "How Management Consultants Help Small Businesses." *Management Aids for Small Business, Annual No. 1.* Washington, D.C.: Small Business Administration, Government Printing Office, Rev. 1958, pp. 177-184.

Chapter 11

The Mini-Proposal

The mini-proposal typically serves as a brief introduction summarizing a business plan. It is designed to help the potential investor to ascertain at the outset whether or not he has any interest whatever in participating in the financing of your enterprise. In many instances, investors develop a high degree of specialization within their portfolios. A properly executed mini-proposal can produce a number of highly positive results: (1) it saves the investor a considerable amount of time by enabling him to determine without having to wade through page after page of introductory material whether or not the investment opportunity is within his area of interest; (2) it saves the entrepreneur the substantial delay normally encountered while an investor carefully reviews an elaborately executed proposal; (3) it reduces the likelihood that your full-blown proposal (maxi-proposal?) will become shopped. There is far less stigma associated with the rejection of a mini-proposal than with the rejection of a detailed, formal plan.

Oftentimes, an investor has a list of basic requirements any proposal must have before he will consider it. This chapter is devoted to an analysis of these important factors.

INVESTOR PREFERENCES

Investors can be crap shooters looking for a fast buck or conservative banker types who aren't satisfied unless they can secure a significant equity in a "sure thing." Some investors are willing to bankroll almost anything that offers the potential for substantial capital gains in a short timeframe. Others restrict their investments in many ways, thus carefully formalizing the process of analysis to which any new business plan is subjected.

An investor engaged in the initial screening of your mini-proposal will probably be concerned with all of the following categories:

Initial Capitalization Required

Many investors—in fact, the majority of investors—have relatively low ceilings on the amount of money they are willing to invest in any one particular project. In the case of private individuals, the figure may be as low as a few thousand dollars; more adequately capitalized investors or agencies might prefer ceilings between $500,000 and $1 million. Professional money managers may not want to get involved in the financing of any business requiring less than $1 million or $2 million. Some of the most successful members of this category have expressed the attitude that it takes as much time, effort, and money to monitor a $50,000 investment as it does to monitor a $1 million investment.

Commonly, investors will have a preference for a particular range of invested dollars; and, while they don't wish to become involved with the problems of a small, penny-ante enterprise, at the same time they may be unwilling or unable to underwrite an entity requiring substantial financing no matter how appealing its prospects may look.

Maturity of the Enterprise

Closely related to the *amount* of financing sought is the matter of the *maturity* of the enterprise. This is often a primary consideration in the willingness of an investor to participate in any new round of financing. Generally speaking, this maturity is defined as a company's degree of development and is described in terms of the type of financing sought by the company. Although there are several additional, more mature financing levels commonly recognized in the investment community, I will concentrate on the following five:

Seed

In this case, all that exists is an idea for a product, possibly a plan, and possibly a proposed company team. This represents one of the highest possible risk investment opportunities.

Start-up

Here there is usually a prototype product (or a well-defined service); a plan and a team exist; but no operating history has been established. Since visualization of the business concept is easier here than it is in the case of seed financing, this situation is more attractive to investors. However, risk is still considered quite high; and the cost of equity financing is also usually substantial in terms of what the founders must surrender to obtain backing.

Mezzanine

In this stage, a company has withstood the rigors of start-up, usually has a record of service billings or product shipments (including an adequate manufacturing capacity and capability), a customer list (albeit a small one), and a financial record (whether profitable or not) that will permit an analysis of progress to date versus dollars spent.

Growth

At this stage, a business has usually established its viability as a commercial operation; but it is unable to generate sufficient cash flow or to attract adequate debt financing at manageable interest rates to permit the rapid growth possible with its proven products (or services) and available staffing. Characteristically, this problem is typified by an inability to handle the cash differential between accounts receivable (on orders shipped) and accounts payable (on raw materials and parts in inventory) while trying to increase sales volume.

Bridge

This type of funding frequently takes the form of debt instruments with warrants or options attached (called "kickers" or "sweeteners") for the later purchase of company stock at a price established at the time the debt is incurred. The term "bridge" derives from the fact that this form of financing is generally used to provide funds to sustain operations while the company is in the process of securities registration for a public offering of stock.

Preferred Industrial Sectors

Many investors prefer to participate in the development of corporations in sectors of the business community where they have established expertise. Thus, you find some investors who will invest in nothing but computer-related industries. Still others have a preference for the retail-clothing industry. Recently a number of investors have chosen to specialize in funding new enterprises devoted to the application of high-technology expertise to the problems of ecology and environmental pollution.

EMPHASIZE THE HIGHLIGHTS

Provided your business plan successfully passes the investor obstacle course in that the amount of capitalization you require, the nature of the market you intend to serve, and the maturity of your enterprise are consistent with investors' objectives, you should next give consideration to providing a brief, accurate, and appealing discussion of each of the following highlights.

Niche in the Market

To improve the chance of success of their new business, the founders should identify a well-protected niche in the market they plan to serve. Ideally, they will provide a needed product or service unlike any currently offered by competitors. Their concept should enjoy the protection of patent coverage, unique founder know-how, trade-secret exclusivity, and/or proprietary characteristics. For example:

The Polaroid camera and film development process represent excellent examples of products enjoying the protection of extensive patent coverage.

The early processes involved in the manufacture of semiconductor devices (transistors and their descendants) enjoyed both patent and founder know-how protection, which enabled their originators to operate profitably and relatively free from competition for a number of years before other suppliers appeared on the scene.

The syrup formula for Coca-Cola is one of the most famous examples of trade-secret protection. Although this drink is bottled at plants in most of the major countries of the world, the syrup is manufactured exclusively by the parent Coca-Cola Company, and its preparation remains a very carefully guarded secret.

Superior Qualifications of the Founders

A brief outline of the qualifications and major accomplishments of the founders is a valuable piece of information to include in the mini-proposal. Patent and/or publication activity, unusual academic or professional standing, sales records, previously successful marketing plans, merger or acquisition negotiation experience, profit-and-loss or product-line responsibility, project managership, and a substantial background in personnel supervision all exemplify the type of information appropriate for this section.

Only superior qualifications and major accomplishments, however, should be indicated here. A more extensive discussion of founder background belongs in the formal business plan.

Market Characteristics

A brief description of the market to be served should include the following information: (1) description of initial products or services (Although all investors are interested in owning part of a corporate giant of the future, most new companies generally begin with a limited number of products or services. The primary features of these items should be mentioned briefly and objectively.); (2) information on the growth rate of the market for this product or service; and (3) a statement indicating the anticipated percentage of market capture. (Ordinarily, to be attractive to an investor, a new company must be in an industry that is growing significantly faster than the gross national product; and the founders should plan for a company growth rate faster than that characteristic of the planned market.)

KEEP IT SHORT AND SWEET

Some large venture capital organizations process more than 100 business plans each month. Typically, one or possibly two of each 100 plans ultimately receive the investor's backing.

In light of the substantial work load involved in processing these many proposals, you can appreciate the importance of stating your case succinctly and alluringly—the mini-proposal is to the formal business plan what an hors d'oeuvre is to a sumptuous repast. Ideally, the mini-proposal should not exceed two pages in length. This will enhance the probability that it will receive prompt attention. Investors are human beings and are just as susceptible to procrastination as any other mortal. The thick proposal that will require hours to read is going to find its way quickly to the bottom of a very large pile. On the other hand, a one-or two-page summary will be read as soon as the envelope is opened.

In essence, the mini-proposal must be detailed enough to covery every major factor, well-enough written to communicate the professionalism of the founding team, and brief enough to invite immediate attention. If you can crank in these three factors, you'll be off to a good start.

Recommended Reading

Bernstein, Maurice S. "Sales Forecasting for Small Business." *Management Aids for Small Business, Annual No. 2.* Washington, D. C.: Small Business Administration, Government Printing Office, Rev. 1958, pp. 57-63.

Bradford's Directory of Marketing Research Agencies and Management Consultants in the United States and the World. Fairfax, Va.: Bradford's Directory of Marketing Research Agencies, biennial.

Frank, N. D. *Market Analysis: A Handbook of Current Data Sources.* New York: Scarecrow, 1964.

Lasser, J. K. *How to Run a Small Business,* 3d ed., rev. and enlarged. New York: McGraw-Hill Book Company, Inc., 1963.

Luck, David J.; Wales, Hugh G.; and Taylor, Donald A. *Marketing Research,* 3d ed. Englewood Cliffs, New Jersey: Prentice-Hall, 1970.

Maynard, Harold B. "Building Growth-Mindedness into Your Business." *Management Aids for Small Manufacturers, Annual No. 9.* Washington, D.C.: Small Business Administration, Government Printing Office, 1963, pp. 1-8.

Salter, Peter G., and Lee, Richard F. "Key Factors in Starting a New Plant." *Management Aids for Small Manufacturers, Annual No. 5.* Washington, D.C.: Small Business Administration, Government Printing Office, 1959, pp. 1-8.

Seymour, Robert G. "How the Small Plant Can Analyze Old and New Markets." *Management Aids for Small Business, Annual No. 1.* Washington, D.C.: Small Business Administration, Government Printing Office, Rev. 1958, pp. 52-59.

Sommer, Howard Ellsworth. "How to Analyze Your Own Business." *Management Aids for Small Business, Annual No. 2.* Washington, D.C.: Small Business Administration, Government Printing Office, Rev. 1958, pp. 35-42.

Chapter 12

The Formal Business Plan

When the founders have managed sufficiently to interest the investors in their mini-proposal, the investors will request that the founders provide them with a formal business proposal. This is the document that in most cases will determine whether or not the investors and founders will reach a point of serious negotiation in the financing of the new enterprise.

Every key aspect of the proposed business should be covered in detail in this document. The founders should endeavor to communicate a sense of thoroughness and a feeling that "We're ready for anything!" This chapter is devoted to a discussion of each of the many items that should receive consideration in preparing the proposal.

INTRODUCTION

A one-page (two if you must) summary of the business proposal should state substantially the same information included in the mini-proposal. Some venture capital organizations are staffed with a number of capable assistants. It is likely that your proposal will be reviewed by one of these staff members. Possibly he did not have an opportunity to review your mini-proposal (some other staff member may have read it); therefore, a restatement of mini-proposal information in your introduction familiarizes the reviewer with your basic plans.

The sequence in which material appears in the proposal should follow that of the exposition in this chapter, unless the founders have a strong desire or a good reason for preferring some other arrangement.

TABLE OF CONTENTS

Depending on the length of your proposal, you may wish to include a table of contents to afford the reviewer ready access to any parts of the proposal he may wish to find quickly. Some analysts with a penchant for accounting may want to look at your financial projections first of all, while others may be more concerned with the resumes of the founders. The table of contents is a convenience and a time-saver for the busy analyst, and it also gives another bit of professional polish to your plan.

THE MANAGEMENT TEAM

In the "old days," one-man operations were very common in the business community. By and large, this fabric of the business community has not changed too much. However, when the launching of a business concept requires substantial funds, the sophisticated investors of today are generally reluctant to invest in a one-man show. Typically, every key management function—marketing/sales, manufacturing, engineering, and finance—must be covered by a man who has demonstrated exceptional capability in his previous business experiences and who has suitable academic credentials. This section of the business plan should give some consideration to each of the following subjects:

Capsule Resumes of the Founders

Condensed resumes of the founders, including name, age education, major accomplishments to date, and recent employment history, will serve to introduce the investors to the management team. The resumes should be limited to a brief exposition on those career highlights that would have an impact on the success of the proposed venture. More detailed information can be included in the resume section of the Appendix.

References

Where possible, each of the founders should obtain anywhere from one to five letters of reference from respected individuals attesting to their character and their business and/or technical expertise. The investor will be less interested in letters written by friends and clergymen than in references from customers, sales representatives, former employers, and other *business* acquaintances. College professors may also provide such letters if they would be appropriate to your circumstances. Ordinarily, the references should not be included in the main body of the proposal; instead, mention following the capsule resumes that letters of reference are included in the Appendix.

Organization Chart

A diagram showing the proposed organizational structure for the new enterprise serves neatly to convey this important information. Each block on the diagram should include a description or title appropriate to the indicated function. The name of the individual occupying each position should also be indicated.

Who Does What, With Which, and to Whom

This section should include a discussion of the primary duties of each member of the founding team. This discussion will serve not only to communicate to the reader the role of various team members but also to promote a clear understanding on the part of each team member of what his function is in making the corporate machine go.

Kenneth Olsen, the President of Digital Equipment Corporation, a very successful New England-based manufacturer of small computers, feels very strongly about the value of job descriptions and clearly defined responsibilities in a new enterprise. In his keynote speech before a group of several hundred would-be entrepreneurs, he emphasized that the operation of his new company was significantly improved when he recognized that the problems he was having were due to a general misunderstanding on the part of his team members regarding their functional responsibilities. Almost every member of his staff expressed surprise when they were formally notified by Ken as to the nature of their responsibilities.

Synergy of the Founding Team

One of the most exciting phenomena in business is that interactive result we call synergy. When the productivity and creativity of a small group of uniquely compatible men is equivalent to the output of a much larger organization, synergy is at work. The business plan should suggest that the talented individuals selected for the business team are capable of working together harmoniously, obtaining inspiration and motivation from each other, and being tremendously productive.

Management Assistance Required

As we mentioned earlier, some investors enjoy and look forward to the opportunity to participate actively in the operation of a new enterprise. If the founders know of their investor's nature in advance and do not object to it, provision may be made in the business plan for the services of the investor or his designee.

In most instances, however, leaving a key position unfilled is the kiss of death for an otherwise excellent business plan. Many investors are fond of the truism "A chain is only as strong as its weakest link." Therefore, failure to designate key positions can prejudice investors against your plan.

A more common problem, which you will surely encounter, is that of filling every executive position with highly qualified manpower without at the same time burdening the new enterprise with such a heavy overhead that an unrealistic first-year sales forecast would be necessary to support it. Arranging for part-time professional services may prove to be a satisfactory alternative to a full-time high-priced staff member.

Watch the Birdie

As an added fillip, you may wish to include photographs of the founding team. The practice is not a common one, but it could prove helpful in early contacts with investors who are located some distance from the founding team and the proposed site for the new company.

THE BOARD OF DIRECTORS

If a business is legally incorporated, statutory provisions will require that the company stockholders elect a Board of Directors. It is the duty of this Board of Directors to represent the interests of the stockholders because, if the number of stockholders is large, it is impractical for them regularly to attend meetings of the company executives to monitor the operations of the business. The Board of Directors has a responsibility to the stockholders to meet on a regular basis with the officers of the company to review corporate progress, to assist in the formulation of policy decisions, and, where necessary, to influence the makeup of the staff of company officers. The Board of Directors, then, is the conduit through which wishes of the stockholders are channeled to the company officers.

Let's clarify the corporate flow of authority. Each company shareholder enjoys voting rights in determining the makeup of the executive staff (the officers) of any company. The distribution of votes to the stockholders is in direct proportion to the number of shares of "voting stock" they own. Thus, if a stockholder personally holds more than 50 percent of the stock in a given corporation, he may very significantly influence the operations of that corporation. The company officers—the President, Vice Presidents, Secretary, and Treasurer—are responsible to the Board of Directors for the day-to-day operation of the company. However, if a majority of the Board of Directors decides that it is necessary to effect a change in the management of the company, changes may be implemented.

A Board of Directors is also responsible for establishing the salaries of the company officers and for providing for the succession of company officers in the event of resignations, firings, or death.

One of the least-appreciated sources of information and guidance available to small businesses is this same Board of Directors. In launching a new enterprise, the founders can use all the help they can get; by establishing an effective Board of Directors, the founders may avail themselves of the objective advice of a knowledgeable group of seasoned businessmen and professionals who will have a continuing interest in the progress of the enterprise.

Since many members of the Board of Directors are not officers of the company, they will be able to obtain a perspective on the business different from that of the company officers. Company officers too often cannot see the forest for the trees. A good Board of Directors can provide a continuing remedy for this visibility problem.

An effective, active Board of Directors may also offer good management counseling services. Ordinarily a small business is not able to afford a large staff of specialists to provide advice and directive guidance to the corporate staff. But members of the Board of Directors who are from outside the corporation can be of valuable assistance. Frequently, if a Board member has some unusual proficiency that is of particular interest to the company officers, private consultations outside of the Board meetings may be arranged.

Fortunately, experienced businessmen are often eager and willing to serve on the Board of Directors of small new companies in order further to broaden their experience, enjoy greater variety in their work routine, and be of service to the business community. In many cases, they are equipped to provide insight into areas of business with which the founders may not be intimately familiar.

In planning for the Board, the entrepreneur commonly asks these questions: How many members it should have? Who should serve on the Board? What qualifications should they have? How do we recruit members? What sort of compensation should these Board members receive? Following are discussions of these queries:

How Many?

No matter how many members there are on the Board of Directors, statutory provisions and common sense require that the number be odd. When the Board transacts official business, key decisions must be submitted to the entire group for a vote. Since a majority vote of the members of the Board is usually sufficient to effect or to ratify any resolutions, the odd number of members ensures that there always *will* be a majority. In most states, the minumum number of Directors required by statute is five. Ordinarily, the Board will include a Chairman, a Treasurer, and a Secretary. The President of the company serves on the Board of Directors; it is also common practice to have one or more of the company Vice Presidents (or senior officers) serve on the Board. As the size of a corporation grows, it may become necessary to enlarge the Board to provide the company with as broad a range of experience and assistance as is financially and administratively practical.

Again, bear in mind that the members of the Board of Directors of a small company are in a position to provide specialized services to that enterprise, which might otherwise require the services of full-time employees. The number of individuals on the Board of Directors of a small business should be sufficient to provide the company officers with guidance and consultative assistance in those administrative areas in which they have the least capability or in which an independent objective appraisal is desired.

Composition—Who?

The members of the Board who are not company officers may represent many sectors of the business community. Ordinarily, the company officers will exercise significant influence in the selection of the Board of Directors. They will often own stock in excess of 50 percent, in which case the composition of the Board of Directors is largely in their hands. Similarly, if the stockholders have confidence in the ability of the company founders to manage the enterprise, they will rely on the judgment of these men in the selection of all or most of the members of the Board.

Since, as mentioned earlier, it is desirable to staff the Board in such a way as to augment, complement, or supplement the capabilities of the operating staff of the enterprise, the nominees offered by the company officers should reflect this desire. For example, substantial investors or their designees may serve on the Board of Directors.

Additionally, one may find on the Board college professors representing disciplines related to the nature of the business.

In no case that I know of is an active banking official permitted to serve on the Board of Directors of a company that is a client of his bank. However, many retired bankers are quite willing to provide assistance to new enterprises by serving on their Boards of Directors. These bankers are able to bring to the company unusually valuable insights into the financial community and to provide access to banking resources that the company officers might not otherwise be aware of. The retired banker will have developed numerous contacts during his career; many of them will be of value to the new enterprise.

Occasionally, individual senior officers of two different companies may agree to serve on each other's Boards. This cross-pollination can prove to be quite valuable to both companies since each individual should be in a position to provide new and different insights into the business problems peculiar to the company on whose Board he sits.

The subject of whether or not any individual providing professional services to a business should sit on its Board is one of the most controversial in industry. A lawyer, certified public accountant, or business consultant who regularly provides service to the company may prove to be a valuable asset in the Board room. However, in the event the company officers decide that the services provided by these individuals are less than satisfactory, the problem of replacing them can be very sticky. For example, when a company is quite small, the services of a small law firm or accounting agency may prove to be adequate for the company's needs. However, if corporate growth is rapid, the small law firm or the small accounting agency may be unable adequately to service the company's accounts; larger firms must be retained. But removal of the smaller firms' staff members from the company Board of Directors can be difficult and embarrassing.

Consider also in selecting a Board of Directors that the presence on the Board of an individual of substantial prominence in his field or specialty will enhance corporate image. A drawback to having such an individual on the Board, however, may be that he is so busy with other commitments that he will be unable to devote the time required to honor his obligations to the company. The name of the Chairman of the Business School of a very large and famous university looks well in the annual report. However, if this individual is regularly unavailable to provide real assistance to the small corporation, the company founders may be better advised to staff this vacancy on the Board with some person of less renown who is in a better position to transmit his knowledge and assistance to the fledgling business.

Recruiting

Retired bankers, active attorneys, college professors, successful businessmen, and individuals from many other sectors of the business and professional community may make valuable members of your Board of Directors. However, such individuals are concerned about their reputations and thus about the enterprises with which they associate themselves. The founders, then, must convince their Board candidates that their business is destined to be successful. The best sales vehicle for communicating this information is the same well-prepared business plan that was presented to potential investors. This plan will not include the names of the Board members, but it *will* include the answers to any questions that potential Board members may have. An entrepreneur who has both confidence that his enterprise will be successful and knowledge of the elements necessary to make it successful has an excellent chance of persuading the individuals of his choice to join his Board.

How does one obtain the names of qualified and appropriate candidates for your Board of Directors? There are no better individuals to contact than those mentioned in Chapter 7 above.

Compensation

A Board member is generally compensated for his services in the form of a fixed payment for each meeting in which he participates. Board members of small companies may receive fees as low as $25 per meeting. However, fees of $50, $100, and more are not at all uncommon. One should bear in mind, however, that the assistance of a Board of Directors should represent an *economy* to the small business; therefore, the fees of the Directors should not represent a greater drain on the company coffers than would the retention of a full-time staff of qualified executives or the retention of the services of professional consultants on a contract basis.

Remember that the individuals that will serve on the Board must have a sincere desire to assist the enterprise and to take a personal interest in it. Therefore, if the proposed Board member seems overly concerned with the fee he will receive for his services, there is an excellent probability that the company would do better to seek the services of someone else.

SUPPORTING PROFESSIONAL SERVICE AGENCIES

Regardless of the kind of business you plan to start, your enterprise will require the services of a law firm, an accounting firm, a bank, and an insurance agency. To be more precise, you will need the services of professionally qualified *individuals*: a *lawyer*, an *accountant*, a *banker*, and an *insurance agent*. In this section, it is imperative that the entrepreneur recognize that in dealing with service organizations, he is dealing with people. Select them carefully.

New businesses generally seem to have far more difficulty in selecting suitable legal and accounting services than in selecting banking and insurance services, evidently because banking institutions and insurance agencies are free to advertise their services; no code of professionalism exists to prevent them from freely and openly competing among one another. On the other hand, the ethics of the legal and accounting professions prohibit the use of advertising. Much of the information that follows is based on research materials supplied the author by the national organizations representing the legal and accounting professions.

How to Select a Law Firm

Based on the reading I have done, the discussions I have had with other businessmen, and my own personal experience in acquiring the services of several different law firms to assist me in business ventures of my own, I have concluded that it is easier to determine the location of a local bordello than it is to locate a qualified law firm. Although many local Bar Associations have established Lawyer Referral Services, which may be found listed in the Yellow Pages of the telephone book under the heading "Attorneys," I would not advise the entrepreneur to attempt to locate satisfactory corporate counsel using such services. According to an article which appeared in the November, 1970 issue of the *American Bar Association Journal*, "The Lawyer Referral Service is the Bar's only organized effort at making competent legal service available to people of moderate means...." In other words, the Lawyer Referral Service exists primarily to assist *individuals* in locating legal counsel to help them with their personal problems. It is hardly a suitable resource to use in attempting to locate satisfactory *corporate* counsel.

If you had a medical problem and wished to locate a specialist, you would probably inquire of your friends and acquaintances to determine the name of someone they knew who had had a similar medical problem. You would then contact the person who had the problem, obtain the name of the physician who attended him, and ascertain whether or not the service he obtained was satisfactory. In the selection of corporate counsel, the same process appears to be useful: Locate a relatively new business engaged in an activity similar to, but not in direct competition with, the one you contemplate. The management of the company should be flattered to have you ask their advice and may be quite willing to provide you with whatever information you ask for regarding their legal counsel. By asking the same questions of several companies, you should be able to compile a list of several competent firms.

Next, make appointments with representatives of each firm. Since it is likely that the attorney will enjoy a worthwhile financial return should he be successful in obtaining you as a client, there is generally no charge for such an introductory meeting. However, this matter should be discussed at the time the appointment is arranged to insure against any misunderstandings.

At the first meeting with a new attorney whose services you are considering, you should be prepared to discuss in some detail the plans you have for your new enterprise. You should also consider in advance the type of questions you wish answered in order to satisfy yourself that the law firm can provide the service your enterprise will require. You should make certain that the firm represents no clients who are competitors of yours, and you should not hesitate openly to discuss the lawyer's fees.

You are entitled to know who the principal clients of the firm are. (Obviously, if the firm provides legal counsel for the local strip joint, it is unlikely that they will provide a suitable service for a store that sells religious artifacts.)

Other factors to be considered have to do with the firm's work load. If the firm is inadequately staffed, it is unlikely that you will receive the kind of service you require. On the other hand, if the firm appears to be seriously lacking business, there may be a very good reason for it. You should determine the experience of the staff, their ages, education, and legal qualifications. Finally, you should determine to your own satisfaction whether or not there is empathy between you and the attorney. If the attorney appears to feel that he is doing you a favor in taking you on as a client, it is doubtful that any ensuing relationship will be mutually satisfactory.

Finally, the entrepreneur should make a point of talking with more than one firm to satisfy himself that he has a basis for comparison and will thus be able to pick the firm with which he feels most satisfied. Additional information on each firm considered may be found in the individual listings in the *Law Directory*,[20] the publication that many recent law school graduates consult in seeking information on possible firms with which they may seek an affiliation as a junior partner.

In discussing your requirements with a candidate attorney, you should attempt to learn whether or not the firm has had extensive experience in dealing with new companies. Determine if the firm has seen many companies through the incorporation phase, if they have drawn up many partnership agreements, if they can be of assistance in locating private sources of venture capital. In other words, you should attempt to learn all of the services that the firm can offer you.

How to Select an Accounting Firm

An accounting firm can provide many necessary and worthwhile services to a new enterprise. Assistance may include but is not limited to:

1. Helping in establishing and maintaining a sound accounting system.
2. Reviewing the company's books in order to advise the company officers regarding their financial progress and the possibility of improving

corporate financial performance. Independent analysis of inventory, budget and working capital problems, and cost accounting and management studies are all within the understanding of a good accountant.

3. Proper handling of tax matters. This service is of the utmost importance to a new company. In many instances, policies regarding the handling of tax matters are very difficult to change later on. For example, determining whether accounting will be on a cash or on an accrual basis and arranging techniques for depreciating capital equipment require a very careful evaluation.

4. Assisting a client company in securing additional financing through a bank or other financial source. The accounting firm is uniquely qualified to help the company prepare a financial presentation for use in a fund-raising effort.

One locates a suitable accounting firm for the new business in much the same way as he locates corporate legal counsel. There are three primary factors to be considered in the selection of an accounting firm:

1. The firm should have a well-established reputation for integrity and competence. The names of such firms may be obtained from established businesses by requesting that they refer you to firms with which they are familiar and which they regard as reputable and competent.

2. Interviews with candidate accounting firms should be arranged. During these interviews the entrepreneur should determine whether or not the experience, professional knowledge, training, and skill of the staff of the firm is sufficient for the needs of the new business.

3. By checking with major clients of the accounting firm and by discussing the subject with representatives of the accounting firm, the entrepreneur should determine if the accounting firm will be in a position to provide the time and service that the new business will require. Accounting firms range in size from small local organizations all the way up to major national firms such as Arthur Andersen and Price Waterhouse. Typically, the fees required by a large firm may be somewhat higher than the fees expected by a smaller firm; and the matter of fees may not be a trivial consideration in the selection of an accounting firm for a small new business.

Auditing is one of the most frequently overlooked services that an accounting firm can provide. Whether the company anticipates a need for additional financing at a later date, whether the company founders anticipate the possibility that they will seek to be merged with or acquired by another corporation, or whether the founders wish to make sure that the company is not being subjected to the handiwork of an embezzler, a regular independent audit will prove to be of enormous value. If only for the reason of this audit, a new firm *must* give serious consideration to engaging the services of an accounting firm.

How to Select a Commercial Bank

When looking for a banking firm, one of the most important considerations a small new company should bear in mind is this: Will the bank be there when you need their help? Consider that any bank can provide the routine services of maintaining accounts, clearing checks, and providing traveler's checks and safe deposit boxes.

As the founder of a new business, you should consider each of the following factors in your evaluation of a commercial banking facility:

Credit and Loan Policies

You should attempt to ascertain how much credit the bank you are considering is prepared to extend to you. You should also attempt to determine the interest rates you may be expected to pay, the extent to which your credit may have to be collateralized, the requirements of the bank regarding compensating balances (i.e., if you borrow $10,000 and the bank requires that you maintain a minimum balance of $2,000 in your account, that $2,000 represents a compensating balance; you are in effect borrowing only $8,000 while paying interest on $10,000).

1. Is the bank familiar with your type of business? Typically, bankers are conservative people; they are much less likely to be liberal in their loan policies when dealing with industries with which they are not familiar than they would be when dealing with industries they understand well. Therefore, it would be wise for the entrepreneur to determine what industries are represented by the bank's existing clientele.

2. Is it the bank's announced policy to encourage small businesses, or does the bank appear to be primarily concerned with the financing of automobiles and appliances?

3. Does the bank make provision for extending credit against accounts receivable? (See discussion in Section Three on the subject of "Factoring.")

4. A bank's financial statement can provide a considerable amount of information about its management attitudes. If most of the bank's assets are in the form of readily liquidated securities, it is probably safe to assume that the bank management is ultra-conservative. Should you require a loan from this bank under marginal circumstances, it is unlikely that you would receive it. On the other hand, if many of the bank's assets are represented by assets not readily liquidated, you may assume that the bank's attitude toward loans is quite liberal. The offsetting factor may be that the liberal bank does not represent as secure a repository for the new company's funds as does the more conservative bank.

Empathic Management

You should attempt to determine whether or not the bank officers have any basic empathic interest in you and the needs of your business. Does the banker appear to be at least willing, if not eager, to render whatever assistance he can to the new enterprise? Is he a young tiger, eager to build new accounts through the encouragement of entrepreneurship in hopes of cultivating the Xerox of tomorrow? Or is he a sedate executive on the verge of retirement, who doesn't want to try *anything* that might jeopardize his imminent pension? Alternatively, is he a young lamb who has no idea as to what he can get away with, who is afraid to try anything? Or is he an old pro who will bend as far as the law will allow, fully confident of his ability to assess the prevailing economic climate and the willingness of the bank to rely on his seasoned judgment? How willing is the banker to assist the entrepreneur in obtaining credit information on customers and suppliers? How willingly does he supply other information that will be of help to the new enterprise?

How knowledgeable is the banker? Does he have a good understanding of the broad services available in the financial marketplace? Does he appear to have insight into private financing? Is he in a position to recommend an accounting firm, a legal firm, or other business services? Is he in a position to provide you with the kinds of business contacts that will assist your company in growing rapidly?

Looking at your own small-businessman's financial needs through the eyes of your banker can give to you an appreciation of the banker's perspective. Consider the investment position of a bank. The bank's main source of income is the interest received from loans. Therefore, the loan interest rates the bank charges represent a very real ceiling on the investment returns. The risk, however, on the types of loans a bank generally makes is necessarily also very low due to strictly enforced federal and state standards—the bank makes low-risk investments and must content itself with low returns. Another reason for this conservatism is that bank deposits are invariably placed on a "demand" basis—a bank patron may withdraw his funds whenever he wishes. Therefore, the banker must make allowance for the possibility that a significant number of his depositors may request the withdrawal of their funds within a short period of time. The bank must thus maintain low-risk investments that can be easily liquidated; equity in a company or a high-risk loan to a new business is not necessarily such an investment. Relative, then, to the other options he has, the banker may find investment in your business to be too risky. He may, however, be able to assist in locating other financing for you—for example, through a bank-owned Small Business Investment Company or the Small Business Administration.

In summary, banking is an industry, a competitive one. Therefore, it is to the entrepreneur's advantage to select the one institution that is in a position to offer the greatest and most flexible resources in satisfying the financial needs of his new enterprise. The entrepreneur should select the most progressive banker he can find, one who can also satisfy the unique requirements of his particular business.

How to Select an Insurance Agency

In today's complex business community, providing broad insurance coverage for any enterprise requires the attention of the trained and knowledgeable staff of a professional insurance agency. The following is a list of some of the services you may wish to have provided by your insurance agency.

There are several different types of business life insurance, each one serving a specialized function:

Key-Man Insurance

Any new enterprise depends very heavily on the unique talents of its founders. The death of any one of them could provide a mortal blow to the foundling business or result in serious financial loss due to the interruption of business or the subsequent retardation of growth. Key-Man Insurance provides an allowance that will enable the company to recruit and train a successor and reduce the loss in profitability during the training period.

Partnership Insurance

Unless legal provision has been made to the contrary, a partnership automatically dissolves at or shortly after death. With foresight, the members of the partnership can make appropriate arrangements to avoid the consequences of this disaster. (A partnership of two or more persons is automatically dissolved upon the death of one of the partners unless legal arrangements provide otherwise. The dissolution of a partnership would make necessary the refiling of fictitious name papers or corporation papers, possibly under the new name; this name change could have unfortunate effects upon the corporate image that was attached to the old name.) By having the business attorney and the insurance agent work together to draw up a partnership insurance policy, provision can be made to retire a deceased partner's interest in the business, to ensure the continuity of business operations, and to supply the deceased partner's beneficiaries with an equitable recompense for his share of the business.

Shareholder Insurance

If a single stockholder retains a substantial equity in the small business, the company officers and remaining stockholders may wish to take steps to protect their interests against the possibility that, should this major shareholder die, a new stockholder whose interests are prejudicial to those of the remaining stockholders and company officers would gain a controlling interest in the company. An insurance policy on the life of a major stockholder can provide for the outright purchase of that stockholder's interest in the event of his demise, thus insuring that the company will maintain its continuity.

Sole Proprietorship Insurance

Approximately 70 percent of the businesses in this country are sole proprietorships. Such businesses often provide regular jobs for many employees. The death of the proprietor can cause significant inconvenience and even hardship for the surviving employees. Sole Proprietorship Insurance can provide for a lump-sum payment to the family or beneficiaries of the deceased while simultaneously insuring the continuity of the business for the protection of the staff.

Other types of insurance include public liability insurance; comprehensive, personal injury, broad-form property damage, blanket contractual, and products insurance; security and theft insurance, including robbery, safe, and alarm system insurance; surety bonds for employees; plate glass insurance; accounts receivable insurance; fire insurance, including extended coverage, special extended coverage ("all risk"), and sprinkler damage insurance; automobile insurance, including physical damage and nonownership of automobile insurance; boiler insurance; earthquake insurance; business interruption insurance; disability insurance; and medical/hospital/surgical insurance.

Having reviewed this bewildering array of various insurance options available to businesses, it should be readily apparent that so complex a field warrants the attention of a qualified specialist—the business insurance broker. As was the case with the law firm, accounting firm, and bank, the insurance broker must be empathetic with the client; and the most effective means of locating such a broker is by obtaining referrals and then investigating them. Bear in mind when looking for the services of an insurance broker that you are not merely buying insurance; you are buying a service. Just as you would not seriously consider acquiring the services of a physician merely because he is the least expensive practitioner whose services are available, you should not evaluate the services of a particular insurance broker solely on the basis of the price of the coverage he offers. Insurance is critical to any business; and the entrepreneur should be very sensitive to the difference between an order-taking insurance clerk and a bona-fide broker equipped with the education, background, and desire to serve his clients.

Remember also that the founders can anticipate and make allowance for everything other than the unexpected. Insurance is a sort of blanket protection against the unexpected; the insurance broker assists the founders in making provision for what they cannot anticipate and, thus, for what many new businessmen overlook. Proper insurance coverage for a new enterprise thus results in the significant reduction of financial risk. Therefore, financing may be obtained much more easily for the well-insured new enterprise.

THE MARKET TO BE SERVED

In this section of your formal business plan, you should provide a detailed analysis of the market to be served by the new enterprise. Here, the founders should provide a showcase of the knowledge and expertise with which they expect to realize substantial competitive advantages in their target market.

Document Your Assertions

The member(s) of the founding team responsible for marketing should investigate every major available source of marketing intelligence. These resources include leading trade, professional, and financial journals, industry and trade associations, the U.S. Department of Commerce [See "UNCLE SAM WANTS (to help) YOU!" in Chapter 6 above], and organizations specializing in the field of market analysis. Several of the primary information sources in this latter category include:

Stanford Research Institute
333 Ravenswood Avenue
Menlo Park, California 94025

Arthur D. Little, Inc.
25 Acorn Park
Cambridge, Massachusetts 02140

Battelle Memorial Institute
505 King Avenue
Columbus, Ohio 43201

Frost and Sullivan, Inc.
106 Fulton Street
New York, New York 10038

Predicasts, Inc.
200 University Circle Research Center
11001 Cedar Avenue
Cleveland, Ohio 44106

For a comprehensive annotated guide to statistical and informational material about business trends and consumer and industrial markets, see *Data Sources for Business and Market Analysis* by Nathalie D. Frank (2nd ed., 1969). This book covers government publications, university programs, research institutions, trade associations, and many other sources. Copies are available at $10 from the Scarecrow Press, Inc., 52 Liberty Street, Box 656, Metuchen, New Jersey 08840.

Finally, the U.S. Department of Commerce, Bureau of the Census, offers an extensive selection of current industrial reports including data on the production, inventories, and orders for 5,000 products representing 40 percent of all U.S. manufacturing. To obtain additional information on these government reports, request Form BC 738 from the Bureau of the Census, Washington, D. C. 20233.

List Major Potential Customers

A valuable aid to inspiring confidence in a potential investor is a roster of potential customers, complete with estimated annual sales to each and a brief justification for this prediction. However, forecasts of the length of time necessary to cultivate customers and to establish the flow of new purchase orders are frequently overly optimistic, and the investor will be understandably suspicious of them. Thus, wherever possible, actual purchase orders or letters of intent expressing the customer's willingness to purchase the products of the proposed new firm should be included in the Appendix of the business plan.

Analyze Major Competitors

A listing of "The Guys in the Black Hats" who represent major competition for the new firm should be included in the business plan, along with a brief discussion of their strengths, weaknesses, estimated market share, and profitability. Provide also an analysis of how your company plans to cope with this competition—and your plans for capitalizing on competitor weaknesses and for meeting the challenges represented by your competitors' strengths. Much intelligence on your competitors' marketing programs can be had by examining their annual reports (if the stock is publicly traded) or by obtaining a report from one of the major independent credit rating services (your banker or your accountant can probably assist you here).

Estimate Market Share

If a new business is to be viable, it must plan to control a certain minimum share of its market. To be a significant force within its market, the volume of its business must be such that its actions are "felt" by the rest of the market. Otherwise, the business is just another "Me, too" company and is subject to the mercy of those firms that dominate the market. Your business plan, then, should include an estimate of the share of the market you plan to capture.

Polish Your Crystal Ball

Anyone involved in the launching of a new enterprise is interested in an assessment of the projected annual growth rate for the market the company will serve. Most investors find the prospect of financing a company that may capture a small percentage of a rapidly growing market far more appealing than the prospect of underwriting a company likely to secure a substantial share of a market with a diminishing annual volume and an uncertain future growth. Sources of such information were suggested earlier in this chapter.

Discuss Product Timing

In these days when "obsolescence" is a man-on-the-street term and when half the products we will be using five years from now haven't been invented yet, *timing* occupies a position of considerable importance in evaluating the prospects for the success of a new product. Almost every industry has its own hula hoop, but remember that today's demand for vacuum-tube hi-fi sets is just about as great as its demand for washboards.

The subject of product-timing invites hours of discussion and pages of exposition. The dilemma is this: You must be neither too early nor too late with your product. The automobile industry provides us with two excellent examples—decades ahead of its time was the Studebaker *Avanti*; born too late and subjected to much ridicule was the Ford Motor Company's *Edsel*.

THE PRODUCTS AND/OR SERVICES

This section of the business plan should provide an in-depth review of the product and/or service to be marketed—the revenue-producing item on which the company founders are willing to stake their future.

The following discussion will highlight the major features to consider in the introduction of a new product or service. The discussion is intended to be comprehensive and practical; however, the peculiar characteristics of any innovative product or service may demand highly individual treatment.

Competitive Features

In preparing a business plan, one must give careful consideration to those factors which will prompt a prospective customer to try your new product or service in preference to the product or service of your competitors.

Size

In many products, size is a factor of considerable importance. Consider, for example, the modern-day transistor radio, which is small enough to fit in your shirt pocket. This reduced size was responsible for a substantially new market for portable radios.

Advances in modern electronics and materials technology have resulted in other new billion-dollar markets that did not exist before the prefix "mini." Portable two-way communications devices, physically implanted pace-makers for heartbeat regulation in cardiac patients, and contact lenses are just three examples of how size reduction due to advancing technology has opened new markets. Bigness, too, is a successful market by-product of technology. Today we have ships with cargo capacities undreamed of decades ago, and each new skyscraper seems taller than its older neighbor across the street. Recently developed surgical techniques can even enlarge the female bosom (one of the nation's leading chemical companies has a very satisfying annual dollar volume in providing chemically inert materials to the medical profession for this express purpose).

Weight

The modern-day inventions of lightweight products and materials has also resulted in the creation of new markets, the expansion of old or existing markets, and the conferral upon various innovators of an encouraging, satisfying share of a new market. Aviation and space exploration were particularly affected by all of this lightweightness—modern-day feats obviously would not have been possible without it. The huge consumer markets have seen the by-products of this new technology in the form, to give one example, of very sturdy, lightweight luggage. Innovation in the freeze drying of foods has eliminated the necessity for carting the proverbial—and heavy—can of beans in your back-pack when you go camping. The agricultural industry provides us with another example of technology's attempts to alter weights—poultry producers have worked for years to produce turkeys and chickens that have more meat per animal and thus a higher weight per bird. Increased weight is also attractive in synthetic diamonds, and a major industry is rapidly emerging in the production of these and other synthetic gem-stones. (Whereas years ago industrial diamonds were typically quite small, gem-quality stones can now be synthesized in the laboratory and offered to the consumer at prices substantially lower than those for genuine African diamonds.)

Durability

As consumer interest groups come of age, federal regulation of product durability is becoming increasingly likely. Consumers are almost always concerned with durability in the products they buy. The entrepreneur who has a product that is more durable than his competitors' products to offer to the market has a fair chance of enjoying substantial market acceptance. Recent years have seen new products such as five-year-lifetime light bulbs, chip-resistant dinnerware that is replaced free of charge if it sustains damage, and reliable space hardware designed to last for years in outer space.

At the other extreme, there is also an increasing demand for products intended for limited use. We have seen the emergence of paper garments, camera flashbulbs, and disposable containers. Today's marketplace, despite its fondness for durability, is enamoured of ingeniously designed "throwaways."

Convenience

Convenience has become a highly marketable concept in this age of affluence and opulence. The automation of toothbrushes, pencil sharpeners, egg beaters, blenders, lawnmowers, hedge trimmers, industrial screw drivers and wrenches, etc., afford the mechanically inclined entrepreneur with product and market opportunities limited only by his ingenuity. Consumer willingness to embrace new products which mechanize formerly manual operations appears to be nearly limitless.

Convenience is one of the primary features of any service enterprise and should be given particular attention in a business proposal that is concerned with a service industry. In such an industry, factors such as location, hours of business operation, and/or availability of personnel may prove to be of the utmost importance. Obviously a hairdresser who keeps his shop open 16 hours a day seven days a week is providing his clientele greater convenience than is the hairdresser who operates five days a week on a nine-hour day. The same also applies to food services.

Quality

Where price remains constant, there is always a market for a properly promoted product that has a higher quality than the product offered by the competition. The convenience food industry, which has always afforded the man with a yen for his own business the opportunity to earn a living, serves as an example—to this day, the quality suggested by the term "homemade" is a significant consumer attraction. In virtually every sector of industry, there is room for new companies that can provide higher quality products than those presently offered at a price equal to or lower than the currently prevailing price. Typically, however, the concept of quality is not easy to sell; a reputation must be established over a period of time. The assertion that one's goods or services are of superior quality must withstand the test of time. Therefore, although quality in the product is extremely important to the *survival* of any business, the reputation for quality cannot be depended upon to leap full-blown from the business plan. *Some* degree of quality is a necessity, but it is *not* a significant competitive advantage for a new enterprise. Maintaining a high level of quality over a sustained period of time will, however, enhance growth of the new enterprise.

Price

Price is a fascinating topic. Everywhere there are markets where one particular product is priced over a broad range. In the food industry, one can pay 15 cents for a hamburger or $25 for a dinner in some swank supper club. One can buy a pair of shoes for $2.50 through a mail-order catalog or have a pair custom-made for more than $200. Considerations involved in the establishment of a price for a given commodity or service are subtle indeed. Even in industries that are highly competitive, such as the cosmetics field, one finds products representing a wide variation in price. Even in the area of governmental procurement, where product specifications are typically very clearly delineated, one frequently finds intense price competition. The entrepreneur preparing his business plan should find an interesting and demanding challenge in his efforts to persuade the investor that his pricing will be such as to promise significant market share while simultaneously providing a satisfactory return on the invested dollar.

Customer Service

Where products are offered, some consideration must be given to customer service. Provision must be made for the repair of broken or defective products either through a nationwide network of repair agencies or by means of a special department at the factory to which customers can return products for replacement, repair, or servicing.

In formulating the business plan, the entrepreneur should give careful consideration to the warranty program he plans to offer with his product. He must also determine what office procedures will be needed to monitor such a program. The long-term success of any business rests heavily on the reputation it is able to establish in the area of customer service.

If the product is a new one, the entrepreneur must plan for the expense and effort necessary to educate the customer in the use of the product. For example, the introduction of a new computer network may require the development of an educational program to instruct the purchaser or lessee in the use of the new equipment.

Standardization-Compatibility

In those industries where the major competitor's product is firmly entrenched in the marketplace, an entrepreneur may successfully compete by offering a line of products compatible with the popular product on a replacement basis. One example of this approach may be seen in the computer industry, where literally hundreds of manufacturers now offer products that are designed to replace parts of the system provided by the original supplier. Viewing this subject from a different point of view, it may be possible to offer to the market a product so designed that it may be readily repaired by removing an easily accessible part and replacing it with a new one.

In a service, standardization is of primary importance. If California-bottled Coca-Cola were to taste differently from Florida-bottled Coca-Cola, there might be some serious problems in the marketing of the product. The means for securing and maintaining standardization in a service industry (which relies heavily on the vagaries of local manpower) is of the utmost importance.

Patents

This subject has been covered at length in previous sections of the book (See Chapter 8). Suffice it to say at this point that possession of a well-drawn patent, coupled with whatever financial resources may be necessary to defend it properly, will provide any new business with a significant advantage in the marketplace, provided that the new product concept itself is a viable one. (A patent, you will recall, is a license for a monopoly affording protection to the holder for a period of 17 years.)

Proprietary Content

In some instances, a product, although not protectable with a patent, may be afforded the protection of covenants of secrecy. Manufacturing processes and secret formulas often have protection of this kind. If the proposed business is in the food industry, for example, certain recipes—like that for Colonel Sanders' Kentucky Fried Chicken—can prove to be of enormous long-term value.

Pictures

In order better to communicate the idea for your product or service to the investment community, it is wise to include illustrations of the product to be offered. If drawings or photographs of individual parts would assist the reader in visualizing the proposed product, include them. Depending on how elaborate the business proposal is, these illustrations may either be in black and white or color. However, it must be borne in mind that the quality of the illustrations is quite important. Poorly rendered drawings may do more harm than good in your efforts to interest a prospective investor.

Manufacturing Process

This section of the business plan should be devoted to a discussion of whatever steps are necessary actually to produce items for sale. If specialized machinery is required in the manufacture of the product, this machinery should be described in detail. Features of the product should be discussed from the standpoint of ease of manufacture. If the product requires the assembly of a number of component parts, some of which may even be procured outside the proposed company, an analysis of these factors is most appropriate. If the procurement of parts, equipment, or raw materials may pose problems, a plan for handling each of these problems should be presented.

Cost Breakdowns

Where appropriate, a list of every part that goes into the product should be prepared. Such a document is commonly referred to as a "Bill of Materials." Pricing on each of these parts in small and large quantities should be indicated. Where practical, a step-by-step sequence of drawings should be prepared to illustrate the various phases in product assembly and testing, all the way up to and including packaging and shipping. Ideally, each step in this process will be separately identified and characterized in terms of time required to perform the indicated operations, cost in terms of raw materials and direct time (the real wage rate paid the individual performing the individual step), and overhead and administrative charges. Since this figure varies widely from industry to industry, more specific references are included in the recommended reading list at the end of this chapter.

State of the Art

In many industries characterized by rapid growth, there is a concept called the "State of the Art," which refers to the condition of the industry in terms of technical advancement or present status and rate of change. In preparing the business plan, the entrepreneur should give consideration to an analysis of his industry and his product. If he is proposing a venture into an industry where products may be obsolete within a short period of time, the proposed venture may turn out to be disastrous. The proposal should contain a realistic evaluation of these factors and a discussion of the founders' plans for dealing with the eventualities of product obsolescence and for keeping up with or ahead of rapidly changing technology. In concluding your discussion of State of the Art, be certain to identify individually those factors that characterize the new company product and that will serve to protect it from a competitive contest with the product of a larger and better-financed corporation.

MARKETING STRATEGY

No doubt many of you have already heard that the days have passed when the world would beat a path to your door if you invented a better mouse trap. Well, they have. A new product today must receive the benefits of careful marketing strategy in order to be accepted and to be successful. Failure to implement proper strategy may provide a capable competitor with an opportunity to produce a similar product that *is* assisted by a superior marketing plan, with the result that the product originators are deprived of any advantage they might have enjoyed had they properly marketed their product in the first place.

Promotional Methods

This section of the business plan should include a discussion of the promotional methods to be employed to bring the product or service to the attention of the end user. These methods may include trade-journal advertising, direct-mail advertising, or newspaper and television advertising. A new-product news release and news releases announcing the formation of the company are musts in providing inexpensive media coverage. Additional sources of publicity for the company, its founders, and its products are technical articles written for publication in trade and professional journals. Whether or not the founders decide to use the services of an advertising agency depends on the financial resources of the founders and the magnitude of the advertising campaign they wish to undertake. Advertising agencies do not always obtain fees directly from their clients; instead, they obtain commissions from the media in which they place the advertising material. In other cases, however, retainers and/or fees are demanded.

Advertising Efforts

When contemplating a promotional campaign, the entrepreneur may be confronted with a bewildering array of communications media including radio, television, newspapers, magazines, billboards, mail, and even intermission spots at the local drive-in theater. When an advertising campaign is crucial to the success of a new business, the business plan should discuss the proposed campaign in detail. It is suggested that the services of a competent advertising agency be engaged to assist with the preparation of such a plan.

Distribution

The subject of product and/or service distribution is fascinating. There are an enormous number of channels available if the individual with marketing responsibility simply exercises his ingenuity in discovering them. The following list is intended merely to suggest a few of the avenues open to the imaginative entrepreneur.

Point-of-Sale-Manufacturing

This is the most basic form of product or service distribution. The man or woman operating a beauty salon is engaged in the business of direct selling. The same is true of a restaurant that prepares food to order for its clientele. Any situation in which a product or service is prepared and supplied at the point of sale is referred to as a direct sale. Variations on this approach are represented in the two following sections.

Direct Mail

In those instances where customers are far removed from the supplier, direct mail may afford the entrepreneur with a satisfactory means of marketing his product. For example, a major manufacturer of vitamins in this country manages to sell a large volume of merchandise by distributing copies of its catalog to potential clients, who then mail their orders to the manufacturer. Computer dating is an example of a service that has been successfully distributed through the mails.

Direct Sales Through Salaried Salesmen

A company can also bring its products to its customers through an organization of company salesmen. In some instances, these salesmen receive compensation not only in the form of wages or salary but also in the form of commissions and bonuses. An example is the sale of Allstate Insurance by the Sears Roebuck and Company—salesmen who offer this service to the marketplace are employees of Sears. Many large manufacturing organizations, such as Hewlett-Packard, an electronics equipment manufacturer, offer their products for sale through their staff of salaried salesmen.

In each of the above instances of direct selling, middleman fees (commissions or discounts offered to persons or organizations outside of the company) are either minimized or eliminated. However, in many instances, the products of a new company require more elaborate distribution organization. The following examples discuss some of these channels:

Wholesalers (Jobbers)

It is often customary for a manufacturer of consumer products to sell his output at a discounted price to a wholesaler or a jobber, who in turn distributes his purchases to numerous retail outlets within his "territory."

Industrial Distributors

These organizations or individuals function in relation to their industrial clients as a wholesaler functions in relation to his retail clients. An industrial distributor typically purchases products for resale to industrial clients. An example of an industrial supplier is the modern-day steel service center. A steel service center may purchase raw materials from a large number of geographically dispersed suppliers and offer them for sale to his local industrial clients.

Private Label

A number of the major retailing organizations in the United States, such as Sears and Roebuck and Montgomery-Ward, regularly sell products that are manufactured by independent suppliers. These independent suppliers build products for major outlets on a contractual basis. A set of product specifications is usually drawn up by the retailer, who then solicits bids from various manufacturers who are qualified to manufacture the desired products. Subsequently a manufacturer is selected to produce the desired products, which will bear the label of the retail organization.

Premiums

A number of products are marketed today as premiums. Wigs, cosmetics, and housewares are often offered by various banking institutions to customers opening new accounts. Similarly, gasoline retailers offer "free" gadgets with the purchase of minimum quantities of merchandise.

Manufacturers' Representatives

In the instances where much contact with the customer is required and the company finances are such that a full-scale company-employed sales force is not practical, the manufacturers' representative provides a very convenient solution. Typically, a manufacturers' representative or a manufacturers' representative organization will carry a broad line of products representing the offerings of several manufacturers. Ideally, these products will complement each other. As an example, a manufacturers' rep or agent supplying manufacturing machinery may carry one manufacturer's lathes, a different manufacturer's drill presses, and still another manufacturer's milling machines.

Some of the advantages of using a manufacturers' representative organization accrue from the fact that the agents work exclusively on a commission basis. Ordinarily, when a sale is completed, the manufacturer bills the end customer and, after receipt of payment from the customer, forwards a commission check to the manufacturers' representative. As a result, if sales are slow, selling costs are also reduced. Thus, the manufacturer is able to determine in advance a significant part of his selling costs. A manufacturers' agent will generally cover a relatively small geographical area with a broad line of products. He is thus in a position to uncover a new market for your product while he tries to interest a potential customer in the purchase of some noncompeting product in his line.

Terms of Sale

In times when money is in short supply (and for new companies this is most of the time), the determination of the terms of sale of the products can be of primary significance in market penetration and in the company's ability to survive financially. To achieve significant market penetration, a new company frequently may find it necessary to resort to financing techniques that will benefit the customer in order to induce potential customers to try the new products. Commonly, two techniques in financing the sale of new products are used.

Net 30 Days

The most common form of sales financing is the maintenance of a 30-day accounts receivable credit basis. Typically, a small discount is offered the customer in return for full payment within a 10-day period. Unfortunately, when the money markets are tight for the customers as well as the new companies, customer credit can extend to 60 and even 90 days or longer. The diligence with which the new company plans to pursue collection of overdue accounts receivable will rest in part on recognition of the fact that some customers may not regard paying their bills as something they care to do. Therefore, a new company may find itself at a competitive disadvantage in insisting on prompt payment of all accounts receivable. Not uncommonly, although sale terms will dictate a 30-day turnover in accounts receivable, a new company must realistically plan on a 60- to 90-day turnover period unless it is prepared to lose those potential customers who make a practice of stretching credit terms.

Product Leasing

In today's marketplace, product leasing is becoming increasingly common as a means of financing the sale of "big ticket" items. Computers and other expensive equipment are rarely sold on a cash basis. Ordinarily, customers are very reluctant to part with a large amount of capital for the purchase of such equipment. Thus, it has become common for the customer to be afforded the option of leasing the desired equipment. In some instances, the manufacturer may be able to make leasing arrangements with a bank or other financial institution. Then the manufacturer sells his product for cash to the financial institution, which in turn leases the product to the end user.

Delivery/Performance Timing

Since the beginning of recorded business history, the customer has demanded "delivery yesterday." A new company planning a program of rapid market penetration must give considerable attention to the problems of supplying customer delivery requirements on a consistently reliable basis.

When a new company is supplying parts to a major user, the importance of delivery cannot be over-emphasized. Consider a situation of a major manufacturer-customer who has hundreds of thousands of dollars tied up in in-process assemblies. If the assembly lines and the delivery of large products or systems are held up due to a shortage of relatively inexpensive parts, the supplier of the late parts will find that the welcome mat has for him been withdrawn, possibly on a permanent basis. And in those instances where a service is to be provided, customers generally have little patience with an agency that does not live up to its delivery commitments.

The characteristics of the market to be served should also be analyzed to determine whether or not it makes economical sense to provide customers with a line of products available from inventory or whether the market demands constant flow of custom-made devices. The latter case can prove to be particularly challenging for a small company. Nevertheless, this kind of a market is one in which a new small company typically finds ready acceptance because of the inability of large corporations consistently to supply custom products in a short period of time. Unfortunately, as a small company grows, speed of delivery typically suffers.

A New Twist

In some instances, acceptance of a new product may depend heavily on the ability of the supplier to provide a new twist to his intended market. Consider if you will the famous case of King C. Gillette, inventor of the first safety razor. Gillette found market acceptance of his new concept practically nil in the age of the straight-edge razor until he got the idea of giving away the blade holder with the sale of each packet of blades. Since the largest market he intended to reach was the market created by the introduction of his disposable blades, his purpose was served and customers accepted the product—a profitable result of Gillette's judgment! More recent examples are the cans and bottle caps which need no special openers and which have proved a boon to the beverage industry; and literally representing new twists for the wire industry were the introductions of paper clips and hair pins.

RESEARCH AND DEVELOPMENT PROGRAM

In order to interest investors and to attract a well-qualified and capable staff, the company founders must give serious consideration at the outset to their plans for growth. A company that offers products to a market must anticipate having to refine their existing products and to develop new products. A company that offers a service must anticipate and provide for growth opportunities. A clearly written statement that describes a program for analyzing and exploiting new opportunities will do much to inspire confidence in the growth potential of the proposed enterprise.

A discussion of possible anti-obsolescence programs and sources of funding for such programs follows.

Product Improvement

When the average enterprise begins operation, the products it offers to the marketplace are only one step removed from their prototypes. In other words, these early products are not particularly sophisticated. The products will no doubt successfully perform the function for which they were designed; however, details such as the cost of the individual parts, the materials used in the fabrication of these parts, and the aesthetics of the product will not have received much attention. The business plan for the new enterprise should include a program of product improvement within the master plan for corporate growth.

Process Improvement

Often, when a business is small, products are built in small quantities. The labor content in each product is typically high and the manufacturing process is usually inefficient. The formal business plan should include some discussion of how the company founders plan to increase their manufacturing efficiency, improve their delivery schedules, and reduce the unit cost of their product. Greater automation in the manufacturing process might be considered. In-house facilities for the manufacture of certain parts might also prove economical. In fact, the development of a brand-new manufacturing technology might result from a suitably planned research and development program, which should be discussed in this section of the business plan.

Development of New Products

The preceding two topics considered product and process improvement. In this section of the business plan, the founders should discuss their plans for the development of new products and new service ideas. Failure to plan for the development of new products is one of the primary factors in arresting the growth of a new enterprise.

After a new business offers a new product or concept to the marketplace, it has a limited period of time in which to enjoy its monopoly. If the company is successful and its product is accepted in the market, the founders may be confident that their competition will make a vigorous attempt to copy their product. Therefore, it behooves the growth-minded founders to plan a program for the exploration and development of new products in order to retain whatever lead they may achieve at the outset.

Who Pays?

Plans for product improvement, process improvement, and new-product exploration and development are all well and good when one wishes to enlist the enthusiastic support of a prospective investor. However, the cost of carrying out these plans can prove to be quite substantial. If the *company* is to underwrite the cost of its internal research and development programs, then substantial profit margins must be realized on the original products in order to sustain the programs. Alternatively, outside capital must be obtained to finance the risky and expensive search for new products.

If the company's staff is well noted for excellence in a particular field, customer contracts may be obtained for development programs. In fact, many research organizations exist today for the exclusive purpose of developing new products for major clients. Your company, if you are lucky, can hitch a ride on this kind of gravy train. For example, if you have a contract to develop a new kind of plastic material that will satisfy the specialized needs of a particular customer, it may be possible for you to retain all rights to the manufacturing process and to the new material, both of which were developed with the customer's money. In return for his investment, the customer may receive a guaranteed price for the material for some contractually specified period of time.

The federal government has, throughout its history, been a major source of research and development funds for businesses. Although the government usually insists that all information resulting from such programs be disclosed, a company fortunate enough to develop a new product or process with federal money still enjoys a unique competitive advantage. They have developed an in-house knowhow that their competitors do not have. A description of a manufacturing process is one thing; mastering the techniques of the process is another.

PLANT LOCATION AND RELATED CONSIDERATIONS

In selecting the location for a new business, many factors must be evaluated. The determination of the location for a retail store is a highly specialized subject and will not be discussed here; however, material treating this subject is included in the Recommended Reading List at the end of this chapter. The following discussion concerns factors influencing the location of industrial enterprises.

Founder's Back Yard

There is often good reason for locating a new business in the founder's "back yard." For example, a new business should be located close to the founder's residence so that he will not have to spend precious working time commuting to and from the business. In addition, starting a new business places many stresses upon the founder's family; and, thus, the founder should avoid the added burden of adjusting his family to a new locale. Also, the founder will have cultivated a number of useful contacts in the community in which he resides.

Customer Proximity

There are those business advisers who maintain that it is best for a new company to develop a local clientele, thereby eliminating travel expenses in sales campaigns. For example, if a company is located on the West Coast and attempts to cultivate new customers on the East Coast, it may cost the new company in the vicinity of $1,000 every time a salesman or other company representative has to visit customers.

On the other hand, there are those business advisers who maintain that it is very difficult for a new company to cultivate local customers when the staff may be very small and the building in which the company is located may be nothing but the residence of one of the founders. Customers who are far removed from the plant site cannot know what it looks like; and thus its frailty, which might frighten customers away, is successfully concealed. The story of Information Machines Corporation (see Chapter 1) again serves as an example. That company's first major customer was in the Midwest; Bud Edelman, IMC's President, believes that, had the customer fully understood IMC's financial status, the company would not have been awarded this critical initial order.

However, the best procedure is probably the most obvious one. The new company should first attempt to develop local customers; if obtaining local customers proves difficult or impossible, then the radius of the company sales efforts should be expanded until customers are obtained.

Supplier Proximity

Many of the factors discussed under "Customer Proximity" are applicable to the topic of supplier proximity. The ability of the new company to maintain an adequate inventory of parts and raw materials and its ability to operate effectively without being in close proximity to major suppliers will determine whether or not the founders will wish to locate the facility close to their suppliers. If highly specialized supporting services are required (such as the fabrication of exotic materials) or, if occasional access to machinery representing prohibitively high capital investments for the small company is required, it may be *necessary* to locate the enterprise near a major supplier. If the new company uses raw materials that are expensive to transport, economy may also require that the plant be located close to the supplier.

Manpower Availability

In formulating the plans for the new business, the founders must consider the availability of manpower. If a large number of hourly semi-skilled or unskilled workers is required, then the founders would be wise to locate in an area noted for its low labor rates. Conversely, if the company products demand the services of highly skilled scientists, engineers, and technicians, the company founders would be well advised to establish their business near a leading college or university.

Transportation Services

The availability of adequate transportation facilities may be very important in the success or failure of the business or in the determination of its growth rate. For example, a major importer of electronics equipment of my acquaintance has his warehouse located in an industrial park adjoining a major international airport. This location permits him to process all shipments while minimizing transportation delays.

Another company I know of is located next to a railroad siding. This firm manufacturers coil springs for mattresses. Although the raw material (wire) for these springs is delivered by truck, the company receives a freight car rate on the wire it buys because the supplier's standard price list reflects a lower rate for all customers, large or small, having access to railroad sidings.

Still another entrepreneur of my acquaintance operates his business within two miles of a small country airport. This founder happens to be an avid pilot, and he makes frequent use of the company aircraft in conducting his electronics business. Thus, he is able to enjoy the comforts and style of residing in the country simultaneously with the financial benefits of operating a high-technology electronics company.

Educational Facilities

High cost of living, availability of skilled manpower, and proximity to a leading university all seem to go hand in hand. In many instances, a nearby university may provide a source of qualified staff members. Furthermore, if the university offers courses that are related to the activities of the new enterprise, professors and other learned men may be available to sit on the company's Board of Directors.

Investor Preferences

Some investors prefer to "plant" their money some place that is close enough so that they can drive their car down to the garden and watch the sprouts. Other investors are content to permit the founders considerable latitude in the utilization of their funds and merely require periodic reports on company progress. But the founders must be prepared for the possibility that the only way they can obtain funding is to locate the enterprise far from the place where they had originally intended to locate it.

Tax Climate

There are many economically depressed areas of this country and there are many foreign governments that are willing to give new industry a very favorable tax advantage to induce it to locate there. Where such opportunities are not inconsistent with the plans and expectations of the company founders, they may find that they will enjoy significant economic benefits from accepting such a government's offer. Details of the inducements that some countries, states, and towns use will be discussed in Section Three.

CONCEPT IN A CAPSULE

While attending a seminar on venture capital at the University of Toronto, I had the great pleasure of hearing a seasoned entrepreneur extol the value of a well-prepared PERT (Program Evaluation and Review Technique) diagram as a tool to help visualize the process of launching a new venture and planning its subsequent growth. The speaker claimed that the PERT diagram was, in his opinion, one of the most important documents in his business plan.

Initially, this entrepreneur prepared an extensive list of his major corporate objectives in terms of product development programs, sales campaigns, establishment of a manufacturing facility, and so forth. Then he prepared another list itemizing all of the steps necessary for its realization. Subsequently, these steps were placed in little blocks on the PERT diagram; the blocks were connected with lines to demonstrate the sequential character of the development process. For example, a step requiring completion of a set of product specifications would have to precede a step calling for the initiation of a development program for the design of that product. The diagram might also show the development steps that can be completed independently rather than sequentially, thus demonstrating a savings in total elapsed time.

In addition to providing the management team with a valuable, worthwhile planning tool, the PERT diagram served another extremely useful purpose: It impressed the hell out of the financiers! ($2.5 million worth!) On one large sheet of paper, it was possible to see every major step in the planned growth of the new company and to observe the relationship of each of these steps to every other step. The ease with which each phase of the planned corporate development could be studied inspired enormous confidence in the minds of the investors, and the founders' presentation of the concept was accepted for what it was: a carefully formulated strategy designed to minimize investor risk and maximize prospects for success. Considering the magnitude of the required funding and the conservatism of the participating investors, this proposal was financed in a remarkably short time. I have made a point of following the progress of this company. After two years of operation, growth has been substantial and prospects for continued success are excellent.

In sum, a PERT diagram, a flow chart, or another graphical representation of the steps involved in corporate growth serves two very important functions: (1) it is an invaluable planning aid and (2) it can be an extremely effective sales tool.

One of the foremost authorities in the country on this subject is Mr. James L. Halcomb, whose company was profiled in Chapter 1 above. For further information on the subject of PERT, the reader is invited to contact Jim or to consult some of the books referenced at the end of this chapter.

Recommended Reading

Allison, David, ed. *The R & D Game: Technical Men, Technical Managers, and Research Productivity*. Cambridge, Massachusetts and London, England: The M. I. T. Press, 1969.

American Marketing Association. *International Directory of Marketing Research Houses and Services*. New York: American Marketing Association. New York Chapter, 1970.

Anthony, Edward L. "Appraising the Market for the Services You Offer." *Small Marketers Aids, Annual No. 2*. Washington, D. C.: Small Business Administration, Government Printing Office, 1967, pp. 29-36.

Anthony, Edward L., ed. "Innovation: How Much is Enough?" *Management Aids for Small Manufacturers, Annual No. 13*. Washington, D. C.: Small Business Administration, Government Printing Office, 1967, pp. 65-73.

Aspinwall, Leo V. "Sizing Up Small Business Locations." *Small Marketers Aids, Annual No. 1*. Washington, D. C.: Small Business Administration, Government Printing Office, 1959, pp. 81-87.

Bank of America National Trust & Savings Association. "Manufacturing." *Small Business Reporter*, Vol. 9, No. 3, 1970.

Beaumont, John A. "How to Write a Job Description." *Management Aids for Small Manufacturers, Annual No. 13*. Washington, D. C.: Small Business Administration, Government Printing Office, 1967, pp. 49-56.

Brosterman, Robert. *The Complete Estate Planning Guide*. New York: McGraw-Hill, 1964.

Brown, Courtney C., and Smith, E. Everett, eds. *The Director Looks at His Job*. New York: Columbia University Press, 1957.

Charm, Sumner D. "Organizing the Owner-Manager's Job." *Management Aids for Small Manufacturers, Annual No. 7*. Washington, D. C.: Small Business Administration, Government Printing Office, 1961, pp. 16-23.

Clewett, Richard M. "Checking Your Marketing Channels." *Management Aids for Small Manufacturers, Annual No. 9*. Washington, D. C.: Small Business Administration, Government Printing Office, 1963, pp. 38-45.

Cloyd, W. W. "Innovations—New Ideas As a Source of Profit." *Small Marketers Aids, Annual No. 5*. Washington, D. C.: Small Business Administration, Government Printing Office, 1963, pp. 1-8.

Dean, Joel. "How to Price a New Product." *Management Aids for Small Business, Annual No. 3*. Washington, D. C.: Small Business Administration, Government Printing Office, 1957, pp. 9-16.

Dudley, Harold M. "How Independent Laboratories Help Small Business." *Management Aids for Small Business, Annual No. 3*. Washington, D. C.: Small Business Administration, Government Printing Office, 1957, pp. 67-74.

Editors of Fortune. *Markets of the Seventies; the Unwinding U. S. Economy*. New York: Viking Press, 1968.

Feuer, Mortimer. *Handbook for Corporate Directors*. Englewood Cliffs, New Jersey: Prentice-Hall, Inc., 1965.

Flanagan, James. "Census Information for Your Business." *Small Marketers Aids, Annual No. 7*. Washington, D. C.: Small Business Administration, Government Printing Office, 1965, pp. 88-95.

Gordon, William C., Jr. "Selecting Marketing Research Services." *Management Aids for Small Manufacturers, Annual No. 9*. Washington, D. C.: Small Business Administration, Government Printing Office, 1963, pp. 69-82.

Greene, Mark R. *Insurance and Risk Management for Small Business*. Small Business Management Series, No. 30. Washington, D. C.: Small Business Administration, Government Printing Office, 1963.

Halcomb, James. *Pert-O-Graph/PERT CPM Kit* (contains Project Manager's PERT/CPM Handbook and Pert-O-Graph II). Sunnyvale, California: Halcomb Associates, 1966.

Hilton, Peter. *New Product Introduction for Small Business Owners*. Small Business Management Series, No. 17. Washington, D. C.: Small Business Administration, Government Printing Office, 1961.

Hobson, Leland S. "The Management Side of Small-Plant R & D." *Management Aids for Small Manufacturers, Annual No. 9*. Washington, D. C.: Small Business Administration, Government Printing Office, 1963, pp. 53-60.

Hummel, Francis E. "Making a Marketing Survey." *Management Aids for Small Business, Annual No. 4*. Washington, D. C.: Small Business Administration, Government Printing Office, 1958, pp. 21-29.

Institute of Life Insurance, N. Y. "Business Life Insurance." *Management Aids for Small Manufacturers, Annual No. 11*. Washington, D. C.: Small Business Administration, Government Printing Office, 1965, pp. 68-73.

Institute of Life Insurance, N. Y. "Sole Proprietorship Life Insurance." *Management Aids for Small Manufacturers, Annual No. 11*. Washington, D. C.: Small Business Administration, Government Printing Office, 1965, pp. 74-77.

Institute of Life Insurance, N. Y. "Partnership Life Insurance." *Management Aids for Small Manufacturers, Annual No. 11*. Washington, D.C.: Small Business Administration, Government Printing Office, 1965, pp. 78-81.

Institute of Life Insurance, N. Y. "Corporation Life Insurance." *Management Aids for Small Manufacturers, Annual No. 11*. Washington, D. C.: Small Business Administration, Government Printing Office, 1965, pp. 82-86.

Kelley, Pearce C., and Lawyer, Kenneth. *How to Organize and Operate a Small Business*, 3d ed. Englewood Cliffs, New Jersey: Prentice-Hall., 1961.

Lewis, Edwin H. "How To Set Up Sales Territories." *Management Aids for Small Business, Annual No. 3*. Washington, D. C.: Small Business Administration, Government Printing Office, 1957, pp. 16-23.

Mace, Myles L. *The Board of Directors in Small Corporations*. Cambridge, Massachusetts: Harvard University Printing Office, 1948.

Mayne, David R. "Specialized Help for Small Business." *Small Marketers Aids, Annual No. 7*. Washington, D. C.: Small Business Administration, Government Printing Office, 1965, pp. 80-87.

McDonald, John. *Strategy in Poker, Business and War*. The Norton Library. New York: W. W. Norton & Company, Inc., 1963.

Metzger, B. L. "Will Profit Sharing Help Your Firm?" *Management Aids for Small Manufacturers, Annual No. 12*. Washington, D.C.: Small Business Administration, Government Printing Office, 1966, pp. 70-78.

The National Observer. *The Seventies: A Look Ahead at the New Decade*. Dow Jones Books. Princeton, New Jersey: Dow Jones & Company, Inc., 1970.

Overmyer, Wayne S. "Picking an Auditor for Your Firm." *Small Marketers Aids, Annual No. 4*. Washington, D. C.: Small Business Administration, Government Printing Office, 1962, pp. 69-76.

Reiter, Edward F. "How to Choose Your Banker Wisely." *Management Aids for Small Business, Annual No. 2*. Washington, D. C.: Small Business Administration, Government Printing Office, Rev. 1958, pp. 69-75.

Research Department, Association of Casualty and Surety Companies. "Business Insurance—I." *Management Aids for Small Business, Annual No. 1*. Washington, D. C.: Small Business Administration, Government Printing Office, Rev. 1958, pp. 62-69.

Research Department, Association of Casualty and Surety Companies. "Business Insurance—II." *Management Aids for Small Business, Annual No. 1*. Washington, D. C.: Small Business Administration, Government Printing Office, Rev. 1958, pp. 70-76.

Research Department, Association of Casualty and Surety Companies. "Business Insurance—III." *Management Aids for Small Business, Annual No. 1*. Washington, D. C.: Small Business Administration, Government Printing Office, Rev. 1958, pp. 76-81.

Research Department, Association of Casualty and Surety Companies. "Business Insurance—IV." *Management Aids for Small Business, Annual No. 1*. Washington, D. C.: Small Business Administration, Government Printing Office, Rev. 1958, pp. 81-86.

Richardson, C. T. "How Directors Strengthen Small Firms." *Management Aids for Small Manufacturers, Annual No. 6.* Washington, D. C.: Small Business Administration, Government Printing Office, 1960, pp. 46-52.

Soper, Goodreau, and Kelly, Linus A. "Research and Development Opportunities with the Federal Government." *Management Aids for Small Manufacturers, Annual No. 6.* Washington, D. C.: Small Business Administration, Government Printing Office, 1960, pp. 1-8.

Special Task Force on Industry Education of the American Marketing Association. "How Marketing Research Helps Small Business." *Management Aids for Small Business, Annual No. 3.* Washington, D. C.: Small Business Administration, Government Printing Office, 1957, pp. 53-60.

Spinney, W. R. *Estate Planning,* 13th ed. Chicago: Commerce Clearing House, 1966.

Staff of the Wall Street Journal. *Here Comes Tomorrow! Living and Working in the Year 2000.* Dow Jones Books. Princeton, New Jersey: Dow Jones & Company, Inc., 1967.

Staff of the Wall Street Journal. *The Innovators; How Today's Inventors Shape Your Life Tomorrow.* Dow Jones Books. Princeton, New Jersey: Dow Jones & Company, Inc., 1968.

Toffler, Alvin. *Future Shock.* New York: Random House, 1970.

Voorhees, Theodore. "Selecting a Lawyer for Your Business." *Management Aids for Small Manufacturers, Annual No. 8.* Washington, D. C.: Small Business Administration, Government Printing Office, 1962, pp. 66-73.

Witschey, Robert E. *Public Accounting Services for Small Manufacturers.* Small Business Management Series, No. 5. Washington, D. C.: Small Business Administration, Government Printing Office, 1954.

Chapter 13

Appendix to the Formal
Business Plan

While the bulk of the formal business plan should suffice to enlist the interest and enthusiasm of the investor and provide the entrepreneur with an opportunity to place all of his thoughts regarding the business concept together on paper, the Appendix to the formal business plan should include a substantial part of the basic documentation necessary to support information presented in the main body of the proposal.

SALES FORECAST

The most basic financial document in the entire business plan should be a conservatively prepared sales forecast. From the standpoint of presentation of the information, it may be displayed in either graph, chart, or tabular form.

It is reasonable to expect that the founders will be able to project with some accuracy the sales they anticipate during the early months of company operation; estimation of sales several years into the future will obviously have to be based on more speculative assumptions.

One of the least imaginative sales presentations or sales forecasts is represented by a simple "straight-line" sales growth pattern. It is preferable, however, to indicate sales figures on a monthly basis for the first quarter of company operation, on a quarterly basis for the next seven to eleven quarters, and semi-annually or annually for two years beyond that point. Where possible, specific customers should be identified in the sales forecast. Particularly desirable would be the inclusion of firm customer orders or letters of intent from key future customers indicating their willingness to buy the company's products, along with some estimate of what dollar volume this would represent. Otherwise, or in addition to this, a list of the names of potential customers should be provided to support the sales forecast.

Also to be included with this information is any other material drawn from market research that describes the total market available in the industry to be served. Such a description places the founders in a position to offer data on their anticipated market share. This is not, however, the place for excessive optimism. For example, a projection of a market position equivalent to between 5 and 10 percent of the total available market for a period of four or five years should appear perfectly creditable to a potential investor. However, when the founders of a new company assert that they expect to enjoy well over 50 percent of their available market in such a short period of time, the investor may laugh and toss the business plan into the wastebasket.

To repeat: the sales forecast is one of the most important documents in the entire business plan. It is the basis for all financial projections. In its preparation, the founders must compromise between the optimism necessary to insure an aggressive assault on the marketplace and the sensible projection that will interest the investor.

PRO FORMA FINANCIAL STATEMENTS

Translated literally from the Latin, *pro forma* means "as a matter of form." However, in the context of contemporary accounting practice, the words pro forma indicate that the information presented is a representation of how things *might* be during some future period covered in a document. Therefore, a pro forma financial statement, for example, is a financial statement that represents projections into the future of current assumptions and information. The information for the pro forma financial statements should always be presented in tabular form. Commonly, this information is placed on spread sheets, which are forms designed especially for the presentation of financial information. Your local business stationer should be able to provide you with a supply of these forms.

To assist individuals in the preparation of pro forma financial statements, an organization called the Robert Morris Associates, which is the national association of bank loan and credit officers, publishes special work sheets called "Projection of

Financial Statements" (Form C-117), which may normally be obtained free of charge through the offices of any first-rate banking organization. An extremely valuable aid in the preparation of these forms is a reprint of the article "Projection of Financial Statements—and the Preparatory Use of Work Sheet Schedules for Budgets" by Chester G. Zimmerman, reprinted from the 1961 issue of the *RMA Bulletin* (now *The Journal of Commercial Bank Lending*), published by Robert Morris Associates. Copies may be obtained at nominal charge by writing to the National Association of Bank Loan and Credit Officers, 1432 Philadelphia National Bank Building, Philadelphia, Pennsylvania 19107.

It is recognized that this section on pro forma financial statements is far from detailed. However, the subject of preparing financial statements is beyond the scope of this book; it is my intention here simply to describe these statements and indicate why they must be included in the business plan. Mention of several elementary texts is made at the end of this chapter under the heading "Recommended Reading." It is advisable, however, for the founders to acquire the services of an accountant to assist with the preparation of the financial materials.

Cash Flow Statement

The cash flow statement is fundamentally a presentation of two types of information: the sources of company funds and an indication of the uses to which these funds are put. Typically, sources of funds include equity money received from the sale of stock, from founder investments, from sales, and from loans. Under the heading "Uses" should be included information regarding purchase or rental of capital equipment, salaries, provision for taxes, cost of materials, etc. The cash flow statement should, in other words, provide the reviewer with a quick picture of the company liquidity. To determine in advance how stable a picture your pro forma cash flow statement presents of your proposed company, it is recommended that you consult books on ratio analysis and also information made available through Dun and Bradstreet on various operating ratios in different industries. It is desirable that your cash flow statement exude a rosy glow of financial health and demonstrate that the new company will always have a comfortable "cushion," or cash reserve, available in the event of unforeseen difficulties.

One of the basic problems with any new company is that a substantial amount of the operating capital may be tied up in inventory or in accounts receivable (orders shipped but not yet paid for by the customer). The young company might be quite profitable; but, if it does not have enough money in the bank account to pay its own accounts payable when they are due, it is in financial difficulty no matter how great the assets represented by inventory and accounts receivable. A supplier cannot be expected to wait indefinitely for payment from you for goods you have disposed of in one way or another. Your supplier does not wish to become the creditor for your customers. He is *your* creditor, and it is *your* responsibility to see that he is paid. You agreed upon certain terms and conditions when you made your original purchases from him, and it is unreasonable to expect a supplier to "hold the bag" until you collect from your customers. Thus, it is important for a new company to insure that it has sufficient *working capital* to bridge the gap between a supplier demanding payment now and a customer insisting upon paying later.

Profit-and-Loss Statement (also called the Income Statement)

Of fundamental importance to anyone involved in business is company profitability. A company that operates for a sustained period of time without realizing a profit is certainly doomed to eventual financial failure; profits are essential to long-term corporate survival. The profit-and-loss statement provides the reader with an indication of the financial performance of the business for the period of time covered in the report. For example, if a quarterly breakdown of profit and loss is provided for the first two years, the statement will indicate the profit (or loss) the company earned in each quarter.

An investor will be particularly concerned about how long after company start-up it will be before the enterprise shows a profit. It would be a gross understatement to say that a company with a sustained record of losses and no periods of profitability is financially unattractive. However, once a company starts realizing profits, its attractiveness to new investors is considerably enhanced.

In this context, the concept of "turn-around" (the point at which the company stops losing money and begins earning money) is of considerable importance. "Turn-around" is the time in the future when the company may look attractive to new investors. The value of the company may subsequently be established by applying the prevailing industry price-to-earnings multiplier to the earnings reflected in the profit-and-loss statement after "turn-around." Thus, the original financial backers may be afforded an opportunity to sell out their interest and realize a substantial capital gain—their reason for investing in the first place!

Balance Sheet

The balance sheet provides a running summary of the assets and liabilities of a business as of each date specified in the statement. An investor may ascertain the net worth of the company by subtracting the liabilities from the company assets. Evaluation of the periodic entries in the balance sheet will enable the investor to visualize the growth of his investment as the company develops and matures.

PROJECTED STAFF AND PLANT REQUIREMENTS

Head Count

A tabulated presentation indicating the total number of employees the company will have during the first five years of operation should be prepared. The time period represented in such a tabulation should correspond to the breakdown provided in the pro forma financial statements. The presentation should include a head count on the number of employees in each specialized category within the corporation—for example, managers, engineers, secretaries, machinists, and salesmen.

Floor Space

As it grows, the new company will need more and more floor space. This section of the business plan should demonstrate that management recognizes the additional demands that business growth will put upon company facilities.

Leasehold Improvements

In most instances, a new or growing business finds that it is necessary to make modifications to the buildings it occupies in order to tailor these facilities to its own specialized requirements. For example, it may be necessary to install additional electrical outlets, walls for offices, modified lighting, and air-conditioning. The business plan should offer some discussion of these needs and an estimate of the cost involved in providing for them.

Major Capital Equipment

As the company grows, it will be necessary to acquire additional capital equipment. The decision to purchase this equipment or to lease it should be discussed in this section of the business proposal, along with the primary factors considered in reaching the decision. Mention should be made of the cost of the equipment, and these expenses obviously should be included in the pro forma financial statements.

LEGAL STRUCTURE OF THE COMPANY

The three most common legal structures for a business are the sole proprietorship, the partnership, and the corporation. The differences among these three basic legal structures involve the personal financial risk to which the participants are vulnerable, the requirements of federal, state, and local tax regulations, and those arrangements necessary to make investment in the enterprise attractive to investors who may not necessarily wish to participate in the day-to-day operation of the business. The basic legal structures are compared below. Obviously, the information presented here is merely intended to serve as an introduction to the subject, and the importance of the retention of qualified legal counsel cannot be overemphasized!

Sole Proprietorship

Approximately 70 percent of the more than 5 million businesses in the United States today are of the legal structure known as a sole proprietorship. In the case of a sole proprietorship, all net income of the enterprise is taxable as the proprietor's personal income. The proprietor maintains individual and personal liability for all financial and legal obligations of the enterprise; and, under most circumstances, the only source of outside financing available to the enterprise is in the form of loans. No one other than the proprietor participates in a distribution of the net income of a business organized under this legal structure.

Partnership

In the case of a partnership, the key individuals in the organizational structure fall into either of two categories: the general partners (there must be at least one) and the limited partners. The general partners typically are responsible for the day-to-day operation of the enterprise, whereas the limited partners exercise no control whatever over routine operations. The general partners must carry the burden of the financial liabilities of the entire enterprise and the personal financial liability of each general partner is virtually unlimited in regard to the business. Furthermore, the general partners are, individually and jointly, completely liable for the financial obligations incurred in the name of the partnership by *any one* of the general partners.

From a fund-raising standpoint, the partnership may wish to recruit limited partners who typically will invest money, land, buildings, patents, etc. (anything except services) in exchange for the right to enjoy a share of whatever profits and/or assets may be generated by the enterprise. Because they do not participate in the management of the partnership, limited partners are sometimes referred to as "silent" partners. Unlike the situation with the general partners, the liability of the limited partners *is* limited—to the amount of their investment. The extent to which the general and limited partners participate in the distribution of the net profits and assets of the partnership are ordinarily specified in the Limited Partnership Agreement, a formal document ordinarily drawn up by the attorney who represents the organization. From a tax standpoint, any income the partnership enjoys is taxable to the individual partners, both general and limited, on a pro-rata basis established in accordance with the partnership agreement and is taxable as ordinary income to each of the designees *whether or not these profits are distributed to the partners.*

Corporation

A corporation is a legal entity separate and distinct from its stockholders, officers, and employees. The corporate legal structure affords the stockholders and officers the greatest possible legal protection against financial vulnerability. In the event the corporation is unable to meet its expenses and its assets are less than its liabilities, bankruptcy may be forced upon the corporate entity without exposing the stockholders and officers to any personal financial liability beyond their investment in the stock of the enterprise.

Depending on the tax bracket in which the corporate stockholder finds himself, he may enjoy significant tax advantages through participation in a corporation rather than participation in a partnership.

From the standpoint of attracting additional financing, the legal structure of the corporation is typically the most attractive of the three discussed herein. The vehicle of stock distribution provides the corporate entity with an opportunity to obtain well-dispersed ownership in the company. Most of the major business entities in this country are organized as stock corporations.

In the event additional financing is required by the corporate entity, such financing may be secured by issuing additional shares of stock. A more detailed analysis of stock offerings will be presented in Section Three below.

In summary, the three most common legal structures for a business enterprise are the sole proprietorship, the partnership, and the corporation; this sequence represents increasing financial and legal complexity. In general, the personal liability of an individual who is both an investor and a participant in the day-to-day operation of a business enterprise is greatest for the sole proprietor and least for the stockholder-officer of a stock corporation.

The type of organizational structure most suitable for a given business entity is in no small way influenced by the financial and other circumstances of the primary participants. Therefore, the services of competent legal counsel should always be retained to provide for a knowledgeable analysis of all the appropriate factors.

FOUNDERS' RESUMES

In the Appendix of the business plan, complete dossiers on the founders, including every vital piece of information in each individual's background, should be presented. A minimum presentation would involve the name of the individual; his address; his birthdate or age; his marital status; his number of children; his place of birth; his formal educational history, including special course work completed; any society memberships; any special honors and awards he has received; any patents that have been awarded him; his national security clearance (where appropriate); and his full employment history, including major career accomplishments and a reverse chronological exposition of all employment. Of course, the length of the employment history in relation to the rest of the business plan should be short; but, for completeness, it must be thorough.

When preparing these resumes, remember that the founders are attempting to persuade the reader that they have particular capabilities that will enable them effectively to function in the positions of responsibility outlined in the business plan. Therefore, it would seem only reasonable that the material in the resumes must be presented in a manner that effectively persuades—that is, in a manner that emphasizes the factors important to the proposed enterprise and minimizes the factors that are only peripherally related to it.

"TO WHOM IT MAY CONCERN:"

In this section of the business plan, the founders should include letters from various references regarding the technical and managerial competence, character, and integrity of each member of the new team.

Such letters may be obtained from former colleagues, managers, members of the banking and financial community, the clergy, etc. In seeking these testimonials, the entrepreneur should make a careful evaluation as to the suitability of each reference source and the appropriateness of each letter as a means of enhancing the image the team wishes to project.

KEY ARTICLES BY MEMBERS OF THE FOUNDING STAFF

If members of the founding staff of the new enterprise have written or published technical, financial, or management articles in fields related to the activities of the new enterprise and if these articles would serve to enhance the author's image in the mind of the reader, include them. In those instances where a founder has been so prolific that inclusion of all of his articles or publications would prove to be unwieldy, use only the most representative writings.

FOUNDERS' PERSONAL FINANCIAL STATEMENTS

Before any knowledgeable investor will commit substantial funds to a new enterprise, he will want—and is entitled—to know the financial condition of the individuals whose plans he is being asked to back. Blank forms for the presentation of such personal financial data may usually be obtained free of charge from the credit department or loan department of your local bank.

FOUNDERS' COMPENSATION

When the time comes for the founders to prepare this part of the business plan, one may truly say that they confront the moment of truth. When venture capitalists get together for tall drinks and taller stories, they often share their own accounts of the "young hustler syndrome," wherein an entrepreneur walks into their offices seeking $1 million with which to start his new business and a salary that is twice that which he currently earns. Soon this guy is confronted by reality for, in most instances, an entrepreneur who is serious about his new business must be prepared to accept a fairly significant *reduction* in income. Usually the salary a founder draws from his enterprise during its early stages of operation will range from no salary at all up to a salary merely sufficient to meet the minimum normal operating expenses of his family. Obviously, if the founder invests all of his liquid assets and goes into personal debt in order to contribute to the capitalization of the enterprise, he will have to draw a higher salary than the founder who has made a minimal personal investment in the business and can afford to maintain himself and his family with previously accumulated savings or other resources.

A company founder may derive compensation from the enterprise in several ways. He may draw a salary, take compensation in the form of stock, or, in the case of a partnership or a proprietorship, participate in the appreciation of the value of the enterprise due to the accumulation of profits retained in the business. The following discussion is intended to cover the primary topics related to founder compensation within a new enterprise:

Tax Aspects

Since the establishment of a new business is frequently intended to provide the founders with substantial long-term financial rewards, it is wise to consider tax planning at the outset of the operation. It is at this point in time that the company founders should seek the advice and services of tax accountants, tax attorneys, insurance agents, tax consultants, and anyone else who can assist with tax problems.

Salaries

As was discussed earlier, the founders of a new business must be prepared to draw salaries substantially lower than those they might have enjoyed with a former employer in a much-less-risky job situation; but the higher, safer salary was also one that offered much less long-term potential. One of the important considerations in the financing of a new company is the expectation that monies invested will appreciate substantially within a period of three to five years. Thus, it would seem reasonable that the founders would avoid drawing out substantial amounts of capital when, by leaving the capital in the company coffers, they can enjoy through their ownership a substantial appreciation in the value of the company.

In addition, one of the very significant factors any potential investor will consider when he is approached for additional financing is the amount of income the founders have withdrawn from the business in preceding years or, alternatively, the amount of money the founders anticipate drawing from the company in the form of salaries in the future. If the founders demand substantial salaries from the outset of the new business, an investor may reasonably conclude that their psychological commitment to the enterprise is probably less than it should be. The likelihood of securing new financing when the founders are not prepared to satisfy themselves with modest salaries is small indeed.

Equity Formula

A stock company is financially attractive primarily because of the prospect of substantial capital gains in the value of the stock. Accordingly, the founders are concerned about:

Control of the Enterprise

In most instances, the entrepreneur who starts a company does so because he desires to exercise substantial control over his own business career.

Substantial Capital Appreciation

Through the successful development of a corporation from start-up to cash-out (the time when much or all of the founders' stock holdings are converted into cash by sale to a private investor, public offering, merger, or acquisition), the entrepreneur hopes to create a substantial personal estate. Not surprisingly, the objectives of the investment community are quite similar. They also wish to enjoy substantial capital appreciation and to build a substantial personal estate. Furthermore, it is not uncommon for an investor to wish to exercise sufficient control in the operation of a new enterprise to guarantee the safety of his investment. Thus, it can be seen that equity participation represents the two primary areas for negotiation between the founders and the financial backers—financial gain and the control of the enterprise. Realize, in addition, that, in any typical financing, neither the financiers nor the founders will be entirely satisfied with the final arrangement. The following discussion will treat some of the considerations in the determination of an equity formula.

The founders must recognize that in all cases it is better to have 30 percent of the future General Motors or International Business Machines than to secure 100 percent of a financially static business entity that has had its growth permanently stunted due to a deficiency of expansion capital and its profits limited due to a lack of the capital assets necessary to achieve a viable business volume.

When the founder attempts to determine how much equity he is willing to exchange for invested capital, he should recognize that it is possible to surrender the majority of the outstanding stock to an investor without surrendering voting control of the company. Voting control can be maintained by issuing nonvoting shares to the investors, thus giving them a status similar to that of the limited partners discussed earlier in this chapter under the heading "Legal Structure of the Company."

In almost every instance, the final arrangements necessary to bring about the capitalization of a new enterprise are *negotiated* between the founders and the financial backers. Therefore, in this section of the business proposal, the founders should simply indicate their position regarding whether or not they intend to demand majority ownership of the outstanding stock and/or voting control of the new enterprise. Stating their position at this point may save considerable negotiating time later; for many financiers will not *consider* investing in a new enterprise unless they can exercise control *and* enjoy majority ownership of the stock.

Finally, the entrepreneur should recognize that there are tens of thousands of different financing arrangements that may be suitable for financing a new enterprise. These arrangements are almost always worked out between the founders and members of the financial community; on large deals, legal counsel frequently participates.

Since the subject of corporate finance is admittedly quite complex, the entrepreneur would do well to acquaint himself with some of the highly specialized terms in the financial jargon. An excellent glossary, "Understanding the Modern Securities Market," may be obtained by writing to the Commodity Research Publications Corporation, 140 Broadway, New York, New York 10005. The cost of this publication is a mere 50 cents, postpaid.

A Standard and Poors, publication, "How to Invest," containing a more abbreviated glossary of financial terms, is available on a complimentary basis by writing to Standard and Poors Corporation, 345 Hudson Street, New York, New York 10014.

SUPPORTING DOCUMENTATION

Formally prepared materials from sources outside the founding staff should be included in this section.

Market Surveys and Reports

If the founders have arranged for a market survey to be prepared by an independent agency, it should be included in the business plan under this heading in the Appendix. Additionally, if marketing analysis surveys and reports have been purchased from agencies that regularly provide such services to the industry, they should also be included in the business plan in this section of the Appendix.

Newspaper and Magazine Articles

Any recently published articles that relate to future prospects for the industry in which the proposed company wishes to participate will enhance and support the authenticity of material presented elsewhere in the business plan; therefore, they should be included in this section.

Credit Reports and/or Annual Reports on Competitors

Where possible, financial data that reflects the economic condition of the major competitors in the proposed industry should be presented. If information is available on similar companies that are only one or two years old, include it also for the purpose of affording the reviewer of the business plan an opportunity to scrutinize the economic condition of a company that has recently preceded the proposed enterprise into the marketplace. Credit reports may be obtained by subscribing to the services of some of the leading national credit information agencies, such as Dun and Bradstreet. An alternative source of credit information would be the annual reports (where available) of your competitors.

Recommended Reading

Anthony, Edward L. "Choosing the Legal Structure for Your Firm." *Management Aids for Small Manufacturers, Annual No. 5*. Washington, D.C.: Small Business Administration, Government Printing Office, 1959, pp. 9-15.

Bank of America National Trust & Savings Association. "Understanding Financial Statements." *Small Business Reporter*, Vol. 7, No. 11, 1969.

Bean, Louis H. *The Art of Forecasting*. New York: Random House, 1969.

Commerce Clearing House. *Tax Choices in Organizing a Business*. New York: Commerce Clearing House, Inc., 1969.

"Common Sale & Payment Terms." *Small Marketers Aids, Annual No. 6*. Washington, D.C.: Small Business Administration, Government Printing Office, 1964, pp. 17-25.

Cox, Alfred A., and Meador, Rowe M. "Pricing Your Services for Profit." *Small Marketers Aids, Annual No. 8*. Washington, D.C.: Small Business Administration, Government Printing Office, 1966, pp. 43-48.

Fagerberg, Dixon, Jr. "Basic Accounting for Small Partnerships." *Small Marketers Aids, Annual No. 3*. Washington, D.C.: Small Business Administration, Government Printing Office, 1961, pp. 34-41.

Feller, Jack H., Jr. "Is Your Cash Supply Adequate?" *Management Aids for Small Manufacturers, Annual No. 13*. Washington, D.C.: Small Business Administration, Government Printing Office, 1967, pp. 74-82.

Fishe, Syman P. "Executive Incentive in Small Business." *Management Aids for Small Manufacturers, Annual No. 5*. Washington, D.C.: Small Business Administration, Government Printing Office, 1959, pp. 22-31.

Fleck, J. S. "Figuring and Using Break-Even Points." *Management Aids for Small Business, Annual No. 2*. Washington, D.C.: Small Business Administration, Government Printing Office, Rev. 1958, pp. 49-56.

Geraci, Joseph J. "Financial Planning in Closely Held Businesses." *Mangement Aids for Small Manufacturers, Annual No. 12*. Washington, D.C.: Small Business Administration, Government Printing Office, 1966, pp. 79-85.

Gould, G. H. B., and Coddington, Dean C. "How Do You Know What Your Business is Worth?" *Management Aids for Small Manufacturers, Annual No. 13*. Washington, D.C.: Small Business Administration, Government Printing Office, 1964, pp. 1-8.

Immer, John R. *Profitable Small Plant Layout*. Small Business Management Series, No. 21 (2nd ed.). Washington, D.C.: Small Business Administration, Government Printing Office, 1964.

Merrill, Lynch, Pierce, Fenner, & Smith, Inc. *How to Read a Financial Report*, rev. ed. Merrill, Lynch, Pierce, Fenner, & Smith, Inc., 1970.

Myer, John N. *Accounting for Non-Accountants.* New York: Hawthorne Books, Inc., 1967.

Myer, John N. *Understanding Financial Statements: A Handbook for Executives, Investors, and Students.* A Mentor Executive Library Book. New York: The New American Library, Inc., 1968.

Office of the General Council, Small Business Administration. "Steps in Incorporating a Business." *Management Aids for Small Manufacturers, Annual No. 8.* Washington, D.C.: Small Business Administration, Government Printing Office, 1962, pp. 60-65.

Peterson, Robert L. "Incentive Techniques for Use in Small Businesses." *Management Aids for Small Business, Annual No. 1.* Washington, D.C.: Small Business Administration, Government Printing Office, Rev. 1958, pp. 157-163.

Pope, John B. "How Distributive Education Helps Small Business." *Small Marketers Aids, Annual No. 2.* Washington, D.C.: Small Business Administration, Government Printing Office, 1960, pp. 70-79.

Reiter, Edward F. "Planning Your Working Capital Requirements." *Management Aids for Small Manufacturers, Annual No. 4.* Washington, D.C.: Small Business Administration, Government Printing Office, 1958, pp. 29-37.

Robert Morris Associates, comp. *Sources of Composite Financial Data, a Bibliography*, 2d. ed. Philadelphia, Pa.: Robert Morris Associates, 1967.

Sanzo, Richard. *Ratio Analysis for Small Business.* Small Business Management Series, No. 20 (3d ed.). Washington, D.C.: Small Business Administration, Government Printing Office, 1970.

Schabacker, Joseph C. *Cash Planning in Small Manufacturing Companies.* Small Business Research Series, No. 1. Washington, D.C.: Small Business Administration, Government Printing Office, 1960.

Sommer, Howard Ellsworth. "Budgeting in the Small Plant." *Management Aids for Small Business, Annual No. 1.* Washington, D.C.: Small Business Administration, Government Printing Office, Rev. 1958, pp. 59-62.

Whyte, William Foote; Dalton, Melville; Roy, Donald; Sayles, Leonard; Collins, Orvis; Miller, Frank; Strauss, George; Fuerstenberg, Friedrich; Bavelas, Alex. *Money and Motivation: An Analysis of Incentives in Industry.* Harper Torchbooks. New York: Harper & Row, Publishers, Inc., 1970.

Zwick, Jack. *A Handbook of Small Business Finance.* Washington, D.C.: Small Business Administration, Government Printing Office, 1965.

Section
Three

Ali Baba and
the Forty
Money Sources

Chapter 14

Introduction to Money Sources

Small businessmen often forget that the position of preeminence enjoyed by this nation in the world of commerce is fundamentally due to our capitalistic system of economics. Through a process whereby public, private, and institutional *capital* sources provide industry with money in exchange for equity or interest, business as we know it is made possible. The material presented in this final section of the book is intended to show the entrepreneur how *he* may join the ranks of the rugged and colorful individualists we refer to as *capitalists*—the men responsible for building and sustaining our land. (*Note:* In this Section, I have chosen to define venture capital in very loose terms: Any monies, regardless of the source, that may be used for the purpose of financing a new or young enterprise.)

MONEY CONCEPTS

This material is intended to provide the reader with a review of basic economic concepts as they relate to the financing of enterprise.

Salt, Beads, and Grain

In primitive times, *barter* was man's only means of securing goods and services from others. The farmer would give so many measures of grain to the blacksmith in exchange for his services, thereby satisfying the farmer's need for blacksmithing services and the blacksmith's need for grain. The blacksmith similarly might offer his services in exchange for the weaver's cloth, again directly satisfying the needs of both individuals. Here, each individual is a seller *and* a buyer since he offers his own goods or services (selling) and receives in exchange (buying) the goods or services provided by another person. As commerce expanded, a more universally acceptable method of transacting business became necessary. Gradually, various *media of exchange*, or forms of *money*, came to be accepted as having a more or less standard value. Thus, the farmer could sell his grain to a grain merchant and receive some form of primitive "money," such as salt or beads, as payment. With this "money," he could *pay* the blacksmith to shoe his horse. The blacksmith could then buy cloth from the weaver with this same money. Now the blacksmith could obtain cloth from the weaver *even if the weaver did not need any blacksmithing services*! In turn, the weaver could hire a carpenter who might be unwilling to build him a house if the only medium of payment was cloth.

As the demands of commerce increased, the use of money and credit expanded enormously, making business as we know it possible. Commerce soon needed experts in the handling and utilization of money—the money changers Christ booted out of the temples were the forerunners of contemporary financial specialists. Today, money and its management constitute our single largest industry.

Supply and Demand

Regardless of the medium of exchange—whether it is salt, beads, grain, or some other commodity—its "value" in terms of what it will buy is subject to variation due to supply and demand. In an economically primitive society where wheat might serve as the medium of exchange, handmade pots hammered out of sheets of metal may have commanded a price of two bushels of wheat prior to the advent of metal stamping equipment. However, with the high volume and low unit labor content made possible through mechanization, similar pots might command a price of only a fraction of a bushel of wheat.

On the other hand, recognize that mechanization has evolved quite slowly through history while the quantity of wheat harvested in any given year is subject to very great fluctuations depending on the weather, parasite damage, or the acreage committed to the crop. Thus, when wheat is plentiful, it may take many more bushels to buy a pot than it would take if the wheat supply were limited. The *medium of exchange*, therefore, is sensitive to the law of supply and demand in a way quite similar to that of the articles and services it buys.

This law of supply and demand applies to money—dollars, for instance—also. Contrary to popular belief, the value of money changes dynamically in terms of what it will buy and the interest rate that must be paid in order to "rent" it. It is extremely difficult to find any commodity to which the value of any kind of money can be related over a long period of time. Thus, when money is in short supply and borrowing demand exceeds reserves available for loans, the cost of money is high. Conversely, when the supply of money is plentiful and loan availability exceeds borrower demands, the cost of money is low.

From the standpoint of the entrepreneur, the cost of money is reflected in the interest rate he must pay in order to borrow it. Similarly, the cost of money may be reflected by the price the common stock of many corporations is able to command. When market conditions result in low price-to-earnings ratios for securities traded on the stock exchanges, you may be certain that the value of shares of stock in small corporations *not* publicly traded will also be adversely affected. Accordingly, the amount of equity in his company that the founder must surrender in exchange for a given amount of capitalization is directly related to prevailing investor psychology as manifested in the level—and the rising or falling of the Dow Jones Industrial Average.

Summarizing, an entrepreneur raising funds with which to start a business during a bull market may have to relinquish a mere 30 or 40 per cent of the equity in his firm to raise *X* number of dollars. In a down or bear market, the same entrepreneur may have to relinquish 60 to 80 per cent of the equity in the same company for the same *X* number of dollars.

Debt Versus Equity Financing

In financing *any* business, it is important to understand the advantages and disadvantages of debt and equity capital.

Debt Capital

In its most common form, debt capital carries with it the obligation for a periodic payment of interest and a lump-sum payment of the principal at maturity. Alternatively, a mortgage-type arrangement may be agreed upon wherein regular fixed payments are made. Mortgage payments made early in the contract period will reflect a *greater* percentage allocated for interest charges than for the reduction of the loan principal. Toward the end of the contract, this same fixed payment will reflect a *smaller* allocation for interest payment than for retirement of the principal.

There are a number of disadvantages in the use of debt financing to meet the financial needs of a new enterprise. Typically, a new enterprise will weather a period of several months or even years before profits are realized. In the case of debt financing, interest and quite possibly payments to reduce the amount of the principal are required on a regular basis. A new enterprise can usually ill afford the cost of "servicing" a large amount of debt. Debt financing also represents a corporate liability, which adversely affects the appearance of financial solvency any company is interested in maintaining. On the plus side, interest payments represent a business expense and are, therefore, tax deductible. Furthermore, it is not necessary to surrender equity in exchange for ordinary debt.

Equity Capital

To secure equity capital, it is always necessary to give up a percentage of the ownership in the enterprise. Thus, the operations of the company become subject to the wishes of *all* of the owners, including those "outsiders" who supply equity capital. Depending on the emotional and financial needs of the founders and of the backers, equity financing may or may not be a desirable means of financing.

One of the major advantages of equity financing is that there is no requirement that monies so invested be repaid. Furthermore, in the eyes of suppliers, a company having a high stockholder equity should be financially sound, representing a good credit risk. And customers will think it unlikely that such a company will be unable to perform on any given contract because of a financial inability to assemble the necessary materials and resources.

Convertible Debt

In the money markets of today, it is becoming increasingly common for suppliers of debt capital to insist on equity "kickers" or "sweeteners" as part of a financial package. Thus, a supplier of debt capital may be able to recover his investment in the enterprise through foreclosure should the business encounter financial difficulty while he enjoys the option of converting his debt into stock in the enterprise should the company prosper and its stock increase in value.

Comparison Shopping

When contemplating the purchase of a house, an automobile, or any other expensive item, people usually attempt to evaluate as objectively as possible the value of their purchase relative to its cost. The same attitude should govern the selection of a money supplier. A thousand dollars borrowed from your Aunt Minnie may cost much less in terms of interest than a thousand dollars borrowed from your commercial banker, which in turn will cost less than a thousand dollars borrowed from the neighborhood hoodlum. Not only that, in the event you have difficulty repaying the debt when originally promised, your Aunt Minnie may be quite forgiving, your banker may drive you to bankruptcy, while the hoodlum may give you a one-way ticket to the morgue.

Just as a commercial banker may charge less for a loan than a finance company, one supplier of equity capital may be willing to pay a much higher price for stock in a new enterprise than another. Unfortunately, just as many people expend very little effort in shopping for loans for their personal needs, many entrepreneurs are equally remiss in their efforts to secure debt and equity financing at the most economical rate for their business. Don't *you* be guilty of this! Remember though, shop discreetly—as I have said before, many bankers and financiers like to feel that they are the only ones with whom you are negotiating.

ARE VENTURE CAPITALISTS *REALLY* THIEVES?

Contrary to the feelings expressed by many of the entrepreneurs with whom I have spoken, venture capitalists taken as a class are *not* thieves. However, one venture capitalist I know who is the president of a New England-based business development firm—and a self-appointed industry spokesman—offered this tongue-in-cheek definition at a recent seminar for entrepreneurs. In his words: "A venture capitalist is a greedy son-of-a-bitch."[21]   And I have had the misfortune of meeting several for whom his epithet is quite appropriate. However, I share with equal conviction the feeling that the vast majority of them are not! The most objective evaluation of the industry would suggest that the typical venture capitalist defies simple classification just as stubbornly as does the ideal woman. Bear in mind while reading what follows that generalizations regarding venture capitalists are expedient at best.

WHAT TO LOOK FOR IN A VENTURE CAPITAL PARTNER

In looking for venture capital partners, the entrepreneur must realize that the relationship he *should* seek to establish will be long term. The following discussion is intended to suggest a number of factors that the entrepreneur would do well to consider in evaluating a potential capital source.

Money

The most obvious test a venture capitalist must meet is whether or not he has funds available for investing in the proposed venture. I have personally had the unfortunate experience of spending several weeks in preliminary talks with a venture capitalist who, a short time later, went bankrupt because of an inadequate supply of working capital. In his desire to participate in every worthwhile proposal that came his way, he had stretched his own credit and that of his company beyond the breaking point. The price of his greed was not only his own bankruptcy but the creation of very serious economic difficulties for the several portfolio companies in whose financing he had participated.

There are some venture capitalists who syndicate private partnerships (see below) for the purpose of financing almost any good deal they may have the fortune to examine. In other words, they organize an investing partnership in which they are the general partner; the other investors participate as limited partners for the express purpose of providing capital for one enterprise. In such situations, the resources of the partnership are only as plentiful as the combined assets of the partners. When working with a venture capitalist such as this, the financing of the deal is fundamentally dependent on his ability to secure the bulk of the required capital from *other* investors.

More Money

The new company that is able to follow its business plan without needing more capital than the founders originally anticipated is the exception, not the rule. Not only do things typically cost more than anticipated, not only do a plethora of unexpected and unanticipated minor expenses manifest themselves until their sum represents a significant percentage of the initial capitalization, but also everything *invariably* takes longer to accomplish than the original schedules planned for. The development of a prototype, the creation of a manufacturing capability, and the penetration of a market consume time with a mystifyingly voracious appetite. Since we all know that time is money, the problem of schedule slippages soon manifests itself on the bottom line of the income statement, and the business is in trouble. If the individual or organization providing the initial capitalization has had extensive experience in working with new enterprises, this need for additional capital will come as no surprise, and provision will have been made for it. However, when dealing with less-sophisticated capital sources (the general public is probably the worst), the ability of the enterprise to secure a capital transfusion when the income statement is having a red-ink hemorrhage may be difficult indeed, if not impossible.

Realistically, however, it is unlikely that an entrepreneur with a high-risk/high-potential package will be successful in securing financing from a venture capital organization that has significant cash reserves. Significant cash reserves generally reflect a conservatism that rules out investment in all but the safest of business propositions. In most cases, this conservatism completely excludes start-up situations.

Availability of Managerial Assistance

One of the salient motivations of the entrepreneur is the desire to call the shots himself, to crack the whip in his own circus. However, the more mature entrepreneur will have an unusual awareness of his own shortcomings and will not be so proud as to refuse to seek assistance in any area of his business operation if and when he needs it. In Henry Ford, the unschooled industrial genius of yesterday, we have an excellent example. Ford gathered around himself a formidable staff of experts in fields as diverse as metallurgy and mass production methodology to compensate for his own shrewdly acknowledged educational deficiencies. Today, Harvard-University-educated Edwin H. Land, brilliant physicist, applied scientist, and inventor of the Polaroid camera, has attracted an enviable stable of astute businessmen who are expert in marketing, financial planning, patent protection, and other areas that are so essential to substantial business success. Obviously, the entrepreneur who has limited financial resources is not in a position to attract and retain such a staff at the outset. He may, however, through judicious selection of a venture capital partner, avail himself of a very substantial reservoir of talent for the purpose of complementing his own unique qualities.

Among the larger and more sophisticated venture capital firms, a staff of seasoned, "graduate" entrepreneurs—men who have met a payroll themselves—is available for the purpose of counseling the officers of the new enterprise on an "as-required" basis, provided the enterprise is successful in meeting or exceeding its orginally stated objectives. This group may provide nothing more than applause unless the founders request their assistance.

In such a situation, the potential for having too many cooks in a kitchen is obvious, and it must be carefully guarded against; similarly, the nonavailability of competent counsel when it is required can prove to be of grave consequence to the survival of the enterprise. The mature entrepreneur will make a sincere effort to determine the complementary nature of the skills and services his venture capital partner-to-be is in a position to provide.

Compatibility of Objectives

It is most important to ascertain whether or not the objectives of the investing parties are compatible with those of the founding team. If capital is provided through nonfinancial channels, such as customers, suppliers, etc., that are possibly motivated by the desire to create or groom an acquisition candidate, catastrophe is only a matter of time if it is the desire of the entrepreneurs (openly acknowledged or furtively concealed) to build a corporate monument for their personal, financial, and psychological aggrandizement. The pacifist entrepreneur who wishes to make fireworks for holiday celebrations will obviously find himself at loggerheads with an investor who wishes to make explosives for the upcoming Arab-Israeli war. The entrepreneur who is sold on the value of employee profit-sharing and stock-option plans will find himself at an impasse with an investor who desires income through dividends.

If more than one individual or capital-supplying firm participates in the syndication of the financial package, it is imperative that the investors' objectives be similar.

Whether these objectives have to do with determination of the geographic location of the firm or whether they have to do with the magnitide of the anticipated return on the investment, investors' objectives must be compatible in order to ensure a harmonious relationship between the financial backers and the company officers and to preclude the needless dissipation of the energies of the founders in the refereeing of boardroom pyrotechnics.

Investors Who Can Keep Their Cool

In his excellent book, *Starting and Succeeding in Your Own Small Business*, Louis L. Allen states:

> The nervous investor who packs up and runs at the sound of trouble is almost always content to take a loss of some kind in order to extricate himself.... The nervous investors are the losers in the venture capital game. They stay in it because they somehow have the idea that they can make their money work for them. They do not know that making the investment should be the first and easiest work they will undertake with their small business client.[22]

It is unfortunate that many investors, particularly those without significant experience in the funding of new enterprises, tend to be nervous about their investment and are prone to abandoning it *and* the unfortunate individuals whom they chose to back when they are most needed—just when financial recovery is imminent but when unprofitable operating history makes the enterprise unattractive to new investors unfamiliar with the extent of the problems the founders have *already* overcome. This abandonment may range all the way from a refusal to supply additional funds up to and including liquidation of the company assets at auction or forced sale. If the only financing that may be secured for the launching of an enterprise is from gutless, spineless, self-fancied money men such as these, the entrepreneurs would be best advised to delay the start of their business until a more propitious time when other sources of financing become available.

A wise investor who has the courage of his convictions and who is satisfied with the integrity, commitment, and business acumen of the company founders will fully appreciate the long-term financial rewards for sticking with *his* commitment as the founders strive to achieve profitability in the face of unexpected difficulties.

Confidence in Team and Concept

It is not enough to satisfy the investors that the proposed venture idea has significant market potential. The investors must also feel confident that the management team is able to achieve the originally proposed objectives. Investors who participate in the financing of a new enterprise just for the hell of it, to make a quick buck, or because they happen to have some spare cash lying around are not in a position to provide the encouragement and understanding the entrepreneurs will require as they weather the storms that batter their corporate vessel in its early years of operation. When the going is rough, an expression of confidence from your investors can provide enormous encouragement.

Reasonable Expectations Regarding Capital Appreciation

The investor who will only be happy if his money quadruples every year can be a real pain in the ass to a hard-working, highly motivated group of aggessive entrepreneurs; the investor who pisses and moans about the fact that he only tripled his money in two years when the original company plan intimated that he would quadruple it is a guy whom the founders can do without. I have personally heard a number of Wall Street gun-slingers explain to me that because of the tight money market and the competition for available capital they are not interested in looking at any deals that don't project at least quadrupling the original investment every year for the next five years. It is unrealistic expectations such as these that prompt unsuspecting novice entrepreneurs to prepare the wildly optimistic financial forecasts that cause them to be laughed out of the offices of the more conservative investors in the capital community.

Same Knowledge of the Market to be Served

The investor in the new enterprise should have more than a passing familiarity with the nature of the market the entrepreneurs intend to enter. Thus, if the company is not doing quite so well as expected but the market is doing better than expected, the investor can remain optimistic in regard to the future of the business because of the favorable market conditions. In the event the enterprise is not doing well due to serious market reversals, the investor is in a position to appreciate that the company's inability to realize its original projections is due not to operational deficiencies but to the vagaries of the marketplace, over which the company officers have no control.

TERMS OF THE DEAL

Depending on how many attorneys are involved, depending on the number of years the investor has participated in financing new enterprise, and depending on the sophistication of the entrepreneur, the written deal may take one to two pages or one to two *hundred* pages. You would be wise to acquaint yourself with such terms as notes, preferred stock, common stock, leases, convertible leases, warrants, options, debentures, subordinated debentures, hypothecation, and a bunch of other jawbreakers you will probably encounter in your negotiations with investors. Your library should have one or two glossaries of financial terms for reference.

Here are some of the considerations normally encountered in structuring the deal:

Risk-Reward Ratios

Whenever the subject of gambling odds comes up, a discussion of risk-reward ratio is inevitable. To provide a simple illustration of the concept, consider the game of roulette. On the American roulette wheel, there are 38 cups into which a little ball may fall. Thus, in the simplest case of one bet on one number, there is one chance of winning and 37 chances of losing out of 38 possible chances. This establishes the risk. In the event a player wins, he receives 35 times the amount of his bet. If he were to play the game long enough, his winnings would average out to $35 for every $38 played. Thus, the risk-reward ratio is slightly less than one. The amount by which this ratio differs from one represents the house winnings.

In the financing of new or unproven enterprises, many money suppliers evaluate investment opportunities in gambling terms. Risk is evaluated as objectively as possible in terms of market projections, capabilities of the founders, excellence and uniqueness of the proposed business concept, and the prevailing whims of the investing public. (For instance, companies in the pollution control field are hot issues today; in the previous decade, computer companies were the darlings of the market; and, much further back, railroads had their day on Wall Street.)

In addition to considering the risk *before* he becomes involved, an astute venture capitalist will endeavor to make expert assistance available to the enterprise to reduce the risk *after* he puts his money into the venture. In some instances, a venture capitalist may insist on majority ownership of the stock so that he may assert himself and impose his own management style upon the enterprise in the event he feels the operational techniques employed by the company officers are jeopardizing his investment.

In assessing the reward for taking the risk, the investor will determine the projected value of the company at some point in the future (typically 3 to 5 years) in terms of annual sales per share, profits per share, and the stock price-to-earnings ratio prevailing in the industrial sector served by the enterprise. For instance, most "growth" companies (firms experiencing rapid increases in sales volume and profitability, which make a practice of plowing back all of the earnings into the enterprise for the purpose of sustaining this growth at the expense of dividends to stockholders) are valued at large price-to-earnings multiples in the marketplace, offering investors very attractive vehicles for capital appreciation. By conservatively estimating the projected value of his holdings at some point in the not-too-distant future, an investor can determine the anticipated reward such an investment would offer. Naturally, investors are concerned with maximizing rewards and minimizing risks. Thus, they hope to gamble in a situation where the risk-reward ratio is considerably *greater* than one.

Regardless of the reward potential, the more conservative an investor is, the less willing he will be to invest in a high-risk proposition. A conservative investor is accustomed to a yield on his equity investment that is not substantially greater than a small multiple of the prevailing prime interest rates. On the other hand, the crap shooters in the business world may be willing to take on a proposition that has five times the maximum risk a more conservative investor would consider. However, these guys expect—even demand—a potential reward of *ten* or more times greater than the reward that will satisfy their more conservative colleagues. In other words, risk-takers accept the risk in exchange for rewards that are as close to being unlimited as possible.

Return on Investment

A concept invariably considered in evaluating the merits of financing a new enterprise is that of return on investment (ROI). It is remarkable how often members of the financial community make reference to ROI and subsequently fail to point out that it is meaningless unless it is considered in the context of risk. Thus, a venture capitalist who contends that he is not interested in participating in the financing of deals that offer an ROI of less than an annual doubling of his investment also means to convey the range of risk he is willing to take.

To give you an idea of the differences in expected ROI prevailing among different members of the financial community, I offer the following quotations for your consideration:

E. F. Heizer, Jr., Chairman and President, Heizer Corporation:

> You might wonder what our objectives are. First of all, in terms of that portion of our money invested in venture capital, we feel that we should earn year in and year out, to be doing our job at all, a 15 percent compound rate of return on our money. Our goal is actually 40 percent compounded on our money that is invested in venture capital. Overall as a corporation, we hope to earn 10 to 20 percent a year.[23]

Charles B. Smith, Associate, Rockefeller Family and Associates; Partner, Venrock Associates:

> Our goal like everybody else's is to make wads and wads of money for the family. If we like a situation, but have to change our criteria to fit, it goes something like four times [our investment] in three years and five times in four and so forth, based on a plausible set of projections, not the entrepreneur's but our own. It never happens but if that sort of gain is at least possible, perhaps you will have a chance of coming out across the board on your portfolio.[24]

Mark Rollinson, Vice President, Greater Washington Investors, Inc.:

> We are looking for a compound return on investment, somewhere between 25 and 30 percent. We don't care how we arrive at that, but we want to have a reasonable opportunity of achieving that sort of performance.[25]

G. Stanton Geary, President, Inverness Capital Group:

> In the venture capital business, the downside risks are very substantial, so the upside potential must be commensurate with this risk; i.e.—there must be an opportunity to make at least ten times the original investment in five to seven years.[26]

Benno C. Schmidt, Managing Partner, J. H. Whitney and Company:

> After balancing the homeruns against the strikeouts, a venture firm. . .should be able at least to double its money every four years. Not an easy goal. Few have achieved it.[27]

Earned Equity

In Section One, I tried to make the entrepreneur aware of the difficulties of building a business. The novice may have begun to think that the task of securing venture capital is the biggest obstacle he will ever have to surmount in starting and building a successful business. 'Taint so! Although imagination and ingenuity are necessary to persuade someone to invest in your enterprise, *building* a successful company separates the men from the boys.

At the many seminars I have attended on starting and financing a new business, I have never failed to hear the question posed from the floor: "How much equity may I retain when I am financed by a venture capitalist?" There is no simple formula. Not only does the answer depend on the entrepreneur and the venture capitalist reaching a satisfactory compromise, but also considerations such as founder salary, founder investment, founder investment *as a percentage of his personal net worth*, patents, copyrights, trademarks, prototypes, capital equipment and other "hard" assets provided by the founders, the business plan, size of the founding team, risk-reward ratio, return on investment, management assistance required, total financing required, competence and maturity of the founders, and many other subjective and objective considerations characteristic of each individual situation must be evaluated.

There is probably nothing wrong with the entrepreneur wanting all of the equity he can possibly get at the outset, particularly if the investors with whom he is working are unsophisticated. However, the more astute investor will require a deal wherein the founders initially own only a modest degree of equity, although they may be provided with the very great incentive of a sliding scale of equity ownership based on successful performance. For example, a founding team may start out owning a mere 20 or 30 percent of the company; if they are successful in building a viable enterprise, they may ultimately obtain significantly more than majority interest. The point I am trying to make is that, since starting a business is much easier than building a *successful* business, the astute investor will insist on a financing package that requires the entrepreneur to *earn* his equity. I feel that this is a fair and reasonable requirement.

"Getting Out"

In almost all cases, investors participating in the financing of new enterprise have as their major objective capital appreciation—in terms of bread, they want to make their dough rise. Investors specializing in the medium- to high-risk situations characteristic of financing new enterprise recognize that within a period of three to seven years the new business will begin to mature and will be unable to sustain the rapid early-years growth in the worth of its common stock. Thus, the investor will be interested in converting his equity to cash so that he may go on to invest in other new, promising, cash-hungry businesses or to retire to a life of mountain climbing or fishing.

There are two common techniques an investor may use to convert his holdings to cash. One is the process of taking the company public (possibly offering some new stock for sale as a means of securing additional capital for the business while at the same time offering most or all of the investor's stock for sale to the public so that he may "cash-out"). The second technique for cashing-out is to arrange to have the enterprise acquired by another firm. In many such instances, the investor may be paid off with common stock in the acquiring company. Usually this new stock is publicly traded and has a value that may be readily ascertained through a phone call to a stockbroker or by consulting the financial pages of the daily newspapers.

In rare instances, the company founders may find it possible to buy out the investors themselves, thus retaining 100 percent ownership of the company. I have a strong personal preference for seeing a deal so structured that the founders may buy out the investors at *any* time, in accordance with a schedule established when the financing was originally arranged. Many investors will balk at having a ceiling on their return. But there are damn few investors who are willing to put their money into a situation where they might suffer unlimited losses; therefore, I see no reason why those same investors should be afforded the opportunity for unlimited *gains*, particularly when the gains are made of the sweat and the ingenuity of the founders.

Recommended Reading

Branch of Small Issues, Division of Corporation, Finance, Securities and Exchange Commission. "How the Securities Act of 1933 Affects Small Business." *Management Aids for Small Manufacturers, Annual No. 4*. Washington, D. C.: Small Business Administration, Government Printing Office, 1958, pp. 8-14.

Mackay, Charles. *Extraordinary Popular Delusions and the Madness of Crowds*. New York: Noonday Press. L. C. Page & Company, Inc., 1932.

Price, William G. F. "Borrowing Money From Your Bank." *Management Aids for Small Business, Annual No. 2*. Washington, D. C.: Small Business Administration, Government Printing Office, Rev. 1958, pp. 75-82.

Senate Select Committee on Small Business and the House Select Committee on Small Business. *Handbook for Small Business; a Survey of Small Business Programs of the Federal Government*. Washington, D. C.: Government Printing Office, 1969.

Small Business Administration. "Helping the Banker Help You." *Management Aids for Small Manufacturers, Annual No. 8*. Washington, D. C.: Small Business Administration, Government Printing Office, 1962, pp. 41-46.

Chapter 15

Forty Money Sources

Mr. Ali Baba worked for the Automaton Personnel Agency, an executive-search firm catering to the nation's top 500 corporations. He had decided several months ago that his conscience could no longer bear the burden of his being a party to sending capable, qualified men into dull, dead-end careers with these faceless frustration factories. In spite of his high income, Al had decided to risk starting a nationwide network of personnel agencies of his own, using resident owner-managers who would cater to small companies, "where the action is." He had spent most of the summer working out a business plan and had just begun what looked like several months' work in reading about the many different sources of funding that might be appropriate for his business.

One weekend, feeling the need for a well-deserved rest, he decided to head for the mountains. Sunday afternoon he was riding his Honda down a remote trail near the end of a canyon when he noticed the faint outline of what looked like a huge door in the canyon wall. Recalling his nursery

205

tales, he decided to give the Arabian Nights' "Open Sesame" bit a try—after all, he was the namesake of the hero of that piece. Well, sure as Shinola, a loud rumbling was heard, the earth trembled, and a gaping hole appeared in the canyon wall where the outline of the door had been.

He scooted his bike inside, uttered the magic words once again, and the opening closed behind him. However, unlike the cave in the story, *this* cave appeared at first glance to be devoid of any treasure. Neither the glitter of gold nor the sparkle of precious gems was in evidence. However, as his eyes became accustomed to the dim light, he could make out a set of forty large tablets inscribed upon the cave walls. At first, he thought they might be some primitive art work. But as his vision cleared, he saw that he had found the key to the treasure he sought—financing for his business. Inscribed on the tablets was the following information—complete with footnotes.

CLOSED-END INVESTMENT COMPANIES

For our purposes, we define, an investment company as an organization, registered under the Investment Company Act of 1940, which

1. is engaged *primarily* in the business of investing, reinvesting, or trading in securities;
2. is engaged in the business of investing, reinvesting, owning, holding, or trading in securities *and* owns or proposes to acquire investment securities having a value exceeding 40 percent of the value of such issuer's total assets (exclusive of government securities and cash items).

Although there are others,[28] the two most common types of investment companies are the closed-end companies and the open-end companies, the latter being popularly known as mutual funds. (A discussion of mutual funds is offered in a separate section below.) The technical distinction between open-end and closed-end companies depends upon the redeemability of the company's shares. Those companies that stand ready to redeem shares whenever called upon to do so (generally at net asset value per share) are classified as *open-end*, and presently about 90 percent of all investment company assets are held by these open-end companies.

Those companies having a relatively fixed capitalization and a normally static number of shares outstanding are classified as *closed-end*. New shares in a closed-end company may, however, be created for the acquisition of additional equity capital or for the payment of capital gains distributions; and occasionally rights to purchase additional shares of stock may be issued to stockholders. Thus, closed-end companies do *not* stand ready to redeem outstanding shares. Instead, new buyers of closed-end shares usually must arrange to purchase them from existing stockholders.

Of the 14 *major* closed-end companies, 12 are listed on the New York Stock Exchange, one is listed on the Boston Stock Exchange, and the shares of the remaining company in this group are traded over the counter. Thus, the prices of closed-end investment company shares are subject to the regular supply-and-demand influences characteristic of any publicly traded stock.

For the most part, the portfolios of major closed-end companies are concentrated in equity-type, common-stock investments. Only in rare instances do they buy the securities of new or relatively young—and therefore unproven—businesses.

One group of closed-end investment companies does, however, make a specialty of providing venture capital for such companies, usually by taking equity in the form of common stock. Often this stock is not registered for public sale and thus cannot readily be liquidated. Arriving at a value-per-share figure for the securities of a young company is a highly subjective process which serves to magnify the risk of such an investment.

The largest closed-end investment company in the venture capital field is American Research and Development Corporation, located in Boston. General Doriot, President of ARD, is a French-born, naturalized American citizen. As explained in an article from *Innovation* magazine:

> Just after World War II he was asked by Senator Ralph E. Flanders of Vermont, then head of the Federal Reserve Bank of Boston, and by Karl T. Compton, president of MIT, and others, to head up an organization to help individuals start companies of their own. It was a period when individual entrepreneurial activity was barely coming to life again. The aim, when ARD was founded in 1946, was not to make money but to assist in the launching of new small enterprises, to keep some of the money that had been accumulating in strictly financial hands from pooling there.

> Despite predictions of failure by such men as Kettering of General Motors, ARD thrived. Over the ... years, it has sponsored nearly 100 companies (Digital Equipment Corporation being an outstanding one), has itself grown to a net worth of over $300 million, and disbursed $18 million to its stockholders. Under Doriot's direction, it continues to back a number of new and existing companies each year.[29]

In 1968, another type of closed-end company appeared on the scene—"Letter Stock Funds." These new investment companies, whose stocks are traded over the counter (Diebold Technology Venture Fund, Fund of Letters, SMC Investment Corporation, and Value Line Development Capital Corporation), had combined initial assets of $344 million. These funds were organized to provide an investment vehicle for individuals who would otherwise not have an opportunity to invest in new or small companies offering high growth potential. The primary strategy of these funds is to purchase "restricted securities," or "lettered stock," in these companies. In this context, a restricted security is one that cannot be sold publicly without registration under the Securities Act of 1933 because it has not previously been registered.

Such securities are acquired either directly from the issuer (known as a "private placement") or from an existing stockholder. Regardless of the source of the stock, the transaction is *privately* (not publicly!) negotiated, and the securities carry an accompanying "letter" contract stating that the stock is being purchased as a "long-term" investment and cannot be offered for resale within a specified period of time, a fact which gives rise to the term "letter stock." Until the original issuer registers the shares for public offering with the Securities and Exchange Commission (SEC), the shares may not be resold on other than a private basis (with the restrictions still attached). Because of federally imposed limitations, letter stock funds are not permitted to devote all of their assets to letter stock investments; they must apportion part of their resources to more readily liquidated securities.

Occasionally, a company, some of whose shares are already publicly traded, may wish to raise additional equity capital without going through the formalities and delays of an SEC registration of new securities. In such an instance, restricted—or letter—stock may be issued in a private placement, possibly with a letter stock fund. The unregistered (or restricted) securities are then sold at a discount below the price of those that are already SEC registered.

For a better understanding of the motivation of letter stock funds, consider this policy statement by the Fund of Letters:

> . . .the Fund views the availability of securities at a discount as an opportunity to invest, at lower prices, in companies in which it would wish to participate, even if the discount were not available. By purchasing Restricted Securities at a discount, the Fund is enabled to acquire large blocks of stock which might otherwise be difficult to obtain, as well as derive the benefit of an added margin of profit if the stock values increase, or a substantial built-in cushion if the market price of the stock declines.[30]

For those desiring additional information on the subject of closed-end investment companies, many libraries subscribe to the publication *Investment Companies*, offered by Arthur Wiesenberger Services. Further information on this publication may be found in Appendix 1.

COLLEGES, UNIVERSITIES, AND OTHER ENDOWED INSTITUTIONS

An endowment is money or property given to an institution such as a college, university, or hospital for the purpose of providing that institution with income. When an endowment takes the form of real estate, the endowed institution may derive income from the lease or rental of the land. (Ordinarily, sale of this land is precluded by the terms of the endowment.) In those instances where cash or securities constitute the endowment, income is derived from dividends and interest on the original portfolio and on new portfolio investments. In rare cases, these institutions might invest in a venture capital situation, but participation would probably be through a professionally managed partnership or some other investment organization of the sort discussed elsewhere in this chapter. *Direct* investment in the stock of a new enterprise is highly unlikely.

However, colleges and universities often own industrial parks, which provide rental income to the institution. (An industrial park is a tract of land developed exclusively for nonresidential and—usually—nonretail business use. Ordinarily, very high standards for building construction and grounds maintenance are observed and a concerted effort is made to insure that the industrial park will remain as attractive as possible.) An endowed institution *may* be of assistance to a new enterprise by providing it with buildings that are within an industrial park.

Also, many university and college professors are, as individuals, in a position to assist the founders of a new enterprise. This assistance may take the form of technical/business consulting or of simple investment in the enterprise. If the vehicle for a new business is to be a product developed as an offshoot of research activity conducted under the supervision of one of the university's professors, his interest in encouraging the success of this enterprise may be quite significant; and he may be more than willing to provide his consulting services in exchange for stock in the company.

In other instances, faculty members who are well acquainted with former students and who feel optimistic about their chances for business success may wish to participate in financing the new enterprise presided over by these former students. (In one of my own business ventures, I was successful in persuading two of my former professors to participate as investors. A third professor was of considerable help in persuading a businessman of his acquaintance to invest in this same venture.)

An event of unusual significance was recently reported in the *Stanford Engineering News*—the Mayfield Fund (a venture capital firm organized in 1969) has pledged a percentage of its capital gains as gifts to Stanford University. In return, a group of the Engineering School faculty will assist in evaluating the technical aspects of business proposals received from companies seeking venture capital. It is also anticipated that companies financed by the Mayfield Fund may enjoy the benefits of faculty consulting assistance at nominal cost since the University may—through participation in the capital gains of the Mayfield Fund—ultimately derive great benefit from the success of these firms.

COMMERCIAL BANKS

If one had to identify the department store or the supermarket of the financial community, he would acknowledge that the commercial bank is the undisputed holder of this unique position. A commercial bank offers the following financing services of interest to the entrepreneur:

Short-Term Loans

Short-term loans generally constitute credit that is extended for one year or less for the purpose of augmenting working capital. Loans may be used to take advantage of often significant trade discounts offered for prompt retirement of accounts payable, to permit a buildup of inventories in preparation for a seasonal increase in sales volume, to cover peak payroll demands, and to satisfy other temporary cash needs. Ordinarily, the funds with which to repay short-term loans are derived from the sale of the goods or services that originally precipitated the need for the loans. Short-term loans are typically unsecured, although the personal guarantee of the proprietors may be required. The bank officer considering the loan request will wish to satisfy himself that there is a high probability that the loan *will* be repayed. Therefore, the applicant should be prepared to give any information necessary to assure the loan officer that the financial health of the firm is excellent.[31]

Intermediate-Term Loans

An intermediate-term loan, or simply *term loan*, provides the small businessman with capital that typically is repaid over a period of from one to five years. The use of intermediate-term financing is an alternative to equity financing (sale of stock in the company) that many a small businessman prefers since he does not have to relinquish ownership in his firm in order to secure it. (See discussion of debt versus equity financing in Chapter 14.)

For example, an entrepreneur may wish to purchase a piece of machinery for the manufacture of salable goods. Since the working life of the machine may be substantially longer than the five-year loan period, there is a high probability that the loan will be self-liquidating over the loan period from the sale of goods manufactured through the use of the machine. This self-liquidating aspect is typical of many intermediate-term loans.

> Intermediate-term loans are also used to purchase existing businesses, to help establish new ones, to provide additional working capital, and to replace long-term indebtedness that may carry a higher rate of interest. They may be either secured or unsecured. Payment may be made monthly, quarterly, semiannually, or annually, often with small early payments and a large final payment called a balloon payment.[32]

Long-Term Loans

Apart from making real-estate loans, commercial banks ordinarily do not make a practice of providing long-term credit to the smaller business. However, your bank's loan officer should be in a position to assist you in securing a nonbank long-term loan in the event the circumstances involved justify such an approach to your financial problem. If nonbank long-term loans are arranged, the lender may require "sweeteners" or "kickers" in the form of options or rights to purchase equity in the company at a later date and at a predetermined price.

Equity Financing

The banking industry is subject to very strict regulation by federal and state agencies. Bank records are subject to regular scrutiny by bank examiners, and the bank is not permitted to commit its depositors' funds to speculative ventures. However, by exercising considerable ingenuity, members of the banking community *have* devised ways of getting a piece of the action in new enterprises that offer the possibility of significant capital appreciation through equity growth.

Small Business Investment Company Subsidiaries and Affiliates

There are at the present time approximately 30 SBICs that are wholly owned by banks. A few examples are Chase Manhattan Capital, owned by the Chase Manhattan Bank; Small Business Enterprises, owned by the Bank of America; Union America Capital Corporation, owned by the Union Bank; and FNCB Capital Corporation, owned by the First National City Bank of New York.

The FNCB Capital Corporation was organized in December, 1967. A brochure describes the investment objectives of this organization:

> (1) to make a profit through capital appreciation; (2) to cultivate new banking relationships which may grow to major account status at some point in the future; (3) to provide additional service to the bank's existing customers; and (4) to continue to participate in and foster a growing American economy by providing capital for new ideas, products, services and techniques.[33]

In addition to those banks having wholly owned SBIC subsidiaries, there are approximately 80 banks that are minority shareholders in SBICs.

Finder

Banks sometimes function as finders or brokers in bringing, for a fee, carefully screened investment opportunities to the attention of customers who are interested in providing venture capital. This is only one of the many services they offer their corporate clients. For instance, the State Street Bank and Trust Company in Boston in this way assists carefully screened small companies to secure venture capital.

In conclusion, I wish to emphasize that banks are *not* in a position directly to provide equity capital to a new enterprise. *However*, your banker can be of enormous assistance in helping you *locate* this type of funding.

COMMERCIAL FINANCE COMPANIES

Commercial finance companies finance receivables, inventory, and equipment in virtually all types of industry. In fact, commercial financing today represents a multi-billion-dollar-a-year business. Commercial financing is often used when a company is short of working capital and cannot qualify for unsecured bank loans, especially if it is already burdened with heavy taxation and inadequate depreciation allowances. However, it should *not* be assumed that all firms using this source are in trouble! Commercial financing is also used for settling estates, providing funds to enable an individual to buy out his partner, or enabling a business to make acquisitions. It provides substantial financial leverage for the promotion of growth and profit at a time when a business may need it most.

Commonly, a commercial finance company provides for regular financing of accounts receivable on a revolving basis. Many companies find that they have large amounts of capital permanently tied up in accounts receivable. The commercial finance company provides cash in exchange for the assignment or hypothecation of these accounts. As fast as goods or services are invoiced, funds can be loaned against the receivables thus created; the collections in this instance are made by the seller, who pays the commercial finance company on receipt of payment from his customer. Thus, the financial burden of carrying accounts receivable is eliminated; and the money derived in this way can be put to profitable use in financing those activities in which the small company has the greatest capability.

Commercial finance companies offer a wide range of financing services in addition to accounts-receivable financing. Some of these services include inventory financing, field warehousing, equipment leasing, and the making of collateral loans on existing capital equipment and machinery. Commercial finance companies provide more working capital for business on a continuing and flexible basis than does almost any other source. However, there are many other advantages commercial financing offers, including: "The increase of capital turnover, a greater return on invested capital, the ability to make advantageous purchases requiring cash, and the improvement of credit standing by discounting suppliers' bills."[34] Furthermore, it may eliminate the undesirable alternative of seeking additional equity capital or taking in partners and diluting the owner's stake in the business.

CONSUMER FINANCE COMPANIES

Consumer finance companies, also known as small loan companies, are not commonly regarded as a source of capital for business. However, in a study conducted several years ago by the National Bureau of Economic Research, it was found that a major small loan company had made approximately 10 percent of its loans to the owners of small businesses. Nothing has occurred in subsequent years to alter this pattern materially, and major consumer finance companies today continue to provide a significant percentage of their loan volume to small businessmen.

Frequently, a loan may be secured from a consumer finance company when no other legally authorized lending agency is willing to provide it, particularly if the amount of the loan is under $1,000. However, administrative and handling charges are often high in relation to the size of these loans; and, in light of the higher risk generally evident in lending to individuals with less than ideal credit ratings, the effective interest rates—or financing charges—for such loans are substantially higher than those levied by commercial banks.

CORPORATE VENTURE CAPITAL DEPARTMENTS OR SUBSIDIARIES

Today, an increasing number of large corporations are creating departments or subsidiaries exclusively devoted to the exploration and exploitation of investment opportunities in new or relatively young ventures. To give you an idea of how extensive this corporate involvement in venture capital is, a listing of several of the involved companies, including their investment subsidiaries (where a subsidiary has been established), follows:

1. Boothe Computer Corporation (Boothe Computer Investment Corporation).
2. Electronic Memories and Magnetics Corporation (division of).
3. Emerson Electric Company (Techno-Ventures, Inc.).
4. Ford Motor Company (division of).
5. General Electric Company (Business Development Services, Inc.).
6. Jenny Oil Company (Resources and Technology Management Company).
7. Monsanto Company (division of).
8. The Singer Company (Diversified Technologies, Inc.).
9. Standard Oil Company of New Jersey (Jersey Enterprises, Inc.).

The elements that motivate a large corporation to enter into the financing of new businesses are as complex and varied as the goals and markets of the corporations involved. The following is an analysis of some of the major motivational factors:

Diversification

By supplying equity capital for the formation of a new company or the expansion of an existing small company, a large corporation may cultivate a potential acquisition candidate that specializes in a field of business in which it is not already engaged.

Growth

As a result of their merger and acquisition activities, many large corporations have come under increasing pressure from the Justice Department. However, by appropriately structuring the financial package that launches a new venture, a major corporation may acquire a minority ownership at the outset, with provision through warrants for the acquisition of majority control in the event the new business is successful and the corporation chooses to exercise its stock options.

Capital Gains

In a number of instances, major corporations enjoy more cash surplus than they can profitably use for expansion in their present product areas. Participation in the financing of new enterprises may afford a large corporation unique opportunities for substantial capital gains, with their attendant tax advantages.

Acquire Technological Leadership

As a result of the considerable interest in entrepreneurship on the part of many of today's highly capable technologists, many large corporations have found it difficult to attract the services of these men because mere salaries do not satisfy them. In addition, the stock in major corporations is not apt to undergo substantial increases in a short period of time, regardless of how hard the young technologists work; therefore, stock options in a major corporation are not particularly attractive. However, if the technologist-entrepreneur is given the opportunity to start a new business that is financed by a major corporation and that has the potential, tied directly to his efforts, for substantial financial success, he may be induced to associate with that major corporation as president and part-owner of a corporate subsidiary or affiliate.

The investment activity of corporate venture capital groups is primarily designed to produce prime acquisition candidates for the future, and the methods used to provide financing reflect this fact. Compromises often subordinate the entrepreneur's desire for independence through majority equity control to his desire for personal wealth. Accordingly, deals can be structured to provide the founders with 30 percent of the equity and the corporate venture capital group with 40 percent, allocating the remaining 30 percent for a "public offering" (See "Investment Bankers" later in this chapter.) in order to arrive at an equitable valuation of the stock. Initial arrangements may set forth the requirement that the founders make their stock available to the investing corporation at some future date at a price equal to that of those shares publicly traded.

Another means of structuring the deal is to establish a buy-out formula that is tied to annual sales, profits, or other performance criteria. Here, the question of majority ownership of equity in the new firm is moot because the founders are committed to relinquish ownership at a later date; the primary area of negotiation is the way in which the buy-out price relates to the performance of the enterprise.

Even though the major corporation may insist upon owning a majority of his business, their financial assistance can offer him many advantages. For example, a large corporation can be expected to show much greater patience with the development of a new enterprise than will a financially oriented investor who is interested merely in a quick buck. A large corporation can also provide marketing channels, manufacturing assistance, accounting support, and general bolstering in every weak area outside the entrepreneur's area of expertise—the expertise that made the venture attractive to the corporation in the first place.

CREDIT UNIONS

There are two basic kinds of credit unions—those chartered by the federal government and those chartered by state governments. Since the federally chartered credit unions substantially outnumber the state-chartered credit unions, this section will be devoted primarily to a discussion of federal credit unions.

Federal credit unions are cooperative associations created for the purpose of promoting thrift among members and of providing a source of credit at reasonable interest rates for worthwhile, productive purposes.[35]

The creation of federal credit unions was authorized by Congress under the Federal Credit Union Act of 1934 (significantly revised in 1959, resulting in added powers for the credit unions and greater opportunities for their members). Under the provisions of amended act, all federal credit unions are regulated by the National Credit Union Administration (NCUA), an agency of the Social Security Administration. The major activities of the NCUA involve the chartering, supervising, and examining of federal credit unions. The activities of the Administration are exclusively financed through charter, supervision, and examination fees, which are paid by the federal credit unions.[36]

Of particular interest to the entrepreneur is the lending function of the credit union. *Eligibility for credit-union loans is exclusively restricted to their memberships.* In order to become a member, one must subscribe to at least one share of stock in the corporation and must pay an entrance fee. Additionally, credit union membership is "limited to groups having a common bond of occupation or association, or to groups within a well-defined neighborhood, community, or rural district."[37]

The ability of a federal credit union to meet loan demands is directly related to the amount of capital available for this purpose in the credit union treasury. For credit unions having a substantial amount of available capital, the statutory limit on an unsecured loan is $2,500. In the event the loan may be secured by collateral, the maximum loan limit is $10,000.[38]

The maximum interest rate that may be charged to the borrower is one percent per month on the unpaid balance. Although loan maturities vary, unsecured loans ordinarily have a maximum maturity of five years; the maturity of large loans made on a secured basis must not exceed 10 years.

Small businessmen may avail themselves of the benefits of credit union membership and borrow money as a personal loan, which will be subject to the reasonable requirement that there be a high probability that the loan will be repaid in accordance with the terms of the original loan agreement. Such loans may prove quite helpful in financing the purchase of equipment for use in a new enterprise.

CUSTOMERS

In a number of instances, customers are able to provide some of the venture capital needed for the launching of a new business. A customer may have a number of reasons for offering financial assistance to a new supplier, and there are many ways in which this assistance may be extended. The following are but a few of the factors motivating customer assistance to a new enterprise:

Encourage Supplier Competition in Virtually Every Industry

A fact of economic existence is that increased competition invariably results in lower pricing. Therefore, customers are almost always happy to see new competition; and some are willing to offer financial encouragement to a new supplier with the expectation that lower prices will result. This heightened competition may also provide better service in the form of more timely deliveries, higher quality standards, and more diverse product offerings.

Obtain "Backyard" Supplier

If the customer is geographically remote from his present suppliers, he may wish to encourage a new supplier to establish a facility in a nearby location. The customer may also wish ultimately to acquire the supplier as a subsidiary.

Obtain Supplier Where None Existed Before

If a market need exists and there is no supplier to satisfy it, the founders of a new venture may be able to persuade a customer that in order to obtain the products he needs, he should assist in the financing of their venture.

The techniques through which financial assistance may be furnished by customers include:

Advance Payments or Deposits

Depending on the product and the market, a new supplier may be in a position to secure deposits or advance payments (partial or full) before any actual work on the order commences. For example, Bud Edelman of IMC (introduced in Chapter 1) was successful in persuading his first major customer to put up a $5,000 advance payment toward the purchase of a $32,000 computer system. In many other sectors of industry, particularly where products are specially manufactured to customer specifications, deposits or advance payments are required as a matter of course.

Progress Payments

In industries as diverse as highway construction and technical research and development, it has become accepted practice for the supplier to demand periodic payment from his customer for work satisfactorily performed to date. Such a financing schedule can significantly reduce the amount of working capital the supplier needs in order to function effectively and solvently.

Loan Guarantees

If a customer desires to purchase a product or service from the lowest bidder in a highly competitive market, the lowest bidder is often a new company trying to enter the marketplace. In some cases, a customer may be willing to guarantee a bank loan to the small supplier in order to obtain the lowest possible price for purchases.

Direct Loans

A customer may also make an outright low-interest loan to a supplier as a means of insuring prompt delivery of his order. Usually, in a situation of this kind, the customer hopes to realize very significant benefits from providing the loan—either in the form of low-cost purchases or in the establishment of a geographically convenient new supplier.

Purchase of Stock in the New Company

In some instances, a customer may develop a "captive supplier" by investing substantially in the common stock of a new supplier's company. In such a situation, stock options may be arranged at the outset to provide for the acquisition of the supplier by the customer at a later date, when the new business has matured and may no longer provide the entrepreneur with the challenges that prompted him to start it.

Lend Equipment

In some highly specialized situations, a customer may provide a supplier with the equipment needed to produce the desired products or to perform the desired services. A common example of this type of support is in the performance of research, development, and manufacturing for the federal government. The government may loan specialized equipment to the supplier to insure the performance of the contracted assignment.

ECONOMIC DEVELOPMENT ADMINISTRATION

The Economic Development Administration (EDA), an agency of the U.S. Department of Commerce, provides business development loans solely for the purpose of assisting economically deprived areas. It is the policy of the EDA to make loans in order to establish viable businesses, with the expectation that new jobs will be created and the local citizenry may enjoy higher personal incomes. Since the economic health of different regions will vary depending on many business and nonbusiness factors, EDA offices maintain regularly revised listings of all eligible communities.[39]

EDA Loan Terms

A significant feature of the EDA loan program is the fact that there is no specific limitation on the dollar amount the agency may lend to any single applicant, although the loan is restricted to no more than 65 percent of the total cost of land, buildings, machinery, and equipment for commercial and industrial enterprises. Depending on the nature of the loan application and the extent to which the host community is economically depressed, the EDA may elect to furnish less than the maximum allowable loan percentage. While EDA business-loan maturity may extend to as much as 25 years, maturity is usually determined by the useful life of the fixed assets being acquired with loan proceeds. Ordinarily, fixed assets acquired by means of an EDA loan will serve as collateral for that loan. Loan repayments generally are made in regular monthly installments. There is, however, no penalty for repayment of an EDA business loan prior to the loan maturity date.[40]

Loan Eligibility Requirements

Eligibility requirements for an EDA loan include:

1. The new business must be located within an area designated by the EDA.
2. EDA loans may be granted to an existing business anywhere for the purpose of *expanding* operations within a designated area. (However, great care must be taken to guarantee that there will be no loss of jobs in the previous business location, lest the EDA open itself to the criticism of economic favoritism toward one community over another.)
3. The required funds must not be available through conventional financing channels.
4. The new enterprise shall be in an industry where long-term growth prospects equal or exceed those of the gross national product—in other words, in an industry where market demand is likely to be greater than the supply for the forseeable future.
5. There *must* be reasonable assurance of loan repayment.
6. Federally established wage rates meeting the requirements of the Davis-Baker Act must be paid to the project construction contractors.
7. Employment policies must comply with the nondiscrimination provisions of the Civil Rights Act of 1964.

8. At least 15 percent of the total eligible project cost must be supplied as equity capital or as a subordinated loan. Subordinated loans must be payable in no shorter a period of time and at no faster an amortization rate than that of the EDA loan. Also, at least 5 percent of the total eligible project cost must be supplied by the state, community, or area organization involved unless unusual hardship exists, in which case the 5 percent community requirement may be waived. However, in this instance, the applicant or other nonfederal source must then supply the 5 percent directly to the project.[41]

The Loan Application

Form EDA-201 is a business loan application for use by proprietorships, partnerships, and corporations. This form is designed to provide the EDA with a full disclosure of all information concerning the proposed business in order to ascertain its commercial viability. Much of the information required is similar in nature to the subject matter discussed in Section Two above, "THE BUSINESS PLAN." In preparing the loan request, the applicant should work very closely with personnel in the EDA area office to make certain that the information furnished is supplied in the detail and format required. Such careful preparation will expedite processing of the loan application.[42]

Loan Restrictions

As a means of providing built-in safeguards for its loans, the EDA generally imposes certain restrictions on the use of loan proceeds. For example, the loan authorization may contain limitations on the salaries that may be paid to company officers and directors. Dividends, bonuses, and other forms of compensation may be restricted. Personal loan guarantees may be required of the principals, and the expenditure of company monies for the acquisition of fixed assets may be subject to EDA review to insure that such acquisitions will not unnecessarily strain working capital reserves.[43]

Loan Processing Time and Expense to the Applicant

Since the justification for obtaining an EDA loan hinges on the ability of the applicant to prove convincingly that permanent new jobs will be created, the evaluation of a loan request may consume considerable time. Although the EDA process loan applications as rapidly as possible, careful study of the many factors involved in an EDA decision cannot be effected overnight.

Depending on the magnitude of the loan requested, the amount of supporting information which must be furnished with the loan application will vary. Any expenses necessarily incurred to secure background information required by the EDA will be borne by the loan applicant. In other words, the responsibility for presenting a convincing justification for an EDA loan is exclusively up to the applicant.[44]

Working Capital Guarantees

Although by law the EDA is enjoined from making direct working capital loans, in unusual circumstances the EDA may guarantee up to 90 percent of the unpaid balance of funds made available by private lending institutions to the EDA borrower. This does not preclude the requirement that the applicant must furnish adequate initial working capital from his own personal resources.[45]

EDA Area Offices

Atlantic: 320 Walnut Street, Philadelphia, Pennsylvania 19106: serving Connecticut, Delaware, District of Columbia, Maine, Maryland, Massachusetts, New Hampshire, New Jersey, New York, Pennsylvania, Puerto Rico, Rhode Island, Vermont, Virgin Islands.

Mideastern: 517 Ninth Street, Chafin Building, Huntington, West Virginia 25701: serving Kentucky, North Carolina, Ohio, Virginia, West Virginia.

Southeastern: 904 Bob Wallace Avenue, Acuff Building, Huntsville, Alabama 35801: serving Alabama, Florida, Georgia, Mississippi, South Carolina, Tennessee.

Midwestern: 32 West Randolph Street, Chicago, Illinois 60601: serving Illinois, Indiana, Iowa, Michigan, Minnesota, Missouri, Nebraska, North Dakota, South Dakota, Wisconsin.

Southwestern: 702 Colorado Street, Austin, Texas 78701: serving Arizona, Arkansas, Colorado, Kansas, Louisiana, Nevada, New Mexico, Oklahoma, Texas, Utah, Wyoming.

Western: 415 First Avenue, North, Seattle, Washington 98109: serving Alaska, American Samoa, California, Guam, Hawaii, Idaho, Montana, Oregon, Washington.

EMPLOYEES

A very significant but often overlooked source of venture capital for the new enterprise is its employees. Employee ownership in the business may provide significant benefits to the firm beyond the obvious easing of corporate cash flow shortages. These benefits to the firm are best analyzed by considering some of the factors that motivate employees to purchase an interest in their firm:

Pride in the Company

Employees can be encouraged to identify with the goals and image of their company if they have a personal interest in its success. Employees who feel a close identification with the objectives, productivity, standards of quality, and all the other characteristics ordinarily associated with pride can benefit both the company *and* themselves.

Security

An employee who owns stock in his company usually finds his feeling of personal security enhanced. Through ownership of stock, he is guaranteed a position from which he can make his wishes known to the company management through the Board of Directors, the corporate entity established exclusively for the representation of stockholder interest.

Build an Estate

Stock ownership can make it possible for an employee to build a personal estate. If he recognizes that his own efforts can be effective in furthering the objectives of the company while thus enhancing *his* equity in the company, he is motivated to work harder. Not only will he be able to realize growth in his financial worth; he is also in a position directly to affect the rate of this growth.

The channels available for employee participation in financing the new enterprise are many:

Direct Loan

An employee may provide capital to his company through the vehicle of a direct loan. As an employee, he is in an excellent position to assess the risk involved in making such a loan. The parent company should, of course, make provision for regular payment of interest to the employee. A separate fund for the purpose of retiring the loan (called a "sinking fund") should be established; and, most important, the loan should be documented with a formally authorized note and with a lien on company property if it is secured by tangible assets.

Loan Guarantee

In some instances, an employee of substantial personal net worth may not wish to make a direct loan or purchase stock in the company but may be willing to guarantee a loan obtained by the company from an outside borrower.

Outright Purchase of Stock

An employee may acquire a stock interest in the company in a number of ways. The simplest of these is the outright purchase of stock through the company treasurer.

Through the mechanism of a *qualified stock option plan*, executive-employees meeting certain limitations established by the Internal Revenue Service may qualify for stock options, which permit them to buy stock in the company at various times in the future at a price established at the time of the initial award of the option.

Still another way of obtaining capital from company employees is through the mechanism of the *employee stock purchase plan*. The terms under which this plan is ordinarily administered afford qualifying employees the periodic opportunity to purchase stock in the company at 85 percent of the fair market value of the stock and in amounts usually proportional to their annual income.

Accept Stock in Lieu of Wages

In some instances, company management may wish to pay certain of its employees with stock in the company instead of with cash. Such a compensation scheme requires the establishment of an escrow account for the accumulation of cash that would otherwise be payable to the employee. This account is maintained until such time as permission is granted by the appropriate government regulatory agency for the issuance of stock to said employees. Subsequently, the money in the escrow account can be returned to the corporate treasury cash account. (An example of compensation provided under this plan was covered in Chapter 1 in the story about Laser Technology.)

Provide Tangible Assets

It is possible for the employees of a new business to provide tangible assets to the company in exchange for stock. Such assets may include land, buildings, raw materials, parts, and equipment, which are exchanged for stock in amounts based on the fair market value of the goods provided and the nominal value of the stock as approved by the appropriate state regulatory agency.

EQUIPMENT MANUFACTURERS

In the face of increasingly stiff competition, many equipment manufacturers have come to appreciate the value of assisting their customers in securing financing for the purchase of their products. Confronted with two potential suppliers who offer comparable equipment in terms of quality and specifications, a small businessman contemplating a major purchase will favor the firm offering the most attractive financing arrangements. Therefore, it is commonplace for many of the large and financially sound suppliers of high-cost equipment, such as electronic computers, road-building machinery, metal-working lathes, end-mills, drill-presses, dry-cleaning presses, or printing presses, to provide their customers with intermediate-term, mortgage-type loans secured by this equipment. Under such an arrangement, customers may realize tax write-offs on both interest expenses and accelerated depreciation allowances while they acquire equity in the equipment purchased. Often, a major equipment manufacturing corporation will establish a wholly owned subsidiary exclusively for this purpose.

Although chattel mortgage and installment financing is often provided, it is also common practice for equipment suppliers to lease equipment to their small business clients. This last arrangement has the advantage in that 100 percent of the rent is an expense for income tax purposes.

From the standpoint of the equipment supplier, there must be a reasonable assurance that the equipment will be a self-amortizing investment: (1) through the revenue produced by the sale of products made with it or (2) through the increased profitability due to higher efficiency resulting from its use.

From the standpoint of the entrepreneur, equipment suppliers may prove to be an extremely helpful source of financial assistance. Information on the availability of such assistance should be secured well in advance of actual need in order to permit proper preparation of cash flow projections.

FACTORING COMPANIES

Factoring companies, or *factors*, as they are sometimes called, perform many financial services for the business community. They trace their origins in this country to a time roughly 150 years ago, when factoring was concerned exclusively with the import of textiles from Europe. Factoring houses represented European textile mills, sold goods, and collected the money from buyers in this country. They assumed the entire responsibility for collections and possible credit losses while at the same time making discounted cash payments to the European mills. Thus, the mills were able to obtain prompt cash payment for goods supplied to customers in this country, and the factoring houses made their profits on their ability to evaluate the credit worthiness of their buyers and to collect fees and interest charges.

Today, factoring companies provide similar, although greatly expanded, services to a large number of industries as diverse as electronics, heavy machinery, durable consumer goods, and many businesses in the service field.

The most commonly known advantages of factoring follow:

1. Factoring frees the capital ordinarily tied up in carrying accounts receivable. The seller does business for cash while his customers get the

terms they require, which permits the seller to use his capital more productively.

2. Factoring eliminates the expense of a credit department.
3. Factoring provides full credit protection and eliminates all risk, as the factor absorbs credit losses.
4. Factoring reduces bookkeeping expenses, maintains accounts receivable ledgers for the client, and absorbs all collection expenses.
5. A factor will usually provide money prior to the shipment of goods to finance a pre-season build-up of inventory [by the seller].
6. A factor may finance machinery.[46]

Through factoring, a service or manufacturing company can substantially increase the volume of business it can handle in relation to the net worth or equity valuation of its enterprise; it can plan cash needs with confidence because it collects receivables whether the customer pays or not; and it is in a strong buying position through the short-term availability of cash, should cash be required to make a purchase on unusually favorable terms. In effect, the businessman is selling for cash while the factor provides his customers with the credit. He is relieved of what might be substantial financial risk and of many of the time-consuming involvements normally associated with the collection process. Thus, he is in a position to devote all of his time to those elements of the business in which he is most qualified.

In addition, factoring may replace the need for additional equity capital, thus avoiding the dilution of the owner's equity in the business. It can also be used to buy out partners and to finance acquisition. In this manner, factoring can provide substantial leverage to a small capital base.

There are two basic kinds of factoring. In nonrecourse or "old line" factoring, the factor purchases the accounts receivable outright (at a discount from face value), subsequently notifying the customer that it has assumed the legal position as a creditor and that payment of the accounts should be made directly to it.

A second form of factoring has come into general use—accounts receivable are purchased *with* recourse. Although a cash payment is made to the manufacturer at the time of assignment of the accounts receivable, a reserve is set aside against the possibility of default. After the customer retires the accounts receivable, the manufacturer will receive the balance due him, minus the factor's discount and interest on the funds advanced. If the customer defaults, the factor, having recourse to the manufacturer, may demand full recovery of the funds originally advanced. In this instance, since the risk to the factor is reduced, the amount of the discount reflects this diminished risk.

The expense involved in using the services of a factor can run as high as 16 percent per annum since receivables are sold at a discount and, in addition, interest must be paid on the funds advanced. However, the business only pays for the financing it needs—unlike the case of a bank loan where some of the funds may not be used or must be set aside as a compensating balance (see Commercial Banks above).

FAMILY INVESTMENT COMPANIES

In this country, one of the oldest sources of high-risk capital for new ventures has been the fortunes of such families as the Rockefellers, the Whitneys, and the Phippses. Today, more and more family fortunes are being made available for the funding of new and young enterprises as the rewards possible in venture capital financing become more widely appreciated. Typically, investment strategy involves pooling the resources of family members and placing them under the management of one or more financial specialists well qualified in the field of venture capital investment.

To illustrate the importance of these family fortunes in underwriting new American industry, consider that the Rockefeller family figured significantly in the financing of the Polaroid Corporation and that the Whitney family fortune, in the hands of heiress Joan Whitney Payson, provided the pool of capital managed by the firm of Payson and Trask. Close to 100 companies have received financing through Payson and Trask in the last 23 years.[47]

Another family venture capital firm, J. H. Whitney and Company, was established 25 years ago and has participated in the financing of approximately 100 ventures, including the very successful California-based Memorex Corporation. The Whitney portfolio also reflects its early investments in companies such as General Signal, Minute Maid, Corinthian Broadcasting, Spencer Chemical, Transcontinental Gas Pipeline, and Global Marine.[48]

Bessemer Securities Corporation, the New York venture capital firm organized to invest the resources of the Phipps family, has supplied venture capital to finance promising business opportunities for the last 16 years. One of its most successful recent investments was in the Measurex Corporation. Measurex is a computerized control systems manufacturer, initially involved in supplying the papermaking industry. Today, its operations are quite profitable, and the growth rate is a source of delight to Bessemer and the very few other venture capital firms that participated in its financing.[49]

One recent entry into the venture capital field is the Gund family, with its three-year-old Gunwyn Ventures of Princeton, New Jersey. Gunwyn's latest investments have been in an electronic test equipment manufacturer, a supplier of specialty food products, and a computer service company. The total capital committed to these three ventures is in excess of $500,000.

Still another recent entry in the venture capital field is the Koch family, which developed Koch Venture Capital, Inc., in Cambridge, Massachusetts. William I. Koch, a young member of the family and an MIT Chemical Engineering graduate with a Doctor of Science degree, is president of the firm. In its three years of operation, the firm has invested $1.25 million in six different companies, two of which have gone bankrupt. Fortunately, these "losers" represent a total loss of less than $50,000. The most successful investment of Koch Venture Capital has been IMLAC, a New England-based computer peripherals manufacturer for which Koch provided start-up capital. Present investment plans for this venture capital firm call for the investment of between $500,000 and $1 million per year.

FINANCIAL CONSULTANTS, FINDERS, AND OTHER INTERMEDIARIES

In the face of the bewildering array of financial sources, the sometimes conflicting requirements of different organizations and individuals supplying venture capital, and a malaise brought about by the apparent mystique characterizing the fund-raising process in general, many entrepreneurs seek the services of financial consultants, finders, and other financial intermediaries in their search for venture capital. A properly qualified finder may be a godsend to the entrepreneur from the standpoint of the services he is in a position to provide:

Determine the Possibility of Obtaining Financing

The initial effort of the financial intermediary will be to ascertain the commercial viability of the proposed business idea with an eye not only to the prospects for commercial success but also to the probability of locating financing. (In many instances perfectly valid business proposals go unfunded because the proposed venture is of a type that is currently not in vogue in investment circles.)

Determine the Amount of Financing Required

An experienced intermediary should be in an excellent position to evaluate objectively the magnitude of the financing required by the proposed venture. He may be of further assistance in evaluating this requirement relative to prevailing capital market conditions (tight money or surplus).

Advise on the Best Financing Technique

The financial intermediary should suggest the best approach to the fund-raising problem. This particular function is especially important in evaluating the pros and cons of equity versus loan financing for the venture.

Assist in Preparation of the Business Plan

In many instances, the intermediary can be of considerable help in assisting the entrepreneur with the preparation of a suitable business plan for his fund-raising effort. One financial consultant I know of charges a flat $1,000 fee for this service.

Locate Capital on a Commission Basis

The primary service a financial intermediary renders to the entrepreneur is the location of venture capital. In most cases, this is done on a commission basis, although a fee in the form of a retainer may also be required.

Syndication

Sometimes in the process of securing a large amount of capital, it may be necessary to persuade many individuals and organizations to pool their resources. The financial intermediary may be of considerable assistance in such a project since his contacts in the financial community will be far more numerous than those of the entrepreneur.

Negotiate the Deal

In most instances, the entrepreneur is a novice in the conduct of financial negotiations; thus, the services of a seasoned financial intermediary can be invaluable.

Although the attitude of venture capitalists toward financial intermediaries is mixed, the involvement of an ethical and knowledgeable financial intermediary is usually welcome in financial circles. If the financial intermediary has previously earned the respect of members of the investment community, he is in a unique position to provide services of value to investors as well as to the entrepreneur.

Screen Propositions

One of the biggest complaints venture capitalists have is that, of the many hundreds of propositions they regularly review, only a very few are acceptable. A financial intermediary can be of great help in culling out all but the very best propositions for the investor's consideration.

Management Consultant

After financial arrangements have been made, the financial intermediary may serve as a management consultant in a liaison capacity between the new enterprise and the investors.

In general, complaints regarding financial intermediaries revolve around three key points:

High Fees in Relation to Services Rendered

If a financial intermediary does nothing more than provide an entrepreneur with a list of venture capitalists whom the entrepreneur himself subsequently contacts, it seems reasonable to conclude that the standard finder's fee of five percent of the eventual deal represents excessive remuneration for the efforts expended.

"Proposal Mills"

Some of the less ethical financial intermediaries have provoked well-deserved ill will among members of the investment community as a result of their operation of "proposal mills." The entrepreneur should be quite leery of any financial intermediary who expresses the attitude "I don't care *what* your product is, kid! We'll work up a good proposal and get financing for you, anyway!"

Some unethical financial intermediaries may also *promise* their clients that they will be successful in locating financing for the proposed venture. However, unless the financial intermediary is personally furnishing the required capital, he is not in a position to make such a guarantee. He can only do his best to secure funds from others.

Wham, Bam, Thank You, Ma'am

If a financial intermediary successfully arranges funding for the new enterprise, it is desirable to structure his compensation in such a way that he has a personal stake in the ultimate success of the new venture, possibly through ownership of stock. All too often, intermediaries successful in locating financing are never seen nor heard of again once the capitalization arrangements have been completed and their fee has been paid. Again, this minimum level of effort is not in consonance with the five-percent-or-more charge that is normally levied under such circumstances.

Financial intermediaries are particularly unique in venture capital financing as a result of their visibility. In the latest New York City telephone directory Yellow Pages, there are more than 150 financial consultants listed. Other Yellow Page headings under which financial intermediaries may be found include Financing, Business Consultants, Business Development, and Investment Management. Also, a classified advertisement offering the services of one particular financial consultant has appeared in every issue of *The Wall Street Journal* for the last year.

FOUNDERS

With rare exceptions, the founders of a new company make a personal capital investment that represents a substantial percentage of their individual net worth. The elements which prompt an entrepreneur to invest his personal assets in his company are largely the same as those which prompted him to launch the venture. (These elements were discussed in some detail in Chapter 2 and will not be repeated here.) Some of the more commonly employed financing techniques are as follows:

Make Direct Loans

Ordinarily, company founders do not make funds available to their company on a loan basis. However, if one of the founders has substantially greater personal assets than the rest of the founders have, he may supply some funds on a direct loan basis. For example, if Mr. Brown and Mr. Smith each have $20,000 to invest in the new venture while Mr. Jones is prepared to invest $100,000, they may all agree to receive an equal number of shares by each investing $20,000 in an equity position. Jones may then agree to provide an additional $80,000 in exchange for a long-term, interest-bearing note. Thus, each of the founders will own the same amount of stock in the venture. Ordinarily, Jones would further agree to subordinate his note, meaning that any other lenders would have priority should it become necessary to liquidate the assets of the corporation.

Guarantee Loans

In some instances, a founder may have assets of substantial value such as unimproved real estate that cannot readily be liquidated or that he does not wish to turn into cash. In such a case, an outside lending agency may accept this individual founder as the guarantor of a loan to the new firm.

Purchase Stock

The most common form of founder investment in a new enterprise is through the cash purchase of common stock. Frequently, this cash is obtained through the sale of previous investments and through substantial individual borrowings. Common secondary sources for loans include:

1. Life insurance policy loans.
2. First or second mortgage on home. Refinancing of home furnishings, automobiles, pleasure boats, etc.
3. Personal loans (signature or character loans).

(It is interesting to note that in many cases a banker may be willing to lend a man several thousand dollars for the purpose of making a vacation trip around the world, but he may be *un*willing to lend this customer the same amount of money for the purpose of starting a business. A leading Chicago-based manufacturer of cosmetics created for the Negro market got his start under just such a set of circumstances— Turned down on a loan request for $500 with which to start his business, he reapplied indicating that he wanted the money for a vacation trip. The loan was granted. However, the hero of our piece was unable to bring himself to squander this money on anything so foolish as a vacation; instead, he started a company. Regardless of the circumstances surrounding the loan application, personal loans are *not* an uncommon source of capital for financing a business.)

Supply Tangible Assets

Very commonly, company founders are in a position to contribute assets to the new venture in exchange for stock. Such assets may include capital equipment, land, buildings, raw materials, and supplies.

Pool Resources

Another technique for raising money when the number of founders involved is large: Establish an organizational chart where the key positions to be filled may number as many as ten or more. The idea is to persuade each of these potential founders to invest a nominal amount of cash in the company—for instance, $1,000, $2,000, or $3,000 each. Thus, sufficient resources may be accumulated to permit the development of a prototype. The founders who do this early work may be the engineering members of the staff; the others may plan to join the venture at a later date. Subsequently, members of the financial community may be approached when the founders are in a much better bargaining position because they have hardware to exhibit. It stands to reason that it is much easier to sell an investor with a piece of hardware than with an eloquent word description of an idea.

One of the fundamental factors any venture capitalist, private investor, relative, friend, neighbor, or other potential source of funds will want to know is the degree of commitment the founders have made to their new enterprise. (Bear in mind that it is extremely difficult to measure, in terms of dollars and cents, the value of hard work and long moonlight hours.) Thus, a consideration of enormous significance is documented evidence that the founders have made a substantial cash investment. This investment does not necessarily have to represent *large* cash amounts; however, it must represent a major percentage of the founders' personal assets. If your car is not in hock, if you don't have a second mortgage on your home, and if you have not borrowed all you can possibly raise from your friendly banker or neighborhood loan company, you may have difficulty convincing *some* investors that you are serious. Fortunately, such an attitude is not held by *all* investors, although *reasonable* evidence of financial commitment is universally expected.

INDUSTRIAL BANKS

Industrial banks—which include institutions referred to as Morris Plan banks—are sometimes difficult to distinguish from ordinary commercial banks, while in other respects they appear to be more like consumer finance companies. Unlike commercial banks, industrial banks are not permitted to offer checking accounts and other key commercial banking services to their patrons. Furthermore, accounts placed with industrial banks are not insured. Under most state laws regulating industrial banks, loan limits range from $1,000 to $5,000 and more, with typical maturities of two or three years.[50] Depending on loan competition with commercial banks, interest rates charged by industrial banks range from slightly above the prime lending rate charged by commercial banks all the way up to the maximum permitted under state law. In almost all instances, loans are retired on the installment basis.

One of the major differences between industrial banks and consumer finance companies is that industrial banks are authorized to accept savings certificates of investment from businesses as well as from private individuals. Policies governing the availability of loan funds from industrial banks are very much like those of consumer finance companies (discussed above), although industrial banks typically handle larger notes than do commercial finance companies.

If the demands of regular finance channels do not fully utilize resources secured from their savings customers, industrial banks explore other avenues of utilizing funds. In those instances where substantial long-term funds have been obtained through debenture issues, extensive diversification programs have been undertaken. As an example, the Morris Plan Company of Cedar Rapids, Iowa organized one of the first small business investment companies in the United States as a wholly owned subsidiary. Additionally, this company is active in the equipment leasing field.[51] Many other industrial banks across the country have expanded their operations to provide services outside the consumer finance field as permitted by individual state regulatory agencies.

Although there are pronounced differences in the investment postures of industrial banks and consumer finance companies, it is interesting to note that in early 1971 the American Industrial Bankers Association merged with the National Consumer Finance Association; the surviving organization is known as the National Consumer Finance Association.

INSURANCE COMPANIES

Historically, insurance companies have been a major source of long-term debt capital for American industry. Life insurance companies in the United States, as of the end of 1970, have combined assets that exceeded $200 *billion*, while property and casualty insurance company assets exceeded $50 billion. Life insurance company investments are primarily in public utility and industrial bonds and in real estate mortgages. Investment standards are typically quite high and new or speculative investment opportunities are rarely considered. Furthermore, life insurance company investments are very carefully regulated by *each* of the 50 states in which they operate. In spite of this fact, however, a few companies have allocated a small percentage of their assets to the venture capital field; and since a "small percentage" of billions of dollars *is* millions of dollars, this is not an inconsequential source of capital. The property and casualty insurance companies, subject to less stringent state regulation, have pioneered in the venture capital field. One of the companies to lead the way was the Allstate Insurance Company, a division of Sears, Roebuck and Company, under the direction of Edgar F. Heizer, Jr., former Assistant Treasurer at Allstate in charge of the Private Placement Division. The Allstate venture capital pool ultimately exceeded $125 million in venture capital investments. As a result of Heizer's remarkable ability to pick winners, Allstate Insurance was an early participant in the financing of such stock market favorites as Teledyne, Memorex, Control Data, and International Industries.[52]

Another insurance firm active in the venture capital field is State Farm Insurance Company, which has allocated "ten million dollars a year for venture capital and has already invested in 20 new companies."[53] State Farm's first venture capital experience, brought to them by the investment banking firm of Drexel Harriman Ripley, Inc., is "paying off better than expected, and they are thinking about increasing venture capital investments sharply, depending on the opportunities."[54]

Other insurance companies now active in the venture capital field include:

> Aetna Life and Casualty Company,
> American Mutual Liability Insurance Company,
> Employers Insurance of Wausau,
> Massachusetts Mutual Life Insurance Company (Groco, Inc.),
> National Liberty Corporation (National Venture Capital Corporation),
> Prudential Insurance Company (Prudential Minority Enterprises, Inc.),
> Connecticut General Life Insurance Company,
> Travelers Insurance Company,
> UBA Corporation (Blythe and Company).

Still other insurance companies participate in venture capital financing as limited partners in venture capital groups. Insurance companies may also participate in the venture capital field through the use of management advisory services. In such an instance, the insurance company will invest its funds in the venture; it will then engage the services of a management consulting firm or investment management firm, as a representative of the interests of the insurance company, to monitor the investment.

INVESTMENT ADVISERS

Under the Investment Advisers Act of 1940, an "investment adviser" is defined to be:

> Any person who, for compensation, engages in the business of advising others, either directly or through publications or writings, as to the value of securities or as to the advisability of investing in, purchasing, or selling securities, or who, for compensation and as part of a regular business, issues or promulgates analyses or reports concerning securities.[55]

According to a Securities and Exchange Commission brochure:

> This is a very broad definition and applies not only to persons who make recommendations concerning securities, but also to persons whose analyses, reports or other materials are to be used by others in making decisions as to what securities to buy or sell or when to buy or sell them.[56]

In addition to providing their clients with newsletters analyzing stock and other financial market trends, the modern investment advisory firm frequently engages in the administration of mutual funds. Most recently, some of these investment management firms have organized pools of venture capital for the purpose of participating in the financing of new (or small) businesses that offer, in their opinion, substantial growth potential.

Of the more than 1500 registered investment advisory concerns in the United States, one of the oldest (founded in 1926) and largest (in terms of client assets under management) is the Boston-based firm of Loomis, Sayles and Company, Inc. According to Walter D. Silcox, a Loomis, Sayles security analyst and vice president, the firm has recently entered the field of venture capital financing in an effort to improve the investment performance of their clients' portfolios. Silcox has stated that:

> While some of us as individuals may look at social goals in helping to finance the entrepreneur, goals such as new products of benefit to society, new employment and the like, our fiduciary responsibility to our clients requires we obtain for them the highest return possible consistent with the risk involved.[57]

In explaining the role his firm plays in the investment scenario, he indicates that:

> Unlike some of the venture capital firms, we are not in a position to supply management, production and marketing know-how or financial controls. We can supply financing advice, but we would not have a man on the board of directors. We supply the money, but leave the running of the business up to the entrepreneur.[58]

As is the case with other large investment counselling firms, the financial resources at the disposal of Loomis, Sayles are derived from a limited number of wealthy, financially sophisticated clients and from institutional capital pools such as pension funds, profit-sharing trusts, and life insurance companies. It is the expressed objective of the Loomis, Sayles organization to participate in the financing of promising companies at all stages of corporate development, ranging from points shortly after start-up through points at which a prospective portfolio company requires additional equity financing for significant expansion. Silcox has indicated the possibility that Loomis, Sayles would even participate in providing seed capital for a *new* enterprise in the event the right man came along with the right product at the right time.

Another of Silcox's remarks provides extremely valuable insight into the process whereby an entrepreneur is afforded the opportunity for contacts with venture capitalists. He says:

> We have met entrepreneurs in many ways. Some are clients of Loomis, Sayles; others are brought to us by stock brokers, finders, friends, and acquaintances.[59]

Silcox has also pointed out that technical consultants occasionally serve as intermediaries in this process.

INVESTMENT BANKERS

Prior to the passage of the Glass-Steagall Banking Act (also known as the Banking Act of 1933), it was the regular practice of banking institutions to provide commercial *and* investment banking services (the purchase and sale of securities) to the business community. However, just as the Securities Act of 1933 (prompted by the 1929 stock market crash) was intended to force corporations and investment firms to adopt higher standards of social responsibility in the solicitation of public financing, the Glass-Steagall Banking Act was devised to insure greater stability and safety in the future of the then failure-plagued banking community. The primary effect of the Glass-Steagall Banking Act was to separate the functions of commercial banking and investment banking.

Investment banking as practiced today is primarily concerned with supplying the *long-term* capital requirements of business while *seasonal* or *short-term* requirements are satisfied through commercial banking and/or other channels. The investment banker functions as a middleman between businesses in need of permanent working capital or funds for the expansion of plant and facilities and the investor with money to supply.

Since investment bankers operate in a sector of the financial community where competition is keen and rewards are high, great circumspection is observed in the conduct of business transactions. In many cases, investment banking firms have spent decades in establishing a reputation for providing investors with worthwhile investment opportunities. Therefore, the small businessman or entrepreneur must recognize the importance of fully disclosing to the investment banker the details of the new or planned venture. A format such as that described in Section Two of this book should be ideal for this purpose.

If the investment banker agrees to assist in financing the venture, the types of notes and stocks to be offered are selected; and the amount, rate, and price are negotiated. Financing through the investment banker may originate in a number of ways:

1. He may provide loan funds from his own account in return for interest and possibly stock warrants.
2. He may secure loan funds from outside investors who are clients of the firm in exchange for a fee and/or stock and/or stock warrants.
3. He may make an equity investment through the outright purchase of stock. In recent years, 30 or 40 different investment banking firms have established pools of capital specially earmarked for venture capital use. In fact, "now it's very hard to find a substantial investment banking company that doesn't have somebody cruising around talking about venture capital."[60]

For example, in 1968, A. G. Becker & Company, Inc., a nationwide investment banking and brokerage firm, and several of its shareholders established Becker Technological Associates, a partnership, for the purpose of investing in technology-oriented companies which are in the developmental stage of growth.[61] The three investment criteria used by BTA may be regarded as being typical of the venturing departments and affiliates of large, reputable investment banking firms:

1. The company should offer products or services which incorporate a high degree of technological or scientific skill. The company's organization should typically include a number of people with advanced competence in more than one technological or scientific skill. The company's organization should include a number of people who have advanced competence in more than one technological area.
2. The company's technological capability should apply to products or services that have relatively large markets. A significant share of these markets should be available to the company due to product or service superiority, uniqueness, or lower cost.
3. A substantial emphasis on profit objectives, management strength, and administrative controls, in balance with the technological capabilities of the organization, should be evident. Management should have the ability to develop the business into a substantially larger enterprise and should possess a meaningful ownership interest.

As a matter of general policy, BTA invests in companies in an early developmental stage of growth. Such a stage can be characterized as that period following:

(a) The initial start-up and organizational efforts,
(b) The design, prototyping, and testing of initial products or services,

    (c)   The initiation of marketing effort,

    (d)   The creation of at least a simple but effective administrative and control system,

    (e)   Sufficient operating history to provide a basis for judgment of management competence,

but before:

    (f)   An assured income-generating capability or financial stability is established,

    (g)   Broad product and market acceptance is achieved.

In exceptional cases, BTA considers investments in new, technologically based ventures that have no previous operating record. Investments of this type are made when the business plans, collective competence, experience, and successful record of a group of entrepreneurs present a potential that far outweighs the absence of an operating history.[62]

4.   The investment banker may undertake to locate equity funds from outside investors—a process commonly referred to as a *private placement*. In discussing this subject in an introductory brochure, the 40-year-old investment banking firm of Bateman Eichler, Hill Richards, Inc. indicates that there are

certain restrictions to this type of placement. Under presently accepted interpretations of the Securities Act, such placement can be offered to only a small group of potential investors, usually not exceeding twenty-five, and a precise record must be kept of those to whom the offering is made. Whether or not the proposed investor buys the issue, he still counts as one of those to whom it has been offered. Offering to more than twenty-five people may well be deemed by the Securities and Exchange Commission as a public offering of unregistered securities and therefore a direct violation of the Securities Act. The average number of investors in most private placements of this type runs between ten and twenty.

Frequently in these placements, the Investment Banker will take his fee principally in warrants, with a relatively smaller amount of cash.

Similar placements might also be made through an Investment Banker to institutional investors, such as one or several insurance companies. Such placements might take the form of common equity, straight debt, debt with warrants, or convertible notes. It can be quite helpful for a company to obtain financing from such sources since it establishes their credit with institutions of recognized and respected reputations which can be impressive to others dealing with the company.[63]

5.   He may choose to do an underwriting of a new stock offering for the company. In his capacity as an underwriter, he may be described in terms of the Securities Act of 1933 as a

person who has purchased from an issuer [the new company] with a view to, or sells for an issuer in connection with, the distribution of any security, or participates or has a direct or indirect participation in any such undertaking, or participates or has a participation in the direct or indirect underwriting of any such undertaking; but such term shall not include a person whose interest is limited to a commission from an underwriter or dealer not in excess of the usual and customary distributors' or sellers' commission.[64]

Individuals in the latter category are usually stock brokers employed by brokerage houses. (Stock brokerage houses are discussed under a separate heading below). A discussion of the steps involved in the making of a full-scale, SEC registered offering is beyond the scope of this work. It should be noted, however, that public offerings of the securities of new or very young companies is almost always ill advised. The investing public is a fickle supporter. In the event there are operating difficulties (and there are *always* operating difficulties in a small company), the ability to raise additional financing through the vehicle of a new issue will, in all probability, be seriously if not fatally impaired. In only the rarest of rare cases will a major, reputable investment banking firm underwrite a new offering for an unproven, unseasoned enterprise. Invariably, one of the first four financing techniques referred to above will be the preferred choice of the wise entrepreneur.

INVESTMENT CLUBS

Investment clubs are formed when a group of friends, neighbors, business associates, or other individuals pool limited financial resources or "dues" for the purpose of investing in common stocks or other securities. Such clubs may or may not be formalized through the medium of a written agreement, charter, or by-laws. In many cases, these clubs operate informally, with members pledging regular amounts paid into the club treasury on a monthly basis.

By the fall of 1951, investment club activity in the United States had reached such proportions that the National Association of Investment Clubs was organized by four investment clubs in Detroit, Michigan. Since that time, the investment club movement has reached more than two million men and women. According to a brochure distributed by the NAIC,

The founders were dedicated to the belief that the investment club was valuable to individuals in that it permitted them to learn how to invest wisely while the amount of funds they were using was small, and, at the same time, offered them an opportunity to build a substantial investment account over a longer period of time. The founders believed, too, that the investment club served a vital national function in that it was a way to create many new investors, to train individuals in successful investment techniques, and through the creation of many new investors provide a substantial and regular flow of capital for the needs of growing industry.

Consequently, the purpose of the National Association of Investment Clubs was to foster the creation of investment clubs and to take all possible steps to assist these clubs to a successful operation.[65]

NAIC provides a variety of services to its member clubs:

The Investment Club Manual is a detailed book showing how to organize a club, how to operate it successfully, and most importantly, provides a sound stock study and portfolio management plan which can serve a club for the lifetime of its members. A movie "Investing Together" is designed to explain what a club is and how it operates.

A film strip "The NAIC Stock Selection Guide" teaches how to use this stock study plan. Complete accounting material meeting the peculiar needs of an investment club is available. Classes, seminars, and information meetings are conducted by NAIC and its divisions in all parts of the country. Stock study forms and aids are prepared by the Association.[66]

One of the significant benefits the NAIC confers upon its members is a subscription to *Better Investing*.

BETTER INVESTING, the official magazine of NAIC and the only publication devoted to the field of investor education and reaching 100,000 investment club members each month, is of major service to investment clubs. It contains discussions of investment theories and techniques developed by club members and professional security analysts, reports of the activities of clubs, suggestions for club meetings and club discussions, ideas for the correction of mistakes made by clubs, and any news affecting tax, legal, or regulatory problems faced by clubs.[67]

Although the NAIC encourages a conservative investment policy among its member clubs, the records indicate that on numerous occasions clubs have chosen to devote a small percentage of their portfolio to investment in new enterprises. In fact, club investments over the years have run the gamut from oil wells to race horses, and investment in a new business should certainly be less risky than either of these propositions.

The Recommended Reading list at the end of this chapter lists additional sources of information on investment clubs. Of course, a primary source of information on investment clubs is the National Association of Investment Clubs, 1515 East Eleven-Mile Road, Royal Oak, Michigan 48067. Specific inquiries regarding NAIC should be directed to this address. Telephone inquiries may be made by dialing (313) 543-0612.

LEASING COMPANIES

Leasing companies provide a very specialized form of financing to small businesses. Through a lease agreement, machinery and office equipment may be rented at a contractually specified monthly rate for a contractually arranged period of time. Leasing arrangements are most attractive to small businessmen because they provide capital assets without the necessity of a capital investment; this constitutes 100 percent financing. However, it is customary for the leasing company to require the prepayment of one, two, or three months' rental on the equipment as an offset against the very high depreciation commonly experienced in the initial months of equipment use.

In most instances, leasing companies prefer to provide equipment that has the following characteristics:

Long Serviceable Life

Equipment offered for lease usually permits long-term depreciation and guarantees sustained resale value should the lessee not wish to renew the lease upon the expiration of the initial contract.

Universal Marketability

Ideally, the machinery or equipment leased will have a continuing ready marketability. For example, items of universal utility such as desks, chairs, lathes, end-mills, paint spray compressors, etc., exhibit the characteristics a leasing agency finds desirable.

Repossessable

If the lessee defaults in the terms of the leasing agreement, the lessor should be in a position to repossess the leased items readily. Thus, it is understood that an oxygen-reduction steel furnace would not qualify under this definition of respossessability; whereas welding equipment, work benches, and laundry and dry-cleaning equipment would qualify quite nicely.

Over the years, lease terms and conditions have become pretty well standardized. Depending on the value of the item leased, its useful life, its repossessability, and its resale value, rent may be arranged on a monthly, quarterly, semiannual, or annual basis. The leasing contract will often make provision for the lessee to purchase the leased item outright on expiration of the lease at a price somewhat less than the fair market value at that time. However, in this instance, the total monies paid over the term of the lease, plus the buy-out amount, typically add up to twice the original simple purchase price.

Leasing affords the small businessman an opportunity to use capital equipment with little or no initial outlay of cash. The productivity resulting from the use of the equipment and machinery will provide sufficient cash flow to meet the rental payments. Increasingly, leasing companies are making available to small businessmen still another option known as the sale-leaseback plan. Under the terms of such an arrangement, equipment that has already been paid for may be sold to the leasing company and then leased back. In this way, the small businessman acquires cash, which may be sorely needed for working capital purposes, in exchange for the equity in his equipment. Financing arrangements of this sort are very much like the refinancing of a house, where the homeowner retires his mortgage in exchange for a brand new mortgage and cash for his previous equity.

Since the leasing of industrial equipment requires a specialized knowledge of the particular industry to be served, it is not surprising that many leasing companies specialize in different industrial sectors. For instance, one company may specialize in medical electronics equipment; another in metals fabrication equipment; and still others in office equipment. Fleet leasing of vehicles is another special type through which a small business may satisfy its transportation and drayage requirements with a minimum initial outlay of capital.

The long-term leasing of real estate (land and buildings) is one of the oldest forms of leasing and represents a significant economic advantage to the small businessman who cannot afford to purchase the fixed assets he may require.

In many instances, the expense involved in lease financing plans depends on the financial credentials of the small business, the risks involved, the marketability of the equipment or machinery leased, and the value of any land and buildings involved. Although leasing expenses run higher than loans, a small businessman may have no other choice in securing the equipment he needs.

MUTUAL FUNDS

"A mutual fund is a company which combines the investment funds of many people whose investment goals are similar, and in turn invests those funds in a wide variety of securities."[68] Typically, a fund will invest in a number of different common and preferred stocks, corporate bonds, and other securities. These securities, taken as a whole, make up the fund portfolio. Because the value of any particular securities holding is subject to daily variation in the capital markets, administration of the portfolio investments of a mutual fund requires the continuous supervision of professionally qualified investment managers.

Mutual funds are open-end investment companies because they make a continuous offering of shares and redeem outstanding shares on demand. Therefore, the number of their shares outstanding varies as new shares are sold to investors and other shares are redeemed.

"Different mutual funds have a wide range of investment objectives, management policies and degrees of risk and profit opportunities."[69] One mutual fund may concentrate its investments in high-risk, short-term investment opportunities; others may specialize in investment situations representing modest but sustained long-term capital appreciation opportunities; still others focus their attention and financial resources on income-producing instruments such as corporate and municipal bonds.

If the management philosophy, objectives, and policies allow, a mutual fund may invest a small percentage of its resources in high-risk "special situations," such as new or relatively young enterprises. It is this mutual fund investment area that should be of particular interest to the entrepreneur. Reference to the mutual-fund directories mentioned in Appendix 1 should enable the capital seeker to ascertain the most likely prospects to approach with his business plan. I should point out, however, that mutual fund investments in new companies *are* quite rare, and these funds should not be regarded as a common source of venture capital.

MUTUAL SAVINGS BANKS

Mutual savings banks are thrift institutions organized for the purpose of providing individuals of relatively small means with a secure repository for their savings. Most mutual savings banks are found in the East and are strictly regulated under the laws of the states in which they are located.

In most instances, mutual savings banks are restricted with regard to the investment vehicles available to them. Mutual savings banks do make industrial and commercial mortgages to qualified borrowers. However, a small businessman is more likely, from this source, to secure a loan on his residence and use the proceeds for business purposes.

PARENT COMPANIES

Laboratories of large corporations often turn out excellent new products that simply do not fit into the corporations' marketing plans. This circumstance may represent a significant loss in research and development dollars and may also result in an even greater loss to the company—the departure of the skilled but frustrated innovator who developed the product. In many cases, this innovator may open up a business of his own centered around the product he created.[70]

In recent years, some of the more progressive firms have come to recognize that the abandonment of good ideas represents needless waste and have taken steps to remedy the situation. The remedy often involves the creation of a corporate subsidiary, with the innovator as president and the "orphan" product as the market vehicle. At a time when mergers and acquisitions have come under increasingly restrictive government regulation, this "spin-off" of fledgling enterprises may provide a very attractive method of effecting corporate growth.[71]

More and more corporate middle-managers are coming to feel that the only way to achieve personal satisfaction in business is to start a firm of their own. Recognizing the entrepreneurial bent of a particular manager, the parent company may decide to underwrite his entrepreneurship—"If you can't beat 'em, join 'em."—and thus avoid the *complete* loss of services and capabilities that the company may have spent years cultivating. In such a situation, the parent company is in a unique position to evaluate the managerial prowess of the potential entrepreneur, thus reducing investment risk. The company may also enjoy some of the handsome financial returns participation in a successful new business offers instead of watching some opportunistic venture capitalist reap the rewards.

The entrepreneur may realize many advantages through having his former employer finance his firm. Most or all of the administrative services of the parent company, such as accounting, marketing surveys, sales organization, etc., may be made available to the new firm at nominal cost. Also, the parent company may become a key customer for the goods and services of the enterprise. The significant financial resources of the parent company may be made available virtually to guarantee the successful launching of the new firm by providing a steady supply of capital (provided prospects for long-term success remain promising) until profitable operation is achieved. Finally, when the time comes for the parent to acquire full control of the enterprise (should the founders wish to sell), the buy-out may take the form of readily marketable securities (usually common stock) in the parent company.

PENSION FUNDS

Pension funds provide individuals with cash reserves to be disbursed as retirement income at some future date. There are many different groups involved in pension funds, including labor union members, corporation employees, state employees, and employees of nonprofit entities such as religious and charitable institutions. Since more information is available on pension funds operated by corporations than on any other type, we will devote our attention to these funds.

Corporate pension funds are of two types: insured (placed with insurance companies at guaranteed rates of return) and noninsured (administered by members of the corporate staff, investment advisers, bank trustees, and others). To give you some idea of the magnitude of funds tied up in pension plan reserves, the Securities and Exchange Commission reported a figure of $104 *billion* as of the end of 1970.[72]

With some corporate pension funds, the employees as well as the employer make contributions. However, whether the employees contribute or not, the *corporation* has the responsibility for administering the funds. This administration is active when a staff is created for the purpose of administering the funds; however, it is more common for the corporation to retain investment counsel or counselors to administer them. Funds may also be turned over to a bank trust department for administration.

Spurred by the spectacular capital appreciation sometimes possible through early investment in growth companies, virtually every individual responsible for money management has become sensitized to the need for *performance*. (As used in financial circles, performance means the rapid appreciation of invested capital.) Now in many cases, the corporation is obligated to increase the pension fund reserve annually for each eligible employee. (The exact amount is based on the number of employees covered, the payments they will receive on retirement, and individual life expectancy.)

This increase may originate from appreciation of portfolio investments (higher valuation of stocks or other holdings) or corporate contributions. Thus, if funds are so invested that portfolio appreciation is in excess of the four to six percent commonly realized from insured investments (referred to above), the magnitude of the corporation contribution may be reduced; and these savings may then be retained as profits. Since the magnitude of the funds tied up in pension reserves frequently is large, the possible advantage of aggressive fund administration is evident to corporate officers and fund managers alike.

Although corroborative information is not currently available, it is reported that a number of pension trusts, including those of Inland Steel, U.S. Steel, and the Champion Paper Company, have moved in the direction of some participation in providing equity financing for promising new businesses. The Memorial Drive Trust, responsible for the administration of the pension reserves of Cambridge, Massachusetts-based Arthur D. Little, Inc., has actively participated in the venture capital field for the last ten years. In 1970, this fund is reported to have invested $2.4 million in a cable television company and another $100,000 in a computer memory manufacturer.

Based on this information, it seems reasonable to assume that pension funds will continue to participate in venture capital at a gradually accelerating rate. Furthermore, participation by all of the many types of funds referred to above is likely as conservative administrators have an opportunity to evaluate the success of more aggressively managed funds. As inflation continues to erode the value of the dollar, the clamor of the pensionees alone should force fund managers to assume a more aggressive role in fund administration.

PRIVATE INDIVIDUAL INVESTORS

According to Schedule Y of the 1970 Federal Income Tax Rates, married taxpayers filing joint returns and certain widows and widowers having annual ordinary income in excess of $200,000 must pay 70 cents in federal income tax on every additional dollar of ordinary income earned. Although entrepreneurs are not usually confronted with tax problems of this magnitude at the time they launch their first venture, there are hundreds of thousands of individuals with incomes that push them into this 70-percent tax bracket. Their willingness to invest in interest-bearing corporate bonds or dividend-producing stocks yielding ordinary income is usually less than enthusiastic; the opportunity to retain 30 cents out of every dollar earned is not much of an investment inducement. By investing in situations offering capital gains prospects, these wealthy taxpayers may significantly reduce Uncle Sam's tax bite—income taxable under the long-term capital gains provisions of the Internal Revenue Code is assessed one-half the tax rate on ordinary income.

Prior to June 30, 1958, losses on common stock investments held in excess of six months were deductible in any given year only to the extent by which they could offset capital gains earned in that same year. Thus, a wealthy investor who had sustained substantial losses in a given tax year might be obliged to carry these losses forward indefinitely until his capital gains offset them. Needless to say, under these circumstances there was little incentive for these individuals to invest substantially in the high-risk situation which is the essence of financing a new business. But, on June 30, 1958, Section 1244 of the Internal Revenue Code was enacted by Congress to encourage the flow of new funds into small businesses. Although a detailed exposition of the ramifications of Section 1244 is beyond the scope of this book, the overall effect can be summarized this way: Qualified private investors participating in the financing of new, small business corporations meeting certain IRS criteria may elect to have capital losses up to $25,000 in any given tax year or $50,000 in the case of a husband and wife filing a joint return for the tax year treated as ordinary losses for tax purposes, while retaining the right to capital gains treatment on the realized appreciation of such investments. This is known as having your cake and eating it too.

The federal government offers still another interesting tax vehicle, known as Subchapter S of the Internal Revenue Code, for the encouragement of small business investment. Qualifying small business corporations having ten or less stockholders and only one class of stock outstanding may elect to be taxed as a partnership instead of as a corporation. Thus, any losses sustained by the enterprise may be apportioned on a pro rata basis among the stockholders and deducted from their individual tax returns as offsets to ordinary income. Once the stockholders elect unanimously to be treated as shareholders in a Subchapter S corporation, this eligibility is effective for all succeeding taxable years of the corporation until it is terminated, either willfully through a vote of the stockholders or through other circumstances as described under Section 1372 of the IRS Code. (Also particularly attractive to moneyed investors is the fact that an *estate* may qualify for Subchapter S treatment. In playing this money game with the IRS, the taxpayer's-eye view may be described as: "Heads I win, tails you lose.")

In summary, Section 1244 stock represents an attractive means of maximizing gains and minimizing losses for the wealthy investor while he participates in a high-stakes crap game involving a qualifying small corporation. Section 1244 is an option available to the stockholders of qualifying corporations, whether the Subchapter S election is made or not. Thus, the financing possibilities available in the capitalization of small businesses provide wealthy investors with two very attractive alternatives. Such investors are worth approaching with your business plans; and they can usually be located through knowledgeable lawyers, bankers, accountants, insurance agents, stockbrokers, investment underwriters, financial advisers, and finders of all descriptions.

Another category of private individual investors is made up of financially and managerially successful entrepreneurs who are ready to participate in the launching of their second or third venture and who may run advertisements in leading financial journals offering a package consisting of financial backing *and* management participation. In other instances, these individuals can be located through the same contacts mentioned above. A team of entrepreneurs successful in persuading a seasoned venturer to participate in their new enterprise should stand a much-higher-than-normal probability of success.

PRIVATE INVESTMENT PARTNERSHIPS

Private investment partnerships (or "limited partnerships") provide wealthy investors with a very attractive means of investing their resources in promising new enterprises. By adopting the role of limited partners, these individuals authorize the general partners to represent them in interacting with the officers of the new enterprise in which the partnership has invested. The general partners in such groups usually qualify for their responsibility by virtue of previous experience in new-enterprise management or as junior members in other venture capital organizations. In many instances, the general partners as well as the limited partners invest their personal resources in the new enterprise. In exchange for their services in managing the resources of the partnership, the general partners often receive salaries or other compensation in addition to their pro rata share of profits resulting from investments of the resources committed by all of the partners.

Participation in such an organization affords the limited partners many advantages. For one thing, they do not have to trouble themselves with monitoring the daily operations of the enterprise in which their money is invested—this is the responsibility of the general partners. Furthermore, because of the tax nature of qualifying partnerships, the individual partners are in a position to treat any losses of the partnership as ordinary losses, while gains receive treatment as long-term capital gains, as explained above in the discussion of Section 1244 of the IRS Code, presented under the heading "Private Individual Investors." Many wealthy people find participation in limited partnerships a practical, rewarding, and satisfying means of investing their funds in new enterprise—a means that does not demand the time-consuming responsibility of regularly monitoring the investment; they often find such partnerships far more satisfactory alternatives to simple participation in new enterprise ownership through the acquisition of common stock, in which tax advantages are not nearly so liberal.

One of the most spectacular achievements of a private individual partnership in recent years was racked up by the San Franciso firm of Hambrecht and Quist. George Quist, formerly head of Bank of America venture capital activity, and William R. Hambrecht, a former vice president of Francis I. DuPont and Company, combined forces and over a period of three years secured limited partners with the resources necessary to provide $9 million for financing the start-up of Information Storage Systems, Inc., a computer peripheral equipment manufacturer in Cupertino, California. Third-year sales for ISS were in the vicinity of $25 million, with pre-tax earnings exceeding ten percent of sales.

In January of 1971, the proposed sale of ISS to Itel Corporation was announced; the sale involved the exchange of some $40 million worth of Itel stock. Several months later, when the sale was finally approved by stockholders of Itel Corporation, the stock had a market value in excess of $50 million. With the press coverage such an achievement received, it is quite understandable why investment community interest in venture capital participation is so widespread.

PRIVATELY OWNED VENTURE CAPITAL CORPORATIONS

Privately owned venture capital corporations are among the largest suppliers of high-risk capital for new and young enterprises in this country. As a separate class of investors, such corporations typically have more advantages to offer their portfolio companies than does any other capital source.

Substantial Reserves of Risk Capital

Although bank trust departments, pension funds, insurance companies, and university endowment funds represent most of the large pools of capital for investment available today, the bulk of these funds are usually tied up in "high-quality," modest-yield, blue-chip stocks, bonds, or other securities. When it comes to risk capital, a relatively small number of closed-end investment companies (including SBICs), private investment partnerships, family investment companies, and investment affiliates have substantial assets reserved for venture capital use. However, a growing number of privately owned venture capital corporations, also with substantial assets, have been formed for the express purpose of investing in promising young companies. Recent examples include Chicago-based Heizer Corporation, which had an initial capitalization of over $80 million raised from 35 institutional investors,[73] and the New Court Private Equity Fund, Inc., which had an initial capitalization in excess of $50 million.

The availability of assets of this magnitude provides an excellent "insurance policy" for portfolio companies. Investors with limited assets may be unable to supply promised capital when required, and shortages may occur whether or not the enterprise is meeting projected performance schedules. Thus, the founders may do a splendid job of building their company only to find themselves in financial difficulty because of an investor's inability to honor his commitments. Conversely, large venture capital organizations are generally able to withstand economic vagaries and to continue to support the young company.

Business Development Assistance

Many small investors may pool their resources to "syndicate" the financing of a deal, but they are not in a position to contribute anything else to the enterprise; on the other hand, privately owned venture capital corporations commonly retain a full-time staff for the purpose of monitoring and, where necessary, assisting portfolio companies with whatever problems they may have, financial or otherwise.

Recently, this process has come to be known as *business development*, and investors who offer this service prefer to be called *business developers* rather than to wear the more commonly applied label of venture capitalist. As defined by the Heizer Corporation, business development is

> the businessman's approach to venture capital. It is the creation of value through the effective combination of men, money, and ideas. It is helping businessmen with good ideas, who are willing to work hard, to be very successful. This is great for them and rewarding for us.[74]

Long-Term Objectives

In the words of Edgar F. Heizer, Jr., president and chairman of the board of the Heizer Corporation,

> a lot of venture capital outfits are pure dice-rollers. . . . It's sort of like going to Las Vegas, except in Vegas you at least know the odds. We're not going into anything on the basis that we might have one winner out of ten.[75] Each company we finance must have the potential of creating an investment quality growth stock.[76]

Thus, for the entrepreneur with a serious desire to build a major corporation over the long haul—as opposed to trying to start a company with the idea of taking it public in one or two years and letting the stockholders hold the bag for a still-green enterprise—the assistance of a privately owned venture capital (or business development) corporation can be of enormous value.

RELATIVES AND FRIENDS

When it comes to having relatives and friends put money into a new and unproven business venture, the matter is largely a case of "damned if you do and damned if you don't." Understand that, if you are successful in persuading individuals in this investor group to participate in financing the new venture, and if for some reason the venture fails (whether it's your fault or not), you may spend the rest of your life having to cope with the unpleasantness of intra-family ill will. Conversely, should the venture be financed by knowledgeable risk-taking venture capitalists who are in a position to sustain a substantial loss without experiencing undue personal hardships, the effect on the entrepreneur's relations with friends and relatives will be largely unchanged.

Unfortunately, it is common for friends and relatives to feel that they have rights of first refusal in deciding whether or not to invest in your ventures. In the event the new enterprise is financially successful and the relatives and friends have not been offered the opportunity to participate in the attendant capital appreciation, ill will of still another sort may result. In this situation, relatives and friends may feel that is is unfair of you to give "total strangers" an opportunity to make substantial financial gains through investing in you while at the same time you deprive *them* of a similar opportunity. My personal attitude in this matter is that relatives and friends should be permitted to invest in the new enterprise only to the extent that they would ordinarily invest in other risk propositions. If your great-aunt has to hock the family jewels in order to participate in the financing of *your* new venture, she should be discouraged.

A number of other authors on this subject suggest that, whenever relatives and friends are invited to participate in the financing of a venture, their investment should take the form of a simple loan. I feel that such an approach is grossly unfair. Friend- and relative-investors have every right to realize a capital return consistent with the risks involved. My feeling is that the terms and conditions offered to the relatives and friends should approximate those which would be exacted by sophisticated investors. Therefore, friends' and relatives' participation in the financing of the venture should take the form of loans with rights attached allowing for the purchase of stock (at a later date and at a predetermined price), of an equity position, or of a combination of the two.

I feel it is safe to say that, in a very large number of instances, relatives and friends play a key role in the financing of new enterprises. Frequently relatives and friends are the only investors who can be persuaded to participate in the early financing of a business, but too often such investments are made emotionally without the participant having any appreciation of the risks involved. Funds are advanced primarily out of the desire to give a helping hand to someone they know well and to whom they wish the best of luck. However, in such situations, people often lose the objectivity that should always characterize financial dealings and often neglect to shore up agreements and understandings with legal documentation. Consider the following two stories which have come to my attention within the last year.

Two bright and very ambitious young men conceived an idea for an exciting new electronics product. The young men decided to organize a company for the purpose of developing a prototype of their product as a prelude to launching a full-scale manufacturing and engineering business. One of these young men persuaded a close friend of his parents, herself a wealthy widow, to provide the necessary seed capital. The financing arrangements were completely informal. Details such as loan interest, the establishment of a corporation, and the creation of equity were not considered at all. Whenever the young men reached a point in the development of their prototype when additional funds were required, they would simply invite the sweet old lady down to their shop to view the progress which they had made to date and then ask for an additional $10,000 or $20,000 loan so that they might continue with their work.

One day when the prototype was very nearly complete, the young men learned of the death of their benefactress. Unfortunately, since no contractual relationship had been entered into at any point, this source of funds was cut off permanently. The widow's heirs expressed the feeling that their relative had been bilked and that they were not about to encourage further squandering of her estate.

Had these young men engaged the services of a competent attorney at the outset, a corporation could have been set up and a reserve of equity funds established by selling the woman stock in the business. In this manner, the traumatic effect on the business created by the death of its primary benefactress could have been avoided. With foresight, they could have made their benefactress a stockholder in the business, with a provision that her life be insured with the company as beneficiary. After the woman's death, funds from the policy could have been used for the purpose of buying out the holdings of the heirs to her estate. Instead, these young men spent almost a full year in trying to raise additional funds on terms they regarded as acceptable.

The second story involves a young man who started a company with money he obtained from a wealthy aunt. This young man was well on his way toward creating a moderately successful, although not yet profitable, enterprise. However, the untimely death of the aunt resulted in numerous unplanned-for difficulties. For one thing, the aunt's estate was placed in probate, and the flow of vital funds was suspended indefinitely. In addition, other heirs regarded the entrepreneur with great animosity, feeling that his efforts in launching his own business had significantly diminished the aunt's estate. Because financing of the enterprise was cut off, the entrepreneur found it necessary to secure full time employment with a major corporation. As of this writing, the company founded by this young man is listed as inactive. Because of rapid advances in technology, the products which he had spent so much time and effort designing are now obsolete. Thus, the potential returns of his labor and the money invested by his aunt have been irretrievably lost.

In summary, relatives and friends *may* be an extremely helpful source of venture capital. Often they are willing to invest in an enterprise at a time when no sophisticated investor would consider doing so. But, in accepting the financial resources of these investors, the entrepreneur should insure that all financing arrangements be legally documented. He should further satisfy himself that participating investors invest only those funds that they are in a position to lose comfortably. Wherever possible, arrangements should be made to insure that these investors will function as silent partners to eliminate the possibility that family squabbles may interfere with the day-to-day operation of the enterprise. (To accomplish this, the investors may be limited partners or may hold preferred stock.)

SALES FINANCE COMPANIES

The increasing use of the "installment plan" for the purchase of automobiles, major household appliances, jewelry, furniture, and many other consumer goods has placed considerable demand on the limited resources of the durable goods retailer. Furthermore, consumers do not represent the only sector of the economy that has come to make use of the installment purchase plan. In industry, such durables as office equipment, heavy machinery, and farm equipment are offered for sale on this basis. Again, the seller of these goods may not have sufficient working capital to permit his resources to be tied up for a long period of time in such contracts.

Enter the sales finance company. The primary activity of the sales finance company is the purchase, at a discount, of installment contracts. For example, a friend of mine who bought some furniture for his home on the installment plan was quite surprised to receive a letter a few weeks later indicating that a sales finance company had purchased his installment contract and that in the future he should forward all of his payments directly to that company. The sales finance company had relieved the seller of all collection responsibilities and the need to maintain a specialized credit department.

Consider this example. An entrepreneur may wish to establish a retail store for the sale of major household appliances. He may make arrangements with his suppliers for 60-day credit terms. In other words, he has 60 days from the receipt of his inventory until the time he must pay the invoice. Next, the retailer offers these goods for sale to the public. Assume that, within this original 60 days, a customer decides that he would like to purchase an appliance at a price representing the normal retail markup over and above the retailer's purchase price. However, the customer indicates that he would like to purchase the appliance on the installment plan. The retailer ascertains the credit worthiness of the customer through a quick check with a local credit information agency; and, in the event the customer proves to be a satisfactory risk, an installment sales contract is drawn up. Subsequently, the retailer offers this contract to a sales finance company at a discount and pays his supplier with these funds. The difference between the amount collected from the sales finance company and the price charged by the appliance manufacturer represents the amount necessary to cover the retailer's operating expenses and to provide him with a profit. Some firms doing a regular business through installment selling often have a *continuous* or *revolving* arrangement with a finance company whereby funds are made available on a constantly renewed pledge of accounts receivable.

Some finance companies, in addition to financing installment sales, also lend on retail inventory, equipment, accounts receivable, and wholesale inventory. Other finance companies will finance major appliances on the "floor plan" basis, where they take title to the inventory, place it on the dealers' sales floor, and take possession of the retail installment contract when the appliance is sold.

In summary, an entrepreneur who has to provide financing for his customers may find the services of a sales finance company of considerable help in selling his merchandise.

SAVINGS AND LOAN ASSOCIATIONS

Savings and loan associations[77] constitute the third largest type of financial institution in the nation. There are now approximately 6,000 such associations in the United States, with combined assets exceeding $200 billion. According to a leading industry publication,

> Associations are private institutions, established and operated under state and federal laws. These laws set the standards for the chartering of new institutions, govern

> operational practices and control the kinds of loans and other investments that can be
> made. In addition to the statutory law, there is a vast body of regulations issued by the
> supervisory officials. Over the years, a complicated web of statutes and regulations has
> been spun around savings and loan operations.
>
> The development of policy governing the conduct of business at the individual institution
> is the responsibility of a board of directors made up of local business and professional
> people.[78]

Although the major financing activity of savings and loan associations is the making
of loans for the purchase or construction of homes, other types of loans are also
available—all associated with real estate. If the demand on their resources for home
loans is less than the supply of available funds, associations may make loans for "other
purposes," as defined by the Federal Home Loan Bank Board:

> This classification contains many diverse kinds of loans. Loans for other purposes include
> apartment house loans, loans on income-producing nonresidential properties, land
> development loans and loans on building lots. This group also embraces advances to home
> owners on existing loans, advances for taxes and insurance which have been added to loan
> balances, and loans made to refinance existing loans. This last category includes the
> refinancing of mortgages previously held by other lenders.[79]

It is in this category of "other purpose" loans where a savings and loan association
may provide financial assistance to the entrepreneur who wishes to convert his
real-estate holdings into cash for use as equity in his own business.

SECURITIES DEALERS

Under the Securities Exchange Act of 1934, a securities "dealer" is defined to be
"any person engaged in the business of buying and selling securities *for his own
account*, through a broker or otherwise. . . or any person insofar as he buys or sells
securities for his own account, either individually or in some fiduciary capacity, but
not as a part of a regular business."[80] In contrast, a "broker" is "any person engaged
in the business of effecting transactions in securities *for the account of others*."[81]

In rare instances, where a new or small company has completed a registration of its
securities with the Securities and Exchange Commission under the appropriate
provisions of the Securities Act of 1933, it may be possible to obtain wide distribution
of the securities of the enterprise (almost always a desirable objective for the purpose
of limiting the holdings— and power—of any one stockholder) through a network of
securities dealers. Thus, it may be possible to sell stock in the company while paying an
amount somewhat less than the substantial and customary fees usually exacted by an
investment banker for providing this service.

As defined above, a dealer is one who normally buys stocks and other securities for
the purpose of later selling them, hopefully at a profit. However, a dealer *may* also

function as an *underwriter*. [In the securities trade, an *underwriter* is an individual who agrees to market all or part of an issue of securities to the public as a service to the seller (usually a corporation). Underwritings usually take one of three forms:

Firm

The underwriter agrees to pay the seller a fixed amount of money per share for an entire issue of securities such as common stock within a specified period of time after the offering date. The price paid to the seller always represents an amount discounted below the offering price—a carefully negotiated element in the underwriting agreement. During the offering period, the underwriter attempts to sell these shares at the specified offering price. Although he is obligated ultimately to pay the corporation for the entire issue, technically he takes title to only those shares that he is not able to sell.

All or None

The underwriter attempts to sell a specified number of shares within the offering period, and all funds collected are maintained in an escrow account until the issue is fully subscribed. In the event all shares are *not* sold, the money collected is returned to the would-be buyers and the offering is termed a failure.

Best Efforts

The underwriter agrees to do his best to sell as many of the registered shares as he can within a specified period of time. Any unsold shares are returned to the company. Because it is possible that the offering may be undersubscribed and the company fail to raise the amount of funds required to achieve the goals described in the prospectus, this type of underwriting is characterized by the greatest risk to the small firm and is the least desirable of the three here described.]

Although the "firm" underwriting is attractive from the standpoint of the new business, it is quite unlikely that *any* underwriter would consider such an arrangement—The certainty of being able to sell the entire issue at the offering price is far from guaranteed and his own risk would be substantial. Since the "best efforts" underwriting is not attractive from the standpoint of the new firm, let's take a closer look at the "all or none" possibility. To illustrate this technique for raising equity capital, consider the recent public offering by Data Recognition Corporation, a California-based high-technology company. A statement in the prospectus regarding dealer fees reads:

> While the offering is not being underwritten, the Company may pay commissions aggregating $52,500 ($.35 per share) [representing 5 percent of the $7 price to the public] to members of the National Association of Securities Dealers, Inc. (NASD), who

sell shares of the Common Stock offered hereby.... The total commissions are computed on the assumption that all shares will be sold, and that all sales will be made through such dealers.[82]

Additionally, the company had to pay 38 cents per share in other expenses incident to this offering.[83] The prospectus further explains that this

is a non-underwritten offering, undertaken by the Company through its officers and directors, without payment of commissions except as set forth above. Because such persons are inexperienced in the sale of securities, there is no assurance that all or any of the shares offered hereby will be sold.[84]

It should be pointed out that although the officers of the Data Recognition Corporation and the securities dealers involved were not underwriters *per se*, they nevertheless functioned in this capacity. Incidentally, the offering described here *was* successful and the desired funds *were* raised.

For a discussion of the pros and cons of public offerings for small companies, see "INVESTMENT BANKERS" above.

SELF UNDERWRITINGS

In some instances, a company with little or no proven operating history may find that it cannot raise sufficient funds either through lending and credit channels or through a private placement of stock. In such a situation, it is rare that any reputable investment banker will underwrite a new offering of securities. Or if the services of an underwriter are available, the management of the enterprise may decide that the underwriting expenses are excessive in relation to the amount of capital required. Alternatively, a public offering of securities may be attempted through a *self* underwriting. As in the case of *any* public offering of stock, retention of the professional services of a qualified attorney is a *must* in navigating the customary Securities and Exchange Commission and state securities regulations and registration labyrinth. Failure to obtain legal assistance could land you in jail because of the strict enforcement of laws reflecting federal and state governmental concern for the safety of the investing public and the protection of our capitalistic system of private enterprise.

In the event that a small or new company wishes to make a public offering of stock amounting to $500,000 or less in any one year, exemption from a full-scale SEC securities registration is available under Section 3(b), as amended, of the Securities Act of 1933 by meeting the conditions prescribed under Regulation A of the SEC regulations. These include the filing with the appropriate SEC regional office of a notification on Form 1-A and the filing and use of a circular that contains basic information about the issues and the security. (In the case of an offering of $50,000 or less, no circular is required.) This filing must take place at least 10 working days prior to the date the offering is to be made.

In computing the maximum offerings for any given year, any offerings previously made within that year must be included. Thus, if an offering is contemplated for November and $200,000 in securities were sold in July, the new offering may not exceed $300,000. Regardless of how such securities are marketed, the $500,000 figure represents *the amount the investing public pays* and *not* the net return after deduction of the legal fees, printing fees, accounting fees, registration fees, postage fees, and any other fees incident to the offering.

Materials filed with the SEC regional office under the Regulation A exemption are carefully examined to make certain that the proposed issue qualifies for the exemption and that all of the required disclosures have been made. Usually, a letter is sent to the offering company indicating areas of noncompliance. If any such areas are present, the offering is suspended until the matter is resolved to the satisfaction of the SEC. If the government determines that the offering circular is seriously misleading or that an attempt has been made to defraud the public, permanent suspension may result. In any event, a hearing may be requested to consider the case, after which a decision will be made regarding retention of the suspension order.

For a complete description of the requirements of a Regulation A exemption status and the filing procedure necessary to qualify, write to the SEC at the address below and request a copy of the publication "Regulation A, General Exemption from Registration under the Securities Act of 1933," SEC document number 486.

Finally, in considering almost any stock offering, it must be remembered that qualifying for the Regulation A exemption merely satisfies certain federal government requirements. Each sovereign state has its own rules (called "Blue Sky" laws) *in addition to* those of the federal government! *Now* won't you please go talk to an attorney?

The staff of the SEC is available to small business owners and managers to discuss problems in regard to securities, such as registration and qualification requirements, exemptions, and disclosures. The Washington, D. C. area address is Room 532, Crystal Mall No. 2 Building, 1921 Jefferson Highway, P.O. Box 2247, Arlington, Virginia 22202.

Regional and Branch Offices are located around the nation as follows:

Zone 1: New York, New Jersey. 26 Federal Plaza, New York, New York 10007.

Zone 2: Massachusetts, Connecticut, Rhode Island, Vermont, New Hampshire, Maine. Suite 2203, John F. Kennedy Federal Building, Government Center, Boston, Massachusetts 02203.

Zone 3: Tennessee, North Carolina, South Carolina, Georgia, Alabama, Mississippi, Florida, and that part of Louisiana lying east of the Atchafalaya River. Suite 138, 1371 Peachtree Street N. E., Atlanta, Georgia 30309. *Branch*: Room 1504, Federal Office Building, 51 S. W. First Avenue, Miami, Florida 33130.

Zone 4: Michigan, Indiana, Ohio, Kentucky, Minnesota, Wisconsin, Iowa, Illinois, Missouri, Kansas City (Kansas). Room 1708, U. S. Courthouse and Federal Office Building, 219 South Dearborn Street, Chicago, Illinois 60604. *Branches:* Room 779, Federal Office Building, 1240 East Ninth at Lakeside, Cleveland, Ohio 44199. 230 Federal Building, Detroit, Michigan 48226. Room 916, Federal Building, 208 North Broadway, St. Louis, Missouri 63102.

Zone 5: Oklahoma, Arkansas, Texas, that part of Louisiana lying west of the Atchafalaya River, and Kansas (except Kansas City). 503, U. S. Courthouse, 10th and Lamar Streets, Fort Worth, Texas 76102. *Branch:* 2606 Federal Office and Courts Building, 515 Rusk Avenue, Houston, Texas 77002.

Zone 6: Wyoming, Colorado, New Mexico, Nebraska, North Dakota, South Dakota, Utah. 7224 Federal Building, 1961 Stout Street, Denver, Colorado 80202. *Branch:* Room 6004, Federal Building, 125 South State Street, Salt Lake City, Utah 84111.

Zone 7: California, Nevada, Arizona, Hawaii. Box 36042, 450 Golden Gate Avenue, San Francisco, California 94102. *Branch:* Room 1403, U. S. Courthouse, 312 North Spring Street, Los Angeles, California 90012.

Zone 8: Washington, Oregon, Idaho, Montana, Alaska. 900 Hoge Building, Seattle, Washington 98104.

Zone 9: Virginia, West Virginia, Maryland, Delaware, District of Columbia, Pennsylvania. Room 532, Crystal Mall No. 2 Building, 1921 Jefferson Highway, P. O. Box 2247, Arlington, Virginia 22202.

SMALL BUSINESS ADMINISTRATION

The Small Business Administration was created by Congress on July 30, 1953. The enabling legislation, known as the Small Business Act of 1953, provides formal governmental recognition of the importance of this country's five million small businesses to the maintenance of a viable economy.

Without a doubt, the most important activity of the SBA is the administration of a financial assistance program for small business. A staff of more than 4,000 government employees, working through a network of 73 field offices, brings the benefits of SBA financial services to all qualified businessmen. Current SBA loans outstanding exceed an aggregate of $1 billion.[85]

Although the SBA offers a number of forms of financial assistance, including disaster loans and lease guarantees, we will restrict our discussion here to four programs of primary practical interest to the average small businessman. A discussion of SBA-licensed Small Business Investment Companies will be presented in the next section.

Bank Participation Loans

Approximately two-thirds of the loans made by the SBA involve the participation of commercial banks or other private lending institutions. If a small business does not qualify for an ordinary bank loan because it fails to meet certain financial criteria, a bank may be willing to lend money to the enterprise provided the Small Business Administration will guarantee the note. Such SBA-guaranteed loans may be used for:

1. Business construction, expansion or conversion.
2. Purchase of machinery, equipment, facilities, supplies, or materials.
3. Working capital.

Provided the loan applicant is able to demonstrate an ability to repay a loan and any other debts out of company profits to the satisfaction of SBA examiners, the SBA may participate in a loan in either of two ways:

1. By guaranteeing up to 90 percent or $350,000 of a bank loan, whichever is less. (In this instance, the SBA merely *guarantees* 90 percent of the bank loan or $350,000, whichever is less; the SBA does not provide an immediate outlay of cash.)
2. By providing $150,000 as the SBA share of an immediate-participation loan with the bank.

The term of the loan may vary, depending on the use to which the funds are to be put. For construction loans, the term may be as long as 15 years. In the case of a working capital loan, the term may be as short as five years or less.[86]

Direct Loans

If a bank or other private lending institution declines to participate in an SBA loan to a new or small enterprise, the SBA may choose to make a direct loan to the business subject to a $100,000 limit. Loan application evaluation criteria, interest rates, maturity dates, and repayment rates for such direct loans are normally the same as those that characterize bank-participation loans.[87]

State Investment Development Corporations

Many states have business-development corporations formed in cooperation with the SBA for the purpose of supplying long-term loans and/or equity capital to small companies. The purpose of such programs is to induce new businesses to locate within a given state, thus enhancing industrial and commercial growth rates and providing employment for its citizens. These state development companies are usually in a position to obtain matching funds from the Small Business Administration to augment their capital. Loans to the development companies from the SBA may be for as long as 20 years. Assistance to state development companies from the SBA for such endeavors are made under the SBA 501 program, authorized under Section 501 of the Small Business Investment Act of 1958.[88]

Local Development Companies

Local development companies are sometimes established within a community in cooperation with the SBA for projects such as industrial parks, downtown renewal, shopping centers, and (of interest to the reader of this volume) financial assistance to small businesses. A group of 25 or more citizens may form a local development company, either as a profit or a nonprofit corporation. These local development companies may obtain as much as $350,000 in SBA funds—for periods of up to 25 years and at very attractive interest rates—for each of the small businesses they wish to aid. Local development companies may also involve the participation of banks; insurance companies; pension-fund groups; and other agencies, authorities, and commissions. The SBA may participate with these groups also. SBA participation in such investments is made under the 502 program, authorized under Section 502 of the Small Business Investment Act of 1958.[89]

SMALL BUSINESS INVESTMENT COMPANIES

Although individual investors have been providing venture capital for new and small business in the United States since the birth of the Nation, no federally-sponsored source of such financing existed until 1958, when Congress passed the Small Business Investment Act. This Act authorized the founding of a special class of investment companies for the encouragement of small business.

> Small business investment companies (SBICs) are financial institutions created to make equity capital and long-term credit (with maturities of at least 5 years) available to small, independent businesses. SBICs are licensed by the Federal Government's Small Business Administration, but they are privately-organized and privately-managed firms which set their own policies and make their own investment decisions.[90]

In return for pledging to finance only small businesses, SBICs may qualify for long-term loans from the Small Business Administration.

> To date, SBICs have disbursed about $1.8 billion by making over 37,000 loans and investments. The concerns they have financed have far out-performed all national averages as measured by increases in assets, sales, profits, and new employment.[91]

The overwhelming majority of all business firms in this country qualify as "small." As a general rule, companies are eligible for SBIC financing if they have assets under

$5 million, net worth under $2.5 million, and average after-tax earnings of less than $250,000 during the past two years. A firm may also qualify as "small" under an employment standard or an amount-of-annual-sales standard. Both of these standards vary from industry to industry. In most cases, a call to your local SBA office or the offices of one of your local SBICs will enable you in short order to resolve the question of eligibility.

All SBIC financing terms are tailored to meet the needs of the individual small business and the particular SBIC fund involved. Thus, the small business and the SBIC negotiate the terms for the financing arrangement—the SBIC might buy shares of stock in the company, might make a straight loan, or might agree upon some combination of the two.

Commonly, SBICs are interested in realizing capital gains from purchasing a stock at a low price and selling it at a later date at a much higher price. Thus, SBICs will purchase stock in a small company or advance funds through a debt instrument (a note or debenture) with conversion privileges or rights to buy stock at a predetermined later date.

According to a publication of the National Association of SBICs, "Industry averages show that for every SBIC dollar placed with a small business concern, two additional senior dollars become available from commercial banks or other sources."[92] Regarding the unique advantages of SBIC financing, this same publication states that

> Before it receives its license, an SBIC must prove that its management and directors are experienced individuals with a broad range of business and professional talents.
>
> This expertise will be applied to assist your business, supplementing the skills of your own management team. Here again, the actual pattern of management and financial counseling will be cut to fit each specific situation.
>
> SBICs can make only long-term loans or equity investments; therefore, their interests and yours will coincide—both of you will want the firm to grow and prosper.[93]

A recent addition to the SBIC program is the Minority Enterprise SBIC (MESBIC). This special class of SBICs was created for the purpose of providing venture capital for socially and economically disadvantaged entrepreneurs. At the present time, only a relatively small number of MESBICs are operational.

For an excellent overview of the first decade of the SBIC industry, readers are referred to the book *SBICs: Pioneers in Organized Venture Capital*, by Charles M. Noone and Stanley M. Rubel. Information on how to secure a copy of this work is available in Appendix 1.

STATE AND LOCAL INDUSTRIAL DEVELOPMENT COMMISSIONS

Many cities, counties, and states across the nation have progressed in recent years in their willingness to provide financial encouragement for struggling new or small businesses. Although the amount of financial assistance offered may vary substantially from community to community and from state to state, the value of encouraging new business is recognized by all, and many localities have set up their own industrial development commissions.

In many instances, the financial assistance offered through state and local industrial development commissions is available in situations where banks or other conservative institutions are not willing to participate in the financing. This is particularly true if the new business does not meet AAA conventional credit requirements. The funds for industrial development commission financing are generally obtained through the issuance of municipal bonds (interest on these bonds is tax-free to the purchasers).

Municipal legislative bodies may also appropriate public funds in their treasuries for the purpose of encouraging new business. Assistance rendered under these programs may include very low-cost, long-term loans for the construction of manufacturing facilities or for the purchase of capital equipment, or it may provide for subsidized employee training programs. In some cases, working capital may be provided. Also, very favorable tax concessions may be offered to encourage new enterprises. Loan repayment periods may run anywhere from 5 to 35 years, depending on the community involved.

Advertisements are regularly run in the leading financial journals by many states and local communities that wish to encourage the growth of new industry within their borders. Information on the advantages of establishing a new enterprise in a given locality may be obtained by writing to the State Industrial Development Commissioner or Chamber of Commerce of any state in which the entrepreneur is interested in locating his facility. The State Commissioner or Chamber of Commerce representative will be more than happy to provide information on the special advantages that would accrue to the founders of a new business choosing to locate in his sovereign state. Information furnished ordinarily includes a discussion of municipal services and utilities, training programs, state and local tax-rate structures, housing, labor supply, availability of raw materials, transportation facilities, specifics on available buildings and building sites, and special financing that might be available through governmental or private sources.

TAX-EXEMPT FOUNDATIONS AND CHARITABLE TRUSTS

A compilation made in late 1968 by the Internal Revenue Service identified some 30,262 foundations.[94] From the standpoint of utility, however, the entrepreneur-capital seeker should find *The Foundation Directory*[95] of far more practical value. Ostensibly, the majority of the foundations in this country have been established for the purpose of serving and enhancing the general well-being of society, although many of these foundations are little more than tax-avoidance mechanisms for their creators.[96] However, there are a large number of foundations which *do* render service to the community.

In some instances, an entrepreneur may wish to launch a business with a product or service that will benefit society; and this entrepreneur may be able to obtain significant financial assistance in the form of grants or loans from an interested foundation. If he does appropriate research on the subject (Start by consulting *The Foundation Directory* mentioned above.), he may be able to identify a foundation dedicated to serving a social need in consonance with the thrust of his planned enterprise. Thus, he may persuade the foundation to assist in the launching of his venture. Three examples illustrate this process:

1. An entrepreneur with a background in medical electronics may wish to launch an enterprise for the purpose of developing and manufacturing a badly needed new medical-electronic instrument. This entrepreneur may be able to persuade the foundation to provide a grant for his company for the purpose of developing such an instrument.
2. An entrepreneur may wish to start a profitable business for the purpose of providing management and technical assistance to minority enterprises. He may persuade an interested foundation to make him a low-interest-rate loan for launching his enterprise.
3. The entrepreneur with plans for the creation of a new business for the purpose of manufacturing products to reduce environmental pollution may afford a foundation a unique opportunity simultaneously to serve society and to realize gains for its portfolio through equity participation in the new enterprise.

These examples are intended merely to suggest only *some* of the avenues by which a tax-exempt foundation or charitable trust may be approached and subsequently induced to participate in financing a deserving venture. With a little imagination, I'm certain you can think of many others. *Remember*: the primary source in identifying a suitable foundation is the directory mentioned above.

TRADE SUPPLIERS

There are many characteristics in the trade supplier-new venture financial relationship that are similar to those of the customer-new venture financial relationship referred to above. Let's consider some of the more important elements that motivate trade supplier assistance:

Develop Customer Loyalty

A new company that receives substantial financial assistance from its trade suppliers will develop a sense of loyalty to those helpers. I have spoken with the presidents of many small firms who acknowledge that loyalty and appreciation remain for years after the new company becomes successful.

Expand Customer Base

By assisting in the creation of new customers, a trade supplier may enlarge its available market and increase the demand for its own output. The result may be greater profitability potential through economies of scale. (The unit cost for 100 widgets should be significantly less than the unit cost for 10 widgets.)

Create Markets for New Products

In some instances, a trade supplier may develop a product for which no market presently exists. For example, a textile manufacturer may produce a new synthetic yarn that existing customers may not be willing to accept. If this supplier encourages the launching of a new cloth or clothing manufacturer, a distribution channel (customer) will have been created.

The means available to a trade supplier for furnishing assistance to a new firm are many:

Extended Credit Terms

The helpful trade supplier may ship goods to his customer on extended credit terms. In some instances, the supplier may offer terms wherein he does not receive payment until the entrepreneur is successful in securing payment from his own customers. Such terms can run anywhere from 30 days to periods in excess of six months.

Loan Guarantees

If a trade supplier wishes to assist a new customer without tying up his own working capital, he may guarantee a bank loan for his customer's account, thereby permitting the customer to pay cash for his purchases. Of course, any interest which the bank or other financial institution may charge must be paid by the customer.

Direct Loans

In some instances, a major trade supplier may agree to provide the new firm with a direct loan.

Purchase of Stock in New Company

Through the expedient of providing equity capital to launch a new customer, a trade supplier may effectively set the stage for an eventual merger or acquisition.

Lend or Lease Equipment

Some trade suppliers are primarily engaged in furnishing customers with raw materials for processing. This processing may require the use of expensive equipment and machinery, which a new company may have difficulty financing. By lending or leasing the equipment to the customer, a supplier may very effectively expand the market for his output.

TRUST COMPANIES AND BANK TRUST DEPARTMENTS

Since trust companies and bank trust departments both function in the same manner, the following discussion will refer only to trust companies, including bank trust departments by inference. (It should be recognized, however, that bank trust departments far outnumber trust companies.)

A trust company is a financial institution organized primarily to administer funds assigned to its supervision for the advantage of the beneficiary. If the trust is discretionary, the trustee is permitted considerable latitude in the manner in which the funds are invested. Although trust company investment policies have always been extremely conservative, clients recently have begun to insist upon the type of portfolio appreciation that is possible only by investment in growth securities. In some instances, trust companies may even invest a part of a client's portfolio in the stock of a new company—particularly if authorized or directed to do so by the client.

Trust companies do not usually interact with the management of small new portfolio companies; instead, they prefer to invest portfolio assets on a limited partnership basis as members of large venture capital organizations staffed with management consultants who monitor the progress of new enterprises.

Although an entrepreneur seeking venture capital is quite unlikely to find it in a trust company, he may reasonably expect assistance from the trust officers in locating more suitable sources of such capital.

VETERANS ADMINISTRATION

Veterans of World War II, the Korean Conflict, the Post-Korean Conflict, and the Vietnam Era who have been discharged or separated under other than dishonorable circumstances and who meet certain other Veterans Administration eligibility requirements may be able to obtain VA-guaranteed loans of up to $2,000 for non-real estate purposes, such as the purchase of capital equipment and supplies and the acquisition of working capital. VA-guaranteed loans of up to $4,000 are available to eligible veterans for the purchase of real estate (other than the purchase of a home, which is a separate service) for business or farm use.

Although these dollar amounts are rather small, properly used they may provide the entrepreneur enough assistance to enable him to complete the development of a prototype or moonlight in some other activity appropriate to his venture while he is still employed elsewhere. Having taken advantage of this opportunity to develop his concept from the idea stage to the hardware or business-plan stage, the entrepreneur may find himself in a much more attractive negotiating position when trying to raise venture capital. Further information on these and other veteran benefits is published by the Veterans Administration Information Service. To obtain a copy of the VA Fact Sheet IS-1, "Federal Benefits for Veterans and Dependents," send 30 cents to the Superintendent of Documents, U. S. Government Printing Office, Washington, D. C. 20402.

Notes

1. Peter F. Drucker, *The Age of Discontinuity*, New York: Harper & Row, 1969, p. 43.

2. The Pert-O-Graph Kit is available from Halcomb Associates, 149 San Lazaro Avenue, Sunnyvale, California 94086, at $24.50 postpaid.

3. "Parents' Creed" is available in a 14 x 16 inch hand-screened felt scroll, in red/blue or blue/green for $3.00 postpaid from the John Philip Company, 1070 Florence Way, Campbell, California 95008.

4. Hannah Campbell, *Why Did They Name it. . . ?*, New York: Ace Books, 1964, p. 190.

5. Dr. Stanley F. Kaisel in a speech presented at the "San Francisco Entrepreneurship Workshop Series on Managing a New Enterprise in Today's Economy," Massachusetts Institute of Technology, Spring 1971, held in Palo Alto, California.

6. Russell Freedman, *Thomas Alva Edison*, New York: American RDM Corporation, 1966, p. 43.

7. Arthur F. Snyder, Senior Vice President of the New England Merchants National Bank, Boston, Mass., speaking on "Panel on Financing New Enterprises," MIT Seminar for Young Alumni, Palo Alto, California, May, 1970.

8. *The Failure Record through 1969*, Dun and Bradstreet, Inc., 1970, p. 2.

9. Laurence J. Peter and Raymond Hull, *The Peter Principle*, New York: William Morrow and Co., 1969.

10. L. Charles Burlage, *The Small Businessman and His Problems*, New York: Vantage, 1958, Preface.

11. Center for Venture Management, 811 East Wisconsin Avenue, Milwaukee, Wisconsin 53202.

12. Zig Ziglar, president, the Zigmanship Institute, 6148 Dilbeck Lane, Dallas, Texas 75240.

13. *Books in Print*, 2 volumes, New York: R. R. Bowker Co., rev. annually.

14. U. S. Department of Commerce, National Bureau of Standards, *State Invention Expositions*, Washington, D. C.: Office of Invention & Innovation.

15. U. S. Department of Commerce, Patent Office, *Q and A About Patents*, Washington, D. C.: Government Printing Office, 1970, p. 3.

16. *Ibid.*, pp. 3-4.

17. U. S. Department of Commerce, Patent Office, *The U. S. Patent Office's "Disclosure Document Program*," Washington, D. C.: Government Printing Office, 1969.

18. U. S. Department of Commerce, Patent Office, *General Information Concerning Patents*, Washington, D. C.: Government Printing Office, rev. 1969. p. 4.

19. C. Howard Mann, "Small Business Profits From Unpatentable Ideas," *Management Aids for Small Business, Annual No. 3*, Washington, D. C.: Small Business Administration, Government Printing Office, 1957, p. 48.

20. Martindale-Hubbell, *Law Directory*, Summit, New Jersey: Martindale-Hubbell, Inc., 1970. (In Five Volumes; 103rd Annual Edition, 1971, printed by R. R. Donnelley & Sons Co., Chicago, Illinois and Crawfordsville, Indiana.)

21. "How to Start and Operate a Small Business," Massachusetts Institute of Technology, Seminar for Young Alumni, 2 days, May 19, 1970, Palo Alto, California.

22. Louis L. Allen, *Starting and Succeeding in Your Own Small Business*, New York: Grosset & Dunlap, 1968, p. 147.

23. E. F. Heizer, Jr., *Proceedings, Venture Capital and Management*, Second Annual Boston College Management Seminar, May 28-29, 1970, Chestnut Hill, Massachusetts: Boston College Press, 1970, p. 79.

24. Charles B. Smith, *ibid.*, p. 88.

25. Mark Rollinson, *NEW BUSINESS: Innovative Technology, Management and Capital*, Boston College Management Seminar, May 22, 23, 1969 Proceedings, Chestnut Hill, Massachusetts: Boston College Press, 1969, p. 89.

26. G. Stanton Geary, "Venture Capital Financing for Small Business—A Symposium," Reprinted from *The Business Lawyer*, Vol. 24, No. 3, April 1969, American Bar Association, 1969, p. 944.

27. Benno C. Schmidt, "The Money is There," *Forbes*, December 1, 1970, p. 45.

28. The other two types of investment companies are face amount certificate companies and unit investment trusts.

29. Nilo Lindgren, "Signposts on the Trail of Venture Capital," *Innovation*, September, 1969, p. 47.

30. Fund of Letters, Inc., *Annual Report*, 1969.

31. Jack Zwick, *A Handbook of Small Business Finance*, Washington, D. C.: Small Business Administration, 1965, Chapter 8.

32. *Ibid.*, p. 60.

33. FCNB Capital Corp., "Introductory Brochure."

34. Meinhard-Commercial Corporation, *Commercial Financing: What It Is and What It Does*, New York: Meinhard-Commercial Corporation, 1969, p. 8.

35. *Handbook for Federal Credit Unions*, Washington, D. C.: Bureau of Federal Credit Unions, 1964, p. 1.

36. *Ibid.*, p. 7.

37. Title 12, Chapter 14, United States Code, Section 1759.

38. *Credit Manual for Federal Credit Unions*, Washington , D. C.: Bureau of Federal Credit Unions, 1969, p. 7.

39. *EDA Business Development Loans. Who Can Borrow. How to Apply*, Washington, D. C.: The U. S. Department of Commerce, September, 1970, p. 3.

40. *Ibid.*, p. 4.

41. *Ibid.*, pp. 5-6.

42. *Ibid.*, pp. 6-7.

43. *Ibid.*, p. 10.

44. *Ibid.*, p. 11.

45. *Ibid.*, p. 13.

46. Meinhard-Commercial Corporation, "Essentials of Factoring," *Factoring; What It Is and What It Does*, New York: Meinhard-Commercial Corporation, 1969, p. 5.

47. Based in part on comments made by Robert D. Stillman, general partner of Payson and Trask, at the Boston College Management Seminar, "New Business: Innovative Technology, Management and Capital," held at the college on May 22 and 23, 1969.

48. "The Money Is There," *Forbes*, December 1, 1970, p. 45.

49. "Has the Bear Market Killed Venture Capital?," *Forbes*, June 15, 1970, pp. 31-37.

50. Conversation with Mr. Harry J. Klein, president of Peoples Industrial Plan, Louisville, Kentucky, on August 7, 1971.

51. Peter F. Bezanson, "Raising Public Funds," *Industrial Banker*, Oct. 1969, p. 6.

52. "What Do You Do With $81 Million?," *Forbes*, July 15, 1970, pp. 42-44.

53. Harvey D. Shapiro, "Managing Money Down on State Farm," *Institutional Investor*, October, 1969.

54. *Ibid.*

55. The Investment Advisers Act of 1940, Section 202(a) (11).

56. United States Securities and Exchange Commission, *Information on Registration and Regulation of INVESTMENT-ADVISERS*, Washington, D. C., January, 1968, p. 1.

57. "Financing New Ventures," *NEW BUSINESS: Innovative Technology, Management and Capital*, Proceedings of Boston College Management Seminar, May 22, 23, 1969, Chestnut Hill, Massachusettes: Boston College Press, 1969, p. 98.

58. *Ibid.*, p. 99.

59. *Ibid.*, p. 100.

60. Thomas J. Davis, Jr., "The New Environment for Venture Capital." *WEMA Perspective*, Summer, 1970.

61. Becker Technological Associates, "Introductory Brochure," 1968.

62. *Ibid.*

63. Bateman Eichler, Hill Richards, Inc., "Financing Fast Growing Companies," Introductory Brochure.

64. Securities Act of 1933, Section 2 (11).

65. National Association of Investment Clubs, *The National Association of Investment Clubs: Its Organization and Its Operation*, Royal Oak, Michigan: National Association of Investment Clubs.

66. *Ibid.*

67. *Ibid.*

68. *1970 Mutual Fund Fact Book*, Washington, D. C.: Investment Company Institute, 1969, p. 5.

69. *Ibid.*

70. See "Orphan Products," Chapter 2 above.

71. See "Corporate Venture Capital Departments or Subsidiaries" above.

72. Securities and Exchange Commission, *Statistical Bulletin*, Washington, D. C., May, 1971.

73. "What Do You Do with $81 Million?" *Forbes*, July 15, 1970, p. 42.

74. Introductory brochure, Heizer Corporation, Chicago, Illinois.

75. *Forbes, op. cit.*

76. Introductory brochure, *op. cit.*

77. Also known as building and loan associations, cooperative banks (in New England), homestead associations (in Louisiana), building associations, and savings associations.

78. *Savings and Loan Fact Book 1968*, Chicago: United States Savings and Loan League, 1968, p. 54.

79. *Ibid.*, p. 89.

80. Section 3(a)(5) of the Securities Exchange Act of 1934.

81. Section 3(a)(4) of the Securities Exchange Act of 1934.

82. Prospectus, Data Recognition Corporation, Palo Alto, California, March 9, 1970, p. 1.

83. *Ibid.*

84. *Ibid.*

85. Addison W. Parris, *The Small Business Administration*, New York: Frederick A. Praeger, Publishers, 1968, p. 57.

86. "Economic Opportunity Loans (EOL)," *Small Business Administration: What It Is; What It Does*, Washington, D. C.: Small Business Administration, p. 6.

87. *Ibid.*, p. 5.

88. *Ibid.*, p. 7.

89. *Ibid.*

90. *Membership Directory*, Washington, D. C.: National Association of Small Business Investment Companies, 1970-1971, p. ii.

91. *Ibid.*

92. *Ibid.*, p. iv.

93. *Ibid.*

94. U. S. Congress, House, Select Committee on Small Business, *Tax-Exempt Foundations: Their Impact on Small Business*, 1968, p. 39.

95. Marianna Lewis, ed., *The Foundation Directory*, New York: Basic Books, Inc., 1971.

96. Joseph C. Goulden, *The Money Givers*, New York: Random House, 1971, pp. 19-50.

Appendix 1

ANNOTATED LIST OF DIRECTORIES AND GUIDES TO
VENTURE CAPITAL SOURCES

This comprehensive list of capital directories and guides is designed to include all the publications that I have discovered in more than a year's research while preparing this volume. As may be expected in a field of such universal interest as "how to make money," the quality and depth of the available material is subject to considerable variation. But since even a *poorly* presented statement of fact—not readily available elsewhere—is better than none at all, the compilation of this list is intentionally unselective. Accordingly, inclusion of a particular title in this list does not necessarily constitute my endorsement thereof.

I have taken every reasonable step possible to indicate accurately the price and availability of each of the following publications. However, since such pricing and availability depends solely on the individual publishers whose names follow each entry, I can assume no responsibility whatever for price changes or the withdrawal of any of these directories and guides from the market.

American Banker, comp. "100 Largest Finance Companies in the U.S." *American Banker*, May 28, 1970.

> This directory should prove quite helpful to the entrepreneur in lending perspective to this sector of the financial community.
>
> Available only through the American Banker, 525 West 42nd Street, New York, New York 10036. Price 50 cents, minimum order $1.

American Bar Association. *Venture Capital Financing for Small Business—a Symposium.* Chicago, Illinois: American Bar Association, 1969.

> This series of articles is designed to acquaint the reader with venture capital financing, the types of assistance available for small business concerns from venture capitalists, who and what they are, and how they operate. The articles are designed primarily to acquaint attorneys with the various factors to be considered when a small business client seeks venture capital.
>
> Reprints of this 30-page series may be obtained through Fred B. Rothman & Co., 57 Leuning Street, South Hackensack, New Jersey 07606. $4.50.

American Institute of Certified Public Accountants. *Financing the Small Business.* New York: The Institute, 1959.

> This book was prepared by the Professional Development Division of the Institute primarily for use as a teaching aid for professional accountants. Since the subject matter has not been considered and acted upon by the counsel of the

Institute, it does not represent an official position of the Institute. Material covered includes cash forecasting, internal sources of financing, equipment financing, bank financing, equity financing, and commercial finance companies.

This book is out of print.

Arthur M. Gelber & Company. *Public Money or Private Placement?* Beverly Hills, California: Arthur M. Gelber & Company, 1970.

This eight-page booklet discusses the problems of start-up, financial management, financial operating difficulties, and expansion. Emphasis is placed upon small businesses that are technologically oriented:

Available free of charge from Arthur M. Gelber & Company, 141 El Camino, Beverly Hills, California 90212.

Bank of America National Trust & Savings Association. "Applying for Minority Business Loans," *Small Business Reporter*. San Francisco, California: 1969.

Although the title suggests that this 28-page report is limited to minority business financing, that isn't the case. This report includes advice on how to obtain a loan and a brief glossary of financial terms.

Available at branch offices of the Bank of America or by mail from *Small Business Reporter*, Department 3120, Bank of America National Trust & Savings Association, San Francisco, California 94120. $1.

Bank of America National Trust & Savings Association. "Financing Small Business," *Small Business Reporter*, Vol. 8, No. 5, 1969.

This eight-page report includes a brief survey of small-business financing. Included are blank forms for profit and loss statements, projected cash budgets, and personal financial statements. Also included is a discussion of the necessary steps to obtain and maintain a credit rating.

Available at branch offices of the Bank of America or by mail from *Small Business Reporter*, Department 3120, Bank of America National Trust & Savings Association, San Francisco, California 94120. $1.

Baumback, Clifford M.; Lawyer, Kenneth; and Kelley, Pearce C. *How to Organize and Operate a Small Business.* 5th ed. Englewood Cliffs, New Jersey: Prentice-Hall, Inc. 1973.

Originally copyrighted in 1940 and now in its fifth edition, this updated classic is encyclopedic in its coverage of small business problems. New material includes obtaining a franchise, concern for the environment, stricter credit regulations, the Federal crime insurance program, and a variety of programs designed to stimulate minority business programs.

Available through bookstores or directly from the publisher at Englewood Cliffs, New Jersey 07632. $11.95.

Berkowitz, Nathaniel C. "Providing Capital for Your Firm," *Management Aids for Small Manufacturers, Annual No. 8*, Washington, D.C.: Small Business Administration, Government Printing Office, 1962, pp. 1-5.

A financial and management consultant outlines several possible money-providing methods. The reader alone must judge which one method or combination of methods would be appropriate to his circumstances.

Available by ordering from Superintendent of Documents, Government Printing Office, Washington, D.C. 20402. 45 cents.

Board of Governors of the Federal Reserve System. *All-Bank Statistics, United States, 1896-1955.* Washington, D.C.: 1959.

A compilation of the total assets and liabilities of state and national banks on a state-by-state basis for a 60-year period.

Available from the Board of Governors of the Federal Reserve System, Washington, D.C. 20551. $4.

Bogen, J. I., and Shipman, S. S., eds. *Financial Handbook*, 4th rev. ed. New York: Ronald Press, 1968.

Contains contributions from experts on financial institutions and all methods of business financing. This edition also deals with the gold crisis.

Available through your local bookstore or from the publisher at 79 Madison Avenue, New York, New York 10016. $17.50.

Bonneville, Joseph H.; Dewey, Lloyd E.; and Kelley, Harry M. *Organizing and Financing Business.* Englewood Cliffs, New Jersey: Prentice-Hall, Inc., 1959.

This book, revised in 1959, is a classic on the subject of the formation of new enterprises. It is written like a textbook; and, therefore, some might find it pretty heavy reading. However, for those willing to take the time, a careful reading should provide considerable insight into the mechanisms of business start-up.

Available through your local bookstore or from the publisher at Englewood Cliffs, New Jersey 07632. $11.50.

Boston College Management Seminar. *New Business: Innovative Technology, Management and Capital.* Proceedings of the First Annual Meeting, May 22-23, 1969. Chestnut Hill, Mass.: Boston College Press, 1969.

This report is a transcript of the seminar proceedings. Major subjects to which the speakers addressed themselves include emerging technologies, successful technical entrepreneurship, managing the new company, financing new ventures, and entrepreneural development.

Available by ordering from Management Institute, Fulton Hall, 405A, Boston College, Chestnut Hill, Massachusetts 02167. $6.

Break, G.F., et al. *Federal Credit Agencies.* Englewood Cliffs, New Jersey: Prentice-Hall, Inc., 1963

This is a collection of research studies prepared for the Commission on Money and Credit.

Out of print, but available in many business libraries.

Bullock, Hugh. *The Story of Investment Companies.* New York: Columbia University Press, 1959.

Discusses the development of British, Canadian, and American investment companies and describes the adaptation of the American investment company to rapidly changing economic conditions.

Available through your local bookstore or from the publisher at 440 West 110th Street, New York, New York 10025. $9.

Business Capital Sources. Merrick, New York: International Wealth Success, Inc., 1970.

This guide to business capital sources includes a 27-page introductory section on the subject "Financing Long and Short Term Needs," which covers elementary business financing. The bulk of this volume is devoted to an annotated listing of loan brokers and investors of all descriptions. In some instances, the only information provided on a loan broker is his telephone number. A better job of editing could have significantly enhanced the value of this 100-page publication.

Available by ordering through the publisher at P.O. Box 186, Merrick, New York 11566. $15.

Business Opportunities Digest. A Special Report. *Financing Sources.* Farmington, New Mexico: Business Opportunities Digest, 1970.

This unusual, 18-page directory includes an assortment of capital sources of all descriptions including factors, finders, and financial consultants, including some that have very intriguing investment preferences.

Available only by ordering directly from the publisher at 301 North Orchard Avenue, Farmington, New Mexico 87401. $2.75.

Carosso, Vincent P. *Investment Banking in America, a History.* Cambridge, Massachusetts: Harvard University Press, 1970.

This excellent, comprehensive history of investment banking is a treasure house of background information either for the novice or the professional who is interested in financial institutions. It is *must* reading for one who wishes to understand the important role of investment banking in the growth of this bastion of capitalism we call America. This work will take much of the mystery out of the role investment banking institutions play as fund-raisers.

Available from your local bookstore or from the publisher at 79 Garden Street, Cambridge, Massachusetts 02138. $14.50.

Casey, William J., and the IBP Research and Editorial Staff. *How to Raise Money to Make Money; the Executive's Master Guide to Financing a Business.* New York: Institute for Business Planning, Inc., 1966.

This loose-leaf publication, written by the man who is now Chairman of the Securities and Exchange Commission, is an authoritatively prepared compendium on the subject of raising money for business ventures. Many examples of business agreements, forms, and other contracts are provided. Many aspects of business finance not treated elsewhere are covered in this volume.

Available only from the publisher at 2 West Thirteenth Street, New York, New York 10011. $39.95.

CIT Corporation. *Financing Idea Book.* New York: CIT Corporation, 1969.

> This publication of the CIT Corporation, the nation's largest independent industrial and commercial financing organization, provides the entrepreneur with an excellent discussion of the rudiments of business financing.
>
> Complimentary copies may be obtained by writing to the corporation at 650 Madison Avenue, New York, New York 10022.

Dauten, Carl A. *Business Finance: The Fundamentals of Financial Management.* Englewood Cliffs, New Jersey: Prentice-Hall, Inc., 1956.

> This textbook includes material on the financial considerations involved in selecting the form of organization of a new business and a review of the more common elements of business financing techniques and financial analysis, planning and control.
>
> Available through your local bookstore or from the publisher at Englewood Cliffs, New Jersey 07632. $10.

Davis, R. A. *The American Sourcebook of Capital.* Los Angeles: R. A. Davis & Associates, June, 1970.

> This directory of 19 different types of financing sources includes the names and addresses of hundreds of individuals and institutions. Unfortunately, no information is provided regarding the investment preferences of those listed.
>
> Available by ordering from the publisher, 11824 Darlington Avenue, Los Angeles, California. $15.

Diener, Royce. *How to Finance a Growing Business.* New York: Frederick Fell, Inc., 1965.

> This book on capital security, written from the viewpoint of the businessman-borrower, not only describes what is available in the field of finance but also provides insight into what goes on in the lender's mind and by what standards the funding source operates. This is an exceedingly readable and understandable basic work on finance. The subject matter is presented without the sensationalism common to get-rich-quick books.
>
> Available from the publisher at 386 Park Avenue South, New York, New York 10016. $6.95.

Directory of Trust Institutions of the United States and Canada. New York: Fiduciary Publishers, Inc., annual.

> This directory provides a geographical list of active trust institutions, heads of trust and investment departments, and trust assets.
>
> Available only from Fiduciary Publishers, Inc., 132 West 31st Street, New York, New York 10001. Included in $15 subscription to *Trusts and Estates.*

Dougall, Herbert E. *Capital Markets and Institutions.* Englewood Cliffs, New Jersey: Prentice-Hall, Inc., 1970.

> This book by the C.O.G. Miller Professor of Finance, Emeritus of Stanford University, provides a clear study of a complex subject: the institutions through which long-term financing is made available to industry. An excellent bibliography is included.

Available through your local bookstore or from the publisher at Englewood Cliffs, New Jersey 07632. $3.95.

Financial Assistance Staff, Small Business Administration. "The ABC.s of Borrowing." *Management Aids for Small Manufacturers, Annual No. 13*, Washington, D. C.: Small Business Administration, Government Printing Office, 1967, pp. 34-48.

Some small businessmen can't understand why a lending institution refuses to lend them money. Others have no trouble getting funds, but they are surprised to find strings attached to their loans. These owner-managers fail to realize that banks and other lenders have to operate by certain principles just as other types of business do.

This *Aid* discusses the following fundamentals of borrowing: (1) credit worthiness, (2) kinds of loans, (3) amount of money needed, (4) collateral, (5) loan restrictions and limitations, (6) the loan application, and (7) standards the lender uses to evaluate the application.

Available by ordering from the Superintendent of Documents, Government Printing Office, Washington, D. C. 20402. 50 cents.

Financing New Technological Enterprise: Report of the Panel on Venture Capital. Arthur F. Snyder, Chairman. Washington, D. C.: U. S. Department of Commerce, September, 1970.

The purpose of this report is to examine the problems associated with the acquisition of venture capital, particularly as related to new technologically oriented businesses, and to recommend steps that may be taken to improve venture capital flow. The report is a summary of the findings of the Panel on Venture Capital, an advisory committee convened by and reporting to the Secretary of Commerce.

Included in the report is a brief listing of major venture capital firms in the United States.

For sale by the Superintendent of Documents, U. S. Government Printing Office, Washington, D. C. 20402. 50 cents.

Finegold, Donaldine S., ed. *International Guide to Directories of Resources in International Development*, 3d ed. Washington, D. C.: Society for International Development, 1971.

This little guide to directories of resources in international development is the most comprehensive I know of in the field. According to information in the foreword, this work "provides an international listing of *directories* of (1) organizations and institutions engaged primarily in operational activities in international development; (2) research and training institutes in international development; and (3) expert personnel in international development."

Available from the Society for International Development, 1346 Connecticut Avenue, N. W., Washington, D. C. 20036. $2.50 ($1 to SID members).

Flink, Solomon J. *Equity Financing for Small Business.* New York: Simmons-Boardman Publishing Co., 1962.

In addition to examining the processes involved in financial management and the various types of loans, this book gives an informative explanation of the steps to be taken in arranging for a stock issue.

This document is out of print.

Flink, Solomon J. *The Role of Commercial Banks in the SBIC Industry.* New York: American Bankers Association, 1965.

This study of the effects of bank affiliation on small business investment companies is concerned with three distinct types: wholly bank owned, public, and private.

Available from the American Bankers Association, 1120 Connecticut Avenue, N. W., Washington, D. C. 20036. $7.50.

Fram, E. H. *Small Business Credit and Finance.* Dobbs Ferry, New York: Oceana, 1966.

This book provides information about capital sources, operating figures, credit for the businessman and his customers, and expansion problems.

Available from Oceana Publications, Inc., Dobbs Ferry, New York 10522. $3.

Grimm, Jay V.; Knauss, Robert L.; and Goodwin, Bernard; eds. *Small Business Financing Library.* Ann Arbor, Michigan: Institute of Continuing Legal Education, 1966.

This three-volume reference is devoted entirely to the subject of financing a small business in circumstances where a public offering of securities is not appropriate. The work is intended primarily as source material for corporate attorneys who are frequently asked to provide financial as well as legal counsel to their clients.

Contact the Institute of Continuing Legal Education, c/o University of Michigan Law School, Hutchins Hall, Ann Arbor, Michigan 48103, regarding availability.

Gross, Harry. *Financing for Small and Medium-Sized Businesses.* Englewood Cliffs, New Jersey: Prentice-Hall, Inc., 1969.

A certified public accountant and professional financial consultant discusses financial planning and capital sources; much of his material is directly applicable to the planning of a new business. Many examples illustrate key points.

Available through your bookstore or from the publisher at Englewood Cliffs, New Jersey 07632. $19.95.

Gross, Harry. *A Guide to Current Techniques in Financing: Ten Methods of Financing for Company Growth.* New York: Pilot Books, Inc., 1961; revised 1967.

This book offers a clear explanation of 10 methods of raising capital and gives step-by-step explanations of the procedures involved. It is a practical guide for the businessman who wants to prevent the economic paralysis that comes from a shortage of working capital.

Available from Pilot Books, 347 Fifth Ave., New York, New York 10016. $2.

Hanson, William C. *Capital Sources and Major Investing Institutions.* Bristol, Connecticut: Simmons-Boardman Publishing Co., 1963.

This directory provides a comprehensive listing of all significant capital sources.

The book is in three parts. Part One describes the various sources of capital and financial institutions. Part Two is a subject index that lists a wide variety of purposes or objects of financing and then indicates the specific sources to be used in locating financing. Part Three provides lists of specific organizations or institutions with names, addresses, and financial resources.

Available by ordering from Simmons-Boardman Publishing Company, Book Division, 508 Birch Street, Bristol, Connecticut 06010. $15.

Hastings, Paul G. "Term Loans in Small Business Financing." *Small Marketers Aids, Annual No. 2.* Washington, D.C.: Small Business Administration, Government Printing Office, 1960, pp. 56-62.

Term loans can have a vital role in small business financing. Running from a year's duration up, they are useful for meeting requirements which fall between short-term bank borrowings and permanent equity capital.

A professor of business administration is the author, and he provides an informative discussion of this important topic in small business financial planning.

Available by ordering from Superintendent of Documents, Government Printing Office, Washington, D. C. 20402. 55 cents.

Hicks, Tyler G. *How to Borrow Your Way to a Great Fortune.* West Nyack, New York: Parker Publishing Company, Inc., 1970.

This book purports to provide information on more than 10,000 sources of capital. The style is of the "getting-rich-quick-is-as-easy-as-falling-off-a-log" school. The author has a knack for making sometimes complex financial topics easier to understand.

Available from your local bookstore or from the publisher at 1 Village Square, West Nyack, New York 10994. $7.95.

Hicks, Tyler G. *Smart Money Shortcuts to Becoming Rich.* West Nyack, New York: Parker Publishing Company, Inc., 1966.

This get-rich-quick book contains many chapters devoted to the raising of other people's money ("OPM," as the author calls it). A large amount of complex source material has been broken down into terms readily understood by the financial novice.

Available from your local bookstore or from the publisher at 1 Village Square, West Nyack, New York 10994. $7.95.

How to Raise Speculation Capital. Santa Rosa, California: Second Income News, 1969.

This 20-page primer on speculation capital does an acceptable job of introducing the novice to the rudiments of securing venture capital.

Available only by ordering directly from the publisher at 4932 Sonoma Highway, Santa Rosa, California 95405. $3.

Hungate, Robert P. *Interbusiness Financing: Economic Implications for Small Business.* Small Business Research Series No. 3. Washington, D. C.: Small Business Administration, Government Printing Office, 1962.

This 157-page booklet provides in-depth coverage of the financial sector of the economy that encompasses the flow of funds among independent nonfinancial business units.

Specifically excluded from this study is any discussion of financial institutions which exist primarily and exclusively to lend or invest money for loan interest or capital appreciation.

Available by ordering from Superintendent of Documents, Government Printing Office, Washington, D. C. 20402. 70 cents.

Hutchison, G. Scott, ed. *The Strategy of Corporate Financing.* New York: Presidents Publishing House, Inc., 1970.

Many leading corporations are turning to new financing techniques to raise the capital they want—techniques such as issuing warrants, convertible bonds, or even their own commercial paper. You can learn all about the advantages and disadvantages of these and other financing techniques in this just-published guidebook.

Individual chapters focus on such critical areas as public equity financing, commercial paper, warrants, convertibles, current trends in the public markets, recent accounting developments, sources of venture capital, techniques for improving cash flows, alternative sources of capital, and many other areas crucial to the financial management of a business organization.

Available by ordering from the publisher at 575 Madison Avenue, New York, New York 10022. $25.

Hutchison, G. Scott, ed. *Why, When & How to Go Public.* New York: Presidents Publishing House, Inc., 1970.

This book, prepared by 15 corporation executives, investment bankers, lawyers, and accountants, describes how to "go public" from start to finish—from selecting your underwriter and pricing the new issue to understanding your new legal obligations and reporting requirements.

Available by ordering from the publisher at 575 Madison Avenue, New York, New York 10022. $22.50.

Investment Bankers Association of America. *Facts You Should Know about Investment Banking.* Washington, D. C.: Investment Bankers Association of America, 1962.

Readers learn how the investment banker fills a dual function by helping businesses to grow and by aiding investors to put their savings to work.

Available free of charge by ordering from Investment Bankers Association of America, 425 Thirteenth Street, N. W., Washington, D. C. 20004.

Jacoby, Neil H. "Getting Money for Long-Term Growth." *Management Aids for Small Manufacturers, Annual No. 10.* Washington, D.C.: Small Business Administration, Government Printing Office, 1964, pp. 1-8.

Getting capital for long-term growth is one of the problems of a new company. Small businessmen in increasing numbers are solving this problem by obtaining equity capital from small-business investment companies (SBIC's).

Pointing out that there are more than 700 SBIC's in the United States, this *Aid* urges small businessmen to select the one that best suits their needs. It then suggests steps that should help owner-managers in their negotiations with SBIC's.

Available by ordering from Superintendent of Documents, Government Printing Office, Washington, D. C. 20402. 35 cents

Klatt, Lawrence A. *Small Business Management: Essentials of Entrepreneurship.* Belmont, California: Wadsworth Publishing Company, Inc., 1973.

Most small business management textbooks are more than you need: sweeping, detailed, often outdated, encyclopedias of everything you always wanted to know about small business management but wish you had been afraid to ask. This one is different. A refreshing introduction to the basics of small business. Paperback.

Available through your local bookstore or from the publisher in Belmont, California 94002. $7.95.

Landrum, Robert K. "Bank Loan Limitations: Living Within Them." *Management Aids for Small Manufacturers Annual No. 12.* Washington, D.C.: Small Business Administration, Government Printing Office, 1966, pp. 1-7.

Loan limitations and restrictions are designed to protect the lender against unnecessary risks. Knowing the why of the limitations can help small businessmen understand those set by banks and other private lenders.

This *Aid* makes suggestions that may be helpful in living within bank-loan limitations. It describes the loan agreement and points out that limitations and restrictions can *help* the owner-manager (for example, the loan agreement protects him on his rate of repayment).

Available by ordering from Superintendent of Documents, Government Printing Office, Washington, D.C. 20402. 35 cents.

Lane, Helen J., and Hutar, Patricia. *The Investment Club Way to Stock Market Success.* Garden City, New York: Dolphin Books, Doubleday & Company, Inc., 1963.

This book discusses the objectives and aims of investment clubs and compares this method of systematic investing to other forms of estate building. Material is included on how to use source materials, analyze an annual report, and evaluate industries and specific companies in relation to their competition. This book is an excellent guide to the inner workings of investment clubs. A 235-entry glossary is included.

Available through your local bookstore or from the publisher at 277 Park Ave., New York, New York 10017. $1.25.

Lechner, A. A. *Industrial Aid Financing.* New York: Goodbody and Co., 1965.

Considers pros and cons, growth, legislative provisions, markets, documents, state-sponsored plans for financial assistance to new industry, and effects of industrial aid on companies and communities.

Available from the publisher at 55 Broad Street, New York, New York 10004. $2.50.

Levy, Robert S., and Granik, T. *Directory of State and Federal Funds for Business Development.* New York: Pilot Books, 1968.

This is a single source for basic data on the financial assistance programs of the 50 states and 12 federal agencies. This concise directory is the starting point for any business, large or small, which seeks to relocate or expand. The book helps management to "shop," compare, select, and discard a wide range of aid programs without collecting and sorting through mountains of promotional literature.

Available from the publisher, 347 Fifth Avenue, New York, New York 10016. $5.

Lewis, Marianna, ed. *The Foundation Directory*, 3d ed. New York: Russell Sage Foundation, 1971.

This directory lists hundreds of major foundations, many of which invest portions of their portfolios in new ventures. Each entry includes a description of the assets and primary areas of interest for the foundations listed.

The directory must be purchased from Basic Books, Inc., 404 Park Avenue South, New York, New York 10016. $12.

List of Companies Registered under the Investment Company Act of 1940. Washington, D. C.: Securities and Exchange Commission, Division of Corporate Regulation, June 1970.

This list includes all companies which are engaged primarily in the business of investing, reinvesting, and trading in securities and which have issued their own securities that are offered to, sold to, and held by the investing public.

Available free of charge to individuals and firms having a demonstrable, bona fide need for this information from the Securities and Exchange Commission at 500 North Capitol Building, Washington, D. C. 20549.

Luckett, D. C., ed. *Studies in the Factor Markets for Small Business Firms.* Small Business Management Research Reports. Ames, Iowa: Iowa State University, 1964.

This article contains seven reports, all of which deal with problems involved in handling the elements of production. The capital market, management recruitment, and labor-management relations are the three areas of major concern.

Available from Iowa State University, Ames, Iowa 50010. $2.

Magee, David, and Staff of Business Development Consultants, eds. *How and Where to Get Capital.* Kerrville, Texas: National Counselor Reports, 1968.

This volume is a fascinating collection of information on capital sources, apparently presented largely without the benefits of editing. Included are capital sources offering everything from automobile loans, educational loans, real estate loans, personal loans by mail, and sources of scholarships and student aid, all lumped together in one alphabetized directory.

Available only from the publisher at Kerrville, Texas 78028. $10.

Makela, Benjamin R., ed. *How to Use and Invest in Letter Stock.* New York: Presidents Publishing House, 1970.

This book includes speeches given at various seminars conducted by Corporate Seminars, Inc., presenting the views of experts who represent three separate viewpoints. Part of the book is devoted to the Wheat Report and proposed SEC rules.

Available through bookstores or directly from the publisher at 575 Madison Avenue, New York, New York 10022. $15.

McNierney, Mary A., ed. *Directory of Business and Financial Services,* 6th ed. New York: Special Libraries Association, 1963.

A selected listing by the Special Libraries Association of more than 1000 business, economic, and financial publications printed periodically, with a regular supplement.

Available by ordering from Special Libraries Association, 235 Park Avenue South, New York, New York 10003. $6.50.

Mangold, Maxwell J. *How Public Financing Can Help Your Company Grow: A Guide to the Advantages and Ways of Securing Equity Capital through Sales of Stock to the Public,* 4th rev. ed. New York: Pilot Books, Inc., 1968.

This is a compact, factual guide to the advantages and ways of securing equity capital through sales of stock to the public. It includes 25 brief case histories of actual public offerings.

Available from Pilot Books, 347 Fifth Avenue, New York, New York 10016. $2.

Markstein, David L. *Nine Roads to Wealth.* New York: McGraw-Hill Book Company, 1970.

An eminently readable book on the subject of money, stocks, bonds, mutual funds, commodity trading, franchising, and municipal and industrial bonds. One chapter is devoted to a discussion of several ways to raise capital.

Available through your local bookstore or from the publisher at 330 West 42nd Street, New York, New York 10036. $6.95.

Meinhard-Commercial Corporation, ed. *Commercial Financing: What it is and What it Does; Export Factoring: What it is and What it Does; Factoring: What it is and What it Does.* New York: Meinhard-Commercial Corporation, 1969.

This series of little booklets offered by Meinhard-Commercial Corporation, the nation's largest factoring organization, provides a concise and informative overview of the role of a commercial factor in the corporate financial game plan.

Available free of charge by ordering from Meinhard-Commercial Corporation, 9 East 59th Street, New York, New York 10022.

Metz, Robert. "Where to Buy Money for a Business." *How to Shake the Money Tree.* New York: Putnam Publishing Co., 1966, pp. 229-250.

This article discusses the various institutions and agencies through which one may obtain loans for starting or expanding a business.

Available through your local bookstore or from the publisher at 200 Madison Avenue, New York, New York 10016. $5.95.

Money Market Directory, 1971. New York: Investment Dealers' Digest, 1971.

This directory lists the 4,600 largest institutional funds, their addresses, telephone numbers, amounts of money managed, and the money managers and investment counselors for each. These investors own securities with a market value of $1 trillion, with annual investment purchases and sales of $200 billion.

Available by ordering from the publisher at 150 Broadway, New York, New York 10038. $125.

Moody's Investors Service, Inc. *Moody's Bank and Finance Manual.* New York: Moody's Investors Service, Inc., 1966.

This book contains financial statements and earnings reports for American and Canadian investment companies and includes several tables classifying investment companies by net assets and management performance. Semi-weekly supplements and weekly indexes keep the manual up to date.

Available from the publisher at 99 Church Street, New York, New York 10007. $115 for a one-year subscription.

Investment Bankers Association of America. *Municipal Industrial Financing.* Washington, D. C.: Investment Bankers Association of America, 1961.

Contains a report on the dangers of using municipal credit to finance construction of industrial facilities and a resolution recommending extreme caution in this type of financing.

Available free of charge from Investment Bankers Association of America, 425 Thirteenth Street, N. W., Washington, D. C. 20004.

"Mutual Fund Directory." *Investment Dealers' Digest.* Sec. II, February 27, 1967.

This directory includes statistical information on 266 mutual funds, 61 contractual plans, and three tax-exempt bond funds.

Available from Investment Dealers' Digest at 150 Broadway, New York, New York 10038. $6.

"Mutual Fund Directory." *Investment Dealers' Digest.* Spring Edition, 1971. New York: Investment Dealers' Digest, 1971.

This directory includes information on the investment activity of most major mutual funds, revised as of December 31, 1970.

Available from the publisher at 150 Broadway, New York, New York 10038. $10.

Naitove, Irwin. *Modern Factoring.* New York: American Management Association, Inc., 1969.

This book describes in detail the various types of services offered by factoring organizations, including such specialized fields as bank participations and the import-export market, as well as the more conventional expansion financing and credit/collection services.

Available from your local bookstore or from the publisher at 135 West 50th Street, New York, New York 10020. $5.

National Association of Mutual Savings Banks. *Directory and Guide to the Mutual Savings Banks of the United States.* New York: The Association, annual.

The major section of this directory is comprised of a geographical listing of savings banks by states, with names of officers, statistical data, and information on deposit interest at each bank. Included is an alphabetical list of savings banks, statistics of the industry, savings bank life insurance, and information on deposit limits in each state.

Available only from the National Association of Mutual Savings Banks at 200 Park Avenue, New York, New York 10017. $5 to libraries, $15 to others.

National Association of Small Business Investment Companies. *Membership Directory.* Washington, D. C.: National Association of Small Business Investment Companies, 1971.

This little directory is a *must* for anyone interested in raising venture capital. The introduction includes a brief but highly informative discussion of SBICs and how they operate. All entries are coded to indicate preferred limit for loans or investments, financing preferences (i.e., equity, loans, or both), and industry preferences.

Available free of charge from the National Association of Small Business Investment Companies, 537 Washington Building, Washington, D. C. 20005.

National Commercial Finance Companies of New York, Inc. *Roster of Membership of National Commercial Finance Conference, Inc., Including Membership of Affiliate-Association of Commercial Finance Companies of New York, Inc.* New York: National Commercial Finance Conference, Inc., April, 1971.

This directory, although free, is available only to authorized individuals and agencies. Should you request a copy of it, you must indicate for what purpose you require it. One of the restrictions the conference has regarding this listing is that it not be utilized for solicitation purposes.

Available from the National Commercial Finance Conference at 29 Broadway, New York, New York 10006.

National Science Foundation. *Federal Funds for Research, Development, and Other Scientific Activities, Fiscal Years 1969, 1970, and 1971.* NSF 70-38, Vol. XIX of Surveys of Science Resources Series. Washington, D.C.: National Science Foundation, Government Printing Office, 1970.

This report provides a comprehensive body of statistical information on the size and scope of federal obligations for scientific activities, the purposes to which funds are directed, and the important trends in major funding areas.

This information can be of considerable assistance in helping the scientifically oriented entrepreneur to identify federal funds to which he may gain access for use in starting his enterprise.

Available by ordering from Superintendent of Documents, U. S. Government Printing Office, Washington, D. C. 20402. $2.

Natural Resource Capital Directory. Birmingham, Michigan: World Resource Investment Digest, 1970-1971.

>This unique directory lists over 150 sources of capital for oil, gas, mining, timber, cattle, real estate, and general business ventures. Listings include investor preferences and name of individual to be contacted.

>Available only by ordering directly from the publisher at P.O. Box 283, Birmingham, Michigan 48012. $10.

Noone, Charles M., and Rubel, Stanley M. *SBICs: Pioneers in Organized Venture Capital.* Chicago: Capital Publishing Corp., 1970.

>A detailed history of the SBIC industry describes how SBICs operate, this book evaluates performance of the industry, analyzes trends and developments, and illustrates successful financings. A directory of more than 200 active SBICs is included.

>Available from the publisher at 10 South LaSalle Street, Chicago, Illinois 60603. $9.50.

Novotny, Carl H., and Searles, David S., Jr. *Venture Capital in the United States: An Analysis.* Cambridge, Massachusetts: New Enterprise Systems, 1970.

>This report is undoubtedly one of the finest and most comprehensive surveys of the venture capital industry of yesterday and today. It contains an extensive bibliography of books and periodicals treating the subject of venture capital. Also included is a 32-page annotated list of firms and individuals in the venture capital field.

>Although the price may seem prohibitively high, any entrepreneur contemplating the substantial financial rewards the successful launching of a new business can provide would find a copy of this report to be a wise investment.

>Available only by ordering directly from the publisher at P. O. Box 29, Cambridge, Massachusetts 02139. $100.

Payne, Jack W. *Capital Sources—The Businessman's Source-Manual of Finance.* Farmington, New Mexico: Business Opportunities Digest, 1963.

>This little directory provides brief descriptions of a large number of different financing sources, including extensive lists of such institutions as investment banking firms, insurance companies, union pension funds, SBICs, etc.

>Although the publication is considerably out of date, much of the basic information is still of value. The publisher, at 301 North Orchard Street, Farmington, New Mexico 87401, has now made this work available at the reduced price of $2.

Payne, Jack. *The Encyclopedia of Little-Known, Highly Profitable Business Opportunities.* New York: Frederick Fell, Inc., 1971.

>This book is a real potpourri of business ideas, providing the names and addresses of hundreds of contacts in business fields as varied, for example, as mines and oil wells, real estate, merger and acquisition brokerage, and franchising. It should make interesting and entertaining reading for the entrepreneur looking for the unusual in business opportunities.

Available from the author at 301 North Orchard Street, Farmington, New Mexico 87401. $9.95.

Person, Carl E. *The Save-By-Borrowing Technique; Building Your Fortune—From Loan to Profit.* Garden City, New York: Doubleday & Company, Inc., 1966.

This work by a graduate of the Harvard Law School, who is now an attorney with a prominent New York law firm, provides a clearly stated, investor's-eye view of techniques for building a substantial personal estate. It should provide the entrepreneur with a valuable perspective in understanding the needs of lay investors.

Available at your local bookstore or from the publisher at 277 Park Avenue, New York, New York 10017. $5.95.

Pfeffer, Irving, ed. *The Financing of Small Business: A Current Assessment.* New York: The Macmillan Company, 1967.

This comprehensive and timely examination of the financial problems— background, financial management, capital sources, requirements—of small business brings together the ideas and research of 18 representatives of government, small business, investment banking, business administration, law, and accounting. The contributions, which are the result of a research seminar conducted by the Graduate School of Business Administration at the University of California, Los Angeles, reflect the increasing attention economists and others are paying to the small business sector of the economy. Throughout this volume, actual requirements, forms, plans, and government programs are illustrated and thoroughly explained.

Available by ordering from the publisher at 866 Third Avenue, New York, New York. $8.50.

R. L. Polk & Co. *Polk's World Bank Directory.* Nashville: R. L. Polk & Co., semi-annual with supplements.

This directory lists all banks in the U.S. by state and city. Financial statements and officers and directors are included for each. Also included are lists of discontinued banks and lists of foreign banks.

Available by ordering from the publisher at 130 Fourth Avenue North, Nashville, Tennessee 37200. Single issue $52.50; five-year contract $35 per issue.

Ricotta, Anthony V., ed. *Corporate Financing Directory for Last Half of 1970.* New York: Investment Dealers' Digest, Inc., 1971.

This unique directory, published annually by one of the leading news magazines of the financial industry, serves as an extremely important source of hard-to-find information for the entrepreneur seeking insight into the operating details of the investment community. Detailed annual summaries are provided on subjects such as rights, exchange and purchase offers, secondary offerings, private placements, and listings of underwriting managers and participations. The information on private placements should be of considerable value to the small businessman seeking equity financing.

Published by Investment Dealers' Digest, Inc., 150 Broadway, New York, New York 10038. $10.

Robinson, R. I. *Financing the Dynamic Small Firm.* Belmont, California: Wadsworth, 1966.

> This text deals with the various aspects of small business finance, among them establishment of the firm, record keeping, capital expenditures, money problems, and mergers.

> Available from the publisher, 10 Davis Drive, Belmont, California 94002. $3.95.

Rohrlich, Chester. *Organizing Corporate and Other Business Enterprises.* New York: Matthew Bender, 1967.

> This legal reference work provides a lawyer's-eye view of the new business formation process. One chapter is devoted to stock subscriptions and promoter's compensation; another offers an extensive discussion of initial capitalization and financing; while still another discusses legal issues in the marketing of securities, including an analysis of blue-sky laws.

> Available from the publisher at 235 East 45th Street, New York, New York 10017. $24.50.

Rosen, Lawrence R. *Go Where the Money Is: a Guide to Understanding and Entering the Securities Business.* Homewood, Illinois: Dow Jones-Irwin, Inc., 1969.

> This book is designed as a cram course to assist individuals in preparing for the National Association of Securities Dealers, Inc., or the Securities and Exchange Commission qualifying examinations for registration as a registered representative. At the end of each chapter is a series of questions similar to those encountered on the NASD or SEC examinations.

> A second purpose of this book, as stated in the introduction, "is to give the reader a full background of the investment business, an understanding of which is important to any individual in formulating his own financial future."

> Available at your local bookstore or through the publisher at 1818 Ridge Road, Homewood, Illinois 60430. $8.50.

Rubel, Stanley M. "Detailed Review of Seminars on 'How to Raise Venture Capital'." *SBIC/VENTURE CAPITAL.* Volume II, No. 5, May, 1971. Chicago: Capital Publishing Corp., monthly.

> An 18-page special report of addresses by Louis L. Allen, G. Stanton Geary, Donald Glickman, Gerald Griffin, Anton H. Rice III, Kenneth W. Rind, Mark Rollinson, Stanley M. Rubel, and Robert D. Stillman, contained in the leading publication in the venture capital field.

> Although single issues are not ordinarily made available, this issue, priced at $30 and available by ordering from Capital Publishing Corporation, 10 South LaSalle Street, Chicago, Illinois 60603, is an exception.

Rubel, Stanley M. *Guide to Venture Capital Sources.* Chicago: Capital Publishing Corp., 1970.

> This guide includes a listing of more than 450 companies and individuals who provide venture capital for industry. The directory includes a description of the kind of venture capital firm characteristic of each entry (i.e., bank-related SBIC, investment banking firm active in venture capital, venture capital corporation subsidiary of operating company, etc.); the maximum dollar investments

considered; types of industries preferred; whether interested as active participant or passive investor; and the name of the individual to contact. This work includes an index of the directory and a worthwile bibliography on the venture capital industry. As directories of this sort go, this is one of the best.

Available from the publisher at 10 South LaSalle Street, Chicago, Illinois 60603. $19.95.

Rubel, Stanley M., ed. *How to Raise and Invest Venture Capital.* New York: Presidents Publishing House, Inc., 1971.

This work includes speeches and proceedings from four venture capital seminars held January through April, 1970. The release date has not yet been announced by the publisher as of this writing, although a Summer, 1971 publication is planned.

Will be available through bookstores or directly from the publisher at 575 Madison Avenue, New York, New York 10022. Price is not available at this time.

SBIC Directory and Handbook of Small Business Finance. Merrick, New York: International Wealth Success, Inc., undated.

Part of the title reads: *SBIC Directory.* The one included in this publication is substantially derived from the free Small Business Administration directory included elsewhere in this bibliography. The last part of the title reads: *Handbook of Small Business Finance.* Approximately half of the pages in this publication have been photographically reproduced directly from the excellent, 45-cent SBA publication, *A Handbook of Small Business Finance.* One might conclude that this IWS publication is overpriced!

Available from the publisher at P. O. Box 186, Merrick, New York 11566. $15.

Shapero, Albert; Hoffman, Cary; Draheim, Kirk P.; Howell, Richard P. *The Role of the Financial Community in the Formation, Growth, and Effectiveness of Technical Companies: The Attitude of Commercial Loan Officers.* Austin, Texas: Multi-Disciplinary Research, Inc., May, 1969.

This is an excellent technical report, which describes in some detail the many considerations involved in determining the degree of bank participation in the financing of small and medium-size technically oriented companies. The report was prepared for the Ozarks Regional Commission and contains an excellent bibliography on the subject of small business finance.

Available only by ordering from the publisher at 1209 Rio Grande Avenue, Austin, Texas 78701. $7.50.

Shapiro, Eli; Solomon, Ezra; and White, William L. *Money and Banking*, 5th ed. New York: Holt, Rinehart and Winston, Inc., 1968.

This excellent textbook, now in its fifth edition, is a classic in its field. Although it is intended for an already knowledgeable audience, a study of its contents, particularly Part IV on "Money and Capital Markets," should prove quite interesting and valuable to the entrepreneur, whose plans may require substantial amounts of funding.

Available at your local bookstore or from the publisher at 383 Madison Avenue, New York, New York 10017. $12.50.

Sinclair, Leroy W., ed. *Venture Capital 1971.* New York: Technimetrics, Inc., 1971.

This up-to-date directory lists more than 400 corporations, partnerships, and finders who provide or locate risk capital for business. Information furnished includes the firm name; individuals to whom initial inquiries should be directed; areas preferred for investment; areas avoided for investment; approximate range of financing; maturity of company desired; whether or not financing is normally syndicated; whether the firm functions primarily as a finder, broker, consultant, active participant, or passive investor; information regarding board membership preferences; and a summary of the most recent venture capital investments.

Available only by ordering directly from the publishers at 527 Madison Avenue, New York, New York 10022. $25.

Small Business Administration. *List of Small Business Investment Companies.* Washington, D. C.: Small Business Administration, Government Printing Office, rev. semi-annually.

This is a list of all functioning small business investment companies, including their branch offices, whose licenses, issued by the SBA, remain outstanding. This list does not purport to characterize the relative merits, as investment companies or otherwise, of the licensees. Inclusion on this list may in no way be construed as an endorsement of a company's operations or as a recommendation by the Small Business Administration.

All entries are coded relative to the size of capital investment preferred.

Available free of charge from the Small Business Administration, Investment Division, Washington, D. C. 20416.

Small Business & Venture Capital Study Center. *Encouraging Venture Capital for Small Business.* New York: Simon & Schuster, Inc., 1967.

This work reports the results of a three-year research project conducted by the Small Business & Venture Capital Study Center, a nonprofit, nonpartisan research organization. Among the recommendations made are: tax changes to increase incentives for venture capital; modifications of existing securities laws; and changes which would serve to improve the administration of the program.

Available from the publisher at One West 39th Street, New York, New York 10018. $2.

Solomon, Ezra, ed. *The Management of Corporate Capital.* New York: The Free Press, 1959.

This work is intended to introduce the executives of tomorrow to a systematic approach to corporate capital decisions. Part III, "The Cost of Debt and Equity Funds," should be of particular interest to an entrepreneur who has a high degree of business sophistication.

Available from your local bookstore or from the publisher at 866 Third Avenue, New York, New York 10022. $7.95.

Solomon, M. P., Jr. "Investment Decisions in Small Business." *Small Business Management Research Reports.* Lexington, Kentucky: University of Kentucky Press, 1963.

> This publication includes results of a survey of the ways in which capital is budgeted and invested by small enterprises and their reasons for choosing among various alternatives.

> Available by ordering from University Press of Kentucky, Lafferty Hall, University of Kentucky, Lexington, Kentucky 40506. $3.

Standard & Poor's Corporation. *Security Dealers of North America.* New York: Standard & Poor's Corporation, semi-annual.

> This work is a geographical listing of all investment firms in the U. S. and Canada, giving the nature of their business, branches, and officers. North American securities administrators, foreign offices and representation, discontinued listings, and an alphabetical list of firms are other useful features.

> Available by ordering from Standard & Poor's Corporation, 345 Hudson Street, New York, New York 10014. $20 per volume. Cumulative revision service available.

Stursberg, Carl W., Jr. *A Guide to Venture Capital Financing.* New York: American Science Associates, 1970.

> This 12-page guide provides an excellent summary of venture capital financing from the viewpoint of a sophisticated investor.

> Available free of charge from American Science Associates (investment bankers to young science-oriented and growth-oriented companies seeking financing through private placement or public offerings), 1345 Avenue of the Americas, New York, New York 10019.

Summers, George W. *Financing and Initial Operations of New Firms.* Englewood Cliffs, New Jersey: Prentice-Hall, Inc., 1962.

> This 64-page report offers an analysis of cash flow and other financing problems with which a new enterprise must successfully cope in order to survive.

> Available through bookstores or from the publisher at Englewood Cliffs, New Jersey 07632. $4.50.

T. K. Sanderson Organization. *Directory of American Savings and Loan Associations.* Baltimore: T. K. Sanderson Organization, annual.

> This directory is arranged geographically by state. It includes mention of officers, assets, and, in some cases, current interest rate.

> Available through your local bookstore or from T. K. Sanderson Organization, 25th and Calvert Streets, Baltimore, Maryland 21218. $30.

U.S. Congress, House of Representatives. Select Committee on Small Business. *Tax-Exempt Foundations: Their Impact on Small Business.* Washington, D. C.: Government Printing Office, 1968.

> Available by ordering through the Government Printing Office, Washington, D.C. 20302. $6.50.

U. S. Department of Commerce. *A Guide to Venture Capital Financing.* Washington, D.C.: U. S. Department of Commerce, 1970.

This pamphlet provides a very brief glimpse of what venture capital is all about. A short list of venture capital firms is included.

Available from the Superintendent of Documents, U. S. Government Printing Office, Washington, D. C. 20402. 30 cents.

United States Securities and Exchange Commission. *Broker-Dealers and Investment-Advisers Directory.* Washington, D. C.: United States Securities and Exchange Commission, rev. semi-annually.

This directory covers all brokers (defined to mean any *person*—banks excluded—engaged in the *business* of effecting transactions in securities for the account of others'; dealers (defined to mean any person—not a bank—engaged in the *business* of buying *and* selling securities for his own account, through a broker or otherwise, or any person insofar as he buys or sells securities for his own account, either individually or in some fiduciary capacity, but not as a part of a regular business); and investment advisers (defined to mean any person who, for compensation, engages in the business of advising others, either directly or through publications or writings, as to the value of securities or as to the advisability of investing in, purchasing, or selling securities, or who, for compensation and as part of a regular business, issues or promulgates analyses or reports concerning securities).

More than 9,000 entries are included in this listing.

This list includes all companies engaged primarily in the business of investing, reinvesting, and trading in securities and whose own securities are offered to, sold to, and held by the investing public.

Xerographically reproduced copies may be obtained at 12 cents per page through the services of Leasco Information Products, 4827 Rugby Avenue, Bethesda, Maryland 20014. (The list generally exceeds 200 pages in length.)

Vancil, Richard F., ed. *Financial Executive's Handbook.* Homewood, Illinois: Dow Jones-Irwin, Inc., 1970.

This is a new compendium of current information on financial matters, consisting of 10 sections and 66 chapters and covering the wide range of responsibilities of today's busy executive in the area of finance and financial management. In its 1,264 pages, this comprehensive book brings together the practical experience of leading corporate executives.

Available through your local bookstore or from Dow Jones-Irwin, Inc., at 1818 Ridge Road, Homewood, Illinois 60430. $27.50.

Venture Capital and Management: The Art of Joining Innovative Technology, Management and Capital. Proceedings of the Second Annual Meeting, May 28-29, 1970. Chestnut Hill, Massachusetts: Boston College Press, 1970.

This report is a transcript of the seminar proceedings. Topics covered are "New Venture Opportunities," "The Role of the Investment Banker and Underwriter," "Managing the New Technology Company," "Government and New

Business," "Venture Capital Sources and Uses," and "The Emerging Role of the Large Institution."

Available by ordering from Management Institute, Fulton Hall, 405A, Boston College, Chestnut Hill, Massachusetts 02167. $10.

Venture Capital Associates. *Complete Guide to Raising Venture Capital.* New York: August, 1970.

This little guide briefly covers many of the major aspects necessary to secure financing from leading venture capitalists in this country. The cursory treatment given each topic suggests that the use of the word "complete" in the title may have been ill advised. The entire work is less than 40 pages in length. A listing of "100 venture capitalists from coast to coast" included in this guide gives only the name and address of each organization, and no mention is made of investor preferences.

Available only by ordering directly from the publishers at 79 Wall Street, New York, New York 10005. $7.

Welfling, Weldon. *Financing Business Enterprise.* New York: American Institute of Banking, Section American Bankers Association, 1960.

This textbook on the role of banks in providing capital for business enterprise assumes a knowledge of commercial law, business administration, and accounting. The material is presented from the viewpoint of the corporate treasurer, and strong emphasis is placed on the major differences between loaning and investing.

Included in the book is a discussion of basic problems in business organization. Two chapters are devoted to a discussion of unincorporated business; other chapters cover short-, intermediate-, and long-term credit, public issues, and private placements.

Out of print.

Wescon. *New Company Start-ups: The Engineer becomes Entrepreneur.* 1969 Wescon Technical Papers presented at Session 5 of the Western Electronic Show and Convention, August 19-22, 1969. Los Angeles: Western Electronic Manufacturers Association, 1969.

This document is a summary of five talks presented at the 1969 Western Electronic Manufacturers Association Show and Convention. Papers offered included "The Many Routes to the Money Market;" "Selling the Package: What They Want to Hear;" "Holding Your Own in the Money Market;" "Why, How and When to go Public;" and "The Mature Company Finances the New Company."

Reprints are available through the Western Electronic Manufacturers Association Show and Convention Offices, Attention: Mrs. Helen Therault, 3600 Wilshire Boulevard, Los Angeles, California 90005. $2.

Western Association of Venture Capitalists. *Directory—Western Association of Venture Capitalists.* San Francisco, California: The Association, 1969/1970.

This is a directory of approximately 25 companies and an additional 25 private individuals in the venture capital field on the West Coast.

Copies of this directory may be obtained from the association headquarters at 1472 Russ Building, San Francisco, California 94104. $1.

Wheat, Francis M., and Blackstone, George A. *Guideposts for a First Public Offering.* New York: Bowne of New York City, Inc., 1960.

This 30-page reprint from the April 1960 issue of *The Business Lawyer*, written by two members of the California Bar, serves as an excellent and authoritative introduction to a subject normally of great interest to the entrepreneur.

Complimentary copies of this booklet are available from the publisher at 345 Hudson Street, New York, New York 10014.

Arthur Wiesenberger & Company, eds. *Investment Companies.* New York: Arthur Wiesenberger Services, Division of Nuveen Corporation, annual.

This is an annual volume on more than 150 open-end and about 50 closed-end funds. Discusses background, policy, and features of each company, with operating results recorded.

Available by subscription at $45 from Arthur Wiesenberger Services, Division of Nuveen Corporation, 61 Broadway, New York, New York 10006.

Willett, Edward R. *Fundamentals of Securities Markets.* New York: Hawthorn Books, Inc., 1970.

This book provides an extensive discussion of the structures and operations of the securities markets. Each market segment—investment banker, broker, stock exchange, over-the-counter market—is subjected to the author's scrutiny. Multiple-choice questions, of the type used in the National Association of Securities Dealers examination, afford the reader an opportunity to check his knowledge of the contents. Recommended to the entrepreneur with a moderate-to-high degree of business sophistication.

Available from your local bookstore or from the publisher at 70 Fifth Avenue, New York, New York 10011. $9.95.

William Iselin & Co., Inc. *Guide to Factoring and Financing.* New York: William Iselin & Co., Inc., 1963.

This guide provides a clear, although brief, discussion of the many services a commercial factor can provide the business community.

Available free of charge by ordering from William Iselin & Co., 357 Park Avenue South, New York, New York 10010.

Winter, Elmer. *Complete Guide to Making a Public Stock Offering.* Englewood Cliffs, New Jersey: Prentice-Hall, 1962.

This excellent, comprehensive guide to making a public offering is presented in a very readable style. Recommended for anyone (including lawyers) interested in the subject of public stock offerings.

Available from your local bookstore or from the publisher at Englewood Cliffs, New Jersey 07632. $17.95.

Woelfel, B. La Salle. "What Kind of Money Do You Need?" *Management Aids for Small Manufacturers, Annual No. 11.* Washington, D.C.: Small Business Administration, Government Printing Office, 1965, pp. 49-55.

A small business needs four kinds of money from time to time: (1) normal trade credit, (2) short-term loans, (3) term borrowing, and (4) equity (investment) capital. This *Aid* discusses the uses of each type of financing. It points out that the purpose for which the funds are to be used is an important factor in deciding the kind of money needed.

Available by ordering from Superintendent of Documents, Government Printing Office, Washington, D. C. 20402. 50 cents.

World Wide Chamber of Commerce Directory. Boulder, Colorado: Johnson Publishing Co., Inc., annual.

This directory includes (1) complete list of chambers of commerce in the U.S., including manager or president; (2) list of foreign embassies and governmental agencies located in the U.S.; (3) list of foreign chambers of commerce with offices in the U.S.; (4) list of chambers of commerce outside of the U.S., arranged alphabetically by country.

Since chambers of commerce regularly function as clearing houses for information regarding community assistance to new and relocating businesses, this directory could be of significant help to the entrepreneur.

Available from the publisher at 839 Pearl Street, Boulder, Colorado 80302. $3.

Zwick, Jack. "A Handbook of Small Business Finance." *Small Business Management Series.* Washington, D. C.: Small Business Administration, Government Printing Office, 1965.

This 80-page booklet provides a starting point for the small businessman who wants to improve his financial management skills. It points out the major areas of financial management and describes a few of the many techniques that can help the small businessman to understand the results of his past decisions and apply this understanding in making decisions for the future.

Available by ordering from the Superintendent of Documents, Government Printing Office, Washington, D. C. 20402. 45 cents.

Appendix 2

SEMINARS AND WORKSHOPS ATTENDED BY THE AUTHOR WHICH
INFLUENCED THE CONTENT OF THIS MANUSCRIPT:

1. "New Company Start-ups: The Engineer becomes Entrepreneur," Western Electronic Show and Convention, August 1969, San Francisco, California.

2. "How to Start & Operate a Small Business," Massachusetts Institute of Technology, Seminar for Young Alumni, two days, October 1969, Cambridge, Massachusetts.

3. Same subject and series as Number 2 above, with different speakers and panelists offering new perspectives, March 1970, New York City, New York.

4. Same subject and series as Numbers 2 & 3 above with different speakers and panelists, offering still *more* varied points of view, May 1970, Palo Alto, California.

5. "How to Obtain Venture Capital and Make Private Stock Placements," Decision Resources Corporation, two days, June 1970, Los Angeles, California.

6. "Seminar for Small Businessmen (Who Want to be Big Ones)," Cossman Seminars, August 1970, San Francisco, California.

7. "Advanced Workshop Seminar," Series of five Workshop/Seminars covering material introduced in Number 6 above in greater depth and expanded scope, September 1970, San Francisco, California.

8. "Venture Capital, An International Look," University of Toronto, two days, September 1970, Toronto, Ontario, Canada.

9. "San Francisco Entrepreneurship Workshop Series on Managing a New Enterprise in Today's Economy," Massachusetts Institute of Technology, seven sessions, February, March, & April 1971, San Francisco, California.

10. "How to Start and Operate a Small Business and Make It Grow," Massachusetts Institute of Technology, two days, March 1971, Anaheim, California.

11. "How to Start a New Business," IEEE International Convention, March 1971, New York City, New York.

12. "Assuring Your Future," Management Games Institute, March 1971, New York City, New York.

13. "How to Successfully Start Your Own Business," New York Management Center, Inc., March 1971, New York City, New York.

14. "The Engineer Starts a Business," IEEE Sacramento Section, Region Six Conference, May 1971, Sacramento, California.

15. "Entrepreneurship III: A Scenario for Survival and Growth," University of Santa Clara, May 1971, Santa Clara, California.

16. "Going Public: Advantages in Public Financing for the Small Business," University of California, June 1971, San Francisco, California.

17. "Workshop for Prospective Business Owners and Managers," Small Business Administration, San Francisco Regional Office, July 1971, San Jose, California.

Appendix 3

DIRECTORY OF THE MEMBERSHIP OF THE NATIONAL ASSOCIATION OF SMALL BUSINESS INVESTMENT COMPANIES

The following comprehensive directory constitutes the membership roster of the National Association of Small Business Investment Companies, with headquarters at 537 Washington Building, Washington, D. C. 20005.

The resources of these companies represent approximately 85 percent of the SBIC industry assets. The announced NASBIC credo is to foster "the development of the highest standards of business conduct. Its code of ethics and trade practice rules, developed and voluntarily adopted by its membership, insures fair dealing within the Association and with the small business community."

This directory of the NASBIC membership includes the corporate name, the name of the chief executive, and the address and telephone number of the company. The investment preferences of each company are also provided and are keyed to the following code:

Preferred Limit for Loans or Investments

A - up to $100,000
B - up to $250,000
C - up to $500,000
D - up to $1 million
E - above $1 million

Investment Policy

* - Will consider either loans or investments
** - Prefers to make long-term loans
*** - Prefers financings with right to acquire stock interest

Industry Preferences

1. Communications
2. Construction and Development
3. Natural Resource
4. Hotels, Motels, and Restaurants
5. Manufacturing and Processing
6. Medical and Other Health Services
7. Recreation and Amusements
8. Research and Technology
9. Retailing, Wholesaling, and Distribution
10. Service Trades
11. Transportation
12. Diversified

NON-SBIC MEMBERS

This Directory also lists several companies which invest in small businesses, but which are not SBICs. These non-SBIC venture capitalists are Associate Members of NASBIC.

ALABAMA

Associated Business Investment Corporation   A * 5,9,12
Mr. B. G. Purvis, Vice President
820 North 18th Street
Birmingham, Alabama 35203
(205) 322-5707

ARKANSAS

Venture Capital Inc.   A *** 12 MESBIC
Mr. Charles E. Simms, President & General Manager
P.O. Box 1343
Suite 300, 212 Center
Union Life Building
Little Rock, Arkansas 72203
(501) 374-9977

ALASKA

Alaska Business Investment Corporation   D *** 1,5,9,11,12
Mr. D. L. Mellish, President
P.O. Box 600
Anchorage, Alaska 99501
(907) 272-5544

Alyeska Investment Company   A * 2,4,9,10 MESBIC
Mr. N. Roy Goodman, General Manager
1815 South Bragaw
Anchorage, Alaska 99504
(907) 279-9584

ARIZONA

First Southwest Small Business Investment Company   A *** 1,2,4,5,7
Mr. Wm. H. O'Brien, President
1611 East Camelback Road
Phoenix, Arizona 85016
(602) 274-3623

CALIFORNIA

BanCal Capital Corporation   B *** 1,3,4,5,6,7,8,10,11,12
Mr. J. Gorham Arend, President
550 South Flower Street
Los Angeles, California 90017
(213) 972-2443

Brantman Capital Corp.   A * 12
Mr. W. T. Brantman, President
1920 Paradise Drive
P.O. Box 877
Tiburon, California 94920
(415) 435-4747

Brentwood Associates, Inc.   D *** 12
Mr. Timothy M. Pennington, President
11661 San Vicente Boulevard
Los Angeles, California 90049
(213) 826-6581

Capital City Equity Company   B *** 1,2,5
Mr. Robert F. Palmer, President
811 North Broadway, Suite 444
Santa Ana, California 92701
(714) 547-5407

City of Commerce Investment Company   A * 5 MESBIC
Mr. Richard J. Olivarez, General Manager
1117-B Goodrich Boulevard
Los Angeles, California 90022
(213) 724-6141

Continental Capital Corporation   C *** 1,5,6,8
Mr. Frank Chambers, President
555 California Street
San Francisco, California 94104
(415) 989-2020

Developers Equity Capital Corporation   A *** 2
Mr. Larry Sade, President
9348 Santa Monica Boulevard, Suite 307
Beverly Hills, California 90210
(213) 878-2533

First Small Business Investment Company of California   D *** 5,8,9,12
Mr. Tim Hay, President
333 South Hope Street
Los Angeles, California 90017
(213) 613-5215

Foothill Venture Corporation
Mr. Russell B. Faucett, President
8383 Wilshire Boulevard, Suite 528
Beverly Hills, California 90211
(213) 655-5620

C *** 1 through 12

Growth SBIC, Inc.
Mr. James W. Howard, President
1500 Orange Avenue
Coronado, California 92118
(714) 435-0171

A *** 2,3,5,7,8,10,12

Krasne Fund
Mr. Clyde A. Krasne, President
9350 Wilshire Boulevard
Beverly Hills, California 90212
(213) 274-7007

A ** 2

Opportunity Capital Corporation of California
Mr. Charles E. Stanley, President
235 Montgomery Street, Suite 1226
San Francisco, California 94104
(415) 398-5696

A *** 1,5,6,10,11 MESBIC

Roe Financial Corporation
Mr. Martin J. Roe, President
6100 Kester Avenue
Van Nuys, California 91401
(213) 787-5330

A *** 9,12

San Joaquin Small Business Investment Corporation
Mr. Morris E. Harrison, President/Manager
P.O. Box 248
34512 Embarcadero Place
Dana Point, California 92629
(714) 496-5540 or 496-6177

B *** 2,3,5,7,12

Branch:
San Joaquin Small Business Investment Corporation
Mr. K. A. Shelton, Vice President
P.O. Box 2083
Bakersfield, California 93303
(805) 323-2284

B *** 2,3,5,7,12

Small Business Enterprises Company
Mr. Steven L. Merrill, Vice President
555 California Street
Bank of America, 41st Floor, No. 3342
San Francisco, California 94104
(415) 622-2271

E *** 1,3,5,6,7,8,11,12

Branch:
Small Business Enterprises Company   E *** 12
Mr. James L. Rawlings, Vice President
555 South Flower Street, Suite 4900
Los Angeles, California 90071
(213) 683-3463

Southern California Minority Capital Corporation   C * 2,4,6 MESBIC
Mr. Marx Cazenave, Senior Vice President
2651 South Western Avenue, Suite 303
Los Angeles, California 90222
(213) 731-8211

Union Venture Corporation   C *** 1,3,5,6,7,8
Mr. Brent T. Rider, President
445 South Figueroa Street
Los Angeles, California 90017
(213) 687-5588

Wells Fargo Investment Company   D * 1,3,5,6,8,12
Mr. Robert G. Perring, President
475 Sansome Street
San Francisco, California 94111
(415) 396-3292

Westamco Investment Company   A * 2,6,12
Mr. Leonard G. Muskin, President
8929 Wilshire Boulevard
Beverly Hills, California 90211
(213) 652-8288

Western Business Funds   D *** 5,6,7,10
Mr. Harold L. Moose, Jr., President
235 Montgomery Street, Suite 2200
San Francisco, California 94104
(415) 989-9677

COLORADO

Central Investment Corporation of Denver   B *** 1,5,6
Mr. Blaine E. D'Arcey, President
811 Central Bank Building
1108 Fifteenth Street
Denver, Colorado 80202
(303) 825-3351

CONNECTICUT

Cominvest of Hartford, Inc.   A * 12 MESBIC
Mr. Vernal R. Mendez, Vice President & Manager
18 Asylum Street
Hartford, Connecticut 06103
(203) 246-7259

Connecticut Capital Corporation   A * 1,2,5,6,7,9,10,11,12
Mr. Albert F. Carbonari, President
419 Whalley Avenue
New Haven, Connecticut 06511
(203) 777-8802

The First Connecticut Small Business Investment Company   D * 2,5,12
Mr. David Engelson, President
177 State Street
Bridgeport, Connecticut 06604
(203) 366-4726
(see New York)

Branch:
First Miami Small Business Investment Company   A ** 1,2,7,10,12
Post Office Box P
Orange, Connecticut 06477
(see Florida)

Hartford Community Capital Corporation   A * 1,5,9 MESBIC
Mr. William F. Connell, President
70 Farmington Avenue
Hartford, Connecticut 06101
(203) 547-2684

Investors Capital Corporation   A * 12
Mr. Edward Helfer, President & Treasurer
144 Golden Hill Street, Suite 525
Bridgeport, Connecticut 06604
(203) 334-0109

Manufacturers Small Business Investment Company, Inc.   A * 5,6,9,11,12
Mr. Louis W. Mingione, Executive Secretary
1488 Chapel Street
New Haven, Connecticut 06511
(203) 777-3042 or 776-8354

Marwit Capital Corporation   E * 12
Mr. Martin W. Witte, President
111 Prospect Street
Stamford, Connecticut 06901
(203) 324-5793

Nationwide Funding Corporation   A * 1 through 12
Mr. Richard Keitlen, Vice President
10A Ambassador Drive
Manchester, Connecticut 06040
(203) 646-6555

Northern Business Capital Corporation   A ** 2
Mr. Joseph Kavanewsky, President
7-9 Isaac Street
P.O. Box 711
South Norwalk, Connecticut 06856
(203) 866-1000

Nutmeg Capital Corporation   A * 5,9,10,12
Mr. Leigh B. Raymond, Executive Vice President
35 Elm Street
New Haven, Connecticut 06510
(203) 776-0643

Small Business Investment Company of Connecticut   A ** 2,4,5,7,9,12
Mr. Kenneth F. Zarrilli, President
1115 Main Street
Bridgeport, Connecticut 06604
(203) 367-3282

DISTRICT OF COLUMBIA

Allied Capital Corporation   B * 1,2,5,6,7,9,11,12
Mr. George C. Williams, President
1625 Eye Street, N.W.
Washington, D.C. 20006
(202) 331-1112

Branch:
Broad Arrow Investment Corporation   A * 4,9,11 MESBIC
1701 Pennsylvania Avenue, N.W.
Washington, D.C. 20006
(see New Jersey and New York)

Capital Investment Company of Washington   C ** 2,6,12
Mr. Irving P. Cohen, Vice President
900 - 17th Street, N.W.
Washington, D.C. 20006
(202) 659-4122

Columbia Ventures, Inc.   C *** 2,3,5
Mr. E. J. Bermingham, Jr., President
1701 Pennsylvania Avenue
Washington, D.C. 20006
(202) 298-9270

Branch:
ESIC Capital, Inc.   B ** 3,5,9,12
1155 - 15th Street, N.W.
Washington, D.C. 20005
(202) 785-4171
(see New York)

Greater Washington Industrial Investments, Inc.   C *** 1,5,6,8,12
Mr. Don A. Christensen, President
1015 - 18th Street, N.W.
Washington, D.C. 20036
(202) 466-2210

MODEDCO Investment Company   B * 1,2,5,8 MESBIC
Mr. Thomas H. Countee, Jr., President
1325 Massachusetts Avenue, N.W., Suite 110
Washington, D.C. 20005
(202) 347-4212

Tech-Mod Capital Corporation   A * 1,3,6,8,9,10,12 MESBIC
Mr. Gary S. Messina, Vice President
1801 - K Street, N.W.
Washington, D.C. 20006
(202) 833-2490

FLORIDA

Burger King MESBIC, Inc.   A *** 4 MESBIC
Mr. Mark A. Smith, Vice President Finance
P.O. Box 520783, Biscayne Annex
Miami, Florida 33152
(305) 274-7500

First Miami Small Business Investment Company   A ** 1,2,7,10,12
Mr. Irve L. Libby, President
420 Lincoln Road
Miami Beach, Florida 33139
(305) 531-0891
(see Connecticut)

Gold Coast Capital Corporation   B ** 1,2,5,6,7,9,10,12
Mr. William I. Gold, President
1451 North Bayshore Drive
Miami, Florida 33132
(305) 371-5456

Growth Business Funds, Inc.   A *** 12
Mr. Alan J. Leinwand, President
One Financial Plaza, Suite 1313
Fort Lauderdale, Florida 33394
(305) 763-8484

Market Capital Corporation   A *** 9
Mr. E. E. Eads, President
1102 North 28th Street
Tampa, Florida 33605
(813) 247-1357

Small Business Assistance Corporation of Panama City, Florida   C *** 2,4,12
Mr. John L. C. Laslie, President
Post Office Box 1627
505 West 15th Street
Panama City, Florida 32401
(904) 769-2371

Southeast SBIC, Inc.   C *** 12
Mr. Warren L. Miller, Treasurer & Investment Officer
P.O. Box 2500
Miami, Florida 33101
(305) 577-4650

Urban Ventures, Inc.   A * 4,5,6,7,9,10,12 MESBIC
Mr. Wm. A. Wynn, Jr., President
Tower 3, 825 South Bayshore Drive
Miami, Florida 33131
(305) 373-4691

GEORGIA

Branch:
Atlanta/LaSalle Capital Corporation   C *** 12
Mr. Ezra Mintz
P.O. Box 4064
Atlanta, Georgia 30302
(404) 522-7597

CSRA Capital Corporation   C *** 2
Mr. A. F. Caldwell, Jr., President
914 Georgia Railroad Bank Building
Augusta, Georgia 30902
(404) 722-7505

Dixie Capital Corporation   A * 2,5,7,10
Mr. William J. Stack, Jr., President
2210 Gas Light Tower
Atlanta, Georgia 30303
(404) 577-5131

ECCO MESBIC, Inc.   A * 2,5,6,7,9,11 MESBIC
Mr. Floyd C. Green, President
Central Administration Building
Mayfield, Georgia 31059
(404) 465-3201

Enterprises Now, Inc.   A * 12 MESBIC
Mr. Al Anderson, Executive Director
898 Beckwith Street, S.W.
Atlanta, Georgia 30314
(404) 753-1163

Fidelity Capital Corporation   D *** 2
Mr. Wayne J. Haskins, Vice President
300 Interstate North
Atlanta, Georgia 30339
(404) 434-1234

First American Investment Corporation   D *** 2
Mr. Jerry J. Pezzella, Jr., President
300 Interstate North
Atlanta, Georgia 30339
(404) 434-1234

Mome Capital Corporation   A * 2,4,5,9
Mr. J. A. Hutchinson, Jr., President
234 Main Street
Thomson, Georgia 30824
(404) 595-1507

Southeastern Capital Corporation   C *** 3,5,9
Mr. J. Ray Efird, President
3715 Northside Parkway, N.W., Suite 505
Atlanta, Georgia 30327
(404) 237-1567

HAWAII

Small Business Investment Company of Hawaii, Inc.   A *** 2,4,9
Mr. James W. Y. Wong, Chairman of the Board
1575 South Beretania Street
Honolulu, Hawaii 96814
(808) 946-1171

IDAHO

First Idaho Investment Corporation   C *** 1,5,8,9,12
Mr. Lloyd Nelsen, Vice President & General Manager
1200 First Street South
Nampa, Idaho 83651
(208) 466-4651

ILLINOIS

Abbott Capital Corporation   A *** 5,12
Mr. Richard E. Lassar, President
120 South LaSalle Street, Room 1100
Chicago, Illinois 60603
(312) 726-3803

Amoco Venture Capital Company   A * 12 MESBIC
Mr. R. H. Anderson, Vice President & General Manager
200 East Randolph Drive
Chicago, Illinois 60601
(312) 856-6523

Androck Capital Corporation   A *** 12
Mr. John R. Anderson, President
1309 Samuelson Road
Rockford, Illinois 61101
(815) 397-4752

Atlanta/LaSalle Capital Corporation   C *** 12
Mr. Daniel J. Donahue, President
150 South Wacker Drive, Suite 575
Chicago, Illinois 60606
(312) 235-1597
(see Georgia)

CEDCO Capital Corporation   A *** 5,6,7,9 MESBIC
Mr. Henry P. Johnson, Vice President & General Manager
162 North State Street
Chicago, Illinois 60601
(312) 368-0011

Chicago Community Ventures, Inc.   A *** 1,2,5,9 MESBIC
Mr. Benjamin C. Duster, President
19 South LaSalle Street, Suite 1114
Chicago, Illinois 60603
(312) 726-6084

Chicago Equity Corporation   A * 12
Mr. Morris Weiser, President
One IBM Plaza, Suite 3625
Chicago, Illinois 60611
(312) 321-9662

Combined Opportunities, Inc.   A * 12 MESBIC
Mr. Frank B. Brooks, Director
5050 North Broadway
Chicago, Illinois 60640
(312) 275-3871

Continental Illinois Venture Corporation   C *** 12
Mr. John L. Hines, President
231 South LaSalle Street, Suite 1738
Chicago, Illinois 60604
(312) 828-8023

First Capital Corporation of Chicago   D *** 12
Mr. Stanley C. Golder, President
One First National Plaza, Suite 2628
Chicago, Illinois 60670
(312) 732-8060

Heizer Capital Corporation   E *** 1,6,7,8,9,10
Mr. E. F. Heizer, Jr., President
20 North Wacker Drive
Chicago, Illinois 60606
(312) 641-2200

North Central Capital Corporation   B *** 1,2,5,6,8
Mr. Willard C. Mills, President
203 Mulberry Street
Rockford, Illinois 61101
(815) 963-8261

The Urban Fund, Inc.   C *** 5,6,9,10 MESBIC
Mr. Peter H. Ross, President
1525 East 53rd Street
Chicago, Illinois 60615
(312) 432-1800

INDIANA

Waterfield SBIC, Inc.   A *** 2,4,5,12
Mr. Richard H. Waterfield, Chairman of the Board
123 West Berry Street
Fort Wayne, Indiana 46802
(219) 422-2466

Branch:
Waterfield SBIC, Inc.   A *** 2,4,5,12
45 North Pennsylvania, Suite 202
Indianapolis, Indiana 46204
(317) 634-6633

IOWA

MorAmerica Capital Corporation   C * 4,5,6,9,10,12
Mr. Robert W. Allsop, Executive Vice President
200 American Building
Cedar Rapids, Iowa 52401
(319) 363-0261
(see Missouri, Nebraska and Wisconsin)

KENTUCKY

Equal Opportunity Finance, Inc.   A * 2,4,6,9,10,11,12 MESBIC
Mr. Frank P. Justice, Jr., Vice President & Investment Manager
224 E. Broadway
Louisville, Kentucky 40202
(502) 583-0601

LOUISIANA

Commercial Capital, Inc.   A ** 12
Mr. Daniel S. Berlin, President
Bogue Falaya Plaza, P.O. Box 808
Covington, Louisiana 70433
(504) 892-4921

The First Small Business Investment Company of Louisiana, Inc.   A ** 3,12
Mrs. Alma O. Galle, President
3626 One Shell Square
New Orleans, Louisiana 70139
(504) 529-5272

First Southern Capital Corporation   B *** 2,3,7,12
Mr. Dennis A. Cross, President
821 Gravier Street, Suite 1216
New Orleans, Louisiana 70112
(504) 529-3177

Gulf South Venture Corporation   A * 12 MESBIC
Mr. Robert P. Aulston, III, President
Suite 1202, 821 Gravier Street
New Orleans, Louisiana 70112
(504) 523-7386

Louisiana Equity Capital Corporation   B *** 2,3,5,9,10,12
Mr. Denis O'Connell, President
451 Florida Street
Baton Rouge, Louisiana 70801
(504) 389-4801

Branch:
Louisiana Equity Capital Corporation   B *** 2,3,5,9,10,12
Mr. Ed Mathews
c/o Ouachita National Bank, P.O. Drawer 1412
Monroe, Louisiana 71201
(318) 325-5892

Branch:
Louisiana Equity Capital Corporation   B *** 2,3,5,9,10,12
Mr. Ralph France
c/o Bank of New Orleans & Trust Co., P.O. Box 52499
New Orleans, Louisiana 70152
(504) 581-7511

Royal Street Investment Corporation,   B *** 12
Mr. William D. Humphries, President
521 Royal Street
New Orleans, Louisiana 70130
(504) 588-9271

SCDF Investment Corporation   B *** 2,5,9,10,12 MESBIC
Reverend A. J. McKnight, President
P.O. Box 3885, 1006 Surrey Street
Lafayette, Louisiana 70501
(318) 232-9206

Southern Small Business Investment Company, Inc.   A * 12
Mr. Gerard H. Schreiber, Secretary & Treasurer
8137 Oleander Street
New Orleans, Louisiana 70118
(504) 482-7861

Venturtech Capital, Inc.   A *** 5,8
Mr. W. A. Bruce, Executive Vice President
Suite 602 Republic Tower, 5700 Florida Boulevard
Baton Rouge, Louisiana 70806
(504) 926-5482
(see New Jersey)

MASSACHUSETTS

Atlas Capital Corporation   B ** 12
Mr. Herbert Carver, President
55 Court Street
Boston, Massachusetts 02108
(617) 482-1218

Eastern Seaboard Investment Corporation   A *** 12
Mr. William Sadowsky, President
73 State Street
Springfield, Massachusetts 01103
(413) 732-8531

Federal Street Capital Corporation   C *** 1,5,8,12
Mr. John H. Lamothe, President
75 Federal Street
Boston, Massachusetts 02110
(617) 542-1380

First Capital Corporation of Boston   C *** 12
Mr. Richard A. Farrell, Senior Vice President
100 Federal Street
Boston, Massachusetts 02110
(617) 434-2440

Greater Springfield Investment Corporation   A *** 12 MESBIC
Mr. William P. Matthews, Executive Director
121 Chestnut Street
Springfield, Massachusetts 01103
(413) 781-7130

Massachusetts Capital Corporation   C * 1,5,6,7,9,10,11
Mr. David V. Harkins, Vice President
1 Boston Place
Boston, Massachusetts 02108
(617) 723-5440

New England Enterprise Capital Corporation   B * 1,5,6,8
Mr. Robert F. Elliott, President
28 State Street
Boston, Massachusetts 02109
(617) 742-0285

Northeast Small Business Investment Corporation   A ** 12
Mr. Joseph Mindick, Treasurer
16 Cumberland Street
Boston, Massachusetts 02115
(617) 267-3983

Pilgrim Capital Corporation   A * 4,5,6,7,9,12
Mr. Bernard G. Berkman, President
842A Beacon Street
Boston, Massachusetts 02215
(617) 566-5212

Schooner Capital Corporation   B *** 12
Mr. Vincent J. Ryan, Jr., President
141 Milk Street, Suite 1143
Boston, Massachusetts 02109
(617) 357-9031

UST Capital Corporation
Mr. Stephen Lewinstein, Senior Vice President
Mr. Robert Scharar, Assistant Vice President
40 Court Street
Boston, Massachusetts 02108
(617) 542-6300

A * 2,5,6,12

WCCI Capital Corporation
Mr. Michael W. Tierney, President
791 Main Street
Worcester, Massachusetts 01610
(617) 791-3259

A * 12 MESBIC

Worcester Capital Corporation
Mr. William A. Gregg, Manager
446 Main Street
Worcester, Massachusetts 01608
(617) 853-7000

A *** 12

MICHIGAN

Branch:
Alliance Enterprise Corporation
Mr. George Berger
23999 N.W. Highway, P.O. Box 304
Southfield, Michigan 48075
(see Ohio, Pennsylvania and Texas)

A *** 12 MESBIC

Doan Associates, Inc.
Mr. Arnold C. Ott, General Partner
Mr. Herbert D. Doan, Ltd. Partner
110 East Grove Street
Midland, Michigan 48640
(517) 631-2471

C * 1,2,5,8,12

Independence Capital Formation
Mr. Dyctis Moses, Vice President
3049 East Grand Boulevard
Detroit, Michigan 48202
(313) 875-7669

A * 1,5,9

Michigan Capital & Service Inc.
Mr. Kenneth Heininger, Manager
410 Wolverine Building, P.O. Box 28
Ann Arbor, Michigan 48107
(313) 663-0702

A *** 12

Motor Enterprises, Inc.   A ** 5 MESBIC
Mr. Herbert F. Lorenz, Administrator
General Motors Building
3044 West Grand Boulevard
Detroit, Michigan 48202
(313) 556-4273

Pooled Resources Investing in Minority Enterprises, Inc.   B * 1,5,10,12 MESBIC
(PRIME, Inc.)
Mr. James F. Hill, President
2990 West Grand Boulevard, Suite M-15
Detroit, Michigan 48202
(313) 872-2212

MINNESOTA

First Midwest Capital Corporation   B * 1,3,5,6,7,8,9,10,12
Mr. A. J. Greenshields, Vice President
1636 IDS Center
Minneapolis, Minnesota 55402
(612) 339-9391

Minnesota Small Business Investment Company   A *** 5,10,12
Mr. Walter L. Tiffin, President
2338 Central Avenue, N.E.
Minneapolis, Minnesota 55418
(612) 789-2471

Northland Capital Corporation   A *** 12
Mr. George G. Barnum, Jr., President
402 West First Street
Duluth, Minnesota 55802
(218) 722-0545

North Star Ventures, Inc.   B *** 1,5,8,10,12
Mr. Gerald A. Rauenhorst, President   o
Suite 2303, Northwestern Financial Center
7900 Xerxes Avenue, South
Minneapolis, Minnesota 55431
(612) 830-4550

Northwest Growth Fund, Inc.   C *** 12
Mr. Robert F. Zicarelli, President
960 Northwestern Bank Building
Minneapolis, Minnesota
(612) 333-2275

Westland Capital Corporation   B *** 1,5,6,9,10
Mr. James B. Goetz, President
2021 East Hennepin Avenue
Minneapolis, Minnesota 55413
(612) 331-9210

MISSISSIPPI

Sunflower Investment Corporation   A ** 9
Mr. Morris Lewis, Jr., President
U.S. Highway 49W at Second Street Extended
Indianola, Mississippi 38751
(601) 887-3211

Vicksburg Small Business Investment Company   A * 12
Mr. David L. May, Treasurer
First National Bank Building
Vicksburg, Mississippi 39180
(601) 636-4762

MISSOURI

Branch:
MorAmerica Capital Corporation   C * 4,5,6,9,10,12
Mr. Larry C. Maddox, Regional Vice President
Suite 2710, Commerce Tower
911 Main Street
Kansas City, Missouri 64105
(816) 842-0114
(see Iowa, Nebraska and Wisconsin)

MONTANA

Capital Investors Corporation   C *** 12
Mr. Alan Bradley, President
Capital Building
Missoula, Montana 59801
(406) 543-7888
(see Oregon and Washington)

Small Business Improvement Company   A ** 9
Mr. T. N. Reynolds, President
P.O. Box 1175, 711 Central Avenue
Billings, Montana 59103
(406) 252-3805

NEBRASKA

Branch:
MorAmerica Capital Corporation   C * 4,5,6,9,10,12
Mr. Russell A. Knudsen, Regional Manager
Suite 1420, One First National Center
Omaha, Nebraska 68102
(402) 346-4212
(see Iowa, Missouri and Wisconsin)

NEW JERSEY

Broad Arrow Investment Corporation   A * 4,9,11 MESBIC
Mr. Charles N. Bellm, President
Route 10 Denbrook Village
Denville, New Jersey 07834
(201) 361-3766
(see District of Columbia and New York)

Engle Investment Company   A * 12
Mr. Murray Hendel, President
35 Essex Street
Hackensack, New Jersey 07601
(201) 489-3583

Main Capital Investment Corporation   A * 2,3,4,12
Mr. S. Sam Klotz, President
818 Main Street
Hackensack, New Jersey 07601
(201) 489-2080
Monmouth Capital Corporation   C * 12
Mr. Eugene W. Landy, President
125 Wyckoff Road
Eatontown, New Jersey 07724
(201) 542-4555

Branch:
Monmouth Capital Corporation   C * 12
First State Bank Building
P.O. Box 480
Toms River, New Jersey 08753

Branch:
Venturtech Capital, Inc.   A *** 5,8
Mr. E. M. Charlet, President
12-16 Bank Street
Summit, New Jersey 07901
(201) 273-2180
(see Louisiana)

NEW MEXICO

New Mexico Capital Corporation
Mr. Ed. Leslie, President
4010 Carlisle NE
Albuquerque, New Mexico 87110
(505) 345-0005

B * 2,4,5,9,10

NEW YORK

BanCap Corporation
Mr. William L. Whitely, President
420 Lexington Avenue, Room 2352
New York, New York 10017
(212) 684-6460

B *** 5,10,12 MESBIC

Basic Capital Corporation
Mr. Paul W. Kates, President
40 West 37th Street
New York, New York 10018
(212) 868-9645

A * 12

Bonan Equity Corporation
Mr. Seon Pierre Bonan, President
60 East 42nd Street
New York, New York 10017
(212) 867-4540

C *** 2

Branch:
Broad Arrow Investment Corporation
Route 5 S, Fort Hunter Road
Amsterdam, New York 12010
(see District of Columbia and New Jersey)

A * 4,9,11 MESBIC

BT Capital Corporation
Mr. James G. Hellmuth, Vice President
600 Third Avenue
New York, New York 10016
(212) 867-0606

D *** 5,12

Capital for Future, Inc.
Mr. Jay Schwamm, President
635 Madison Avenue
New York, New York 10022
(212) 759-8060

B ** 2

CEDC MESBIC, Inc.
Mr. H. Kendall Nash, Vice President
106 Main Street
Hempstead, New York 11550
(516) 292-9710

A * 12 MESBIC

The Central New York Small Business Investment Company, Inc.   A * 10,12
Mr. Robert E. Romig, President
738 Erie Boulevard East
Syracuse, New York 13210
(315) 475-1631

Citicorp Venture Capital Ltd.   E *** 1,3,5,6,8,9,10,11,12
Mr. F. A. Roesch, President
399 Park Avenue
New York, New York 10022
(212) 559-0405

Chase Manhattan Capital Corporation   D * 1,5,7,8,11
Mr. Louis L. Allen, President
1 Chase Manhattan Plaza
New York, New York 10005
(212) 552-6811

Branch:
Clarion Capital Corporation   D *** 1,5,6,9,12
Mr. Milton D. Stewart, President
Two Penn Plaza
New York, New York 10001
(212) 594-2280
(see Ohio)

CMNY Capital Company, Inc.   B *** 1,2,5,6,9,10,12
Mr. Robert Davidoff, Vice President
77 Water Street
New York, New York 10005
(212) 437-7078

Coalition Small Business Investment Company Corporation   A * 12 MESBIC
Mr. Ralph L. McNeal, President
800 Second Avenue
New York, New York 10017
(212) 661-4060

Equitable Small Business Investment Corporation   A * 6,12
Mr. David Goldberg, President
350 Fifth Avenue
New York, New York 10001
(212) 564-5420

ESIC Capital, Inc.   B ** 3,5,9,12
Mr. George H. Bookbinder, President
420 Lexington, New York 10017
(212) 684-0020
(see District of Columbia)

Fairfield Equity Corporation   B *** 5,6,12
Mr. Matthew A. Berdon, President
295 Madison Avenue
New York, New York 10017
(212) 532-1700

15 Broad Street Resources Corporation   C *** 1,5,6,8
Mr. Duane E. Minard, III, Vice President
15 Broad Street
New York, New York 10015
(212) 483-2579

Finest Capital Corporation   A **, 5, 12 MESBIC
Mr. Abraham H. Fruchthandler, President
1416 Avenue M
Brooklyn, New York 11230
(212) 627-2500

Branch:
The First Connecticut Small Business Investment Company   D * 2,5,12
680 Fifth Avenue
New York, New York 10019
(see Connecticut)

Forum Equity Corporation   A *** 12 MESBIC
Mr. Hiram C. Cintron, Executive Vice President
214 Mercer Street
New York, New York 10012
(212) 533-0100 Ext. 206

J. H. Foster & Company   C * 12
Mr. John H. Foster, President
One Battery Park Plaza
New York, New York 10004
(212) 742-5158

The Franklin Corporation   D *** 1 through 12
Mr. Herman E. Goodman, President
One Rockefeller Plaza, Suite 2614
New York, New York 10020
(212) 581-4900

The Hamilton Capital Fund, Inc.   B *** 3,5,12
Mr. Joel I. Berson, President
660 Madison Avenue
New York, New York 10021
(212) 838-8382

Intercoastal Capital Corporation   C * 2,5,10,12
Mr. Herbert Krasnow, President
18 East 48th Street
New York, New York 10017
(212) 758-0209

Lake Success Capital Corporation   A * 2
Mr. Herman H. Schneider, President
100 Garden City Plaza, Suite 516
Garden City, New York 11530
(516) 746-2828

The Loud Venture Capital Corporation   A *** 5,10,12
Mr. Douglass N. Loud, President
630 Fifth Avenue
New York, New York 10020
(212) 582-6760

M & T Capital Corporation   C *** 12
Mr. Harold M. Small, President
One M & T Plaza
Buffalo, New York 14240
(716) 842-4881

Midland Capital Corporation   C *** 12
Mr. C. Edgar Schabacker, Jr., Chairman and President
110 William Street
New York, New York 10038
(212) 732-6580

Minority Equity Capital Company, Inc.   A *** 12 MESBIC
Mr. Patrick Owen Burns, Executive Vice President & General Manager
470 Park Avenue South, Suite 300
New York, New York 10016
(212) 889-0880

Nelson Capital Corporation   D * 12
Mr. Irwin B. Nelson, President
Mr. Elliott S. Nelson, Executive Vice President
591 Stewart Avenue
Garden City, New York 11530
(516) 294-9595

New York Business Assistance Corporation   B ** 2
Mr. Lawrence A. Blatte, President
98 Cutter Mill Road
Great Neck, New York 11021
(516) 829-9666

North Street Capital Corporation
Mr. Antony B. Mason, President
250 North Street, W1-3
White Plains, New York 10625
(914) 694-4250

A *** 12 MESBIC

NYBDC Capital Corporation
Mr. Marshall R. Lustig, President
41 State Street
Albany, New York 12207
(518) 463-2268

A *** 5

Pioneer Capital Corporation
Mr. L. Wm. Bergesch, President
1440 Broadway
New York, New York 10018
(212) 594-4860

A *** 12 MESBIC

R & R Financial Corporation
Mr Sylvan Schoenberg, Vice President
1451 Broadway
New York, New York 10036
(212) 564-4500

A *** 12

Royal Business Funds Corporation
Mr. Stephen M. Pollan, President
250 Park Avenue
New York, New York 10017
(212) 986-8463

C *** 2,4,6

Branch:
Royal Business Funds Corporation
600 Old Country Road
Garden City, New York 11530
(516) 248-9354

C *** 2,4,6

Small Business Electroncis Investment Corporation
Mr. Leonard B. Randell, President
120 Broadway, P.O. Box 599
Lynbrook, New York 11563
(516) 593-5151

B ** 12

Southern Tier Capital
Mr. Irving Brizel, President
219 Broadway
Monticello, New York 12701
(914) 794-2030

A * 4,12

Struthers Capital Corporation   D *** 12
Mr. Victor Harz, President
630 Fifth Avenue
New York, New York 10020
(212) 757-3427

Tappan Zee Small Business Investment Corporation   A *** 1,2,5,12
Mr. Irving A. Garson, Chairman of the Board
120 North Main Street
New City, New York 10956
(914) 634-8822

Union Small Business Investment Company, Inc.   A * 1,2,4,5,7,9,10,11,12
Mr. Robert A. Rosen, Chairman & President
1727 Veterans Memorial Highway
Central Islip, New York 11722
(516) 582-6700

Winfield Capital Corporation   C * 12
Mr. Stanley Pechman, President
237 Mamaroneck Avenue
White Plains, New York 10605
(914) 949-2600

NORTH CAROLINA

Cameron-Brown Capital Corporation   B *** 12
Mr. J. Randolph Gregory, Vice President
4300 Six Forks Road
Raleigh, North Carolina 27609
(919) 782-3911

Delta Capital Inc.   B * 2,5,9
Mr. A. B. Wilkins, Jr., President
202 Latta Arcade
320 South Tyron Street
Charlotte, North Carolina 28202
(704) 372-1410

Forsyth County Investment Company   A * 1,4,5 MESBIC
Mr. James F. Hansley, President
305 Pepper Building
Winston-Salem, North Carolina 27101
(919) 724-3676

NORTH DAKOTA

First Dakota Capital Corporation
Mr. Roger A. Bye, Executive Vice President
Suite 110, Professional Building
100 South 4th
Fargo, North Dakota 58102
(701) 237-0450

A *** 1,2,5,8,12

OHIO

Branch:
Alliance Enterprise Corporation
Mr. John Paff
3060 Eggers Avenue
Cleveland, Ohio 44105
(see Michigan, Pennyslvania and Texas)

A *** 12 MESBIC

Clarion Capital Corporation
Mr. Peter D. Van Oosterhout, Chairman of the Board
2011 Union Commerce Building
Cleveland, Ohio 44115
(216) 687-1096
(see New York)

D *** 1,5,6,9,12

Community Venture Corporation
Mr. Richard H. Stowell, President
Suite 1515, 88 East Broad Street
Columbus, Ohio 43215
(614) 228-2800

A *** 5,8,9

Dayton MESBIC, Inc.
Mr. L. A. Lucas, Executive Director
12 North Ludlow Street
Dayton, Ohio 45402
(513) 223-9405

B *** 12 MESBIC

Dycap Inc.
Mr. A. Gordon Imhoff, General Manager
88 East Broad Street, Suite 1660
Columbus, Ohio 43215
(614) 228-6641

A *** 12

Glenco Enterprises, Inc.
Dr. Edward L. Wilkerson, President
1257 East 105th Street
Cleveland, Ohio 44106
(216) 721-1200

A *** 6,8 MESBIC

Gries Investment Company   B *** 12
Mr. Robert D. Gries, President
2310 Terminal Tower Building
Cleveland, Ohio 44113
(216) 861-1146

OKLAHOMA

Alliance Business Investment Company   C *** 3,5,7,12
Mr. Elliott Davis, Chairman of the Board & Chief Executive Officer
500 McFarlin Building
Tulsa, Oklahoma 74103
(918) 584-3581
(see Texas)

American Indian Investment Opportunities, Inc.   A * 12 MESBIC
Mr. Alfred C. Block, General Manager
515 Constitution
Norman, Oklahoma 73069
(405) 329-8110 & 329-8111

Bartlesville Investment Corporation   A * 2,3,5
Mr. J. L. Diamond, President
827 Madison Boulevard
Bartlesville, Oklahoma 74003
(918) 333-3022

Capital, Inc.   A *** 3,5,9
Mr. I. Jack Stephens, President
2106 City National Bank Tower
Oklahoma City, Oklahoma 73102
(405) 236-3729

First Oklahoma Venture Corporation   C *** 12
Mr. J. R. K. Tinkle, President
P.O. Box 25189
First National Center
Oklahoma City, Oklahoma 73125
(405) 272-4569

Investment Capital, Inc.   A * 2,9,12
Mr. Lloyd O. Pace, President
1301 Main Street
Duncan, Oklahoma 73533
(405) 255-3140

OREGON

Branch:
Capital Investors Corporation   C *** 12
1221 Oregon National Building
610 S. W. Alder Street
Portland, Oregon 97205
(503) 223-4128
(see Montana and Washington)

Cascade Capital Corporation   C *** 1,5,6,7,8,10,12
Mr. Jack S. Flowers, President & Chairman
421 S. W. 6th Avenue
Portland, Oregon 97204
(503) 225-4281
(see Washington)

Trans Pac Capital Fund, Inc.   B *** 1,6,9,10,12
Mr. Norriss Webb, President
1800 S. W. First Avenue
Portland, Oregon 97201
(503) 221-1280

PENNSYLVANIA

Alliance Enterprise Corporation   A *** 12 MESBIC
Mr. Ed L. Willis, President
1616 Walnut Street, Suite 802
Philadelphia, Pennsylvania 19103
(215) 732-2812
(see Michigan, Ohio and Texas)

Capital Corporation of America   B *** 5,6,7,12
Mr. Barton M. Banks, President
Mr. Martin M. Newman, Vice President
1521 Walnut Street
Philadelphia, Pennsylvania 19102
(215) 564-2843

Delaware Valley Small Business Investment Company   C * 1 through 12
Mr. Wm. J. Wolf, President
Wolf Building - Market Square
Chester, Pennsylvania 19013
(215) 876-2669

Branch:
Delaware Valley Small Business Investment Company
Mr. George J. Banet, Vice President
1604 Walnut Street, 5th Floor
Philadelphia, Pennsylvania 19103
(215) 546-0135

Equal Opportunity Corporation of Pennsylvania   A * 4,9 MESBIC
Mr. Earl J. Brandt, President
2145 Market Street
Camp Hill, Pennsylvania 17011
(717) 737-8000

Greater Philadelphia Venture Capital Corporation, Inc.   A *** 12 MESBIC
Mr. Guyon W. Turner, General Manager
920 Lewis Tower Building
Philadelphia, Pennsylvania 19102
(215) 732-3415

Osher Capital Corporation   B *** 1,2,5,9,10,12
Mr. L. Cantor, President
Wyncote House
Township Line Road & Washington Lane
Wyncote, Pennsylvania 19095
(215) 624-4800

Philadelphia Ventures, Inc.   B * 1,5,6,8
Mr. Joseph B. Heimann, President
Suite 625, One Plymouth Meeting
Plymouth Meeting, Pennsylvania 19462
(215) 825-9036

Progress Venture Capital Corporation   A * 12 MESBIC
Mr. William A. Campbell, General Manager
45 West Haines Street
Philadelphia, Pennsylvania 19144
(215) 849-2206

Sharon Small Business Investment Company   A * 9
Mr. H. D. Rosenblum, President
385 Shenango Avenue
Sharon, Pennsylvania 16146
(412) 981-1500

PUERTO RICO

Popular Investment Company, Inc.   B *** 5
Mr. Jose E. Carballo, Vice President & Manager
Banco Popular Center - Suite 835
Hato Rey, Puerto Rico 00936
(809) 765-6441

RHODE ISLAND

Industrial Capital Corporation   B * 5,8,12
Mr. John A. Burchett, President
111 Westminster Street
Providence, Rhode Island 02903
(401) 278-6258

Narragansett Capital Corporation   D,E *** 1,5,10,12
Mr. Harvey J. Sarles, President
40 Westminster Street
Providence, Rhode Island 02903
(401) 751-1000

SOUTH CAROLINA

Falcon Capital Corporation   A * 12
Mrs. Mona G. Sokol, President
89 Broad Street
Charleston, South Carolina 29401
(803) 723-8624

TENNESSEE

C & C Capital Corporation   A *** 12
Mr. C. E. Quimby, President
P.O. Box 90
Knoxville, Tennessee 37901
(615) 637-1363

Financial Resources, Inc.   A *** 5,8,12
Mr. Milton C. Picard, Chairman
1909 Sterick Building
Memphis, Tennessee 38103
(901) 527-9411

TEXAS

Admiral Investment Company, Inc.   A *** 2,12
Mr. W. H. Harris, Vice President
2200 West Loop South
Houston, Texas 77027
(713) 621-8140

Branch:
Alliance Business Investment Company   C *** 3,5,7,12
Mr. Leon Davis, President
4850 One Shell Plaza Houston, Texas 77002
(713) 228-5143
(see Oklahoma)

Branch:
Alliance Enterprise Corporation   A *** 12 MESBIC
Ms. Varma Mitchele
Room 2520 Southland Life Building
Dallas, Texas 75221
(see Michigan, Ohio, and Pennsylvania)

Capital Marketing Corporation   B ** 9
Mr. Harry S. Cook, General Manager & Director
9001 Ambassador Row
Dallas, Texas 75222
(214) 638-1913

CSC Capital Corporation   C *** 1,5,9,10,12
Mr. Clifford J. Osborn, President & Chairman of the Board
1800 Mercantile Dallas Building
Dallas, Texas 75201
(214) 747-5117

Enterprise Capital Corporation   C * 2,5,12
Mr. Paul Z. Brochstein, President
Suite 465W, 4635 Southwest Freeway
Houston, Texas 77027
(713) 626-7171

First Dallas Capital Corporation   D *** 1,2,3,4,5,6,8,9
Mr. Thomas O. Hicks, President
714 First National Bank Building
Dallas, Texas 75283
(214) 744-8050

First Texas Investment Company   A *** 2,5,8,9,10,12
Mr. Tom F. Steele, President
13025 Champions Drive
Houston, Texas 77069
(713) 444-1731

MESBIC Financial Corporation of Dallas   A *** 12 MESBIC
Mr. Walter W. Durham, President
P.O. Box 6228
Dallas, Texas 75222
(214) 637-0445

Interstate Venture Capital Corporation   B *** 5,8,12
Mr. Lamar E. Ozley, Jr., President
510 Capital National Bank Building
Houston, Texas 77002
(713) 237-9167

Permian Basin Capital Corporation   A *** 12
Mr. Wm. B. Johnston, President
P.O. Box 1599
Midland, Texas 79701
(915) 683-4231

Republic Small Business Investment Company   B *** 12
Mr. Michael A. Stone, Executive Vice President
P.O. Box 5961
Dallas, Texas 75222
(214) 653-5942

The Small Business Investment Company of Houston   A * 12
Mr. William E. Ladin, President
640 West Building
Houston, Texas 77002
(713) 223-5337

Texas Capital Corporation   C *** 5,12
Mr. John Gatti, President
2424 Houston Natural Gas Building
Houston, Texas 77002
(713) 222-8861

Trammell Crow Investment Company   A *** 2,5,9
Mr. Robert E. Glaze, President
2001 Bryan, Suite 3200
Dallas, Texas 75201
(214) 742-2000

United Business Capital, Inc.   A ** 12
Mr. Ben Fleming, President
1102 South Broadway
La Porte, Texas 77571
(713) 471-5550

West Central Capital Corporation   A *** 2,5,12
Mr. Howard W. Jacob, President
P.O. Box 412
Dumas, Texas 79029
(806) 935-3902

Western Capital Corporation   A ** 2
Mr. Harold L. Knop, President
300 Zidell Building
7007 Preston Road
Dallas, Texas 75205
(214) 528-4590 or 528-4788

UTAH

Intermountain Capital Corporation
Mr. John M. Whiteley, President
10 West First South
Salt Lake City, Utah 84101
(801) 532-1800

A * 12

VERMONT

Vermont Investment Capital, Inc.
Mr. Harold Jacobs, Vice President
Route 14
South Royalton, Vermont 05068
(802) 763-8878

A *** 2,5,6,7,8,10,12

VIRGINIA

Equity Investment Funds, Inc.
Mr. Gerald J. Friedman, President
213 East Main Street
Norfolk, Virginia 23510
(804) 627-2386

A ** 12

Inverness Capital Corporation
Mr. Harry S. Flemming, President
417 North Washington Street
Alexandria, Virginia 22314
(703) 548-1700

C *** 1,2,5

Metropolitan Capital Corporation
Ms. M. A. Riebe, President
2550 Huntington Avenue
Alexandria, Virginia 22303
(703) 960-4698

A *** 12

Virginia Capital Corporation
Mr. Robert H. Pratt, President
515 Ross Building, P.O. Box 1493
Richmond, Virginia 23212
(804) 644-5496

B *** 12

WASHINGTON

Branch:
Capital Investors Corporation
Mr. Richard F. Everett, Area Executive Officer
1041 Dexter-Horton Building
Seattle, Washington 98104
(206) 622-2193
(see Montana and Oregon)

C *** 12

Branch:
Capital Investors Corporation
Mr. Mike Jones, Area Executive Officer
828 Old National Bank Building
Spokane, Washington 99201
(509) 456-3493
(see Montana and Oregon)

C *** 12

Branch:
Cascade Capital Corporation
1100 Second Avenue
Seattle, Washington 98101
(206) 587-2236
(see Oregon)

C *** 1,5,6,7,8,10,12

Northwest Capital Investment Corporation
Mr. Robert M. Harris, President
1111 West Spruce, Suite 31B
P.O. Box 2425
Yakima, Washington 98902
(509) 457-6173 or 457-6174

A *** 3,6,12

Washington Capital Corporation
Mr. T. B. Dame, Vice President
1417 - 4th Avenue
Seattle, Washington 98101
(206) 682-5400

C ** 2,4,5,6,7,10,12

WISCONSIN

Commerce Capital Corporation
Mr. Edward L. Machulak, President
6001 North 91st Street
Milwaukee, Wisconsin 53225
(414) 462-5310

D *** 2,5,12

Branch:
Commerce Capital Corporation
Mr. Richard F. Wartman, Manager
106 West Second Street
Ashland, Wisconsin 54806
(715) 682-2786

D *** 2,5,12

Branch:
Commerce Capital Corporation
Mr. Hubert R. Murphy, Manager
9 South Main Street
Fond du Lac, Wisconsin 54935
(414) 921-2420

D *** 2,5,12

Branch:
Commerce Capital Corporation   D *** 2,5,12
Mr. G. R. Viele, Manager
126 Grand Avenue
Wausau, Wisconsin 54401
(715) 845-2151

Branch:
MorAmerica Capital Corporation   C * 4,5,6,9,10,12
Mr. Paul D. Rhines, Regional Vice President
122 West Washington Avenue
Madison, Wisconsin 53703
(608) 251-7794
(see Iowa, Missouri and Nebraska)

NON-SBIC MEMBERS

Allis-Chalmers Financial Corporation   B ***
Mr. Rodger F. Smith, Vice President - Investments
P.O. Box 512
Milwaukee, Wisconsin 53201
(414) 475-2591

BACA, Inc.   C *** 12
Mr. Jerry P. Rosenblatt, Vice President
1444 Linden Street
Bethlehem, Pennsylvania 18018
(215) 691-8844

BARDCO Inc.   B * 3,5,12
Mr. Arthur J. Crawford, President
30 East 63rd Street
New York, New York 10021
(212) 628-3830

Barnhill and Company   C * 1,5,8,9
Mr. R. B. Barnhill, Jr., Partner
1931 Greenspring Drive
Timonium, Maryland 21093
(301) 252-5610

Charter New York Corporation   D * 1,3,6,8
Mr. Allen R. Freedman, Vice President
1 Wall Street
New York, New York 10005
(212) 487-6265

First Missouri Development Finance Corporation   C *** 12
Mr. Jerry Stegall, Executive Vice President
302 Adams Street, P.O. Box 252
Jefferson City, Missouri 65101
(314) 635-0138

First Piedmont Capital Corporation   A *** 5,8,12
Mr. Peter J. McCord, President
P.O. Box 3028
Greenville, South Carolina 29602
(803) 242-5883

Merrill Lynch & Company
Mr. Gene F. Mag
2 Penn Plaza
New York, New York 10001
(212) 790-1243

New South Investment Company   C *** 1,5,6,9,10,12
Mr. A. Richard Wilson, President
Suite 1540 Commerce Square
Memphis, Tennessee 38103
(901) 526-8463

Talcott Venture Company   D *** 12
Division of James Talcott, Inc.
Mr. Paul H. Levine, Vice President
1290 Avenue of the Americas
New York, New York 10019
(212) 956-2932

Urban National Corporation   C *** 12
Mr. R. Courtney Whitin, Jr., President
177 Milk Street
Boston, Massachusetts 02109
(617) 482-3651
MINORITY INVESTMENTS ONLY

Appendix 4

SIX BUSINESS START-UP CHECKLISTS

CHECKLIST NO. 1: INFORMATION REQUIRED FROM APPLICANT FOR FINANCING.

Goodman and Mautner, Inc., 5250 Century Boulevard, Los Angeles, California 90045.

CHECKLIST NO. 2: A 24-POINT CHECKLIST FOR PREPARING A BUSINESS PLAN.

Robert R. Kley Associates, Inc., 2920 Aurora, Ann Arbor, Michigan 48105.

CHECKLIST NO. 3: DEVELOPMENT OF A MARKETING PROGRAM.

William E. Hill and Company, Inc., 640 Fifth Avenue, New York, New York 10019.

CHECKLIST NO. 4: MARKETING FUNCTIONS CHECKLIST.

William E. Hill and Company, Inc.

CHECKLIST NO. 5: INFORMATION NEEDED FROM PROSPECTIVE PORTFOLIO COMPANIES MAKING APPLICATION FOR INVESTMENT BY THE SBIC OF NEW YORK.

Small Business Investment Company of New York, 64 Wall Street, New York, New York 10005.

CHECKLIST NO. 6: CHECKLIST FOR ORGANIZING AND OPERATING A SMALL BUSINESS.

Prentice-Hall, Inc., Englewood Cliffs, New Jersey 07632

ADDITIONAL CHECKLISTS—A SHORT BIBLIOGRAPHY

CHECKLIST NO. 1:

INFORMATION REQUIRED FROM APPLICANT FOR FINANCING

The following checklist has been provided through the courtesy of Goodman & Mautner, Inc., a leading private venture capital firm in Los Angeles. It outlines the information that a company seeking financing through Goodman & Mautner must supply and suggests a format for the presentation of this information.

A. *Corporate Structure*

1. Give the name of the company, the state in which it was incorporated, and the date of its incorporation.

2. Predecessor companies: if any, give their particulars and their history up to the incorporation of the subject company.

3. Subsidiaries of subject: show the degree of ownership by the subject company and identify any minority interests. Also give the dates and state of the incorporation of any subsidiaries.

4. Outstanding securities, including bank loans involving the subject company and any subsidiaries that are not 100 percent in the ownership of the subject company: state the principal terms of such securities. Wherever bank loans or institutional obligations exist, identify lender, and name, if possible, the individual at the lending institution who is most familiar with the account.

5. Name and state the other holdings of the principal holders of subject company's common stock and/or other types of equity securities (convertible debt or preferred stock). If any such principal holders are not members of executive management, identify them and describe briefly the history and reasons for their stock purchases; also state if such holders have been in the past or are currently suppliers, vendees, or lessees or if they have any other business relationships with the subject company. If they do have such relationships, describe them in full, including the financial details of any transactions with the subject company.

6. Give a chronological record of the subject company's sales of its equity securities, stating prices, number of buyers, identity of principal buyers, and any other pertinent facts.

B. *Executive Management and Work Force*

1. Provide an abbreviated schematic diagram of the organization.

2. Provide personal resumes, including academic and business backgrounds, of all executive officers and any other supervisory personnel who may be considered of special value to the organization (for example, director of research, production manager, etc.). Business backgrounds should be as specific as possible regarding the positions held and the functions of such positions. Name three business references for each executive officer. State the present salaries and/or other remunerations.

3. If a restricted stock option plan is in effect or is contemplated, deliver a copy of such a plan or an outline of the proposed plan, along with a schedule of options granted or to be granted, exercise prices, and grantees.

4. Include a statistical table showing for the last five years, if applicable, the number of employees at year-end and the total payroll expense. If profit-sharing or bonus plans were in effect for this period or any portion thereof, show such payments or appropriations in separate columns.

5. Include a statistical table that shows the departmental breakdown of the work force at the most recent date available. Show a further breakdown for the research department, if any, between engineers and nonengineers.

C. *Business*

1. Prepare a narrative description of historical development of the business, including the dates of any significant changes, such as acquisitions, introduction of new products, etc.

2. Describe the present product lines, providing as full a quantitative analysis as possible of the relative importance of each. If possible, provide a sales analysis for the past several years. Provide an evaluation of each product with respect to quality, performance, etc., in comparison with competitors' products. Identify competitors in each line of products and compare percent of market possessed by subject company's product(s) with percentage possessed by the products of competitors in each product line. Describe in what ways the subject company believes its products have special competitive advantages over those of other producers.

3. Where products are of a technical nature, describe briefly the uses to which each principal product is put.

4. Describe marketing methods, including any significant changes in methods introduced in the last five years and the reasons for them. Provide a list of principal distributors, dealers, manufacturers' representatives, foreign agents, etc.

5. Identify and describe any patents believed to be of value to the subject; give expiration dates.

6. Provide an analysis of 20 principal customers in each of the last five years, giving annual dollar sales made to each. Describe any special agreements with any such customers. Give briefly the background facts explaining any relatively sharp gain or decline in sales to each of such customers in the last five years.

7. With respect to proprietary items, describe pricing policies on each important product line, including the current prices to distributors and the distributors' prices to ultimate consumers or users. Compare subject company's prices with those of the principal competitors.

8. Describe as concretely as possible management planning in regard to product and market development over the next five years.

D. *Industry*

1. Where possible, give a statistical record of the industry or sub-industry in which the subject operates; indicate the sources of such statistical data.

2. Evaluate future prospects for the industry or sub-industry of the subject company. Any judgments should be supported by logical reasoning which leads to the conclusion.

3. Describe any technological trends or potentialities in or out of the subject company's industry that might materially and/or adversely affect the subject company's business.

E. *Financial Statements and Operating Statistics*

1. Furnish annual audited statements for the last five years. If audits are short forms only (i.e., no supporting schedules for major balance sheet items, cost of sales, and expense categories), also furnish internal fiscal year-end reports.

2. Furnish the most recent interim financial statements (need not be audited) in comparative form.

3. If the financial statements contain items or involve methods of treatment peculiar to industry or to the subject company, describe them.

4. Where applicable, furnish historical operating statistics as to unit sales, average realized prices, costs per unit, etc.

F. *Financing Sought*

1. Describe as specifically as possible the financing sought, including the amount, suggested form, and other concurrent financing if this is part of a larger plan.

2. As concretely as possible, describe the application of financing. If funds are to be used in whole or in part for construction or capital additions, provide detailed estimates of the cost of the program.

3. Furnish independent engineering reports, if any, which have been prepared in connection with the contemplated financing or business program.

4. If financing is in whole or in part for the purpose of buying out in whole or in part the subject company's stockholders, give details as to the individuals desiring to divest themselves of their holdings.

5. Estimate as concretely as possible the incremental earning power to be generated by the application of financing proceeds.

6. If further financing requirements are anticipated for the purpose of carrying out the subject company's future program, state the amount, timing, and management's thinking as to the form of the financial arrangements.

7. Furnish a balance sheet showing the projected effects of the financing that is presently sought.

8. Furnish cash flow and/or profit and loss forecasts covering the 24 months succeeding this financing. Describe all pertinent reasoning that supports such forecasts.

CHECKLIST NO. 2:
A 24-POINT CHECKLIST FOR PREPARING A BUSINESS PLAN

The following checklist has been provided through the courtesy of Robert R. Kley Associates, Inc., an Ann Arbor-based private venture capital firm that is engaged in Regional New Business Opportunity Development in the southeastern Michigan area.

The items listed below represent the salient points to be considered in planning and financing a new venture that is centered around the development of a new product. They are presented in the order in which a business plan is normally arranged.

1. Provide a one-page summary of the idea, the market need, and the amount of money required.

2. Describe the key goals and objectives—specify what you are setting out to achieve, particularly in the sense of sales and profitability.

3. Provide an in-depth market analysis, and cite external sources of market research data.

4. List the names of six close competitors.

5. List for each product the anticipated selling price to an ultimate consumer, and present a brief summary that compares these prices with those of major competitors.

6. Provide a list of potential customers who have expressed an interest in the proposed products.

7. Provide a one-page summary of the functional specifications for the new product.

8. Illustrate the physical forms of the products with drawings and/or photographs.

9. Provide a profile of the most important patents.

10. Categorize and list the key technologies and skills required to develop and manufacture the proposed products, and indicate which technologies and skills the company plans to emphasize.

11. Describe the alternative channels of sales distribution, e.g., direct sales, sales through manufacturers' representatives, sales through original equipment manufacturers (OEMs), etc.

12. Describe the basis for determining, from the purchaser's point of view, if the new products are typically "lease" or "buy" items.

13. Describe the type and geographical distribution of the anticipated field service organization.

14. Describe the building block modularity of the new products (a module is something which can be independently manufactured, is testable, and can be inventoried).

15. Portray the cost vs. volume curves for each module, and illustrate the cost breakdown for material, labor, and factory burden.

16. Describe the manufacturing process involved; illustrate it by means of a block diagram.

17. Describe the types and quantities of capital equipment needed, and determine when this equipment will be required.

18. Portray a Flow-Event-Logic-Feedback chart that illustrates achievement milestones and portrays stepped levels of when and how additional funds should go into the venture.

19. Project staff and plant space requirements over a five-year period.

20. List the rationale for choosing a particular manufacturing plant location.

21. Provide cash flow projections by month for 24 months and then every quarter for the following three years.

22. Provide pro-forma balance sheets for five years.

23. Provide pro-forma profit and loss statements for five years.

24. State the degree of ownership control being sought and the limits to which these can be varied in regard to time and profitability.

Several examples of growth industries to which this checklist has been applied are:

Health Sciences	Power and Energy
Education	Metals and Alloys
Computers and Peripherals	Chemicals and Plastics
Solid State Electronics	Pollution Control
Electronic Communications	Infrared, Optics, and Holography.

CHECKLIST NO. 3:
DEVELOPMENT OF A MARKETING PROGRAM

This marketing checklist has been provided by special arrangement with the international management consulting firm of William E. Hill and Co., Inc., a subsidiary of Dun and Bradstreet, Inc.

A. *PLANNING STAGE*
   1. *Identify and Measure Market Segments:*
      a) Identify total market, including size and growth.
      b) Break market down into meaningful "business" segments, again including size and growth.
      c) Identify (typical) customers in each segment.
      d) Identify (typical) competitors in each segment, including profit and growth records of competitor.
   2. *Identify Market Characteristics for Each Segment* (through Field Research):
      a) Identify end-user functional requirements (e.g., prestige, appeal).
      b) Identify end-user product requirements (types, extent of line, prices, quality, packaging service, product service, warranties, etc.).
      c) Determine end-user buying practices.
      d) Determine competitor marketing practices.
   3. *Determine Major Requirements for Success in Each Segment:*
      a) Determine concept of the business or basic business policies.
      b) Determine product line.
      c) Plan marketing.
      d) Plan operations or production.
      e) Plan engineering, research, and new product development.
   4. *Project the Business and Our Company Profit Potential:*
      a) Project growth forces in the market (or lack of same).
      b) Project technical trends (including product/process obsolescence).
      c) Project competitive trends (including capacity, vertical/horizontal integration).
      d) Project market trends (including approaching saturation, population shifts, changes in merchandising, changes in buying habits).
      e) Make market and industry projections (physical units and dollar volume).
      f) Make projection of pricing climate (factors causing improvement or decline).
      g) Make projection of "our share" of market attainable.
      h) Project costs, investment, return on investment (5-year pro forma financial statements).

5. *Develop Marketing Objective and Strategies:*
   a) Evaluate company objectives versus profit opportunities, company skills and resources, and company needs.
   b) Develop marketing objectives and strategies for each market segment.

B. *EXECUTION STAGE*
   1. *Determine Sales Force Requirements:*
      a) Established customers: determine requirements in regard to frequency and types of calls, persuasive selling, engineering selling, personal selling, executive selling, technical service, etc.
      b) Potential customers: identify prime and secondary potential customers and their needs; determine requirements in regard to frequency and type of primary sales contacts; bird dogging.
   2. *Determine Sales Administration to Facilitate Above Functions*
      a) Decide upon a policy for determining sales "territories" and for distributing salesmen's accounts.
      b) Develop sales organization and management.
      c) Plan method for sales compensation and for review of salesmen's performance, quotas, or other standards; customer contact.
      d) Plan methods of stimulating salesmen.
   3. *Determine Requirements for Service to Fill Customer Needs*
      a) Plan for price and delivery quotations, order processing, scheduling and expediting of deliveries, and order follow-up.
      b) Plan for technical service of product, if necessary.
      c) Plan for shipping and physical distribution.
      d) Plan for distributing sales correspondence, product information, and advertising literature.
   4. *Determine Advertising and Sales Promotion Requirements*
      a) Advertising must reach both present and potential customers.
   5. *Determine Marketing Administration to Facilitate Above Functions*
      a) Market research determines market trends and forecasting, makes sales analyses, identifies prime prospects, analyzes competitors, and obtains trade intelligence.
      b) The marketing administration must work in conjunction with the developers of new products so that the new products can be marketed effectively.
      c) Plan for advertising and sales promotion.
      d) Positive pricing administration.
      e) Select distributors and/or dealers carefully.
      f) Recruit adequate personnel, then train them well, compensate them adequately, and frequently review their performance.
      g) Plan marketing budgets, cost controls, and inventory control.

h) Plan to take care of both credits and collections.
i) Evaluate trade association affiliations.
j) Determine whether or not product or market managers can act as specialized assistants in marketing administration.
k) Plan for the handling of national or multi-salesman accounts.
l) Plan the total organization structure of marketing activities.

CHECKLIST NO. 4:

MARKETING FUNCTIONS CHECKLIST

This checklist, also provided by special arrangement with William E. Hill and Co., Inc., indicates the many functions that must be considered in establishing a well-rounded marketing organization.

    A. *Sales Operations*
        Customer maintenance
            Periodic follow-up
            Engineering selling
            Personal selling
            Executive selling
            Service selling
        New customer development
        Bird dogging
        Customer service
        Intelligence feedback
    B. *Marketing Research and Planning*
        Sales analysis by product
        Market share analysis
        Territory analysis
        Distribution analysis
        Account profitability analysis
        Market measurement
        Market forecasts
        Market characteristics
        Identification and classification of potential accounts
        New products research
        Test marketing
        Product planning
        Package planning
        "Long-range" planning
        Competitive, technical, and market trends
        Market intelligence center
    C. *Sales Management*
        Sales organization
        Territories
        Use of account or other specialists
        Quotas and other performance standards
        Performance review

        Salesman stimulation
        Time and expense controls
        Call reports
        Compensation review

D. *Advertising and Sales Promotion*
        Advertising
            Creative development
            Media selection
            Sales coordination
        Sales promotion
            Salesman aids
            Merchandise displays
            Trade promotion literature
            Public relations

E. *Customer Service*
        Quotation and estimating
        Order processing
        Scheduling
        Expediting and delivery
        Specials
        Technical service
        Sales correspondence
        Warranties
        Adjustments

F. *Physical Distribution*
        Warehousing
        Shipping
        Repackaging
        Inventory control

G. *Marketing Management*
        Marketing objectives
        Market segments to pursue
        Volume and profit goals
        Overall marketing concept
        Marketing strategy selection
        Sales policies
        Pricing policies
        Policies in other areas
        Credit, allowances
        Budget and cost controls
        Inventory control

Trade association membership
New product marketing-customer liaison
Use of product and/or market specialists
Key account aid
Overall marketing organization
H. *Marketing Personnel*
Selection
Recruitment
Training
Personnel records
Manpower planning

CHECKLIST NO. 5:

INFORMATION NEEDED FROM PROSPECTIVE PORTFOLIO COMPANIES MAKING APPLICATION FOR INVESTMENT BY THE SBIC OF NEW YORK

The following checklist has been provided through the courtesy of the Small Business Investment Company of New York, a publicly held SBIC affiliated with the International Bank.

1. Short introductory statement giving facts as to incorporation of company (date, state), location of executive offices, and *brief* description of business (What is made, how it is used, who uses it).

2. Statement regarding amount of funds needed from SBIC-NY and use to which said funds are to be put.

3. Statement regarding amount of capital already supplied by applicant. How much in cash? How much in the form of patents, processes, or property? How much as compensation for past services rendered?

4. Statement regarding capitalization of company, listing short-term debt, long-term debt, preferred stock, common stock, and surplus (or deficit). Specify interest rates and term on debt (options?).

5. Summary of earnings and a projection of earnings for coming years; also a cash flow statement if it seems appropriate.

6. More detailed outline of business, indicating products, method of manufacture, markets, method of sales, research and development, patents, competition, plant, property, equipment, and backlog.

7. Description of management, including previous experience, education, and age.

8. Accounting of remuneration of management if over $20,000 per year.

9. List of principal shareholders, with amounts held.

10. Audited financial statements for past five years or whatever is available.

CHECKLIST NO. 6:
CHECKLIST FOR ORGANIZING AND RUNNING A SMALL BUSINESS

This checklist is reproduced from the book *How to Organize and Operate a Small Business*, Fifth Edition, 1973 by Clifford M. Baumback, Kenneth Lawyer and Pearce C. Kelley, through the courtesy of the publisher, Prentice-Hall, Inc.

A. The Decision for Self-Employment
   1. Have you rated yourself and had some acquaintances rate you on the personal qualities necessary for success as your own boss, such as leadership, organizing ability, perseverance, and physical energy?
   2. Have you taken steps to improve yourself in those qualities in which you are weak but which are needed for success?
   3. Have you saved money, made business contacts, taken special courses, or read particular books for the purpose of preparing yourself for business ownership?
   4. Have you had training or experience in your proposed line of business or in one similar to it?
   5. Are you (*a*) good at managing your own time and energy? (*b*) not easily discouraged? (*c*) willing to work harder in your own business than as an employee?
   6. Have you estimated the net income from sales or services you can reasonably expect in the crucial "first two years"?
   7. Have you compared this income with what you could make working for someone else?
   8. Are you willing to risk the uncertainty or irregularity of your self-employment income during the early years of the enterprise?
   9. Would you worry less as an employee than you would as the owner of your own business?
   10. Have you carefully considered and enumerated the reasons why you want to enter business on your own?
B. Buying a Going Concern
   1. Have you checked the proposition against the specific warnings issued by Better Business Bureaus and other authorities as discussed in Chapter 5?
   2. Are the physical facilities in satisfactory condition?
   3. Are the accounts receivable, inventory, and goodwill fairly valued?
   4. Have you determined why the present owner wants to sell?
   5. Have you compared what it would take to start a similar business of your own with the price asked for the business you are considering buying?
   6. Has your lawyer checked to see that the title is good, that there are no liens against the business and no past due taxes or public utility bills?

7. Have you compared several independent appraisals of the business, arrived at by different methods?
8. If it is a bulk sale, has the sale provisions of the Uniform Commercial Code been complied with?
9. Have you investigated possible developments, such as those discussed in Chapter 5, that might affect the business adversely?

C. Justifying a New Business
1. Have you analyzed the recent trend of business conditions?
2. Have you analyzed conditions in the line of business you are planning to enter?
3. If your business will be based on an entirely new idea, have you attempted to secure actual contracts or commitments from potential customers instead of merely getting their polite approval of your idea?
4. Have you discussed your proposition with competent advisors who are in different occupations or who have different viewpoints?

D. Acquiring a Franchise
1. Have you viewed the franchise offer in the light of the material presented in Chapters 6 and 7?
2. Have you contacted personally several of the company's franchise holders to see how they like the deal?
3. Have you asked for a business responsibility report on the franchise promoter from you local Better Business Bureau or Chamber of Commerce?
4. Have you engaged the services of a lawyer to go over all provisions of the franchise contract?

E. Selecting the Profitable Location
1. Did you compare several different locations before making your final choice?
2. Did you use one or more detailed checklists to guide your selection?
3. Have you arranged for legal counsel before signing the lease and any similar contracts?
4. Are you, and the members of your family affected, satisfied that the community in which you plan to locate will be a desirable place in which to live and rear your children?
5. If your proposed location is not wholly suitable, are there sound reasons (not merely your impatience to get started) why you should not wait and try to secure a more nearly ideal location?

F. Building and Layout
1. Have you studied your proposed building with function, construction, and modernization in mind?

2. Have you made a personal inspection of the physical plant of other successful businesses similar to the one you plan to start, including both independents and the branches of large organizations?

3. Have you made a scaled layout drawing of your store or shop?

4. If the proposed building does not meet all of your important needs, are there any *good* reasons for deciding to use it?

G. Financing and Organizing the Business

1. Have you written down a complete, itemized list of all capital needs for starting your kind of business, including a fair allowance for operating expenses and your own living expenses until the business is able to support itself *and* provide a substantial reserve for the "one serious error" most businessmen make during their first year of operation?

2. Have you discussed this financial prospectus with a banker and a successful businessman in your proposed field?

3. Have you used as a guide the standard operating ratios for your business in calculating your capital requirements?

4. Have you considered all the factors for and against each legal form of organization?

5. If you plan to secure much of your initial capital from friends or relatives, are you *certain* that your business will remain free of "friendly" domination?

H. Establishing the Business Policies

1. Have you made an objective investigation of the probable success of your proposed policies?

2. Have you written down the main provisions of your general and major policies?

3. Have you discussed your proposed policies with competent advisors to counteract the beginner's tendency to offer what *he* likes and wants instead of what his potential *customers* like and want?

4. Have you written down an adequate statement of the reputation you want your business to acquire with customers, suppliers, and competitors?

5. Have you made adequate provisions to insure that your policies will be understood and enforced and that you will receive ample warning of the need for policy adjustments?

I. Management and Leadership

1. Have you considered the way you will organize duties and responsibilities?

2. Have you made up a tentative plan or schedule to guide the distribution of your own time and effort?

3. Have you thought about how you would go about preparing standards, budgets, schedules, and other management aid as discussed in the text?

4. Have you provided some check on your own actions to insure that you do adequate management planning before making commitments or important decisions covering future activities of the business?

5. Have you arranged to use periodically some checklist covering detailed activities regarding customer relations, maintenance, safety, or whatever type of activity will require close attention to details in your particular business?

J. Insurance and Risk Management
1. Have you evaluated all the hazards to which your business will be exposed?
2. Have you determined the hazards for which you should provide insurance coverage?
3. Have you determined how much of each kind of insurance you should purchase, and the costs of this insurance?
4. Have you made allowances in your budget of estimated expenses for losses resulting from predictable, uninsured risks (such as shoplifting and bad debts)?
5. Have you considered the nature of the protective devices and precautionary control measures you will need to reduce the business risks you will face?

K. Personnel and Employee Relations
1. Will you be able to hire employees, locally, who possess the requisite skills?
2. Have you prepared your wage structure, and are your wage rates in line with prevailing wage rates?
3. If you plan to employ friends and relatives, are you sure you have determined their qualifications objectively?
4. Have you planned working conditions to be as desirable and practical as possible?
5. Are you certain the employee incentives you plan to use represent the workers' viewpoint rather than what *you* think they want?
6. Have you planned your employment, induction, and training procedures?

L. Procurement and Supplier Relations
1. Have you considered each of the desirable objectives in choosing a particular supplier, as discussed in Chapter 17, before selecting the companies you plan to deal with?
2. Have you carefully analyzed the points for and against concentrating your purchases with one or a few vendors, taking into account your personal skill and ability as well as conditions in your line of business?
3. Have you given adequate attention to each of the fundamentals of buying, as discussed in Chapter 17, in making your plans for this function?
4. Have you investigated your field of business with reference to the existence of cooperative buying groups, and the advantages of affiliating with one of these groups?

M. Pricing for Profit
1. Have you thought through the advantages and disadvantages of acquiring the price reputation you plan for your business?

2. Have you considered the probable reaction of competitors to your pricing practices?

3. Have you compared the relative importance in your business of each major marketing instrument, including price?

4. Have you investigated possible legal limitations on your pricing plans?

5. Have you considered possible applications of price-lining to your business?

6. Have you decided on the formula or method you will use in pricing each class of goods and services?

7. Have you decided how and to what extent you will meet probable price competition?

N. Advertising and Sales Promotion

1. Have you analyzed your probable competition in connection with the direct and indirect sales promotional methods you plan to use?

2. Have you planned definite ways to build and maintain superior customer relations?

3. Have you defined your potential customers so precisely that you could describe them in writing?

4. Have you decided how you can measure and record the degree of success achieved with each sales promotion so that you can repeat the "hits" and avoid the "duds"?

5. Have you considered different features of your business that would be appropriate for special promotions timed to your customers' needs and interests?

6. Have you made a list of all the media suitable for advertising *your* business, with some evaluation of each?

7. Have you selected the most promising reasons why people should patronize your business, and have you incorporated them in plans for your opening advertisement?

8. Have you made use of all appropriate sources in the preparation of a good initial mailing list?

9. Have you given careful thought to the advertising value of the proposed names for your firm, products, and services?

10. Have you made plans for some unusual gesture of welcome and appreciation for all customers during the opening days of your business?

11. Have you planned how you can measure the effectiveness of your advertising?

O. Credit and Collections

1. Have you carefully investigated the need for credit extension by your business?

2. Have you planned specifically the various ways you will secure and use information obtainable from your charge account customers?

3. Have you made a personal investigation of the services and costs of affiliating with the local credit bureau?
4. Have you planned the basic procedures you will *always* follow before extending credit to any applicant?
5. Have you formulated plans to *control* all credit accounts?

P. Inventory Control
1. Have you determined carefully what constitutes a *balanced* inventory for your business?
2. Have you recorded on paper the exact information you will need for effective inventory control?
3. Have you planned the best methods for securing this information?
4. Have you selected the most appropriate inventory control *system* to use?
5. Have you planned the best procedures to use for stock or stores keeping?
6. Have you listed the purposes and uses of the information you plan to secure from your inventory control system?

Q. Production Control
1. Have you prepared a production control routine or "system" suitable to your manufacturing processes?
2. Have you anticipated future production requirements, and have you made plans for increasing the capacity of the plant as needed?

R. Profit Planning and Expense Control
1. Do you know what your "break-even" volume is?
2. Have you made an estimate of what your volume is likely to be during the early years of your business?
3. Have you investigated the standard systems of expense classifications used in your type of business and selected the most appropriate one for your use?
4. Have you determined what are usually the largest items of expense for your type of business and made definite plans for controlling these expenses from the very beginning of the business?
5. Have you determined which, if any, expense items, though normally small for your type of business, very easily become excessively large unless carefully controlled *at all times*?
6. Have you prepared on paper a *flexible* expense budget for two or three different probable amounts of volume of business, including provisions for frequent operating expense reports to be compared with planned figures in your budget?
7. Have you determined the standard operating ratios for your field that you plan to use as guides?
8. Have you compared the expense of "farming out," or having certain activities of the business done by outside agencies, with what it would cost you to do the work yourself?

S. Regulations and Taxes
1. Have you ascertained from reliable sources all regulations that must be complied with in your business?
2. Have you provided for an adequate system of record keeping that will furnish essential information for all taxation purposes?
3. Have you checked the police, health, fire, and other safety regulations that apply to your business?
4. Have you provided for securing all information from employees required by law?
5. Have you obtained a Social Security number?
6. Have you complied with regulations governing the use of a firm or trade name, brand names, or trademarks?

T. Records
1. Have you decided what records will be adequate for each division and need of your business?
2. Have you secured the necessary forms to enable you to start keeping adequate records from the first day of operation of the business?
3. Have you planned your record system so that appropriate use will be made of standard operating ratios?
4. Have you investigated the possibilities of using simplified record-keeping systems for some of your needs?
5. Have you considered applications of the "one-book" system to your business?
6. Have you decided by whom each record needed will be kept?
7. Have you investigated the record-keeping system recommended by the trade association in your field?

Business Operations:

Advertising, Vol. 9 No. 1, Pub. 1969.

Opening Your Own Business, Vol. 7 No. 7, Reissued 1969.

Small Business Success, Vol. 7 No. 5, Reissued 1969.

How to Buy or Sell a Business, Vol. 8 No. 11, Pub. 1969.

Understanding Financial Statements, Vol. 7 No. 11, Reissued 1969.

Financing Small Business, Vol. 8 No. 5, Pub. 1969.

Franchising, Vol. 9 No. 9, Pub. 1970.

Personnel for the Small Business, Vol. 9 No. 8, Pub. 1970.

Small Business—a Look Ahead, Vol. 8 No. 1, Pub. 1967.

Steps to Starting a Business, Vol. 8 No. 8, Pub. 1969.

Applying for Minority Business Loans, Special issue. 28-page illustrated kit. Pub. 1970.

Professional Management:

Establishing a Dental Practice in California, Pub. 1969.

Establishing a Medical Practice in California, Pub. 1970.

Ota, Leslie, and Rodgers, Nancy M., ed. "How to Establish and Operate Your Own Small Business: Thirty-Nine Varieties." *Business Literature*, April-June 1962, pp. 35-40.

This is an extensive annotated bibliography listing books treating the details of starting and operating 39 different types of small businesses.

Available from The Business Library, 34 Commerce Street, Newark, New Jersey 07102. 60 cents.

Small Business Administration. *Checklist for Going into Business.* Small Marketers Aids No. 71. Washington, D.C.: U.S. Government Printing Office, 1970.

Free.

Small Business Administration. "Starting and Managing Series." Available from the Superintendent of Documents, Government Printing Office, Washington, D. C. 20402.

Titles include:

Starting and Managing a Small Business of Your Own	35 cents
Starting and Managing a Small Credit Bureau and Collection Service	60 cents
Starting and Managing a Service Station	45 cents
Starting and Managing a Small Bookkeeping Service	35 cents
Starting and Managing a Small Building Business	50 cents
Starting and Managing a Small Motel	40 cents
Starting and Managing a Small Duplicating and Mailing Service	35 cents
Starting and Managing a Small Restaurant	65 cents
Starting and Managing a Small Retail Hardware Store	30 cents
Starting and Managing a Small Retail Drugstore	40 cents

Starting and Managing a Small Dry Cleaning Business   35 cents
Starting and Managing a Small Automatic Vending Business   40 cents
Starting and Managing a Carwash   45 cents
Starting and Managing a Swap Shop or Consignment Sale Shop 35 cents
Starting and Managing a Small Shoe Service Shop   45 cents
Starting and Managing a Small Retail Camera Shop   40 cents
Starting and Managing a Retail Flower Shop   55 cents
Starting and Managing a Pet Shop   30 cents
Starting and Managing a Small Retail Music Store   55 cents

Appendix 5

SMALL BUSINESS ADMINISTRATION AND U.S. DEPARTMENT OF COMMERCE FIELD OFFICE LOCATIONS

SBA FIELD OFFICE ADDRESSES

Boston, Massachusetts 02203
  John Fitzgerald Kennedy Federal Building
Holyoke, Massachusetts 01040
  326 Appleton Street
Augusta, Maine 04330
  Federal Building
  U. S. Post Office
  40 Western Avenue
Concord, New Hampshire 03301
  55 Pleasant Street
Hartford, Connecticut 06103
  Federal Office Building
  450 Maine Street
Montpelier, Vermont 05601
  Federal Building
  2nd Floor
  87 State Street
Providence, Rhode Island 02903
  702 Smith Building
  57 Eddy Street

New York, New York 10007
  26 Federal Plaza
  Room 3930
Hato Rey, Puerto Rico 00919
  255 Ponce De Leon Avenue
Newark, New Jersey 07102
  970 Broad Street
  Room 1636
Syracuse, New York 13202
  Hunter Plaza
  Fayette & Salina Streets
Buffalo, New York 14203
  Federal Building
  Room 9
  121 Ellicott Street
Albany, New York 12297
  91 State Street

Philadelphia, Bala Cynwyd, Pennsylvania 19004
  1 Decker Square
Wilmington, Delaware 19801
  U. S. Customs House
  6th and King Streets

Baltimore, Maryland 21201
  1113 Federal Building
  Hopkins Plaza
Clarksburg, West Virginia 26301
  Lowndes Bank Building
  119 N. 3rd Street
Charleston, West Virginia 25301
  3410 Courthouse & Federal Building
  500 Quarrier Street
Pittsburgh, Pennsylvania 15222
  Federal Building
  1000 Liberty Avenue
Richmond, Virginia 23240
  Federal Building
  400 N. 8th Street
Washington, D. C. 20417
  1405 I Street, N. W.

Atlanta, Georgia 30309
  1401 Peachtree St., N. E.
Birmingham, Alabama 35205
  908 S. 20th Street
Charlotte, North Carolina 28202
  Addison Bldg.
  222 South Church Street
Columbia, South Carolina 29201
  1801 Assembly Street
Jackson, Mississippi 39205
  245 East Capitol Street
Gulfport, Mississippi 39501
  2500 14th Street
Jacksonville, Florida 32202
  Federal Office Building
  400 W. Bay Street
Louisville, Kentucky 40202
  Federal Office Building
  600 Federal Place
Miami, Florida 33130
  Federal Building
  51 S. W. 1st Avenue
Tampa, Florida 33602
  Federal Building
  500 Zack Street

Nashville, Tennessee 37219
   500 Union Street
Knoxville, Tennessee 37902
   502 South Gay Street
Memphis, Tennessee 38103
   Federal Building
   167 North Main Street

Chicago, Illinois 60604
   Federal Office Building
   219 South Dearborn Street
Springfield, Illinois 62701
   502 Monroe Street
Cleveland, Ohio 44199
   1240 E. 9th Street
Columbus, Ohio 43215
   50 West Gay Street
Cincinnati, Ohio 45202
   5026 Federal Building
   550 Main Street
Detroit, Michigan 48226
   1249 Washington Blvd.
Marquette, Michigan 49855
   502 West Kaye Avenue
Indianapolis, Indiana 46204
   36 South Pennsylvania Street
Madison, Wisconsin 53703
   25 West Main Street
Milwaukee, Wisconsin 53203
   238 W. Wisconsin Avenue
Eau Claire, Wisconsin 54701
   510 South Barstow Street
Minneapolis, Minnesota 55402
   816 2nd Ave. South

Dallas, Texas 75202
   1309 Main Street
Albuquerque, New Mexico 87101
   Federal Building
   500 Gold Ave., S. W.
Los Cruces, New Mexico 88001
   1015 El Paso Road
Houston, Texas 77002
   808 Travis Street
Little Rock, Arkansas 72201
   377 P. O. & Courthouse Building
   600 W. Capitol Avenue
Lubbock, Texas 79408
   Federal Office Building
   1616 19th Street
El Paso, Texas 79901
   109 N. Oregon Street
Marshall, Texas 75670
   505 East Travis Street
New Orleans, Louisiana 70130
   124 Camp Street

Oklahoma City, Oklahoma 73102
   30 N. Hudson Street
San Antonio, Texas 78205
   301 Broadway
Lower Rio Grande Valley
Harlingen, Texas 78550
   219 E. Jackson Street
Corpus Christi, Texas 78401
   Post Office & Custom House Building

Kansas City, Missouri 64106
   911 Walnut Street
Des Moines, Iowa 50309
   New Federal Building
   210 Walnut Street
Omaha, Nebraska 68102
   Federal Building
   215 N. 17th Street
St. Louis, Missouri 63102
   Federal Building
   210 North 12th Street
Wichita, Kansas 67202
   120 South Market Street

Denver, Colorado 80202
   721 19th Street
Casper, Wyoming 82601
   300 North Center Street
Fargo, North Dakota 58102
   653 2nd Avenue, North
Helena, Montana 59601
   Power Block Bldg.
   Main & 6th Avenue
Salt Lake City, Utah 84111
   2237 Federal Building
   125 South State Street
Sioux Falls, South Dakota 57102
   National Bank Building
   8th and Main Avenue

San Francisco, California 94102
   Federal Building
   450 Golden Gate Avenue
Fresno, California 93721
   Federal Building
   1130 O Street
Honolulu, Hawaii 96813
   1149 Bethel Street
Agana, Guam 96910
   Ada Plaza Center Building
Los Angeles, California 90014
   849 South Broadway
Las Vegas, Nevada 89101
   300 Las Vegas Blvd., South
San Bernardino, California 92401
   532 North Mountain Avenue

Phoenix, Arizona 85004
   122 N. Central Avenue
Tucson, Arizona 85701
   Federal Building
   155 East Alamenda Street
San Diego, California 92101
   110 West C Street
Seattle, Washington 98104
   506 Second Avenue
Anchorage, Alaska 99501
   1016 West Sixth Avenue

Fairbanks, Alaska 99701
   510 Third Avenue
Juneau, Alaska 99801
   Federal Building
Boise, Idaho 83702
   216 North 8th Street
Portland, Oregon 97205
   921 S. W. Washington Street
Spokane, Washington 99210
   Courthouse Building
   Room 651

U. S. DEPARTMENT OF COMMERCE FIELD OFFICE ADDRESSES

Albuquerque, New Mexico 87101
   U. S. Courthouse-Room 316
   William E. Dwyer, Director
   Area Code 505 Tel. 843-2386
Anchorage, Alaska 99501
   412 Hill Building
   632 Sixth Avenue
   H. Phillip Hubbard, Director
   Area Code 907 Tel. 272-6531
Atlanta, Georgia 30303
   Room 400, 75 Forsyth Street, N. W.
   David S. Williamson, Director
   Area Code 404 Tel. 526-6000
Baltimore, Maryland 21202
   415 U. S. Customhouse
   Gay and Lombard Streets
   Carroll F. Hopkins, Director
   Area Code 301 Tel. 962-3560
Birmingham, Alabama 35205
   Suite 200-201
   908 South 20th Street
   Gayle C. Shelton, Jr., Director
   Area Code 205 Tel. 325-3327
Boston, Massachusetts 02203
   Room 510, John F. Kennedy
      Federal Building
   Richard F. Treadway, Director
   Area Code 617 Tel. 223-2312
Buffalo, New York 14203
   504 Federal Building
   117 Ellicott Street
   Robert F. Magee, Director
   Area Code 716 Tel. 842-3208
Charleston, South Carolina 29403
   Federal Building, Suite 631
   334 Meeting Street
   Paul Quattlebaum, Jr., Director
   Area Code 803 Tel. 577-4171

Charleston, West Virginia 25301
   3000 New Federal Office Building
   500 Quarrier Street
   J. Raymond DePaulo, Director
   Area Code 304 Tel. 343-6181, Ext. 375
Cheyenne, Wyoming 82001
   6022 O'Mahoney Federal Center
   2120 Capitol Avenue
   Joseph D. Davis, Director
   Area Code 307 Tel. 778-2220, Ext. 2151
Chicago, Illinois 60604
   Room 1486, New Federal Building
   219 South Dearborn Street
   Gerald M. Marks, Director
   Area Code 312 Tel. 353-4400
Cincinnati, Ohio 45202
   8028 Federal Office Building
   550 Main Street
   Thomas E. Ferguson, Director
   Area Code 513 Tel. 684-2944
Cleveland, Ohio 44114
   Room 600, 666 Euclid Avenue
   Charles B. Stebbins, Director
   Area Code 216 Tel. 522-4750
Dallas, Texas 95202
   Room 3E7, 1100 Commerce Street
   C. Carmon Stiles, Director
   Area Code 214 Tel. 749-3287
Denver, Colorado 80202
   Room 161, New Customhouse
   19th and Stout Streets
   John G. McMurtry, Director
   Area Code 303 Tel. 837-3246
Des Moines, Iowa 50309
   609 Federal Building
   210 Walnut Street
   Kenneth A. Byrns, Acting Director
   Area Code 515 Tel. 284-4222

Detroit, Michigan 48226
  445 Federal Building
  Frank A. Alter, Director
  Area Code 313 Tel. 226-6088
Greensboro, North Carolina 27402
  258 Federal Building
  West Market Street, P. O. Box 1950
  Joel B. New, Director
  Area Code 919 Tel. 275-9111
Hartford, Connecticut 06103
  Room 610-B, Federal Office Building
  450 Main Street
  Richard C. Kilbourn, Director
  Area Code 203 Tel. 244-3530
Honolulu, Hawaii 96813
  286 Alexander Young Building
  1015 Bishop Street
  H. Tucker Gratz, Director
  Area Code 808 Tel. 546-8694
Houston, Texas 77002
  1017 Old Federal Building
  201 Fannin Street
  Edward T. Fecteau, Jr., Director
  Area Code 713 Tel. 226-4231
Jacksonville, Florida 32202
  Post Office Box 35087
  400 West Bay Street
  Wm. Bruce Curry, Director
  Area Code 904 Tel. 791-2796
Kansas City, Missouri 64106
  Room 1840, 601 East 12th Street
  George H. Payne, Director
  Area Code 816 Tel. 374-3141
Los Angeles, California 90024
  11201 Federal Building
  11000 Wilshire Blvd.
  Stanley K. Crook, Director
  Area Code 213 Tel. 824-7591
Memphis, Tennessee 38103
  Room 710, 147 Jefferson Avenue
  Bradford H. Rice, Director
  Area Code 901 Tel. 534-3214
Miami, Florida 33130
  Room 821, City National Bank Building
  25 West Flagler Street
  Roger J. LaRoche, Director
  Area Code 305 Tel. 350-5267
Milwaukee, Wisconsin 53203
  Straus Building
  238 West Wisconsin Avenue
  David F. Howe, Director
  Area Code 414 Tel. 224-3473
Minneapolis, Minnesota 55401
  306 Federal Building
  110 South Fourth Street
  Glenn A. Matson, Director
  Area Code 612 Tel.725-2133

New Orleans, Louisiana 70130
  909 Federal Office Building, South
  610 South Street
  Edwin A. Leland, Jr., Director
  Area Code 504 Tel.527-6546
New York, New York 10007
  41st Floor, Federal Office Building
  26 Federal Plaza, Foley Square
  Arthur C. Rutzen, Director
  Area Code 212 Tel. 264-0634
Philadelphia, Pennsylvania 19107
  Jefferson Building
  1015 Chestnut Street
  Raymond R. Riesgo, Acting Director
  Area Code 215 Tel. 597-2850
Phoenix, Arizona 85025
  5413 New Federal Building
  230 North First Avenue
  Donald W. Fry, Director
  Area Code 602 Tel. 261-3285
Pittsburgh, Pennsylvania 15222
  431 Federal Building
  1000 Liberty Avenue
  Lewis E. Conman, Director
  Area Code 412 Tel. 644-2850
Portland, Oregon 97204
  217 Old U. S. Courthouse
  520 S. W. Morrison Street
  J. D. Chapman, Director
  Area Code 503 Tel. 226-3361
Reno, Nevada 89502
  2028 Federal Building
  300 Booth Street
  Jack M. Howell, Director
  Area Code 702 Tel. 784-5203
Richmond, Virginia 23240
  2105 Federal Building
  400 North 8th Street
  Weldon W. Tuck, Director
  Area Code 703 Tel. 782-2246
St. Louis, Missouri 63103
  2511 Federal Building
  1520 Market Street
  Charles E. Gore, Director
  Area Code 314 Tel. 622-4243
Salt Lake City, Utah 84111
  1201 Federal Building
  125 South State Street
  Ray L. White, Director
  Area Code 801 Tel. 524-5116
San Francisco, California 94102
  Federal Building, Box 36013
  450 Golden Gate Avenue
  Philip M. Creighton, Director
  Area Code 415 Tel. 556-5864

San Juan, Puerto Rico 00902
    Room 100, Post Office Building
    George R. Delgado, Director
    Phone: 723-4640
Savannah, Georgia 31402
    235 U. S. Courthouse & Post Office Building
    125-29 Bull Street

James W. McIntire, Director
    Area Code 912 Tel. 232-4321
Seattle, Washington 98104
    8021 Federal Office Building
    909 First Avenue
    Judson S. Wonderly, Director
    Area Code 206 Tel. 442-5615

Appendix 6

BUSINESS AND FINANCIAL PERIODICALS

American Stock Exchange Investor (10 issues yearly). 86 Trinity Pl., New York, New York 10006.

Arizona Modern Business (monthly). 4044 East Lewis Avenue, Phoenix, Arizona 85008.

Arkansas Banker (monthly). Arkansas Bankers Assn., Publishers, 1027 Pyramid Bldg., Little Rock, Arkansas 72201.

Bank and Quotation Record (monthly). William B. Dana, 25 Park Pl., New York, New York 10007.

Bankers Monthly (monthly). Rand McNally and Co., P. O. Box 7600, Chicago, Illinois 60680.

Banking (monthly). Journal of the American Bankers Assn., 90 Park Avenue, New York, New York 10016.

Banking Law Journal (monthly). Warren, Gorham and Lamont, Inc., 89 Beach Street, Boston, Massachusetts 02111.

Barrons National Business and Financial Weekly, 30 Broad Street, New York, New York 10004.

The Bond Buyer (weekly). The Bond Buyer, Inc., 67 Pearl Street, New York, New York 10004.

Boston Globe (daily). 135 Wm. T. Morrissey Blvd., Boston, Mass. 02107.

Burroughs Clearing House (monthly). P. O. Box 418, Detroit, Michigan 48232.

The Business Lawyer (monthly). 1155 East 60th Street, Chicago, Illinois 60637.

Business Management (monthly). 22 West Putnam Avenue, Greenwich, Connecticut 06830.

Business Opportunities Digest (monthly). 301 N. Orchard Avenue, Farmington, New Mexico 87401.

Business Week (weekly). 330 West 42nd St., New York, New York 10036.

Chicago Daily News (daily). 401 North Wabash Ave., Chicago, Illinois 60611.

Chicago Sun-Times (daily). 401 North Wabash Ave., Chicago, Illinois 60611.

Chicago Tribune (daily). Tribune Square, Chicago, Illinois 60611.

Cleveland Trust Company Business Bulletin (monthly). Euclid and E. 9th, Cleveland, Ohio 44101.

Commerce Magazine (monthly). 30 West Monroe St., Chicago, Illinois 60603.

Commercial and Financial Chronicle (monthly). 25 Park Pl., New York, New York 10007.

Commercial West (weekly). 6601 West 78th St., Edina, Minnesota 55435.

Consumer and Finance News (monthly). National Consumer Finance Assn., 1000 16th St. N. W., Washington, D. C. 20036.

Credit and Financial Management (monthly). National Assn. of Credit Management, 475 Park Ave. S., New York, New York 10016.

Dallas Morning News (daily). A. H. Bello Corp., Publishers, Young and Houston St., Dallas, Texas 75222.

Dun's Review and Modern Industry (monthly). Dun & Bradstreet Publications Corp., P. O. Box 3088, Grand Central Station, New York, New York 10017.

Electronic News (weekly). 7 East 12th Street, New York, New York 10003.

Exchange (monthly). New York Stock Exchange, 11 Wall Street, New York, New York 10005.

Federal Reserve Bank of New York (monthly). 33 Liberty St., New York, New York 10045.

Federal Reserve Bulletin (monthly). Board of Governors of the Federal Reserve System, Division of Administrative Services, Washington, D. C. 20551.

Financial Analysts Journal (bi-monthly). 477 Madison Avenue, New York, New York 10022.

Financial World (weekly). 17 Battery Place, New York, New York 10004.

First National City Bank Economic Letter (monthly). First National City Bank of New York, 399 Park Ave., New York, New York 10022.

Forbes (semi-monthly). 60 Fifth Avenue, New York, New York 10011.

Fortune (monthly). Time & Life Bldg., Rockefeller Center, New York, New York 10020.

Generation, The Magazine of Young Businessmen (monthly). Generation, Inc., 120 North Green Street, Chicago, Illinois 60607.

Harvard Business Review (bi-monthly). Soldiers Field, Boston, Mass. 02163.

Industrial Banker (monthly). American Industrial Bankers Assn., 1629 K Street N. W., Washington, D. C. 20006.

Industrial Research (13 issues per year). Industrial Research Blvd., Beverly Shores, Indiana 46301.

Institute of International Finance Bulletin (irregular). University of New York, 100 Trinity Pl., New York, New York 10006.

Institutional Investor (monthly). 140 Cedar Street, New York, New York 10022.

Investment Dealers' Digest (weekly). 150 Broadway, New York, New York 10038.

Investor. Wisconsin's Business Magazine, 312 East Wisconsin Avenue, Milwaukee, Wisconsin 53202.

Journal of Commerce (daily). 99 Wall Street, New York, New York 10005.

Journal of Small Business. Journal of the National Council for Small Bus. Mgmt. Development, c/o Lillian B. Dreyer, Secretary-Treasurer NCSBMD, 351 California Street, San Francisco, California 94104.

Journal of Taxation (monthly). 125 East 56th Street, New York, New York 10022.

Kansas Banker (monthly). Kansas Bankers Assn., 420 First National Bank Bldg., Topeka, Kansas 66603.

Kentucky Banker (monthly). Kentucky Bankers Assn., 425 S. Fifth, Louisville, Kentucky 40202.

Los Angeles Times (daily). Times Mirror Square, Los Angeles, California 90053.

Magazine of Wall Street and Business Analyst (weekly). Ticker Publishing Co., Inc., 120 Wall Street, New York, New York 10005.

Miami Herald (daily). 1 Herald Plaza, Miami, Florida 33101.

Michigan Investor (weekly). Michigan Investor Publishing Co., 1629 W. Lafayette Blvd., Detroit, Michigan 48216.

Mid-Continent Banker (13 issues per year). 408 Olive Street, St. Louis, Missouri 63102.

Midwest Industry Magazine (monthly). Kansas Business Publishing Co., Inc., 4125 Gage Center Drive, Topeka, Kansas 66604.

Mid-Western Banker (monthly). 161 W. Wisconsin Ave., Milwaukee, Wisconsin 53203.

Milwaukee Journal (daily). Milwaukee Sentinel, 333 West State Street, Milwaukee, Wisconsin 53201.

Mississippi Banker (monthly). Mississippi Bankers Assn., 504 First National Bank Bldg., Jackson, Mississippi 39201.

Modern Data (monthly). 3 Lockland Avenue, Framingham, Mass. 01701.

Morgan Guaranty Trust Company Survey (monthly). 23 Wall Street, New York, New York 10015.

Mortgage Banker (monthly). Mortgage Bankers Assn. of America, 1707 H Street N. W., Washington, D. C. 20006.

Mountain States Banker (monthly). 1720 California Street, Denver, Colorado 80202.

Municipal Finance (quarterly). Municipal Finance Officers Assn., 1313 East 60th Street, Chicago, Illinois 60637.

Nation's Business (monthly). Chamber of Commerce of the U. S., 1615 H. Street N. W., Washington, D. C. 20006.

New Englander (monthly). 150 Causeway Street, Boston, Mass. 02114.

New Jersey Banker (quarterly). New Jersey Bankers Assn., P. O. Box 573, Princeton, New Jersey 08540.

New York Times (daily). 229 West 43rd Street, New York, New York 10036.

Newsletter from the National Small Business Association. 1225 19th Street N. W., Washington, D. C. 20036.

Northwestern Banker (monthly). Malcolm K. Freeland, 306 15th Street, Des Moines, Iowa 50309.

Ohio Banker (monthly). Ohio Bankers Assn., 33 N. High Street, Columbus, Ohio 43215.

Robert Morris Associates Bulletin (monthly). Philadelphia National Bank Bldg., Philadelphia, Pa. 19107.

SBANE. Small Business Assn. of New England, Inc., 69 Hickory Drive, Waltham, Mass. 02154.

SBIC/Venture Capital (monthly). Capital Publishing Company, 10 South LaSalle Street, Chicago, Illinois 60603.

Savings and Loan News (monthly). U. S. Savings and Loan League, 111 E. Wacker Drive, Chicago, Illinois 60601.

Savings Bank Journal (monthly). Thrift Publishers, Inc., 200 Park Ave., New York, New York 10017.

Second Income News (monthly). 4932 Sonoma Highway, Santa Rosa, California 95405.

Securities Magazine. 80 Williams Street, New York, New York 10038.

Smaller Manufacturers Council. Chamber of Commerce Building, Pittsburgh, Pennsylvania 15219.

Southern Banker (monthly). McFadden Business Publishers, 2119 Warren Drive, Norcross, Atlanta, Georgia 30071.

Survey of Current Business (monthly). Superintendent of Documents, U. S. Government Printing Office, Washington, D. C. 20402.

Tarheel Banker (monthly). North Carolina Bankers Assn., P. O. Box 2826, Raleigh, North Carolina 27602.

Texas Banker Record (monthly). Texas Bankers Assn., P. O. Box 2007, Austin, Texas 78767.

Trusts and Estates (monthly). Fiduciary Publishers, Inc., 132 West 31st Street, New York, New York 10001.

Tulsa Tribune (daily). 315 South Boulder Avenue, Tulsa, Oklahoma 74102.

U. S. Investor (weekly). Frank P. Bennett and Co., Inc., 286 Congress Street, Boston, Massachusetts 02210.

The Wall Street Journal (daily). 30 Broad Street, New York, New York 10004.

Washington Post. 1515 L. N. W., Washington, D. C. 20005.

World Resource Investment Digest (monthly). P. O. Box 283, Birmingham, Michigan 48012.

Applause

The author would like to take this opportunity to thank the many people who provided information and assistance in the preparation of this manuscript. Although a comprehensive listing is not practical and no slight is intended toward those whose names are not included, I would like to acknowledge the particularly helpful assistance of the following individuals and organizations (listed alphabetically):

Alameda County Library, Hayward Business Branch

American Bankers Association

American Bar Association

American Institute of Certified Public Accountants

Center for Venture Management

Library of Congress, National Referral Center for Science and Technology Division

Massachusetts Institute of Technology, Alumni Association

National Consumer Finance Association

Newark Public Library, Business Branch

San Francisco Public Library, Business Branch

San Jose Public Library

San Jose State College Library

University of Toronto, School of Business

The technical advice and assistance of Dr. Herbert E. Dougall, C.O.G. Miller Professor of Finance, Stanford University Graduate School of Business proved invaluable in the preparation of Chapter 15. (Any errors in the text, however, are *entirely* my own responsibility.) The comments of Mr. Karl S. Kropf, Manager, Special Industries Group and Vice President, Wells Fargo Bank were most helpful in the formulation of my discussion of commercial banking. The editorial assistance of Joan Rogers, Director of Grammatical Sciences and an entrepreneur in her own right, who coddled my commas, smoothed my syntax, and mended my split infinitives, saved me months in the preparation of this book. The secretarial services provided by Elsie L. Kuntz and Iris M. Tralle, two cheerful ladies who typed this manuscript, were invaluable in helping me keep production on schedule. The Index was prepared by Janette Leppe.

Index

Accountants, 65, 153
  Certified Public, 69, 85, 121, 143
  tax, 183
Accounting, 70
Accounting firm, 144, 149
  selection of, 146, 147
Accounts:
  payable, 131, 177, 209
  receivable, 16, 46, 131, 148, 177, 212, 223, 224
Acquisition, 133, 147, 184, 213, 217, 241
Acquisition candidate, 197, 214
Activity, patent, 181
Advertising, 159
  classified, 19, 59, 91
  direct mail, 159
  newspaper and television, 159
  trade journal, 74, 159
Advisers, business, 166, 232
Agency:
  insurance, 150, 151
  professional service, 144
Agent, insurance, 183
Allen, Louis L., 198
Allstate Insurance Company, 160, 232
American Bar Association Journal, 145
American Industrial Bankers' Association, 231
American Management Association, 66
American Research and Development Corporation, 207
Analyst, investment, 138
Anthrope, Phil, 27
Armstrong, Neil, 21
Arthur D. Little, Inc., 243
Articles:
  newspaper and magazine, 186
  published, 182
  technical, 159
Assets, 178, 207
  capital, 184, 239
  personal, 229, 230
  tangible, 221, 222, 230
Assistance, management, 140, 196
Assistance in preparation of business plan. (*See* Business Plan, preparation of)
Associations:
  alumni, 82, 181
  industry, 83
  professional, 82, 181
  trade, 83
Attorney, 5, 69, 85, 90, 121, 144, 145, 180, 199, 249
  company, 109, 146, 150
  patent, 69, 100
  tax, 183

Audacity, 12, 82
Auditing, 147
Authenticity, 185
Authority (as a founder attribute), 118
Automaton Personnel Agency, 205
Autonomy, 29

Board of Directors, 140
  compensation of, 144, 219
  composition of, 142
  recruitment of, 144
  replacement of a member of, 143
  selection of, 142
  size of, 142
Bonds,
  corporate, 243
  municipal, 259
Bonus, 33
Bordello, location of, 145
Book clubs, 73
Books, 70
  (as idea source), 70, 93
Bookstore, 72
Boston Stock Exchange, 206
Brentano's, Inc., 72
Brochure, 118
Brokerage houses, 237
Brokers, stock, 211, 237
Budget, 37
Bull market, 193
Bureau of Census, U. S. Department of Commerce, 152
Burlage, L. Charles, 55
Business:
  new, 153
  starting a, 46, 47, 65
Business associates, 59
  former, (*See* Partners)
Business cards, 110
Business consultants, (*See* Consultants, business)
Business development, 246
Business magazines, (*See* Trade magazines)
Business plan, 16, 121, 122, 124, 125, 131, 132, 133, 144, 151, 153, 158-159, 164, 165, 168, 176, 177, 179, 196, 219
  another company's, 121
  Appendix to, 139, 152, 175, 181
  cosmetics of, 122
  formal, 133, 137, 175
  illustrations in, 158
  importance of, 117
  Introduction to, 138

(is a Sales Document), 118
packaging of, 122
preparation of, 120, 160, 205, 226
review of, 226
Business proposal, 27, 138, 185
Business stationery, 70, 109
Business Week, 11, 31
Buyer's agent, 96
Buy-out, 242
Buzz words, 109

Campaign, advertising, 159
Capital, 16, 65, 163, 183, 196, 197, 198, 234 (*See also* Equity capital and Venture capital)
expansion, 184
high-risk, 225, 246
invested, 184
seed, 248
working, 16, 209, 212, 217, 219
Capital:
appreciation, 184, 199, 211
assets, (*See also* Assets), 184
community, 199, 234
equipment, 33, 179, 212, 259
gains, 178, 184, 206, 214, 244
market, 75, 125
source, (*See also* Source, capital), 195
Capitalists, 191
Capitalization, 20, 130, 132, 183, 193, 206
Carpet Critters, 14
Cash, 208
Cash-flow, 6, 46, 177
"Cash-out," 203
Cash reserves, 46, 177
Chambers of Commerce, 259
Characteristics,
market, 133
proprietary, 157
unique, 99
Chase Manhattan Bank, 211
Chase Manhattan Capital, 211
Checklist, 41
Children, 51, 54
Civil Rights Act of 1964, 218
Clearing house, 85
Closed-end investment companies, (*See also* Investment companies, closed-end), 206
Clubs,
service, 82
Toastmasters, 78
Coca Cola, 90, 132
Collateral, 148, 212
College, 66, 208
College community, 79
Colonel Sanders' Kentucky Fried Chicken, 158
Colossal Conglomerate, 27
Commerce, U. S. Department of, (*See* U. S. Department of Commerce)
Commercial bank, (*See also* Bank, commercial), 209, 210, 212, 230
selection of, 148

Commercial factor, 16
Commercial finance company, 211
Commission,
finder's, 227
representatives, 162
underwriter's, 253
Commissioner of Corporations, 21
Commitment, founder, 230
Communications, inadequate corporate, 32
Community,
banking, 182
financial, 48, 75, 78, 143, 182, 209, 230
investment, 131, 184, 227
Companies,
closed-end investment, 206, 246
commercial finance, 211
consumer finance, 212, 231
family investment, 225
factoring, 223
insurance, 231, 236
leasing, 240
life insurance, 231, 233
local development, 217
new, 141, 162, 163, 167, 169, 176, 183
sales finance, 249, 250
open-end investment, 240
Company:
legal structure, 179
stock, 131
Compensation, 58
board of directors', 219
business consultants', 228
founders, 182
stock as, 222
Competence, 41
Competition, 99, 165
external, 216
internal, 32
Competitors, 58, 74, 152, 186
Compromise, 176
Compton, Karl T., 207
Computer dating, 94
Confidence, 118, 169
Consultants, 75
business, 58, 85, 121, 143, 209
financial, 226
management, 10, 65, 227, 262
professional, 144
tax, 183
technical, 209, 234
Contacts, business, 68, 82, 85, 149
Contracts, employment, 90
Contributions versus rewards, 33
Control Data Corporation, 232
Convertible debentures, 258
Copyright, 15, 70
Corporate bonds, interest-bearing, 243
Corporate venture capital departments, 213
Corporations, (*See also* Commissioner of Corporations), 181

legal structure of, 179
   venture capital, 213
Cost breakdowns in Business Plan, 158
Counsel, 197
   corporate legal, 145, 147
   investment, 242
Covenants of secrecy, 157
Crap-shooters, 130, 201
Creativity, 119
Credibility, 118
Credit, 44, 118, 261
   bank, 148
Credit:
   information, 186
   rating services, 153
   reports, 149, 186
   Unions, 215
Creditor, 55, 224
Criticism, constructive, 119
Crystal Ball, 153
"Cushion," (*See also* Cash reserves), 177
Customers, 29, 44, 83, 109, 110, 118, 154, 176, 194,
   215, 261
   credit for, 223
   credit information on, 149, 186
   list of, 176
   potential, 176
   proximity of, 166, 167

Dale Carnegie Institute, 79
Data Recognition Corporation, 252
Datrix, 93
Davis Baker Act, 218
"Deal,"
   structure of, 200
   terms of, 199
Dealer, securities, 237
Debenture, 258
   issues, 231
Debt:
   capital, 193, 194, 231
   convertible, 194
   financing, 131
   instruments, 131, 258
   long-term, 258
   straight, 236
   with warrants, 236
Decision, investment, 125
Dedication of founders, 42
Department of Commerce, U. S. (*See* U. S. Depart-
   ment of Commerce)
Department of Housing and Urban Development, U. S.
   (*See* U. S. Department of Housing and Urban
   Development)
Deposits, customer, 216
Depreciation, 147, 223
Design News Annual, 94
"Designing around," 101
Desire of founders, 42
Dible, Donald M., Seminars, 68

Digital Equipment Corporation, 139, 207
Directory of Economic Development Administration
   Offices, 220
Directors, (*See also* Board of Directors), 107
Disclosure of idea, 102
Disclosure Document Program, 100
Discount, factor's, 224
Dissertations, doctoral, 92
Distribution channels (product and service): 160
   direct mail, 160
   direct sale by salaried salesmen, 160
   distributors, 83, 84
   independent suppliers, 161
   industrial salesmen, 161
   point-of-sale manufacturing, 160
   private label manufacturing, 161
   wholesaler or jobber, 161
Dividends, 200, 208
Divorce, 53, 54
Document, Sales, 118
Documentation, supporting, 185, 249
Doriot, General, 207
"Doughty-Dough Makers," 60
Drawings (in business plan), 158
Drexel Harriman Ripley, Inc., 232
Drucker, Peter F., 1
"Dry-run," 120
DTI Security, 3
Dun and Bradstreet, 177, 186
Du Pont, Francis I., & Co., 245

Envelopes, business 110
Environmental pollution (*See* Pollution, environmental)
Equipment:
   equity for, 230, 240
   leasing of, 179, 212, 231, 237, 262
   loan of, 218
   suppliers of, 222, 223
Equity, 130, 184, 191, 193, 194, 203, 210, 212, 221
   common, 236
   earned, 202
   founder, 21
Equity:
   capital, 194, 195, 206, 208, 211, 213, 219, 224,
      227, 256
   financing, 131, 210, 243, 249
   formula, 184, 226
   growth, 211, 223
   participation, 184
   position, 47, 214, 229, 248
Estate, personal, 184, 221
Expenses,
   fixed, 46
   EDA loan processing, 219
Facilities, 166-168
   educational, 168
   transportation, 167
Factoring, 223
   advantages of, 224
   nonrecourse, 224

Factors, 223
Faculty, college, (*See* Professors)
Faithless, Fred, 27
"False starts," 122
Fame, 30
Family, 13, 51, 52
Family Investment Companies, 225, 246
Family jewels, 248
Federal Home Loan Bank Board, 251
Federal Reserve Bank of Boston, 207
Fees, 254
  finder's, 228, 235
  lawyer's, 146
  simple, 97
Finance, corporate, 185
Finance company, 195
  commercial, 211
  consumer, 212
Financial:
  intermediaries, 226, 227
  resources, personal, 47
  rewards, 33
    long-term, 183
  statements,
    personal, 182
    pro-forma, 176, 179
Financiers, 169, 185
Financing,
  bridge, 6, 131
  equity, 194
  growth, 131
  inventory, 212
  lease, 163
  mezzanine, 131
  mortgage-type, 223
  new, 184
  new enterprise, 185, 192
  private, 149
  start-up, 125
Finders, 211, 226, 234
First National City Bank of New York, 211
First refusal, rights of, 247
Flanders, Ralph E., Senator, 207
Floor space, 179
FNCB Capital Corporation, 211
Ford, Henry, 197
Forecasting, 46
Former business associates (*See* Partners), 57
Formula, equity distribution, 199-203
Founders, 20, 32, 46, 47, 51, 53, 57, 61, 109, 110,
  119, 138, 140, 144, 154, 159, 164, 166, 167, 168,
  169, 175, 177, 182, 183, 184, 185, 195, 197, 198,
  216, 228
  backyard of, 166
  family of, 166
  investment of, 230
  responsibility of, 119
  resumes of, 138, 181
Foundations, tax-exempt, 259
Fraternity, 82

Friends, 58, 59, 230, 234, 246
Fund of Letters, 208
Fund, Mutual (*See* Mutual Fund)
Fund raising, 124, 147, 180

Gain, financial, 184
Gambling, 200
Gall, Gilbert, 28
Garage, 19, 45
Gargantuan Growth Group, Incorporated, 26
Geary, G. Stanton, 202
General manager, 17
General Motors, 184, 207
Genius, creative, 102
"Getting Out," 203
Gillette, King C., 163
Glass-Steagall Banking Act (*See also* Banking Act of
  1933), 234
Glossary, 185
Good Humor Man, 43
Goose, Old Lady, 60, 61, 89
Government Printing Office, 70
Greater Washington Investors, Inc., 201
Greed, 196
Gross national product, 133, 218
Growth, corporate, 153, 164, 200
Gun-slingers, 199
Gund family, 225
Gunwyn Ventures, 225
"Gut-feel," 125
Guts, 20, 42

Halcomb, James, 9, 169
Halcomb Associates, 9
Hambrecht, William R., 245
Hambrecht and Quist, 245
Harvard Student Agencies, Inc., 94
Head-count, 179
Heizer, E. F., Jr., 201, 232, 246, 247
Help, 81, 86, 124
Hewlett-Packard, 160
Highlights, emphasis of in mini-proposal, 132
Hill, Napoleon, 42
Hobby, 19
Housing and Urban Development, U. S. Department of
  (*See* U. S. Department of Housing and Urban
  Development)
Hula hoop, 153
Hypothecation, 212

Ice cream, 43
Idea, 26, 33, 68, 69, 100, 110, 118, 119, 121, 226
  product, 89, 91, 95
  unpatentable, 102
Illustrations in business plan, 158
Image, 118
  building of, 109
  corporate, 107, 122, 143, 150
  employee identification with company, 221
  projection of, 107, 108, 182
  Townsend, R., commentary on, 110-112

IMLAC, 226
Import-export, 65
Incompetence, 42
Incorporation, 146
Independent dealer, 96, 161
Industrial:
  Banks, 231
  Development Commissions, state and local, 217-220
  park, 208
  Research "100" Award, 23
  sectors, preferred, 132
Inflation, 243
Information, credit (*See* Dun and Bradstreet)
Information Storage Systems, Inc., 245
Infringement, patent, 101
Ingenuity, 19, 118, 119
Innovation, 33
Insomnia, 47
"Installment plan," 223, 231, 249
Institute for New Products, 92
Institutions,
  endowed, 208
  thrift, 250
Insurance, 151
  business life, 150
  key man, 150
  partnership, 150
  shareholder, 150
  sole proprietorship, 151
Insurance agency, selection of, 144, 150
Insurance companies (*See* Companies, insurance)
Integrity of legal counsel, 147
Intelligence:
  business, 76
  marketing, 153
Interest rate, 45, 148, 149, 191, 193, 200, 213, 215, 231
Intermediaries, financial, 226, 234
Internal competition (*See* Competition, internal)
Internal Revenue Code, 243, 244
  Section 1244, 244, 245
  Subchapter S, 244
Internal Revenue Service, 3, 222
International Business Machines, 184
Invention, 26, 33, 95, 100, 125
Inventors, 69, 96, 100, 104, 125
  warning to, 102
Inventors' Congress, 95
Inventors' Fair (*See* Inventors' Congress)
Inventors' Show (*See* Inventors' Congress)
Inventory, 163, 167, 177, 212
Inverness Capital Group, 202
Investment, 118, 125, 130
  cash, 230
  criteria for, 231, 235
  founder, 177, 228, 229
  low-risk, 149
  opportunities for, 200
  return on, 198
  safety of, 184
  self-amortizing, 223

Investment:
  advisers, 232, 242
  Advisers Act of 1940, 232
  banker, 234, 251
  banking, 234, 237
  clubs, 237
  community (*See also* Community, investment), 184
  Company:
    closed-end, 206
    open-end (*See* Mutual Funds)
  Company Act of 1940, 206
Investor, 45, 69, 118, 122, 124, 129, 130, 132, 133, 140, 158, 169, 179, 182, 185, 199, 200, 209, 227, 243
  basic requirements of, 130
  control by, 184
  objectives of, 132, 231
  preferences of, 130, 168
  private, 184
  prospective, 110, 165, 183, 234
  psychology of, 193
  solicitation of, 109, 124
  sophisticated, 138, 244
  specialization of, 130-132
Issue, new stock, 237
Itel Corporation, 245

Jobbers, 161
John Philip Company, 15
Journal of Commerce, The, 93
Journal of Commercial Bank Lending (*See* RMA Bulletin)

Kaisel, Stanley F., Dr., 31
Kettering, 207
Key words, 93
"Kickers," 131, 194, 210
"Kiss of death," 140
Know-how, 165
Koch, William I., 225
Koch family, 225
Koch Venture Capital, Inc. 225

Laboratory, university, 209
Lady, sweet old, 248
Land, Edwin H., 197
Las Vegas, 247
Laser, 18, 20
Laser Technology, Inc., 19, 222
Law firm, selection of, 144, 145, 149
Lawsuit, 121
Lawyer, 5, 65, 90, 109, 121, 143, 180, 184, 199
Lawyer Referral Services, 145
Leads, sales, 83
Lease, 21, 223, 231, 238, 262
Lease agreement, 163, 238
Lease-purchase plan, 238
Leasehold improvements, 179
Legal counsel (*See also* Lawyer and Attorney), 180, 185

Legal documentation, importance of, 248, 249
Letter, sales, 70, 121
Letter stock funds, 207, 208
Letter of intent, 152, 176
Leverage, 212, 224
Levitation Laboratories, 27
Liabilities, 178
　financial, 180, 193
　personal, 180, 181
Libraries, 72, 76, 122
　college and university, 71
　community, 71
　professional and trade association, 72
Library of Congress, 97
Licensee, 96, 104
Licensing, 90, 92
　business, 109
　patent, 95, 96, 102, 104
　regulations for, 109
Lien, 221
Life insurance policy loan, 229
Limited partnership agreement, 180, 232
Liquidity, 177
Little Red Hen, 60, 89
Loan, 177, 180, 231
　application for, 218, 219
　bank, 226, 229
　bank participation (SBA), 256
　customer, 217
　collateral, 212
　direct, 217, 221, 229, 261
　high-risk, 149
　intermediate-term, 210
　long-term, 210, 229, 256
　personal, 229
　short-term, 209
　simple, 211, 248
　subordinated, 219, 229
Loan:
　guarantee, 217, 261
　guarantor, 221, 229
　maturities, 231
　restrictions, 219
Location, plant, 71, 166, 216
Logotype, 109
Longtimer, Larry, 26
Loomis, Sayles and Company, Inc., 233
Loren, Sophia, 17

McLaughlin, H. B., 19-23
　wife of, 19, 21, 22
Maltby, John Philip, 15
Maltby, Shirley (Mrs. John Philip), 15-17
Maltz, Maxwell, 42
Management Consultant (*See* Consultant, management)
Manager,
　fund, 243
　investment, 240
　marketing, 59

Manpower, availability of, 167
Manufacturers, equipment, 222
Manufacturing process, 158, 164
Manuscripts, 93
Market, 52, 151
　capture of, 133, 153
　growth rate of, 133, 153
　knowledge of, 118
　niche in the, 132
　penetration of, 154, 163, 196
　tight money, 199
　virgin, 100
Market:
　research, 176
　share, 176
　survey, 74, 118, 185
　value (fair), 222
Marketing, 74, 84, 96
　reports on, 185
　strategy in, 159
　trends in, 95
Massachusetts Institute of Technology (MIT), 207
Master and Servant Law, 90
Materials, raw, 167
Mayfield Fund, 209
Measurex Corporation, 225
Media of exchange, 192, 193
Memorex Corporation, 225, 232
Memorial Drive Trust, 243
Merger, 19, 133, 147, 184, 213, 241
"Me Too!" company, 153
Millionaire, 68
Minority Enterprise SBIC (MESBIC), 258
Mistress, 52
Molasses, 71
Money, 192, 193
　cost of, 193
　equity, 177
　managers of, 130
　supply of, 193
　value of, 193
Monopoly, 165
Montgomery Ward, 161
Moon rocks, 18, 21
Moonlight, 230
Morris Plan, 230
Mortgage, 193, 223, 229, 241
Motivation, 31, 38, 42, 43, 64
Multiples, price-to-earnings, 192, 199, 200, 201
Mushroom Theory of Management, 26
"Mustang," 37
Mutual Fund, 206, 233
　management philosophy of, 240, 241
Mutual Savings Banks, 241
Name, company, 109
National Association of Bank Loan and Credit Officers
　(*See also* Robert Morris Associates), 177
National Association of Investment Clubs, 237
National Association of Securities Dealers, 252
National Bureau of Economic Research, 212

National Consumer Finance Association, 231
National Credit Union Administration (NCUA), 215
National Referral Center, 97
National Technical Information Service (NTIS), 76
Negotiation, 133, 227
Neighbor, 230
Nepotism, 35, 53
Net worth, 178, 224
New products, 93, 95, 165
New Products and New Sales Ideas, 93
New Products Digest, 92
New Products Newsletter, 92
New York Stock Exchange, 206
New York Times Book Review, The, 73
News, release, 22, 159
Newsletters, 75, 233
Newspapers, 76, 110
Nimble, Jack B., 25, 32, 35
Nimble Whizbanger Laboratories, 27
Nolte, Dorothy Law, 15
Noone, Charles M., 258
Note,
   convertible, 236
   long-term, 229, 258
   subordinate, 229
NTIS (*See* National Technical Information Service)

Objectives, compatibility of, 197
Offering, public, 236, 253, 254
Officers,
   company, 107, 140-142, 147 150, 181, 197-200, 219, 243
   loan, 210
Official Gazette, 91
Olsen, Kenneth, 139
One-man show, 138
Open-End Investment Companies, 240
Operating history, 131
Operation Breakthrough, 10
Opportunity, 71
Option, stock, 210
Organization chart, 139, 230
Organizational structure, 181
Orphan Products, 36, 241
Over-the-counter, 207
Owl, 60, 61, 89

Papa Fortune, 43
Papers, financial, 75
Parent company, 91, 241-242
Parents' Creed, 15
Partners, 45, 57, 91, 212
   general and limited, 180, 185 232, 245
   recruitment of, 57
   "silent," 180, 232, 245, 249
   venture capital, 195, 197
Partnership, 83, 91, 179
   agreements for, 146
   limited, 245, 262
   Private Investment, 196, 245, 246
   venture capital, 245

Patent: 26, 27, 33, 70, 96, 99-101, 133
   agreements, 90
   brokers, 96, 97
   coverage, 132
   holder, 96
   rights sale, 96, 102
   validity, 102
Patent Office, U. S. (*See* U. S. Patent Office)
Pawtucket, Rhode Island, 60
Payson, Joan Whitney, 225
Payson and Trask, 225
Peale, Normal Vincent, 42
Pension funds, 233, 242
   corporate-insured, 242
   corporate-noninsured, 233, 242
People, 41, 44
Performance, 242
Periodicals, 73, 75
   new-product, 91
Persistence, 12, 19, 82, 117
Personal fortune, 30
Phipps family, 225
Photographs, 140, 158
Physical well-being, 46
Piece of the action, 211
Pizzazz, 119
Placement, private (*See* Private placement)
Plan, business (*See* Business plan)
Planning, 124, 125
Plant, requirements for, 179
Polaroid camera, 132
Polaroid Corporation, 119, 225
Pollution, environmental, 132, 200
Pool, capital, 235, 237
Portfolio, 125, 196, 207, 208, 240, 243, 246
Portfolio diversification, 238
Premiums, 161
Presentation, financial, 147
President, 19, 52
Presidentson, Mr., 26
Price-to-earnings multiplier, 108, 193, 200
Pride, 81
Principal, 83, 193
Private Individual Investors, 85, 243, 251
Private Investment Partnerships (*See* Partnership, Private Investment)
Private partnerships, syndication of, 226, 234, 245
Private placement, 207, 232, 236, 253
Probate, 249
Problems, financial, 53
Process improvement, 164
Procrastination, 35
Pro forma financial statements, 176, 179
Product, 89, 241
   acceptance of new, 163
   convenience of, 155
   custom designed, 163
   customer service of, 156, 163
   development of, 76, 231
   durability of, 155

features of, 154
initial, 133
improvement of, 164, 231
leasing of, 163
price of, 156
promotion of, 159
proprietary, 52, 157
protection of, 157, 159
quality, 156
size of, 154
specifications of, 154, 161
standardization-compatibility of, 157
timing of, 153, 163
weight of, 154
Production, 26
Professors, 65, 85, 139, 143, 144, 209
Profit-sharing trusts, 197, 233
Program Evaluation and Review Technique/Critical
    Path Method (PERT/CPM), 9, 168, 169
Progress payments, 216
    Projections, financial, 121, 138
"Proposal mills," 228
Proposals, (*See also* Business Plan), 26, 118, 175
    business, 83, 139
    mini, 129, 130, 133, 137, 138
    "shop-worn," 122
    virgin, 122
Proprietary content of product, 132
Prospectus, (*See also* Business Plan), 118, 119, 120
Protection, product, 89, 99, 100
Prototype, 36, 69, 70, 124, 131, 164, 196, 230, 263
Public,
    general, 196
    investing, 237
Public offering, (*See* Offering, public)
Public speaking, 78, 79
Publications,
    bank, 74
    trade, 21, 133, 159
Publicity, 11, 12, 20, 21, 22, 70, 159
Publisher's Clearing House, 74
Purchase orders, 152
Purchasing agent, 19

Quist, George, 245

Raborn, William F. (Red), Admiral, 9
"Raiding," 58
Ratio,
    price-to-earnings, 108
    risk-reward, 200
Ratio analysis, 177
Recruiting partners (*See* Partners, recruitment of)
Red tape, 35
References, founder, 139, 182
Referrals, 59
Registration, securities, 132
Regulation A, 253, 254
Relatives (as investors), 230, 247
Report, Annual, 143, 153, 186

Representatives, manufacturers', 16, 69, 83, 84, 161
Requirements, cash, 46
Research and development, 22, 92, 164, 241
Resources, 29, 44, 231
    banking, 143
    financial, 117
    personal, 41
Responsibility, 51, 119
    functional, 139
    product-line, 133
    profit-and-loss, 133
Retainer, 97, 227
Return on Investment, 201
Rewards, maximizing, 200
Rights, 206, 210, 248, 258
    conversion, 91
    of first refusal, 247
Risk, 45, 200, 240
    capital, 131, 221
    credit, 194
    downside, 202
    financial, 179
    high, 201
    investment, 242
    minimizing, 200
RMA Bulletin, 176
Robert Morris Associates (RMA), 176
Rockefeller Family, 201, 225
Rollinson, Mark, 201
Roulette, 200
Royalty, 91, 97, 104
Rubel, Stanley M., 258

Salary, 59, 141, 183
Sale, terms of, 253
Sale-leaseback, 239
Sales forecast, 175
Sales Letter (*See* Letter, sales)
Savings, founder, 183
Savings and Loan Associations, 250
Schedules, 196
Schedule Y (IRS Code), 243
Schmidt, Benno C., 202
School of Hard Knocks, 68, 117
Schools, business, 85
Science Information Exchange, 98
Sears Roebuck and Co., 161, 232
Securities, 208, 237
    restricted, 207
Securities Act of 1933, 236, 251, 253
Securities and Exchange Commission (SEC), 120, 233,
    236, 237, 242, 253
    regional and branch offices, 254, 255
Securities dealers (definition of), 251
Securities Exchange Act, 251
Security, 33, 221
Seed capital, 131
Seller's agent, 96
Seminars, 64, 65, 66, 67
Serfdom, 59

Service, 89, 154
  consulting, 208
  initial, 133
  management counseling, 141
Sesame Street, 54
Sheen Fulton J., Bishop, 42
Sheriff, 3, 46
Shoestrings, 47
Shopped (proposal), 122, 123, 129
Silcox, Walter D., 233
Sinking fund, 221
Sleep, 82
Small Business Act of 1953, 255
Small Business Administration (SBA), 16, 65, 70, 76,
      77, 91, 149, 255-257
  501 Program, 257
  502 Program, 257
  loan, 16, 255, 256
Small Business Investment Act of 1958, 257
Small Business Investment Company (SBIC), 149,
      231, 257, 258
Small Business Reporter, 75
Small businessman, 73, 75
Small loan companies, 212
Smith, Charles B., 201
Smithsonian Institution, 98
Sole proprietorship, 83, 91, 179
Source,
  capital, 195, 196
  financial, 147
  money, 205
Speaking, public, 13
Specialization, 129
Spin-offs, 91, 241
Spleen, Stanley, 28
Spread sheets, 176
Staff,
  competitor's, 58
  inadequacy of, 146
  projected requirements for, 179
Stamina, 46, 63
Stanford University, 209
Start-up, 46, 47, 131, 178, 184, 196, 235
State Farm Insurance Company, 232
State Industrial Development Commissioner, 258, 259
State Invention Expositions, 95
State Investment Development Corporations, 256
State-of-the-art, 158
State regulatory agencies, 231, 232
State Street Bank and Trust Company of Boston, 211
Statement,
  cash flow, 177
  income, 178, 196
  profit-and-loss, 178
Stock, 21, 45, 58, 131, 142, 181, 194, 214, 222, 228
  common, 193, 237, 252, 253
  employee, 221
  ownership of, 200, 221
  position in, 91
  public offering of, 120, 132, 184
  sales of, 177

Stock:
  brokers, 85, 120, 203, 234, 237
  exchanges, 193, 206
  holdings, 184
  option, 59, 60, 218, 222
  option plan, qualified, 222
  purchase plan, employee, 197, 222
Stockholders, 52, 140, 142, 150, 181, 194, 206, 207,
      249
Stockholders Delight Division, 26
Stork, 89
"Strike three," 42
Studebaker Avanti, 154
Subsidiary, 27, 91
Super-serendipity, 125
Supplier, 44, 83, 84, 118, 177, 194, 216, 223
  captive, 218
  independent, 161
  proximity of, 167, 216
  trade, 223, 260, 261
Supply and demand, 192, 207
"Sure Thing," 130
Survival, 178
"Sweeteners," (*See also* "Kickers"), 131, 194, 210
Syndicate, 196, 246
Syndication, 197, 227, 235, 237
Synergy, 68, 140
System, accounting, 147

Table of Contents, 138
Taxes, 15, 31, 46 181, 194, 214
  planning for, 147, 183
  problems of, 183
  regulation of, 179
Tax advantages, 168, 181
Team, founding, 58, 139, 197, 198
Technological leadership, 214
Teledyne, 31, 232
Time, 11, 13, 46, 53, 123, 129, 138, 158, 162, 169,
      178, 179, 185, 196
Toastmasters Clubs (*See* Clubs, Toastmasters)
Toastmasters International, 78
Track record, 5, 59, 108, 119, 124
Trade:
  associations, 65, 72, 73
  discounts, 209
  journals, 12, 20, 74, 75, 159
  secrets, 90, 99, 132
  shows, 94
Trademark, 11, 70, 110
Tradesmen, 83
Transportation services and facilities, 167
Trial runs, 122
Truman, Harry S., 120
Trust companies, 242, 262
Trust departments, bank, 242, 262
"Turn-around," 178
Twist, new, 93, 163

Ulcer, 47, 82
Unbeliever, 124

Uncle Sam, 3, 31, 76
Underwrite, 130, 253
Underwriter, 118, 252
  definition of, 236
  insurance, 125
Underwriting, 236
  all or none, 252
  best efforts, 252
  firm, 252
  self, 253
Union America Capital Corporation, 211
Union Bank, 211
University Microfilms, 93
University of Toronto, 168
Universities, 66, 93, 119, 208
Upward Spiral Industries, 27, 37
U. S. Department of Commerce, 64, 70, 76, 95, 217
U. S. Department of Housing and Urban Development, 10
U. S. Patent Office, 92, 100

Varian Associates, 10
Venrock Associates, 201
Venture, 118, 120, 125, 159, 198, 211, 216, 225
Venture capital, 11, 20, 133, 146, 168, 191, 198, 202, 206-263
Venture capital corporations, privately owned, 246
Venture capitalist, 47, 57, 69, 78, 118, 121, 124, 125, 182, 195, 200-202, 227, 230, 247

Veterans Administration, 262
  guaranteed loans, 262
  Information Service, 263
Vice President of Historical Planning, 26
Virgin proposal (*See* Proposal, virgin)

Wall Street, 200
Wall Street Journal, The, 31, 91
Warehousing, field, 212
Warrants, 6, 213, 235
Whitney Family, 225
Whitney, J. H. & Co., 202, 225
Whizbanger, Willie, 27, 36
Who pays?, 165
Wholesalers, 161
Widow, wealthy, 248
Wife, 5, 13, 15, 17, 19, 21, 22, 27, 28, 31, 51, 52, 54, 57, 64
Winning, importance of, 31
Women's Lib, 61
Working capital, (*See also* Capital, working), 178, 209, 212, 217, 249, 259

Xerox, 93, 119, 149

Yellow Pages, 110, 228

Ziglar, Zig, 70